Elizabeth H. Pleck is a Fellow of the Bunting Institute, Radcliffe College.

Joseph H. Pleck is Program Director of the Wellesley College Center for Research on Women.

The american man

Elizabeth H. Pleck

Joseph H. Pleck

A SPECTRUM BOOK

PRENTICE-HALL, INC., Englewood Cliffs, New Jersey 07632

Library of Congress Cataloging in Publication Data

Main entry under title:

The American man.

   (A Spectrum Book)
   Includes bibliographical references.
      1. Men—United States—Addresses, essays, lectures.
2. 2. Masculinity (Psychology)—Addresses, essays,
lectures.   3. Sex role—Addresses, essays, lectures.
4. Men—United States—Sexual behavior—Addresses,
essays, lectures.   I. Pleck, Elizabeth H.   II. Pleck,
Joseph H.
HQ1090.3.A45   301.41'1'0973   79-26171
ISBN 0-13-028159-X
ISBN 0-13-028142-5 pbk.

Editorial/production supervision and interior design by Carol Smith
Manufacturing buyer: Cathie Lenard

A SPECTRUM BOOK

Printed in the United States of America

10 9 8 7 6 5 4 3 2 1

PRENTICE-HALL INTERNATIONAL, INC., *London*
PRENTICE-HALL OF AUSTRALIA PTY., LIMITED, *Sydney*
PRENTICE-HALL OF CANADA, LTD., *Toronto*
PRENTICE-HALL OF INDIA PRIVATE, LIMITED, *New Delhi*
PRENTICE-HALL OF JAPAN, INC., *Tokyo*
PRENTICE-HALL OF SOUTHEAST ASIA PTE., LTD., *Singapore*
WHITEHALL BOOKS, LIMITED, *Wellington, New Zealand*

SSH
R

1.95pa.

Contents

period I
Agrarian Patriarchy (1630-1820)

v

period **II**

The Commercial Age (1820-1860)

Notes on the Contributors

T. H. Breen is Professor of History and Director of the American Culture Program at Northwestern University. He has written *The Character of the Good Ruler: A Study of Puritan Political Ideas in New England, 1630-1730,* edited *Shaping Southern Society: The Colonial Experience,* and is the author of many articles in American colonial history.

Joe L. Dubbert is Associate Professor of History at Muskingum College, where he teaches courses in American social and intellectual history. His most recent work is *A Man's Place: Masculinity in Transition.*

Marc Fasteau is a graduate of Harvard Law School who has litigated in the area of sex discrimination. He was an assistant in foreign affairs to Senator Mike Mansfield. He is the author of *The Male Machine.*

Peter Gabriel Filene teaches history at the University of North Carolina, Chapel Hill. He is assembling a book of autobiographical essays by men, focusing on their work and family lives, and is learning to be a photographer.

Eugene D. Genovese is Professor of History at the University of Rochester. He has been president of the Organization of American Historians and is a Fellow of the American Academy of Science. His most recent book, *Roll, Jordan, Roll: The World the Slaves Made* won the Bancroft Prize in American history.

Michael Gordon is Professor of Sociology at the University of Connecticut. He is the author of *The American Family: Past, Present, and Future.* His edited collections include *The American Family in Social-Historical Perspective,* second edition and *The Nuclear Family in Crisis: The Search for an Alternative.*

Jeffrey P. Hantover is Director of the Council on Accreditation of Services for Families and Children. He received his Ph.D. in sociology from the University of Chicago in 1976. His current research interests are sex roles and family policy analysis.

Blanche Glassman Hersh is coordinator of the Women's Studies Program at Northeastern Illinois University. She was one of the founders of the National Women's Studies Association. Her book is entitled *The Slavery of Sex: Feminist-Abolitionists in America.*

Jon M. Kingsdale is Senior Health Policy Analyst at the Government Research Corporation in Washington, D.C. He is completing his Ph.D. dissertation at the University of Michigan on the economic history of hospitals in the United States from 1870 to 1940.

Mirra Komarovsky is Chair of the Women's Studies Program at Barnard College and Columbia University. She has written *Leisure: A Suburban Study, The Unemployed Man and his Family, Women in the Modern World, Blue Collar Marriage,* and *Dilemmas of Masculinity: A Study of College Youth.* She received the Jessie Bernard Award in 1977 from the American Sociological Association for research in the area of family and sex roles.

Elliot Liebow is Chief, Center for Studies of Metropolitan Health Problems, National Institute of Mental Health. He is the author of *Tally's Corner: A Study of Negro Streetcorner Men.*

Mary Beth Norton is a member of the history department at Cornell University, specializing in the study of the American Revolution and of women. She has written a number of articles on both topics and is the co-editor with Carol Berkin of *Women of America: A History.* Her first book, *The British Americans: The Loyalist Exiles in England, 1774-1789* won the Allen Nevins Prize. A forthcoming book is *Liberty's Daughters: The Revolutionary Experience of American Women, 1750-1800.*

Robert Oaks has taught American history at the University of Texas at Arlington and Austin, California State University, Los Angeles, and San Jose State University. He has written for the *Journal of Homosexuality* and is a member of their editorial board.

Joseph H. Pleck is a Program Director at the Wellesley College Center for Research on Women. His books include *Men and Masculinity* and *The Male Role: Sex Role Identity and Sex Role Strain* (forthcoming).

Charles E. Rosenberg is Professor of hisotry at the University of Pennsylvania. His publications include *The Trial of the Assassin Guiteau: Psychiatry and the Law in the Gilded Age, The Cholera Years: The United States in 1832, 1849, and 1866* and *No Other Gods: On Science and American Social Thought.* He is finishing a book on the origins of the hospital in the United States from 1800 to 1920.

Henry Nash Smith's most recent book is *Democracy in the Novel: Popular Resistance to Classic American Writers.* He is also the author of *Mark Twain: The Development of a Writer* and *Virgin Land,* and he edited *Popular Culture and Industrialism, 1865-1890.*

We wish to express our thanks to Michael Hanagan for assistance in research and for his helpful comments on a previous draft of the introduction. Estelle Freedman, Michael Gordon, and Maurine Greenwald also provided further comments useful in revision.

Introduction

Men are male only part of the time, women are female always, said Rousseau in *Émile*. The activity and behavior of men are seen as human activity, that of women as distinctly female. Historians (mostly men) have considered at length the public deeds and quests of (selected) men. Many of the facts about men's lives in the past are thus already known. However, these facts are badly in need of a new, sex-conscious reinterpretation. This project requires reviewing men's historical experience, not as human history but as the history of only one of the two sexes and, specifically, that of the more privileged sex.

The history of masculinity is a relatively new subject of inquiry with a small but growing literature.[1] It has its roots in the increasing sophistication and growing acceptance of "so-

1

cial history" and in the reemergence of women's history, itself an outgrowth of the feminist movement. This dual lineage has shaped the questions and style of investigation in men's history.

THE DUAL LINEAGE OF MEN'S HISTORY: SOCIAL HISTORY AND WOMEN'S HISTORY

The origins of social history can be traced to the *Annales* school of French historical scholarship (taking its name from its major journal, *Annales: Economies, Sociétés, et Civilisations*, which began publication in the 1920s). This genre of historical writing, rejecting the traditional emphasis on past politics as the major topic of inquiry, centered on the social life and customs of ordinary people in past cultures. In the United States a similar historical interest in the social experience of the "masses" appeared in the 1960s, compelled in part by the impact of the New Left on politics and on academic scholarship. This new American social history, devoting special attention to workers, slaves, immigrants, and protest groups, proclaimed an ambition to rewrite the past as "history from the bottom up."

About the same time, Phillippe Aries' *Centuries of Childhood,* a study of the evolution of the concept of Western European childhood from medieval to modern times, promoted the development of family history as a branch of social history and reverberated with the youth movements that were so much a part of the 1960s. Historians in the United States, influenced by Aries, began to study the family and the private side of life, from sexuality and adolescence to marriage customs and death rituals. Taking its lead from the social sciences, the traditional narrative form was often abandoned in favor of a more analytical approach, which often involved developing and testing a hypothesis, sometimes with the use of quantitative data derived from poll tax records, city directories, or federal manuscript census schedules. As new questions began to be asked, historians left behind their traditional documents of newspaper accounts, diplomatic correspondence, and the like and ventured into hitherto unexploited sources, ranging from medical advice literature to court records and folklore.

Spurred by the reemergence of feminism in the late 1960s, new work on the history of women provided a rich and revelatory set of insights about the past lives of women, which began to challenge many of the traditional assumptions of historians. Women's history was rooted in the fundamental discoveries that women's historical experience was different from men's, that much of women's past experience was unknown, and that the route to understanding that past was not biological inevitability but history itself.

Most important for things to come, women's history introduced a new way of thinking about the historical experience of the genders. In a virtual credo of the new women's history, Joan Kelly Gadol has stated, "We consider the relation of the sexes, as those of class and race, to be socially rather than naturally constituted, varying with changes in social organization. Our use of sex as a social category means that our conception of historical change itself, as change in the social order, is broadened to include changes in the relation of the sexes."[2] This new analysis paved the way for a men's history. Women's history grasped the significance of analyzing both men and women rather than studying women exclusively. Addressing the Berkshire Conference on Women's History in 1975, Natalie Zemon Davis, a historian of medieval and early modern Europe, urged that "we should now be interested in the history of both women and men. We should not be working on the subjected sex any more than a historian of class can focus exclusively on peasants. Our goal is to understand the significance of the *sexes*, of gender groups in the historical past."[3]

GENDER HISTORY

Women's history generated the study of "sex as a social category," a history of gender that incorporated two different but complementary subjects, the history of women *and* men. At its broadest and most schematic level, this history embraces three kinds of gender-based relationships (and subcultures): woman to woman, woman to man, and man to man. As commonly practiced, women's history studies the first two of these topics; the relationships between women and those of women with men, and the history of masculinity is concerned with the last two, the relations of men with women and those of men with other men.

Women's and men's history take the same and different routes to the common destination of a history of gender. Each studies same-sex and cross-sex relationships; each identifies a relationship unique unto itself, that among members of one sex—all-male relationships in men's history, all-female relationships in women's history. A common domain, the history of men's relations with women, is shared by both, but women's history looks to this subject as a guide to women's experience, and men's history finds here the implication for men. A subject of interest in both histories, for instance, is the history of male beliefs of the inferiority of women, which in women's history can be understood as a reason for women's confinement and in men's history as a source of men's greater freedom.

There are, of course, important differences between women's and men's history. Both research and interpret parts of human experience that have gone neglected in previous research. But in women's history, the study of previously unknown topics takes precedence over the need for reinterpretation of already investigated subjects, whereas in men's history, new research is less vital than developing new interpretations of previously studied events, activities, and ideologies. The two gender histories also differ in the sources of previous inattention. The relative absence of women from the historical profession and the silence of the feminist movement contributed to the decline in historical writing about women. Denying women a history was part of a larger acquiescence about women's condition. Women's history reemerged as self-conscious feminists sought to re-discover their past as a means toward reshaping their future. The neglect of men's history as a suitable topic for study has other roots—in the avoidance of self-awareness common to powerful and privileged social groups. The interest in the history of masculinity awaited the demands of social movements—the men's and gay liberation movements—which offered a critique of socially accepted sexual relations and raised new topics for inquiry. The history of the very social movements that breathed life into history will be con-sidered briefly in this essay; it is worthwhile to remember that it is their continuing influence on historical scholarship that generates the interest in and the subject matter of histor-ical investigation.

The historical essay that follows has a necessarily mod-est goal of identifying some of the important changes and sources of change in male–female and male–male relation-ships: It relies especially on the new insights from social history and women's history in order to review the history of masculinity. No general theory about changing gender rela-tions is proposed here out of the belief that no single theory embraces the complexity of changing sex roles. We do not find any single path of influence between male–male and male–female relations; since each set of gender relations has helped to reshape the other, the influences between each have been mutual and reinforcing.

FOUR PERIODS OF
UNITED STATES MEN'S HISTORY

All efforts at historical periodization are, in a sense, arbitrary, an attempt to demarcate from a continuous stream of past history the turning points of significance. We have identified four periods in the history of masculinity: agrarian patriarchy (1630–1820), the commercial age, (1820–1860), the strenuous life (1861–1919) and companionate providing (1920–1965). Our own times stand as the probable beginning of a new epoch in the history of gender relations. Women's history has rightfully objected that many of the traditional periods of American history, for example, the Era of Good Feelings or the Gilded Age, have little force as applied to women's history. For that reason, it might seem that these would serve well as epochs of significance in a history of men. But the exclusive focus on selected political events makes periods like these equally unsuitable in charting the history of the average man. We have tried to identify periods that correspond to much broader and far-reaching changes in American politics and warfare and to new directions in economic, religious, and family life. Our decisions are tentative ones, weighted toward the political and military end of the spectrum; as new research begins to shed light on the private side of men's history, a new periodization, which takes these trends into account, will surely shift the emphasis toward the other end of the spectrum.

The articles we have chosen for inclusion in this anthology present a diverse range of topics in the history of male–female and male–male relationships in the four periods of American history. They consider the private and public sides of men's lives, what men were expected to do, and what men actually did. Some of the articles show the imprint of feminism and/or the men's liberation movements; others were written prior to these movements but can be now more fully appreciated, such as Elliot Liebow's report on black streetcorner men in Washington, D.C., Mirra Komarovsky's investigation of unemployed husbands in the Great Depression, or Henry Nash Smith's insights into the image of the frontiersman in American popular literature. They range as well across social groups and regions—from slaves in the South to scoutmasters in Chicago—for, whereas masculinity has been a common bond among all men, the unities of age, region, class, and race have divided men. The very diversity of men's historical experience—the fact that there has been no model American man but a range of manhoods—forces us to move continually between dominant themes and important variations, between the accepted norm and what constituted deviance from it. This tendency to emphasize social deviance is especially influenced by the men's and gay liberation movements, which have so often found themselves challenging accepted standards of manhood and finding value in the less manly and the nontraditional.

Period I: Agrarian Patriarchy

As sons of Adam, men in the colonies were more sinned against than sinning. The Biblical view of Eve as the temptress, responsible for the fall of Adam, had helped shape the religious-minded colonists' views of the proper relations between the sexes. From the ribs of man had come woman and from woman, sin. The judgment of God was that Adam was to rule over Eve, as every subsequent husband should command every wife. Although both sexes belonged to the churches (whether Puritan, Anglican, or Congregationalist), only men were permitted to speak in church meetings because they were the one sex capable of fully comprehending religious doctrine. The Quakers were the exception, believing that men's spiritual claims were no greater than women's, and the separate-but-equal basis of the monthly meetings divided religious authority between the sexes. Even outside of Quakerdom, by the eighteenth century, ministers' sermons (at least in New England) began to present women's spiritual capacity in a more favorable light, as the proportion of men attending churches declined.[4] Still only men were allowed to speak in church, to be ministers and religious elders.

Colonial men were also favored in legal and economic transactions, and few women held independent title to land. Under English common law, married women suffered "civil death," that is, the husband, as head of the family, owned joint property outright. Only men had the right to sign contracts, and in cases of legal separation, husbands usually were granted custody of the children. It is true that husbands often bestowed on their wives generous provisions in wills and testaments, sometimes much more than the customary one-third, but the widow's portion, whether small or large, still served as proof not so much of her worth as of her deceased husband's merit as a provider.

The canon of sexual conduct during this period was the familiar double standard, the underlying tenet of which Keith Thomas explained as "the view that men have property in women and that the value of this property is immeasurably diminished if the woman at any time has sexual relations with anyone other than her husband."[5] The norms of male forwardness in sexual initiative were well established, but women were considered to be more prone to passion (the spiritual daughters of Eve), since their sense of rational control was thought to be weaker. In the seventeenth century, Puritan reformers urged a single standard of marital fidelity for men as well as for women, but their advice went largely unheeded in law and in practice.[6]

Because most American colonies did not grant legal divorce, husbands as well as wives were, in a sense, bound together equally until death. But the frequent advertisements of colonial husbands disowning the debts of "runaway" wives suggest that the absence of divorce was a smaller hardship for husbands than for wives. When divorce was granted, it operated according to the double standard. Whereas in the Southern colonies divorce was nonexistent, in New England the Puritans and their descendants viewed marriage as a civil contract based on mutual consent and permitted divorce, although the actual number of divorces granted was minimal. Any Massachusetts man who could prove his wife adulterous could receive a divorce. A wife charging her husband with adultery was only allowed "bed and board," a form of legal alimony without divorce. At least by the mid-eighteenth century, an increasing number of Massachusetts wives charging husbands with adultery could secure divorces rather than simply bed and board. Coming at the time of the American Revolution, this change suggests that Revolutionary ideas about equality before the law were having an effect on the double standard of justice.[7]

In a society like the colonies, with so few institutions outside the family, the church, and the courts, men's behavior toward women had to be modified to take into account women's crucial economic role. The facts of economic interdependence between the sexes in colonial society have led historians to conclude that husbands and wives were more or less equal partners in a common enterprise. But upon closer scrutiny, it is clear that wives in the colonies did not work alongside their husbands in the fields, except among the poorest whites and Africans. More generally, Mary Beth Norton's research on eighteenth-century Loyalist marriages (Chapter 3) serves as a further caution against a simple economic interpretation. Among this large sample of former colonists (who fled to England after the Revolution), the wife's former work, even if she tended a garden and raised livestock, was still the care of the household, and the husband's world involved the management of finances and property. In claims to the British government for lost property, Loyalist widowers failed to remember their lost household items, and Loyalist widows mentioned missing clocks and china pots but could not accurately list family financial holdings. In this society at least, the definitions of goodness and sin were not simple economic ones but judgments divinely ordained and legally certified.

As this narrow world of the colonies expanded in size and in scope, men were granted the special privilege of schooling. In seventeenth-century New England—the one region where figures on literacy are available—women were only slightly more likely to be illiterate than men. The introduction of common schooling helped decrease male illiteracy, but since few daughters were sent to school, the sexual gap in education widened.[8] College education for the colonial elite was another realm of male privilege: The first college for men was established in 1636, the first for women not until 1837. For more than 200 years then, an intellectual and ministerial elite of Harvard and Princeton graduates helped secure male educational superiority and advantages in finance, politics, and religion.

It might be justly claimed that the dominance of husbands over wives and that of fathers over sons were the twin cornerstones of colonial social relations. Fathers wanted sons to bear their name, to help in working the land, and to attend to them in old age. Despite the fact that mothers and older children were expected to care for infants, ministers beamed their advice to fathers, not mothers, in supplying the discipline and education necessary for a son's future direction, and told them, "he that spares the rod, hates his son."[9] In all the colonies, transmission of property defined the rights and obligations between father and son. The Southern colonies practiced strict primogeniture, but New Englanders often divided land equally among sons, with a double share for the eldest. The timing of a father's division of property to his sons varied between colonies. In seventeenth-century Andover, Massachusetts, fathers managed to retain power over adult sons, first by dictating the choice of a son's wife and then by retaining legal control over his farm. Quaker fathers in the middle colonies were seemingly more generous in giving land to their sons upon marriage (and money to their daughters), but they expected sons to work the farm and repay them.[10] Even in the cities, fathers were, in a sense, transmitting property to sons in the form of training in a craft. Only very poor white men, perhaps the bottom 10 percent of white male society, were left outside this system and thus found themselves neither in control of their sons' futures nor in expectation of the usual filial obligations.

This system of property inheritance depended on a man's ability to secure a wife and to father sons. It was somewhat precarious in both respects. Wives were in short supply in the colonies; men outnumbered women throughout the seventeenth century and well into the next. As a response to this imbalance, some men delayed marriage until they were propertied, and others turned to younger women as brides. In the Southern colonies some prospective grooms, by paying off the indenture of a servant, in effect purchased a wife. In this competition for wives, landless men fared worse than others and African men worst of all, especially in the Southern colonies, where they outnumbered African women nearly two to one.[11] Matters were aggravated by white masters, who often claimed sexual rights to slave women, thereby precipitating one of the central and lasting antagonisms between white masters and slave men.

To secure labor for the farm and care in old age, it was necessary for a man to father several children because so few survived to adulthood. Since potency was a prime test of virility, impotence demonstrated insufficient manliness. Wives able to prove a husband incapable of siring children were granted annulments, although rarely were they given divorces.[12] Since divorce was uncommon, few impotent males were held up to public ridicule, but the expected standard of sexual prowess was still well known.

The ideal of a stable social hierarchy ruled by natural male leaders was accepted not only as family practice but as political doctrine that placed masters over servants, older ahead of younger, and wealthier above poorer. Most of the colonies had simply followed the English custom of restricting the franchise to propertied men. But with the widespread male ownership of land, at least half and perhaps as many as two-thirds of adult white men in the colonies were eligible to vote. The apathy of the male electorate and their apparent willingness to rely on the same group of wealthy men for leadership reflected the patriarchal principle as applied to colonial politics. This ideal was honored in eighteenth-century Virginia and Connecticut, where landed gentry virtually ruled the colonies for generation after generation, though it was never quite maintained in other colonies, where the rule of the older, wealthier men was subject to intense competition, quarrels, and even occasional outbreaks of violence.

The patriarchal principle in political and social life actually permitted and encouraged male competition, for had not one son of Adam murdered his brother? Colonial Cains were urged against Abels in drinking bouts, cockfights, horse races, and duels to the death. Although Puritans and Quakers severely punished gambling, drinking, and brawling, after the early years of settlement they were unable to compel nonbelievers in these codes. Forms of male aggression and competition in colonial society were highly patterned cultural events similar, for instance, to those among the gentry of eighteenth-century Virginia, as analyzed by Timothy Breen in Chapter 2. Although Virginia aristocrats were eager to gamble huge sums of money and spur their race horses to the finish line, they also sought to limit gentlemanly competition by prohibiting duels and urging aggrieved gamblers to take disputes to the courts.

This separate cultural world of men also encouraged manly intimacy and affection, a love between equals, which was often lacking in sentiments toward the other sex. In the military, for example, young gentlemen often formed close male friendships, which we can learn about from their correspondence. As an officer in George Washington's Revolutionary Army, Alexander Hamilton wrote lengthy, passionate letters to John Laurens, a man of his rank and of about the same age (early twenties). For three years (until Laurens' death), they wrote to each other frequently, referring to each other as "My Dear," and writing "I love you" at the close of their letters. Hamilton, who had written five or six letters without receiving a response, described himself as a "jealous lover." He often closed by telling Laurens that the other officers sent "their love." All this occurred while Laurens was married and Hamilton engaged. No one will ever be able to tell if these men were sexually intimate, but the expressions of love found in these letters appear to have been an accepted part of the nobility of sentiment that men of high station shared.[13]

Love between men was acceptable as long as it did not extend to sexual contact. The greatest punishment was reserved for men who had sexual relations with other men. Colonial statutes punished *male* homosexuality with death, but lesbianism, with the exception of one statutory provision, was not a crime. It is surprising that men, viewed as the less passionate sex, were singled out; perhaps an explanation is that Puritan fathers believed only men capable of sexual attraction toward their own sex.[14]

In the isolated settlements spread across the colonial landscape, the one common denominator was the rule of older, wealthier men. Despite the importance of having a wife and children and their economic contribution to the family, the religious norms and legal codes of colonial society sanctioned male superiority. The relations between men were equally governed by patriarchy: paternal power in the home and in the world of politics and religion, the power as well to define proper standards of male behavior and to punish deviance.

Period II: The Commercial Age

The single vertical scale of colonial society was replaced by a vertical one in the commercial age, duly marked off in two equal halves, one for each sex. A new social order removed the mantle of authority from older, wealthier men. Women stood to gain because the dominant middle-class ideology of this period, enunciated by ministers and women magazine writers, proclaimed the doctrine of separate but equal spheres for the sexes. The husband's sphere was to be the world of business and public affairs; his wife's the world of the home (and the church). Men, with their keen sense of practicality and innate desire to win, were suited for the mundane pursuits of industry, government, and warfare; women, delicate in physique but superior in sensibility, piety, and virtue, were to be situated in the home. The husband, although expected to be a good provider, was asked to make his home a refuge from the business world.

The doctrine of separate spheres was closely connected with the beliefs in sexual purity for women and men. Whereas the pure woman was elevated in status to her separate sphere, the outcast and fallen woman was excluded. In the slave South, white masters and overseers helped to place white women on a pedestal but took concubines from among the slaves. Was it true, as has been suggested, that white Southern men were so motivated by guilt about their sexual relations with slave women? In the North, working women, the young domestic in the home or the prostitute on the streets, were defined as suitable prey, the kind of women virtuous men never wanted to marry.

Now males were viewed as the more passionate sex, and the goal of the good woman was to help man control his passions for his own sake and for the good of society. Instead of fathers providing discipline, mothers were now expected to supervise the sexual education of sons. Male masturbation, which had been rarely mentioned as a source of parental concern in Enlightenment marriage and child-rearing tracts, now dominated the advice literature; the mother was especially advised to watch her son in order to help him reject the traditional double standard and remain a virgin until marriage.[15]

This new sexual ideology (for it was belief and not practice) was closely connected with the doctrine of the separate spheres and emerged from profound religious and economic change. In a wave of religious revivals between 1790 and 1835 called the Second Great Awakening, the staid form of worship gave way to a new, exuberant, and distinctively American style of reaching salvation. Fatalism and ministerial imperative declined, and emotional feeling and winning souls through dynamic preaching grew. Every county, town, and large city on the East Coast had its own revival and its favorite preacher. The parishioners, instead of passively awaiting salvation, actively sought it through personal responsibility, community activism, and reform of society. Evangelical religion led to the growth of missions, temperance societies, and Sunday schools and left as its legacy a greater emphasis on piety, self-restraint, discipline, and frugality: a new style of manliness. More than a century before, the First Great Awakening had much the same effect; for example, among yeomen in eighteenth-century Virginia, where it contributed to the disavowal of drinking, gambling, dancing, and cardplaying.[16] The *Second* Great Awakening was distinctive only in the simultaneous appearance of three social changes: heady prescriptions about male sexual conduct, new-found religious piety, and a get-rich commercialism characteristic of a speculative era.

Control over sexuality nicely fitted the business ethic of this age. An entire economy of the body emerged: A man needed to save his limited amount of semen, to practice frugality, or he would bankrupt himself.[17] Sexual advice writers believed that excess sexual energy robbed man of his stamina for work and suggested hard work as the best cure. Reverend John Todd's *Student Manual* (1835), which sold hundreds of thousands of copies, maintained that mental power depended on strict conservation of bodily and sexual energies. Masturbation or sexual excess of any kind posed great threats to sanity, social achievement, and individualistic striving. Control of fertility, of course, was part of this emphasis on sexual control, and advice, freely given, appeared to be readily adopted in this period, as fertility declined, especially among the urban middle classes. Was it husbands, anxious to limit the family finances, or wives, eager to lessen the burden of childbearing, or both who sought smaller families? Whatever the middle-class man's reasons for continence (often achieved by withdrawal before emission), he did not accede without some strains on his sense of manhood, for he may have eased his economic burdens at the expense of defining himself as less potent and thus less manly.

Such were the demands of the new ideology of separate spheres and sexual purity on the middle-class man. Outside of the cities, the Northeast, and the middle class, did these new beliefs matter? They were important in setting the standard for the dominant social groups and in defining social deviance for the mosaic of outsiders from all points of view who, in the antebellum decades, found themselves in rebellion against deeply held social values.

The Mormons, the first American-made religion, sprang from a rejection of American Protestantism. Largely recruited from New York and the Middle West, from the economically dissatisfied, from small farmers who had been displaced by commercial agriculture, and from tradesmen and merchants bypassed by economic expansion, they subscribed to the ultimate patriarchal religion. By the authority of Aaron and his sons, Joseph Smith had a divine revelation calling him to form his own church (which he did in 1830). Divine authority also permitted "celestial marriage," the right of Mormon men to marry several women. Still, this new church, which retreated farther and farther from civilized America in order to establish its own utopia, was among the staunchest upholders of the Protestant Ethic (despite their communal economy) and strictly opposed adultery, homosexuality, and drinking.[18]

At the other extreme, slave men lacked rights to marry, migrate, own property, sign contracts, testify in court, or participate in voluntary associations. As human chattel, slave men and women were equally circumscribed and thus, by force of circumstances, were the most removed from confinement to rigid sex roles. In practice, it proved impossible for white masters to treat slave men as genderless or for slave men to view themselves that way. As the selection from Eugene Genovese's *Roll, Jordan, Roll* (Chapter 6) indicates, both slave husbands and masters tried to preserve male dominance in the quarters, but for different reasons. Masters, wanting to make a profit from their investment, endeavored to encourage slave men to work, with coercion as their last resort. Imbued with the belief in the superiority of slave society, masters sought to further their self-images as benevolent patriarchs, preserving the family and male authority among the slaves. Slave men were not simply pawns in the master's game, because they had their own goals: to make family decisions and discipline their children, even as they recognized that the threat of sale hung over them. Often they were able to manipulate manly competition between the master and the overseer or the patriarchal ideals of the master to their own and their family's limited advantage.

Born from the social turmoil of the commercial age, an organized feminist movement, representing another form of deviance from accepted patterns, forwarded a serious critique of masculine privilege. The Seneca Falls Declaration of Principles, formulated in 1848, boldly stated that "the history of mankind is a history of repeated injuries and usurpations on the part of man toward woman, having as its direct object the establishment of an absolute tyranny over her." Two suffragists and abolitionists, Lucy Stone and Henry Blackwell, chose to make their marriage ceremony in 1855 a public attack on the laws that gave husbands guardianship of the children, exclusive ownership of property and earnings, and "the whole system by which the legal existence of the wife is suspended during marriage. . . ."[19] Henry Blackwell was among the small group of antebellum American men, influenced by feminism, who sought to renounce his right to wifely obedience and to overthrow what he saw as domestic slavery. He was not alone; one-third of the signers of the Declaration of Principles at Seneca Falls were men.

Alongside these reassertions and challenges to manly superiority over women, the relations between men were equally subject to change, for paternal authority was being eroded by economic and social forces. In a wave of enthusiasm following the Revolution, state legislatures abolished laws of primogeniture favoring oldest sons. It was a new tendency, even a trend, for many men to marry without their fathers' permissions, often choosing wives of their own selection. The decline in apprenticeship undermined fatherly instruction of boys, and the rising proportion of female teachers placed young men under a woman's authority for nearly the whole of their early years. Many adult sons moved away from their fathers' farms to begin new homesteads in the Midwest or the Lower South, and others left their fathers' farms for the city. The system of ranks, favoring older, wealthier men, was giving way to an open competition between men. From 1775 to 1836, successive Massachusetts towns abolished the seating arrangement in the meeting house that gave preference first "to a person's age, second to estate" and began to sell seats at auction, with the best bench going to the highest bidder.[20] Each adult male was on his own and could no longer find a father to protect—or control—him.

Without a father's patronage or even a genteel education, the man who rose above his humble origins through fair competition was not only the common man, he was the best man. This cherished belief in Jacksonian America had little to do with the realities of widening economic inequality or continued slavery. Almost untouched by the gap between rich and poor and depending instead on the examples of a selected few, the gospel of success held that with sufficient effort every white man should be able to overcome handicaps of background in securing wealth. (Black men, slave or free, were considered inferiors, ill-suited for this competition.) Since the majority of American men were farmers, they were gambling that next year's harvest would repay their debts to the local bank and give them enough profit to buy more land or farm equipment. Speculation in land was as prevalent in the city as on the farm, where a form of male bravado, boosting their town as a means of boosting themselves, was especially common. Although the frontiersman and the cowboy remained the unrivalled American heroes, the travails of the young urban man also made a claim on the American imagination, especially through Horatio Alger's books for boys.[21] Directed toward the small urban population, these books championed the cause of the respectable clerk or merchant, who was often honored by an older established patron for his honesty, diligence, and frugality (and simple good luck) and rewarded by being given the man's daughter in marriage.

In this period, men's separate culture grew almost as fast as the speculation in greenbacks. In the colonial era, men met at the court house, the church, the blacksmith's shop, or at city taverns or coffeehouses. They sought places to arrange business deals and places to escape from business:

lodges, debating clubs, and lyceums for the urban middle class and militia or volunteer fire companies for the working class.

Older forms of male camaraderie and competition continued in visits to prostitutes, undisciplined work habits, and jovial drinking bouts in taverns. Alongside this older ethos emerged another men's culture, committed to voluntary association and based on adherence to principles of sobriety, self-discipline, and temperance. This male working class in antebellum Northeastern cities was, in fact, split between these two, not so much along sheer economic lines as along religious ones. A study of antebellum Boston indicated that temperance workingmen were no wealthier or higher in occupational status than older-style workingmen but that they were more likely to be reform Protestants, Unitarians, or Congregationalists.[22]

The commercialism of antebellum society and the effects of the Second Great Awakening had taken masculinity out of its older patriarchal mold. Men were no longer the link in the Great Chain of Being just above women; now they played to their own separate but no longer superior sphere. Although this placement was accepted and even espoused by some, it was challenged by feminists, who demanded the right to political power in the men's sphere, and by more tradition-minded women, who sought to reshape and control men's sexuality along purer lines. In a society where fundamental values were being so continually called into question, a range of alternatives, from feminism to the reassertion of religious patriarchy, found adherents.

The new social arrangements had opened men to even greater brotherly competition as paternal authority had been abrogated. If all white men were equals, then it followed that each was in competition with his brother. Outside of the plantations and the islands of communalism dotting the countryside, there was little permanent respite from the new race for commercial success.

Period III: The Strenuous Life

Between the Civil War and World War I, the stated goal of much sexual doctrine was to raise men to women's standard. In this period, expectations had the same blend of hypocrisy and moral purity as in the commercial age. If anything, men's absence from the household and moral impurity was even more subject to scrutiny. But with the desecularization of American life, the prescriptive emphasis on male purity was taken up more by doctors than by ministers; these physicians gave a more somatic basis to sexual ideology and a more technical rationale for its existence. Once ministers had frightened men with visions of hell; now doctors predicted blindness and impotence and furnished scientific proof that masturbation and homosexuality often led to insanity. These changes were not entirely sanguine, given the nineteenth-century medical doctor's resort to tortuous contraptions and devices to prevent masturbation and spermatorrhea.[23]

The dominant idea of male–female relations in these years was still separate spheres for each sex. Mothers civilized sons, wives provided husbands with a refuge from the world of work. The middle-class Victorian ideal could be seen in the standard biography of George Washington offered between 1864 and 1900. The Virginia aristocrat was portrayed as muscular, self-restrained, and self-reliant, a man who never cared about reasoning (anti-intellecutalism had become associated with masculinity in the 1870s). Gilded Age biographers transformed Washington into a self-made man, who after his father's death at the age of twelve, was forced to support his family. He emerged in this literature as a husband faithful to Martha but "too much of a man to have his marriage lessen his liking for women" and as a benevolent master who never whipped his slaves. The working-class equivalent of the George Washington myth could be found in temperance tales, such as the "Romance of

Labor," published in labor newspapers across the country. After a young man marries an heiress, he soon falls into an idle life, losing his wife's respect and his own sense of worth: He becomes a machinist's apprentice, regains his self-esteem, and ultimately becomes a proprietor of a large iron works. Most important of all, the "Romance" tells us, he had conquered his wife, won her affection, and "compelled her to acknowledge a physical strength and moral purpose greater than her own."[24] Although the dominant image of masculinity had percolated down to these working-class newspapers, it was still reaching only the acculturated segment of American society, for in these years of massive immigration, American males were not only Yankees, but Europeans, Asians, and Mexicans who had their own reasons for believing men were divinely and naturally different from women, reasons that had little to do with beliefs in success through work or evangelical piety.

By the 1890s, the "new woman," who rode a bicycle, loosened the lacing of her corset, and took a job before marriage, emerged in American magazines as deeply threatening to men. A growing number of women's magazines were openly asserting the deficiencies of men. Women were sapping male strength; they were seeking to enter his bastions of power and his secret preserves; some of them were even taking jobs away from men. Women became the other that men never wanted to become. In fact, by the late nineteenth century, the word "manliness" itself came to signify less the opposite of childishness than of femininity.[25]

The economic threat was slight, but the fear of working women was great. In a few jobs, such as typists, librarians, and sales clerks, a process of feminization was at work, as larger numbers of women entered previously all-male jobs. The few men who remained in them were then defined as effeminate and unmanly, but even the husband employed in muscular work who allowed his wife to work was seen as meek and submissive. Differences in physical strength were used to justify the exclusion of women from many jobs. What began as a reform designed to lift the burden from working women actually helped to reserve the best jobs for men. In *Muller v. Oregon* (1908), the Supreme Court, giving voice to the fears and prejudices that had been building for decades, upheld a ten-hour workday only for working women. "The two sexes differ in structure of body, in the functions to be performed by each, in the amount of physical strength, in the capacity for long continued labor, particularly when done standing, the influence of vigorous health upon the future well-being of the race, the self-reliance which enables one to assert full rights, and in the capacity to maintain the struggle for subsistence."[26]

The final stronghold of male public privilege was the voting booth, which, after a fifty-two-year long campaign, was integrated by sex after the ratification of a national constitutional amendment in 1920. Because men held political power, the campaign for suffrage involved persuading a male electorate to enfranchise women. Because arguments based on appeals to man's sense of equal justice seemed to fall on deaf ears, suffragists found it more expedient to rely on traditional appeals to race and ethnic prejudice and on men's sentimentalization of motherhood—women would keep the governmental house clean as they had done at home. In other words, suffragists sought not to challenge traditional definitions of sex roles but to use them to further their own ends. Even so, the male supporters of suffrage often had to brave the view that they were betraying their sex. A *New York Times* editorial in 1912 in support of women's suffrage was nonetheless willing to suggest that the 800 men joining a suffrage parade had an ulterior motive: "There must be strong inducement to make men march in a woman's parade. Some may be looking for customers. We suspect both the waistmakers and the dentists, for instance."[27]

Perhaps because relations with women had become threatening and fearful, men turned to other men for convi-

viality and comradeship. In these years between the Civil
War and the armistice after World War I, a belief in the
"strenuous life" found in male bonding not just a way to
pass the time but a positive social value. Although the
slaughter of 500,000 American men in the Civil War produced a national war weariness, it awakened in some an
almost permanent nostalgia for the campfire and the bar-
racks life and had the unintentional effect of pressing men to
search for its peacetime equivalent. Charles Francis Adams
longed to find in civilian life what he had found in war, the
"close contact with nature and a roughing it among men and
in the open air, which I especially needed."[28] Continued
wars against the Indians; pitched battles with organized
labor; and armed interventions in Hawaii, Panama, the
Philippines, Cuba and Mexico fed the military spirit. At the
height of American expansionism, in the 1890s, the male
hero in American magazines was the great tycoon, Carnegie
or Morgan, portrayed as a great soldier who fights "the battles where they must now be fought, in the markets of the
world, not in the fields, or forest."[29]

All of this love of soldiering served to initiate a cult of
body building. Daniel Eddy published several editions of his
highly popular advice book for young men. In the first edition, which appeared prior to the Civil War, he advised men
to develop character and manly self-restraint and give their
bodies a rest. By the second edition, published immediately
after the war, he was saying, "What mudsills are to building,
muscular development is to manhood."[30]

The rise of organized athletics was one feature of this
cult. Whereas prior to the war collegiate athletics had been
discouraged, soon after it manly competition was encouraged, and Harvard and Yale began football teams. Financed
by wealthy gentlemen of the Northeast, baseball had already
become the national pastime by the coming of the war. During lulls in Civil War battles, soldiers played baseball and
organized prize fights. As large urban stadiums served by

public transport were constructed, baseball became the average man's sport, and with the shortening of the workday, more leisure time to attend games became available. The prototypical sports hero was a man of the people—violent, uneducated, lower class in origin; in the late nineteenth century, he was an Irish immigrant; by the early twentieth century, he had become a black, like Jack Johnson, who at first was heralded as the century's best athlete until his much publicized interracial love affair. This hero worship of muscular, lower-class men was channeled, accepted, and even forwarded by middle-class men, such as Ernest Thompson Seton, the founder of the Boy Scouts: "I do not know that I have met a boy that would not rather be John L. Sullivan than Darwin or Tolstoi. Therefore, I accept the fact and seek to keep in view an ideal that is physical. . . ."[31] Although organized athletics accepted the style of male aggression common to the lower classes, these games still had to be controlled by gentlemen. After a particularly bloody Stanford versus Berkeley football game followed by riots in San Francisco, Theodore Roosevelt ordered football civilized by the wearing of helmets or else he would issue a presidential proclamation abolishing the game.

Men's desire to be men and to make boys into men found its most creative outlet in the establishment of adult male clubs designed for boys. Ernest Seton of the Boy Scouts blamed female influence for boys' flabby muscles and weak character. He worried about "the boy who has been coddled all his life and kept so carefully wrapped up on the 'pink cotton wool' of an over-indulgent home, till he is more effeminate than his sister, and his flabby muscles are less flabby than his character."[32] Distaste for sports was a clear sign of effeminacy; as Zane Grey put it, "Every boy likes baseball. And if he doesn't he's not a boy." The effeminate boy was identified by body type (skinny, hairless, glasses, pale skin, and protruding Adam's apple) and behavior (avoids fights, is anxious to please, enjoys the company of women). Becoming involved in sports could transform the effeminate boy into a man. But scouting was more than a cure for the boys: It was also good for the men, as Jeffrey Hantover's analysis of male scoutmasters (Chapter 10) shows. Scoutmasters found in this largest of boys' organizations a means of validating their masculinity through the training of boys and through their own participation in outdoor life.

Scoutmasters could not find in the office and in paper work a suitable means for affirming their sense of manhood. The middle-class man worked in a feminine environment— clean, safe, and homelike—and precisely because of the virility impulse of the age, his culture heroes were not only John L. Sullivan but the American workingman who faced dangers on the job. In ideals and in reality, the American farmer was on the decline, and the worker was on the rise. In 1860, six out of every ten American workingmen were farmers; by 1920, only a third were farmers. At the same time, the percentage of men employed in manufacturing and construction rose from 18 percent in 1860 to 31 percent in 1920.

The air of camaraderie in the factory was often enhanced by the dangers of working in steel mills or iron works. Large factories had all the atmosphere of a men's separate club, and even union meetings were often held in the backrooms of saloons. But whether men should seek relief from work in drink was still an open question. On the one hand, Pittsburgh Irish Catholic labor leaders could urge temperance, an act by which "a man proclaims himself to be a man,"[33] whereas on the other, saloons flourished across the country and attracted workingmen throughout the day: The greater the proportion of workingmen in the city, the more saloons were to be found there. In 1911, the city with the largest per capita number of saloons—one for every eighty-eight people—was Gary, Indiana, an entirely new, mostly male company town built on the Indiana sand dunes for the purpose of supplying the Midwest with the steel it needed.

As Jon Kingsdale's article (Chapter 9) shows, the neighborhood working-class saloon, in Gary and elsewhere, functioned as a lunchroom, as a men's political club, and even as a union hall. With its photographs of John L. Sullivan, flanked by portraits of nude, fleshy beauties, the saloons reinforced a masculinity dependent on gambling and bravado. Along with the saloons, fraternal lodges, such as the Odd Fellows, Moose, or Eagles, or the Knights of Columbus for Catholics, constituted the major working-class male institutions. In 1901, five and a half million American men belonged to lodges, about five times the number of union members. The regular meeting of the lodge was an opportunity for men to drink and trade jokes, and lodges organized male social life, from sport teams and parades to dances and picnics.

A replica but also a rejection of this heterosexual men's culture, a separate urban homosexual subculture also developed and flourished in a few large American cities. By the late nineteenth century, a few American cities had become large and diverse enough to allow a few isolated villages of homosexuality, generally located near centers of bohemian life. Although police harassed homosexuals, they also permitted dance halls, Turkish cafes, baths, and bars to remain open in exchange for cash payments. New York City's gay population, located near Greenwich Village, was probably the largest for its day; other communities could be found in Philadelphia, Boston, Chicago, and Denver. City newspapers sometimes carried discrete advertisements, and male prostitutes in Philadelphia or New York wore a "red tie" to indicate their availability. A more settled, older community coexisted alongside this visible younger one, which even by this time had identified certain occupations as homosexual: musician, art dealer, teacher, actor, florist, and woman's tailor.[34]

In sum, between the Civil War and World War I, the ideology of the separate spheres that had emerged in the commercial age continued to be an important means for defining male–female relations. The middle-class man was still expected to uphold a high standard of sexual morality, but at the same time, the large number of brothels and high rates of venereal disease in Victorian society testified to a huge discrepancy between social norms and actual behavior. In this neatly separate world of the sexes, the shrill cry against the entry of the new woman into a man's world was given concrete expression in male actions, popular literature, and male-only organizations. Whereas the dominant ideology of the earlier period had sanctioned honest economic competition between equals, in tune with the martial spirit, men were now asked to forego competition (except in foreign markets) in favor of comradeship and to strive for success by making war and leading the strenuous life. The martial spirit made male friendship into a cult of comradeship whose effects were to be seen in the cult of body building and in the blossoming of paramilitary organizations for boys. The form and content of this men's separate world varied between social groups but flourished everywhere in male-only institutions, which made these years the heyday of men's public culture.

Period IV: Companionate Providing

Einstein, by theorizing that space was curved, not flat, advanced a new theory of relativity; Stravinsky's balladic suites had exciting rhythms accompanied by jarring, sour tones; the nudes of Picasso, although recognizable as human forms, were little more than bold angular swaths of thick paint slapped across a canvas; a Viennese doctor told the millions that infants had sexual feelings and that children dreamed of having sex with their parents. The assault on Victorianism, begun in the early part of the twentieth century, had swept away almost an entire cultural ethos by the 1920s. Older definitions of masculinity were as outmoded as the spitoon and the straight razor. The final blow to Victorianism came from World War I. If the definition of manhood required being gassed and catching typhoid in the trenches, then why be a hero?

In the modern postwar world, men hung up their rifles and put away their medals in favor of a hip flask and a ukulele. Both the liquor and the strumming were necessary to modern man's new quest, romancing a young woman. The popularity of cabarets and, later, speakeasies in major cities testified to the desire of each sex to find public meeting places in which to drink, dance, and be entertained. Fewer college yearbooks carried pictures of varsity letter men arm in arm, and more ran drawings of bathing beauties and campus homecoming queens.[35] Men were spending more time with women, not only in the youthful peer culture, which had its own sports events and schools, but in school, now increasingly coeducational. Eventually co-ed schooling altered marriage patterns: By the 1940s grooms were selecting brides roughly similar in age, mostly as a result of men choosing brides from ex-schoolmates.[36] In the sexual revolution of the 1920s, male friendship took a back seat to dating. Social surveys reported that the proportion of men visiting a prostitute was half that for men born after 1910 compared with those born earlier; the proportion of men having extramarital affairs with a woman of their own class rather than a prostitute rose; by the 1930s, three-quarters of American men were prepared to marry a woman who was not a virgin.[37]

Sick and well were the polar opposites in the modernist view of male sexuality and the male sex role. In the early twentieth century, Havelock Ellis claimed to find no evidence linking masturbation to serious mental or physical disease. Ellis, an extreme modernist, had taken masturbation from the realm of secret vices and placed it in the category of healthy and recreational behavior, along with reading comic books and collecting cards of baseball players. It was only one step further to the belief that masturbation was not only benign but a positive good and that those who sought to curb it were themselves pathogenic. Whereas once ministers and medical doctors had set the standard for male sexual purity, by the early twentieth century, Freudian-influenced psychiatrists held that men must develop "sex-role identity" from suitable male role models and from reinforcement in learning masculine behaviors. Acting overtly masculine reflected insecurity in the male role; sexual attraction to other men was considered disturbed role identity. (The story was often told of the psychoanalyst who believed the homosexual to be definitely crazy and the heterosexual to be probably so.) Since identifying with a male role model was considered the primary means for acquiring proper sex-role identity, failure along the way led to such problems as poor school performance, juvenile delinquency, and sex offenses.[38]

In marriage manuals, psychiatrists and medical doctors had a forum for espousing their views of proper male sexuality. The ideals for the nineteenth-century American husband of sexual continence and control had been replaced by an ethic of sex-as-recreation. In marriage manuals of the 1920s, the husband was asked to awaken sexual yearnings in his wife and once having done so to advance toward the goal of simultaneous mutual orgasm. The husband was still seen as the sexually aggressive partner and his wife was seen as in need of awakening, although some manuals (again in the 1930s) were giving wives hints about techniques for male arousal. In 1948, the actual behavior of American men was scrutinized with the publication of Alfred Kinsey's *Sexual Behavior in the Male,* based on more than 5,000 case histories. Kinsey, who began his early career as a zoologist, took a similarly taxonomic approach to male sexuality or, to be more precise, that form of sexual activity that led to orgasm. Toward this end, he reported that 86 percent of American males had engaged in premarital sex, 40 percent had carried on extramarital affairs, and 37 percent had on some occasion engaged in homosexual activity. As a theorist, Kinsey presided over the creation of a new view of masculinity. First, simply by reporting the incidence of homosexuality in the male population, he helped Americans to realize its ordinariness. Kinsey went further by suggesting that homosexuality was potential in all men but was actualized only in some, because of social sanctions against it. Second, he championed the cause of the adolescent male, whom he believed to be restrained by traditional sexual mores against premarital sex and by outmoded views toward masturbation. (Kinsey's findings of a lower incidence of sexual activity among adolescent females had led to the reductionist conclusion that women were *innately* less drawn to sex than their male counterparts.)[39]

An ethic that praised sex as a leisure time activity fitted well with changing social trends. The average man had, in fact, more leisure time than ever before. The average male work week declined from fifty-nine hours in 1900 to forty-two hours in 1948, although since the 1950s, the male work week has stabilized at this level. Men were working fewer hours but were making more money, as measured in terms of the growth in real wages and in the mass consumption of American families, who were now able to subsist solely on the husband's wages. But the definition of good providing also rose dramatically: a revolution of rising expectations for the male breadwinner, expectations to be met by purchases of cars and home electrical goods, from washing machines to refrigerators to lamps and radios. A good provider came to be defined as a husband who paid his bills on time.[40]

The man unable to purchase these goods for his family was deficient as a man. By that definition, millions of American males in the Great Depression did not measure up. Men postponed marrying and fathered fewer children, gave up career plans and took lower-status jobs. As Mirra Komarovsky's report, written during the worst years of the depression (Chapter 13), indicates, male unemployment set off a chain reaction of family quarrels, alcoholism, wife-beating, and child abuse; it often led to male impotence, desertion, and marital breakup; wives nagged, and husbands sulked. The predictable response to these economic burdens was an increase in visits to prostitutes: Polly Adler, a Chicago madam, claimed that her business nearly doubled during the depression.[41]

These troubles lasted one decade but not two because World War II, the greatest mass participatory war in American history, put men in uniform or sent them back to work in wartime industry. In the long run, the war redistributed income and benefits to the men who fought it and away from the noncombatants (women, boys, and older men). More important, a grateful government passed the Servicemen's Readjustment Act in 1944 (the G.I. Bill of Rights), which subsidized college education and home purchases for more than 7.5 million veterans, an unprecedented governmental largesse that tranferred 14.5 billion dollars to G.I. Joes. At least partially in response to this federal subsidy, men could marry earlier, thereby precipitating the "marriage rush" at the end of World War II, which resulted (permanently) in a falling age at first marriage for American men.

But although World War II ended the widespread deficiencies of a large class of white men as family breadwinners, the experience of the majority of black workingmen can be considered as a form of permanent Great Depression. Despite the increase in real wages and the improved occupational status of black workingmen since the end of World War II, the rate of black unemployment has remained at an almost constant level—twice that of white men—and wages for black men (with much more variation) average about 60 percent those of white men. Trying to provide and failing to do so has been a central dilemma for poor black husbands and fathers, with some predictable consequences in the higher incidence of marital breakup among black than white men. In the excerpt from *Tally's Corner* (Chapter 14), Elliot

Liebow, an anthropologist, describes the life of black street-corner men in Washington, D.C. during the 1960s. They moved back and forth between different unskilled jobs, sometimes earning enough to support a family and then losing the job or quitting and thus failing to provide. Still, what the men wanted was what most other men had: an interesting job and one that provided a good standard of living.[42]

Although black streetcorner men experienced failure as providers, the men who were extremely successful, freed from worries about day-to-day subsistence, were in a sense prisoners of success. William H. Whyte's *The Organization Man*, published in 1956, found the corporate wife married to the man but the man married to the job: In order to rise in the corporation, he had to neglect his wife and children. Many men expressed concern that the job gave them no time for their families, but most actually preferred the office to the home. With expense account trips and business lunches, the Organization Man had a higher standard of living on company time than with his family. Moreover, the corporation forced the husband to grow and develop, whereas the wife, as one executive put it, "stayed home—literally and figuratively," creating the problem of the "outgrown wife," about which few managers chose to speak.[43]

Although companionship may have been a characteristic feature in the modern ideology about male–female relations, the emphasis on male–male relations returned to competition, an almost complete reversal of the belief in camaraderie that was part of an earlier age. The form of male competition or cooperation was structured by the world of work and therein divided men who had careers from those who had jobs. For career men, an involvement in work was far more absorbing than their involvement in family or leisure. The training of middle-class men began in school, where the basis of competition was not just physical but mental ability and the form of aggressiveness verbal as well as athletic. Corporate work required no physical strength,

although athletics was always claimed to be the necessary
training ground for managerial skill, thereby linking forms of
adolescent and adult male competition in the business class.
The managerial style emphasized interpersonal skills, coolness and suppression of affect, efficient and rational planning. Although managers retained ultimate responsibility in
the organization, they also needed to maintain its smooth
functioning by promoting cooperation and group effort,
even among likely competitors. This middle-class view of
men's work seems to have emerged from popular literature
by the 1920s. In the *Manliness of Christ*, published in 1911,
Jesus appeared as a well-developed athlete, aggressive and
slightly warmongerish—"No Prince of Peace at Any Price."
By 1925, in Bruce Barton's *The Man Nobody Knows*, Jesus had
come to resemble an advertising executive, the carpenter's
son who built his own organization and managed a group of
twelve subordinates with executive ability and personal
charisma.

For the ordinary man, machine technology had
supplanted reliance on brute physical strength. The village
blacksmith, who depended on his muscles to hammer out
tools of iron, had been replaced by the machine, which
stamped out patterns at a pace faster than hundreds of individual blacksmiths could ever have achieved. No longer toiling with his hands, the male worker now tended, repaired,
fed, assembled, or steered a machine. A declining number of
men were employed in occupations requiring muscular
strength—longshoremen, miners, fishermen, unskilled
laborers—and more men were truck and bus drivers, park-
ing lot attendants, and factory operatives. (Indeed, knowing
how to repair machines or how to change an automobile tire
became a means of validating masculinity.) Some men found
these jobs of interest and their relationships with coworkers
of importance; others found the work boring, a monotony of
routine operations easily learned. Still, most workingmen

seemed to find the work intrinsically satisfying and a necessary means of providing for their families.

In the modern era, intimate male–male relationships could still be found—they were the norm for male adolescents—but the world sustaining a separate men's culture had faded. It was maintained past adolescence most strongly among men of lower social standing, who met and befriended each other at the workplace or at taverns, corner gas stations, bowling alleys, or on streetcorners. In the working class, this men's culture was, in fact, a separate and closed social system, best described in William Foote Whyte's *Street Corner Society,* a brilliant reconstruction of working-class Italian–American male society in the 1920s. Here, the men's social world consisted of four interlocking, mutually interdependent groups who maintained regular contact: mobsters, police, streetcorner gangs, and politicians. Whyte's portrait of male society was derived from men living in an old ethnic neighborhood of Boston; even in the 1920s, upward occupational mobility and suburban residence was helping to destroy it.[44] By the 1950s, a study of an Italian neighborhood less than a mile from the one Whyte had written about no longer found an intact male social system, but a fragmented culture. Instead of joining their friends on the streetcorner, Italian–American men were now often inside with their wives watching television. What had happened to the boys' night out? Even when men attended sports events, they took their wives as often as their male buddies. Although the workplace often remained the last bastion of a men's culture, the autonomous, virtually separate life of men so evident in lodges, taverns, and other public institutions had increasingly become peripheral to men's daily lives.

In sum, the modern ideal man was a good provider, a friendly companion, and a skilled lover. He had always been expected to be a breadwinner, but now he was asked to be the mainstay as well of a new style of mass consumption. The Great Depression threatened man's ability to provide these goods, and the emergence of more bureaucratized forms of work made paid work stressful in new ways. The relationship of man to man, no longer a great comradeship, was now a mere acquaintance at school or work. Many male social institutions had gone the way of the barbershop quartet: They are now quaint artifacts or, if still accepted, the joint property of both sexes.

EPILOGUE: SINCE THE 1960s

In the early 1960s, blacks in the South—boycotting segregated schools, organizing voter registration drives, and marching in every major city to secure the passage of new civil rights laws—demanded an end to generations of apartheid. Earlier historical experience had already proven the close connection between the cause of blacks and that of women. In the 1830s, abolitionist women, moved by the similarities between themselves and the slaves, demanded freedom for women. In the 1960s, involvement in the civil rights movement began to ripple outward, affecting women and many other social groups, who came to view themselves and their social movements in terms of liberation from traditional constraints.

Changes in the accepted definitions of manhood were forwarded by three social movements, each of which in turn began to criticize long-standing features of the male role: the women's movement, the gay movement, and the men's movement. The re-emergence of the women's movement in the 1960s grew from two constituencies: professional women, confronting differentials in pay, promotion, and positions of leadership, who founded NOW (the National Organization of Women) in 1965; and younger, mostly college-educated women, dissatisfied with a secondary role in the civil rights movement, the New Left, and anti-war groups. The NOW membership was much larger and more immediately influential, but the New Left women led the way in introducing a much wider range of issues, seeing in sexuality, socialization, and the division of labor in the home the sources of women's inequality.[45] The feminist movement had clear implications for the analysis of men's roles. From Doris Lessing to Marge Piercy, feminist novels portrayed their male characters as emotionally frozen, unable to express feelings, or as immature and irresponsible. Women activists were relegated to female tasks—typing memos, bringing coffee, and doing all the cleaning and childcare— and found that men monopolized political discussion and decision making.

The gay liberation movement, like the women's movement, drew much of its constituency from younger, mostly college-educated men and women who had been part of the civil rights and anti-war movements. Gay liberation's critique of the Western taboo against male expression of intimacy and affection raised unresolved issues for all men, irregardless of sexual orientation. Its precursor was the Mattachine Society, founded in the 1950s as a response to McCarthyite persecution of homosexuals.[46] For almost two decades, Mattachine pressed for legal changes and relied on quiet persuasion, but in the heightened social atmosphere of the late 1960s, gay liberation, boisterous and proud, entered. Its origins are usually dated to the Stonewall Resistance of 1969, when gay men and lesbians in Greenwich Village openly fought against police harassment.

The third of these social movements, the men's movement, began the next year with the formation of a Men's Center in Berkeley. That year Jack Sawyer, a psychologist previously active in civil rights and anti-war movements, published a short article, "On Male Liberation," in *Liberation* magazine. A men's newspaper, *Brother: A Forum for Men against Sexism*, began in Berkeley in 1971. Men's consciousness-raising groups appeared with increasing regularity in the early 1970s, and four books representing a new perspective on the male role were published in 1974: Warren Farrell's *The Liberated Man*, Marc Feigen Fasteau's *The Male Machine*, Joseph Pleck and Jack Sawyer's *Men and Masculinity*, and Jack Nichols' *Men's Liberation: A New Definition of Masculinity*. A feature-length documentary film, "Men's Lives," by Will Roberts and Josh Hanig was released that year. Local groups sponsored several national conferences in Knoxville, Tennessee; State College, Pennsylvania; St. Louis, Missouri; Ramapo, New Jersey; and Los Angeles, California; which in turn led to the formation of the first national men's organization, The Man's Awareness Network (MAN), and then to Men Allied for Liberation and Equality (MALE) and MAN for ERA.

During the initial phase of organization, the main activity was meeting in consciousness-raising groups modeled after similar women's groups. In the belief borrowed from feminism that "the personal is political," men in these groups sought to identify sexual–political issues through the examination of their lives. Warren Farrell's nationwide lecture tours to promote his book led to the formation of men's groups across the country, especially on college campuses. Gradually the men's movement began to develop public education actitivies: Numerous resource centers emerged in several cities as well as the national conferences and the national organizations already noted. Projects, representing a diversity of concerns, were begun: childcare collectives; a men's music collective, producing and distributing a record on the Folkways label; a mail-order distribution service for men's awareness materials; the Malebox; and groups concerned with such issues as rape, wife abuse, and the need for men to take greater responsibility for contraception.

The men's movement was both a response to the social changes represented by the women's movement and a social movement in its own right. Insofar as women and men live in an intimate association, changes for one sex required and contributed to changes for the other. Because women were beginning to act in ways that no longer complemented many traditional male behaviors, some men began to experience a kind of strain in their own roles. This new situation led directly to the emergence of the men's movement. In its early days, the men's movement focused on new and more egalitarian forms of male–female relationships. In this sense, the men's movement was a response to the women's movement. But the emergence of the women's movement along with the additional impetus from the gay movement also created a climate wherein long-standing issues in the male role could eventually be discussed. In that sense, the men's movement was responding not only to feminism but also to many issues in the male role that were unconnected with women. As the question of relations between men began to receive more attention, it became essential to confront prejudice toward homosexuals, as gay liberation had urged, along with other issues among men—competition and intimacy between men, a son's relationship with his father, and fears of emotional expressiveness. One of the central arguments of the men's liberation analysis was that men create and foster hierarchies of competition. Women function as rewards for that competition and as refuges from it. Competition between men also brings forth male aggression and violence, even as other men seek to constrain and limit it. Male friendships gave some superficial intimacy but were often devoid of deeper expressions of love and affection. Men's fear of love for and sexual relations with other men, the men's liberation viewpoint argued, often resulted in the repression of all emotional feelings and in the hatred and fear of homosexuals.[47]

By the middle 1970s, the retreat from social activism was underway, but all three of these social movements continued to reshape American cultural and family life. On the one hand, many of the long-sought reforms—an equal rights amendment to the Constitution, access to free abortions for indigent women, an end to discrimination against homosexuals—failed to pass or were blocked. Despite more than a decade of affirmative action programs, men continued to dominate most of the prestigious, well-paying jobs and to push the levers of power in politics and in corporations. On the other hand, across the country, even among those previously untouched by an earlier decade of social activism, there was a growing acceptance of new definitions of masculinity. Homosexuals felt freer than ever before to claim their identity openly, demanding not simply tolerance but recognition and political power. Men were entering nontraditional jobs, from nursing to midwifery, or were drawn to work with young children in day care centers and kindergartens. Some men, taking fathering more seriously than men had in the past, wanted to be present in the delivery room, sought paternity leaves from their jobs in order to spend more time with their children, and were seeking to raise sons and daughters free from many of the traditional definitions of masculine and feminine behavior. For the first time, national surveys in the mid 1970s began to find that men with employed wives were spending increasing amounts of time in housework.[48] As much as any single indication of altered sensibility, a new gender-conscious vocabulary helped to identify and promote sex-role change.

This awareness has generated the interest in and the need for a history of the sexes, which, in its investigation of the past, holds out great hope for the future. For if "man" has not been singular but diverse and has been fashioned not by divine creation but from concrete experiences, then man's new life can diverge from his heritage. What more important lesson can be learned from the study of men's past?

NOTES

[1]Two general books on men's history are Alan M. Kirshner, *Masculinity in a Historical Perspective: Readings and Discussions* (Washington, D.C.: University Press of America, 1977) and Joe L. Dubbert, *A Man's Place* (Englewood Cliffs, New Jersey: Prentice-Hall, 1979). Joan Mellen's perceptive analysis of masculinity in American movies, entitled *Big Bad Wolves:*

Masculinity in American Film (New York: Pantheon, 1977) serves as the foundation for any survey of twentieth-century American manhood. Donald Spoto's *Camerado: Hollywood and the American Man* (New York: New American Library, 1978) should also be consulted. Jonathan Katz' *Gay American History: Lesbians and Gay Men in the U.S.A.* (New York: Thomas Crowell, 1976) is a superb collection of documents. G. J. Barker-Benfield's *The Horrors of the Half-Known Life: Male Attitudes Toward Women and Sexuality in Nineteenth Century America* (New York: Harper and Row, 1976) and Peter Gabriel Filene's *Him/Her/Self: Sex Roles in Modern America* (New York: Harcourt Brace Jovanovich, 1974) contain extended discussions of the male as well as female roles. A general overview of the history of the male workrole is Donald Bell's "Changing Men: Paths to a New Male Consciousness," in Robert A. Lewis, ed., *Men in Difficult Times*, forthcoming, 1980. A selective social science bibliography that summarizes current research, compiled by Kathleen Grady, Robert Brannon, and Joseph H. Pleck, is *The Male Sex Role: An Annotated Research Bibliography* (Rockville, Maryland: National Institute of Mental Health, 1979). Articles on current and historical aspects of the male role can be found in David S. Ferriero, *Bibliography of the Men's Studies Collection*, third edition (Cambridge: Humanities Library of the Massachusetts Institute of Technology, 1977). Joseph Kett's *Rites of Passage: Adolescence in America; 1970 to the Present* (New York: Basic Books, 1970) contains a wealth of interesting material about male child rearing, schooling, and youth culture. The difficulty is that Kett does not use sex as a category of analysis, and thus he fails to analyze male adolescence as the history of a gender group. Philip Greven's *The Protestant Temperament: Patterns of Child-Rearing, Religious Experience, and the Self in Early America* (New York: Knopf, 1977) divides early American Protestant males into three types: the evangelicals, the moderates, and the genteels. The framework in understanding these "ideal types" of American manhood is the "sex-role identity" perspective. The major difficulty here is that Greven is applying modern categories and concerns (anxiety, father absence) to a distinctively premodern society. Furthermore, many of the crucial assumptions of the sex-role identity perspective, when adequately put to the test, have failed to be validated.

[2]Joan Kelly-Gadol, "The Social Relation of the Sexes: Methodological Implications of Women's History," *Signs: A Journal of Women in Culture and Society*, v. 1 (Summer, 1976), p. 814.

[3]Natalie Zemon Davis, "Women's History in Transition: The European Case," *Feminist Studies*, v. 3, Nos. 3–4 (1976), pp. 83–103.

[4]Lonna M. Malmsheimer, "Daughters of Zion: New England Roots of American Feminism," *New England Quarterly*, v. 50, No. 3 (September,

1977), pp. 484–504; Ben Barker-Benfield, "Anne Hutchinson and the Puritan Attitude Toward Women, *Feminist Studies*, v. 1, No. 2 (Fall, 1972), pp. 65–69. A different point of view can be found in Laurel Thatcher Ulrich, "Vertuous Women Found: New England Ministerial Literature, 1668–1735," *American Quarterly*, v. 28, No. 1 (Spring, 1976), pp. 20–40.

⁵Keith Thomas, "The Double Standard," *Journal of the History of Ideas*, v. 20, No. 2 (April, 1959), p. 210.

⁶Nancy F. Cott, "Eighteenth-Century Family and Social Life Revealed in Massachusetts Divorce Records," *Journal of Social History*, v. 10 (Fall, 1976), pp. 20–43; Nancy F. Cott, "Passionless: An Interpretation of Victorian Sexual Ideology, 1790–1850," *Signs: A Journal of Women in Culture and Society*, v. 4, No. 2 (Winter, 1978), pp. 219–236; Carroll Smith-Rosenberg, "Sex as Symbol in Victorian Purity: An Ethnohistorical Analysis of Jacksonian America," in John Demos and Sarane Spence Boocock, eds., *Turning Points: Historical and Sociological Essays on the Family* (Chicago: University of Chicago, 1978), pp. 212–247.

⁷D. Kelly Weisberg, "Under Great Temptations Heer: Women and Divorce in Puritan Massachusetts," *Feminist Studies*, v. 2 (1975), pp. 183–194; Nancy F. Cott, "Divorce and the Changing Status of Women in Eighteenth-Century Massachusetts," *William and Mary Quarterly*, v. 33 (October, 1976), pp. 586–614.

⁸Kenneth Lockridge, *Literacy in Colonial New England: An Enquiry into the Social Context of Literacy in the Early Modern West* (New York: Norton, 1974), pp. 13–27.

⁹Benjamin Wadsworth, *A Well-Ordered Family*, in David J. Rothman and Sheila M. Rothman, eds., *Sources of the American Social Tradition*, v. 1 (New York: Basic Books, 1975), p. 45.

¹⁰Philip Greven, *Four Generations: Population, Land, and Family in Colonial Andover, Massachusetts* (Ithaca: Cornell University, New York, 1970); Barry Levy, "Tender Plants: Quaker Farmers and Children in the Delaware Valley, 1681–1735," *Journal of Family History*, v. 3, No. 2 (Summer, 1976), pp. 116–135; Linda Auwers, "Fathers, Sons, and Wealth in Colonial Windsor, Connecticut," *Journal of Family History*, v. 3, No. 2 (Summer, 1978), pp. 136–149.

¹¹Lois Green Carr and Lorena S. Walsh, "The Planter's Wife: The Experience of White Women in Seventeenth-Century Maryland," *William and Mary Quarterly*, 3rd series, v. 34 (1977), pp. 542–571; Herbert Moller, "Sex Composition and Correlated Cultural Patterns in Colonial America,"

William and Mary Quarterly, 3rd series, v. 2 (1945), pp. 113–153; Robert V. Wells, "Quaker Marriage Patterns in a Colonial Perspective," *William and Mary Quarterly*, 3rd series, v. 29 (1972), pp. 415–442; Allan Kulikoff, "The Beginnings of the Afro-American Family in Maryland," in Aubrey C. Land, Lois Green Carr, and Edward C. Papenfuse, eds., *Law, Society and Politics in Maryland* (Baltimore: Johns Hopkins, 1977), pp. 171–196; Russell R. Menard, "Immigrants and Their Increase: The Process of Population Growth in Early Colonial Maryland," in Land, Carr, and Papenfuse, eds., *Law, Society and Politics*, pp. 88–110.

[12]Martin Duberman, "Male Impotence in Colonial Pennsylvania," *Signs: A Journal of Women and Culture*, v. 4, No. 2 (Winter, 1978), pp. 395–401.

[13]Jonathan Katz, ed., *Gay American History: Lesbians and Gay Men in the U.S.A.* pp. 451–456.

[14]Only in Pennsylvania, where the Quaker religion opposed the death penalty, was the penalty less severe: Homosexuality was punishable by six months' imprisonment. After the Quaker influence receded in Pennsylvania, the legislature adopted a stricter tri-partite punishment for sodomy: imprisonment for single white men, castration and imprisonment for married white men, and the death penalty for black men. Both Pennsylvania and Virginia adopted separate statutes for each race. Louis Crompton, "Homosexuals and the Death Penalty in Colonial America," *Journal of Homosexuality*, v. 1, No. 3 (Spring, 1976), pp. 277–294. For patterns of persecution in the British navy, see Arthur N. Gilbert, "Buggery and the British Navy, 1700–1861," *Journal of Social History*, v. 10, No. 1 (Fall, 1976), pp. 72–98 and for those in the American navy, see Harold D. Langley, *Social Reform in the United States Navy, 1798–1862* (Urbana: University of Illinois, 1967), pp. 172–174.

[15]Carroll Smith-Rosenberg, "Sex as Symbol," pp. 212–247; Lewis Perry, " 'Progress, not Pleasure, Is Our Aim': The Sexual Advice of an Antebellum Radical," *Journal of Social History*, v. 12, No. 3 (Spring, 1979), pp. 354–367; Linda Gordon, "Voluntary Motherhood: The Beginnings of Feminist Birth Control Ideas in the United States," in Mary S. Hartman and Lois Banner, eds., *Clio's Consciousness Raised: New Perspectives on the History of Women* (New York: Harper and Row, 1974), pp. 54–71; Daniel Scott Smith, "Family Limitation, Sexual Control, and Domestic Feminism in Victorian America," in Hartman and Banner, eds., *Clio's Consciousness Raised*, pp. 119–136.

[16]For the impact of the *First* Great Awakening, consult Cedric B.

Cowing, "Sex and Preaching in the Great Awakening," *American Quarterly*, v. 20, No. 3 (Fall, 1968), pp. 624–644 and Rhys Isaac, "Preachers and Patriots: Popular Culture and the Revolution in Virginia," in Alfred F. Young, ed., *The American Revolution* (Dekalb, Illinois: Northern Illinois, 1976), pp. 127–156.

[17]Peter T. Cominos, "Late-Victorian Sexual Respectability and the Social System," *International Review of Social History,* v. 8 (1963), pp. 18–48, 216–250 and Ben Barker-Benfield, "The Spermatic Economy: A Nineteenth Century View of Sexuality," *Feminist Studies*, v. 1, No. 1 (1972), pp. 45–67.

[18]Kathleen Marquis, "Diamond Cut Diamond: Mormon Women and the Cult of Domesticity in the Nineteenth Century," *The University of Michigan Papers in Women's Studies*, v. 11, No. 2 (1976), pp. 105–124. The persistence of the ideology of domesticity, even on the frontier, is discussed by Johnny Faragher and Christine Stansell in "Women and their Families on the Overland Trail, 1842–1867," *Feminist Studies*, v. 2, Nos. 2–3 (1975), pp. 150–166.

[19]As quoted in Eleanor Flexner, *Century of Struggle: The Woman's Rights Movement in the United States* (New York: Harvard University, 1968), pp. 77, 64.

[20]David Hackett Fischer, *Growing Old in America* (New York: Oxford, 1977), p. 79. Daniel Scott Smith has studied the declining parental control over marriage in this period by comparing the age at marriage of sons whose fathers died early with those whose fathers lived to an old age. He assumed that the greater the difference in age at first marriage between the two groups of sons, the stronger the force of paternal control would be. By the end of the eighteenth century, he found a declining age difference between the two groups of sons, indicating declining parental involvement in the choice of marriage partners. Daniel Scott Smith, "Parental Power and Marriage Patterns: An Analysis of Historical Trends in Hingham, Massachusetts," *Journal of Marriage and the Family*, v. 35 (August, 1973), pp. 419–428.

[21]Ray Allen Billington, *America's Frontier Heritage* (New York: Holt, Rinehart, and Winston, 1966), pp. 139–157; John G. Cawelti, *Apostles of the Self-Made Man* (Chicago: University of Chicago, 1965), pp. 9–38; Theodore Green, *American Heroes: The Changing Models of Success in American Magazines* (New York: Oxford, 1970); Judy Hilkey, "Masculinity and the Self-Made Man in America, 1850–1900," unpublished paper delivered at the Berkshire Conference on the History of Women, Radcliffe College, October, 1974; Irwin G. Wyllie, *The Self-Made Man in America: The Myth of*

Rags to Riches (New York: Free Press, 1954); Moses Rischin, ed., *The American Gospel of Success* (Chicago: University of Chicago, 1968).

[22]Jill Siegel Dodd, "The Working Classes and the Temperance Movement in Ante-Bellum Boston," *Labor History*, v. 19, No. 4 (Fall, 1978), pp. 510–531. See also Bruce Laurie, "Nothing on Compulsion: Life Styles of Philadelphia Artisans, 1820–1850," *Labor History*, v. 15, No. 3 (Summer, 1974), pp. 336–337 and Alan Dawley and Paul Faler, "Working-Class Culture and Politics in the Industrial Revolution: Sources of Loyalism and Rebellion," *Journal of Social History*, v. 9, No. 4 (Summer, 1976), pp. 466–480. Unfortunately, none of these authors make explicit the fact that this is a *male* working-class style.

[23]John S. Haller and Robin M. Haller, *The Physician and Sexuality in Victorian America* (Urbana: University of Illinois, 1976), pp. 190–234; Regina L. Wolkoff, "The Sex Revolution Revisited: Ideas about Male Sexuality in America, 1890–1930," unpublished paper delivered at the Organization of American Historians, April, 1978, pp. 1–20; R. P. Neuman, "Masturbation, Madness, and the Modern Concepts of Childhood and Adolescence," *Journal of the Social History*, v. 8, No. 3 (Spring, 1975), pp. 1–27; Jeffrey Weeks, " 'Sins and Diseases': Some Notes on Homosexuality in the Nineteenth Century," *History Workshop*, v. 1 (Spring, 1976), pp. 211–219; H. Tristam Engelhardt, Jr., "The Disease of Masturbation: Values and the Concept of Disease," *Bulletin of the History of Medicine*, v. 48, No. 2 (1974), pp. 234–248; Arthur N. Gilbert, "Doctor, Patient and Onanist Diseases in the Nineteenth Century," *Journal of the History of Medicine and Allied Sciences*, v. 3, No. 3 (July, 1975), pp. 217–234; Vern L. Bullough and Martha Vogt, "Homosexuality and the 'Secret Sin' in Pre-Freudian America," *Journal of the History of Medicine and Allied Sciences*, v. 28, No. 2 (April, 1973), pp. 143–155. A general summary of male mistreatment by Victorian doctors is provided by Gail Pat Parsons in " 'Equal Treatment for All': American Medical Remedies for Male Sexual Problems, 1850–1900," *Journal of the History of Medicine and Allied Sciences*, v. xxxii, No. 1 (January, 1977), pp. 55–71.

[24]Howard N. Rabinowitz, "The Washington Legend, 1865–1900: The Heroic Image in Flux," *American Studies*, v. 17, No. 1 (Spring, 1974), pp. 5–21; Francis J. Convares, "Labor and Leisure in Pittsburgh: Some Tendencies in Late Nineteenth–Century Working–Class Culture," unpublished paper, October 1977, pp. 1–25. On the ideal husband, see Michael Gordon and M. Charles Bernstein, "Mate Choice and Domestic Life in the Nineteenth-Century Marriage Manual," *Journal of Marriage and the Family*, v. 32, No. 4 (November, 1970), pp. 655–674 and Herman R. Lantz, M.

Schultz, and M. O'Hara, "The Changing American Family from Prein-dustrial to the Industrial Period: A Final Report," *American Sociological Review*, v. 42 (June, 1977), pp. 406–421. A similar investigation of British norms and practices is Carol Christ's "Victorian Masculinity and the Angel in the House," in Martha Vicinus, ed., *A Widening Sphere: Changing Roles of Victorian Women* (Bloomington, Indiana: Indiana University, 1977), pp. 146–162.

[25]Joseph Kett, *Rites of Passage: Adolescence in America, 1790 to the Present*, p. 173. For some case studies, see James R. McGovern, "David Graham Phillips and the Virility Impulse of the Progressives," *New England Quarterly*, v. 39 (1966), pp. 334–355; Gerald L. Marriner, "A Victorian in the Modern World: the 'Liberated' Male's Adjustment to the New Woman and the New Morality," *South Atlantic Quarterly*, v. 76 (1977), pp. 190–203.

[26]*Muller v. Oregon*, 208 US 412, 422–23 (1908).

[27]*New York Times*, May 3, 1912, column 2, p. 10.

[28]Quoted in Joseph L. Dubbert, *The Masculine Mystique*, p. 16. Dubbert extensively explores the impact of the Civil War on American manhood. See as well George M. Fredrickson, *The Inner Civil War: Northern Intellectuals and the Crisis of the Union* (New York: Harper and Row, 1965).

[29]As quoted in Peter Filene, *Him/Her/Self*, p. 80.

[30]As cited in Joseph Kett, *Rites of Passage*, pp. 162–163.

[31]Ernest Thompson Seton, *Boy Scouts of America: A Handbook of Woodcraft, Scouting and Life-Craft* (New York: Doubleday and Page, 1910) as quoted in Roderick Nash, ed., *The Call of the Wild 1900–1916* (New York: G. Braziller, 1971), p. 23.

[32]Joseph Kett, *Rites of Passage*, p. 224. A full-scale study of these boys' organizations is David Irving MacLeod, "*Good Boys Made Better: The Boy Scouts of America, Boys Brigades, and YMCA Boys' Work, 1880–1920*," unpublished Ph.D. dissertation, University of Wisconsin, 1973.

[33]As quoted in Francis J. Convares, "Labor and Leisure in Pittsburgh," p. 7.

[34]Jonathan Katz, ed., *Gay American History*, pp. 39–52. See also Vern L. Bullough, "Challenges to Societal Attitudes Toward Homosexuality in the Late Nineteenth and Early Twentieth Centuries," *Social Science Quarterly*, v. 58 (June, 1977), pp. 291–304.

³⁵Joseph Kett, *Rites of Passage*, p. 36.

³⁶John Modell, Frank F. Furstenberg, Jr., and Theodore Hershberg, "Social Change and Transitions in Adulthood in Historical Perspective," *Journal of Family History*, v. 1 (Autumn, 1976), pp. 7–32.

³⁷A. C. Kinsey, W. B. Pomeroy, and C. E. Martin, *Sexual Behavior in the Human Male* (Philadelphia: Saunders, 1948), pp. 595–609; Paul Robinson, *The Modernization of Sex: Havelock Ellis, Alfred Kinsey, William Masters and Virginia Johnson* (New York, 1976), pp. 1–41.

³⁸The best single modern summary of the sex-role identity perspective is supplied by Henry B. Biller in *Paternal Deprivation: Family, School, Sexuality, and Society* (Lexington, Massachusetts: Lexington Books, 1974). A brief critique of this perspective is Joseph H. Pleck's "The Male Sex Role: Definitions, Problems, and Sources of Change," *Journal of Social Issues*, v. 32, No. 3 (1976), pp. 155–164. The detailed criticism of this perspective will be available in *The Male Role: Sex Role Identity and Sex Role Strain*, by Joseph H. Pleck, to be published by M.I.T. Press in 1980.

³⁹Michael Gordon, "From an Unfortunate Necessity to a Cult of Mutual Orgasm: Sex in American Marital Education Literature 1830–1940," in James M. Henslin, ed., *Studies in the Sociology of Sex* (New York: Appleton-Century-Crofts, 1971), pp. 53–77; Paul Robinson, *The Modernization of Sex*, pp. 42–119.

In the nineteenth century the double standard was declining because men were being asked to remain pure. In the twentieth century, women's sexual standard had come closer to men's. Nonetheless, there is still a substantial difference in behavior. College men in the late 1960s and early 1970s believed that men should have more premarital sexual freedom than women, and they practiced what they preached.

The extramarital double standard also remains in place. In Kinsey's data (from 1938 to 1953), half of all husbands but only 20 percent of all wives had affairs. In a 1973 *Playboy* survey, 41 percent of husbands and 8 percent of wives had an outside lover. Modern husbands appear slightly more monogamous than the Kinsey men, but this may have been due to the slightly younger age of the *Playboy* sample. Mary Z. Ferrell, William L. Tolone, and Robert H. Walsh, "Maturational and Societal Changes in the Sexual Double Standard: A Panel Analysis (1967–1971; 1970–1974)," *Journal of Marriage and the Family*, v. 39, No. 2 (May, 1977), pp. 255–272 and Morton Hunt, "Sexual Behavior in the 1970's: Extramarital and Postmarital Sex," in Chad Gordon and Gayle Johnson, eds., *Readings in Human Sexuality: Contemporary Perspectives* (New York: Harper and Row, 1976), p. 244.

[40]Elaine Tyler May, "The Pressure to Provide: Class, Consumerism, and Divorce in Urban America, 1880–1920," *Journal of Social History*, v. 12, No. 2 (Winter, 1978), pp. 180–193. An interesting analysis of the relative stability in the male work week since the 1940s is John D. Owen's "Hours of Work in the Long Run: Trends, Explanations, Scenarios, and Implications," unpublished paper delivered at the Conference on Work Time and Employment, National Commission for Manpower Policy, Washington, D.C., October, 1978.

[41]Other studies with information on the male role during the Great Depression include Robert Lynd and Helen Merrell Lynd, *Middletown in Transition: A Study in Cultural Conflicts* (New York: Harcourt Brace, 1937), pp. 178–179; Louis Terkel, *Hard Times: An Oral History of the Great Depression* (New York: Pantheon, 1970), pp. 196–197; Ruth Milkman, "Women's Work and Economic Crisis: Some Lessons of the Great Depression," *Review of Radical Political Economics*, v. 8, No. 1 (Spring, 1976), pp. 81–85; Andrea Boxer, "The American Father and the Great Depression," unpublished Master's thesis, Bryn Mawr College, 1976.

[42]For an overview of many issues pertaining to the American black male, see Doris Y. Wilkinson and Ronald L. Taylor, eds., *The Black Male in America: Perspectives on His Status in Contemporary Society* (Chicago: Nelson Hall, 1977) and Robert Staples, "Masculinity and Race: The Dual Dilemma of Black Men," *The Journal of Social Issues*, v. 34, No. 1 (1978), pp. 169–183.

[43]William H. Whyte, Jr., *The Organization Man* (Garden City, New York: Doubleday, 1957).

[44]William F. Whyte, *Street Corner Society* (Chicago: University of Chicago, 1943).

[45]Sara Evans, *Personal Politics: The Roots of Women's Liberation in the Civil Rights Movement and the New Left* (New York: Alfred A. Knopf, 1979); Barbara Easton, "Feminism and the Contemporary Family," *Socialist Review*, v. 8, No. 3 (May–June 1977), pp. 11–36.

[46]John D. Emilio, "Dreams Deferred," *The Body Politic* (November, 1978; December, 1978–January, 1979), pp. 24–29.

[47]Phyllis Chesler, *About Men* (New York: Simon and Schuster, 1978); Joseph H. Pleck, "My Male Sex Role—and Ours," in Deborah David and Robert Brannon, *The Forty-Nine Percent Majority: Readings on the Male Role* (Lexington, Massachusetts: Addison-Wesley, 1975), pp. 253–264.

[48]Joseph H. Pleck and Linda Lang, "Men's Family Role: Its Nature and Consequences," Working Paper, Center for Research on Women, Wellesley College, 1978; John Robinson, *Changes in Americans' Use of Time, 1965–1975* (Cleveland: Communications Research Center of Cleveland State University, 1978).

period

1

(1630-1820)

Agrarian
Patriarchy

chapter 1

"Things Fearful to Name":

Sodomy and Buggery in Seventeenth-Century New England

by Robert Oaks

Before the introduction of Christianity, the "blood brotherhood" between Indian men often included sexual relations, and homosexuals commonly held positions of respect and status in most native American cultures. Elsewhere in North America, homosexuals have been hanged, castrated, jailed, and lobotomized, a history of almost unrelieved persecution. But the manner of persecution and the justifications for it have changed dramatically in American history. Robert Oaks examines the context of homosexual persecution within seventeenth-century Puritan culture. With their Biblical views of sex only in marriage, the Puritans watched out for any form of deviant sex and even punished those married couples found to engage in nonprocreational acts. In studying the persecution of homosexuals, Oaks must rely on court cases involving sodomy or bestiality—at the most, nineteen cases. Despite the paucity of evidence, Oaks finds that some were more deviant than others: Puritan statutes made male but not female homosexuality a crime, and men convicted of bestiality were more likely to be hanged than male homosexuals. Oaks suggests some of the reasons for these differences. The Puritans, who defined man in terms of his place in the Great Chain of Being, may have believed that the practice of bestiality made man too much like an animal. Oaks does not offer a similar explanation for the statutory punishment of male homosexuality but not of lesbianism. It seems likely that, despite the general view that women were the more passionate sex, the Puritan fathers found it difficult to believe that womens' passions were aroused by other women. Their extreme punishment of sodomy in males was a recognition that men were capable of feeling and acting upon homosexual attractions.

In recent years, historians have begun to study the long neglected story of human sexuality. The previous neglect of a subject that affects virtually every individual stemmed both from a reluctance to discuss such a sensitive topic and from the difficulties involved in research. Several demographic studies of 17th-century New England recently have begun to probe such questions as the incidence of adultery, divorce, and pre-marital sex, but as yet there is very little information on variant sexual activity such as homosexuality and bestiality.[1]

Research into these areas is more difficult because one of the major sources for the historian of heterosexual activity—birth records—is obviously absent. The most important source for variant sexual activity in colonial New England is court records. This evidence should be used cautiously since it provides information only about people caught in specific acts. One could argue that court records for this period no more reflect the true nature of homosexuality and bestiality in Puritan society than the records of the New York Police Department do of homosexuality in the late 20th-century New York City. Nevertheless, these records do show that this type of activity existed in colonial New England and also suggest that some of the few speculations that historians have made are inaccurate. It is not true, for instance, as Edmund Morgan claimed many years ago, that "Sodomy [was] usually punished with death."[2] Nor do the records of Plymouth substantiate Geoffrey May's claim that "between one-fifth and one-fourth [of all sex offenses] were for various homosexual practices."[3] On the other hand, these records do reveal Puritan attitudes toward variant sexual activity and suggest that even extreme attempts to suppress it could not eliminate it.[4]

"Things Fearful to Name": Sodomy and Buggery in Seventeenth-Century New England" by Robert F. Oaks. Reprinted by permission of the author and publisher from the *Journal of Social History*, v. 12, No. 3 (Winter 1978), 286–281. Copyright © 1978 by Peter N. Stearns.

There was some confusion of terminology in describing variant sex crimes in colonial America. The two terms used most often—buggery and sodomy—sometimes meant different things to different people. Usually, the Puritan colonies used the term sodomy to refer to homosexuality and buggery to refer to bestiality. But occasionally, buggery also meant homosexuality, sodomy referred to besitality, and, on one occasion, Massachusetts authorities tried without much success to stretch the definition of sodomy to apply to heterosexual child molestation.[5]

Both crimes were capital offenses in all the New England colonies. Homosexuality had been capital in England since the days of Henry VIII, but the Puritan colonies, where laws regulating moral behavior were often severe, patterned their laws not on the English statutes, but on the Old Testament. The one exception was Rhode Island, where the law drew on the New Testament.[6] Plymouth, the first colony specifically to make sodomy and buggery punishable by death (1636), included these crimes with other capital offenses, such as murder, rape, treason, witchcraft, and arson.[7] The law only applied to men, however. Lesbianism usually did not come under the definition of sodomy. John Cotton wanted to include lesbianism as a capital crime in a proposed legal code he drew up for Massachusetts in 1636, but his code was not accepted. Only in New Haven after 1655, when the colony did accept Cotton's code, was female homosexuality a capital crime, and even that exception ended when Connecticut incorporated the colony ten years later.[8]

Yet despite the harsh penalties for sodomy and buggery, Puritan leaders often refused to apply them, especially for homosexual activity. As with other types of crimes, the courts often employed the concept of remission of sentences for many sex crimes. Remission may have resulted from an enlightened attempt to move away from the traditional concept of punishment for retribution, it may have reflected economic realities in an area where labor was scarce, or it may have stemmed from a reluctance to apply capital punishment to crimes feared to be rather common. It is significant that Puritan authorities, despite the penalties on the books, apparently regarded homosexuality—though not bestiality—as not much worse than many "ordinary" sex crimes. Adultery, for example, was also a capital offense, but the death penalty was rarely inflicted in New England for that crime either.[9] This reluctance to punish illicit sexual activity of all types grew stronger in the latter decades of the 17th century.

The first recorded incident of homosexuality in New England occurred in 1629, when the ship *Talbot* arrived in Massachusetts. During the voyage, "5 beastly Sodomiticall boyes . . . confessed their wickedness not to be named." Unwilling to deal with anything so distasteful, Massachusetts authorities sent the boys back to England, arguing that since the crime occurred on the high seas, the Bay Colony had no jurisdiction.[10]

The colony of Plymouth seemed to have more homosexuality than other areas of New England, though this may simply indicate a greater willingness to prosecute such crimes, or, perhaps, less opportunity for privacy. There may have been problems with homosexuality in Plymouth as early as the mid-1620s. The well-known story of Thomas Morton of Merrymount could have homosexual overtones. William Bradford's description of the "great licentiousness" of Morton and his men hints that such activity may have taken place:

> And after they had got some goods into their hands, and got much by trading with the Indians, they spent it as vainly in quaffing and drinking, both wine and strong waters in great excess. . . . They set up a maypole, drinking and dancing about it many days together, inviting the Indian women for their consorts, dancing and frisking together like so many fairies, or furies, rather: and worse practices. As if they had anew revived and celebrated the feasts of the Roman goddess Flora, or the beastly practices of the mad Bacchanalians.[11]

Morton does not specify their "worse practices," but it is not unreasonable to assume that some of those Englishmen vol-·untarily living in isolation from all women except a few Indians would have practiced homosexuality. For some, it may have been situational, stemming from limited opportunities for heterosexual activity: but for others, homosexuality may have been the preference, as it undoubtedly was for English pirates in the West Indies later in the century.[12]

Several years later, in 1636, Plymouth held the first trial for homosexuality in New England. John Alexander and Thomas Roberts were "found guilty of lude behavior and uncleane carriage one [with] another, by often spendinge their seede one upon another." The evidence was conclusive, since the court had a witness and confessions from the accused. Furthermore, Alexander was "notoriously guilty that way," and had sought "to allure others thereunto." This was a clear-cut case, and, it would seem, an obvious time to apply the death penalty, adopted by the colony only a few months earlier. But instead, the court issued a more lenient sentence. Alexander was whipped, burned in the shoulder with a hot iron, and banished from the colony. Roberts, a servant, was whipped, returned to his master to serve out his time, and forbidden from ever owning land in the colony. Apparently there was some dispute over this last restriction, because the phrase "except hee manefest better desert" was inserted in the records, then crossed out.[13]

The leniency extended to the two men is perhaps surprising. Alexander's banishment suggests that the court was not worried about a labor shortage. Nor would a death sentence be out of line with penalties in other areas of English rule. In the mid-1620s, Virginia executed Richard Cornish for sodomy. Though there is some evidence that the charges may have been trumped up to rid the colony of a troublesome individual, the fact that sodomy was even chosen as an excuse for execution indicates that the 17th-century Englishman had few qualms about imposing death as punishment for that crime.[14] And in England, in 1631, the Earl of Castlehaven was found guilty and executed for crimes "so heinous and so horrible that a Christian man ought scarce to name them." Not only did Castlehaven abet the rape of his wife by one of his servants, but he also committed sodomy with several servants. This latter act brought the death sentence. Here, too, there was some remission when the Earl appealed directly to Charles I for mercy, but not nearly to the same degree granted by Plymouth to Alexander and Roberts. The King commuted the Earl's sentence from hanging to the more humane beheading, and then postponed the execution for a month to give Castlehaven "time for repentence."[15]

The Roberts and Alexander case also suggests that Plymouth officials prosecuted with some reluctance. They "often" engaged in such conduct, and Alexander was "notoriously guilty that way." If Alexander was so notorious, why had he not been punished before? Perhaps the magistrates were willing to overlook homosexuality unless it became too obvious, an attitude not unlike that of 20th-century America. It is even possible that the death penalty was an attempt to discourage widespread activity. The fact that it was not applied to such an obvious case only a few months after it went on the books suggests that it was meant only as a warning, and no one seriously thought of using it.

Another Plymouth sodomy case, in 1642, resulted in even more lenient treatment. The court found Edward Michell guilty of "lude and sodomiticall practices" with Edward Preston. Michell was also playing around with Lydia Hatch, and Preston attempted sodomy with one John Keene, but was turned down. To complicate matters even further, Lydia was caught in bed with her brother Jonathan. The sentences imposed for these various activities are particularly interesting since homosexuality in this case received approximately the same punishment as illicit heterosexuality. Lydia Hatch was publicly whipped. Michell and Preston were each whipped twice, once in Plymouth and again in

Barnstable. John Keene, because he resisted Preston's advances and reported the incident, was allowed to watch while Michell and Preston were whipped, though the record intriguingly states that "in some thing he was faulty" too. Jonathan Hatch, regarded as a vagrant, was whipped and then banished to Salem.[16] These penalties were not only extremely light, but were not much harsher than penalties imposed for the relatively common heterosexual crime of fornication.[17]

Lesbian activity was scarcely punished at all. There were no prescribed penalties on the books, which may explain why there is only one recorded case in New England. In 1649, Mary Hammon and Sarah Norman, both from Yarmouth, were indicted for "leude behavior each with other upon a bed." Mrs. Norman was also accused of "divers Lasivious speeches." Her sentence required that she make a public acknowledgement "of her unchast behavior" and included a warning that such conduct in the future would result in an unspecified harsher punishment. Inexplicably, Mary Hammon was "cleared with admonision." It is difficult to understand how one woman could be guilty and the other innocent, though it is possible that the court was more disturbed by Mrs. Norman's "lasivious speeches" than they were by her "leude behavior."[18]

There was undoubtedly much more homosexual activity than the court records indicate. By the early 1640s, Governor Bradford lamented the great number of sex crimes, not only heterosexual offenses, "But that which is even worse, even sodomy and buggery (things fearful to name) [which] have broke[n] forth in this land oftener than once." Bradford tried to explain what seemed to be a virtual crime wave. He suggested that the Devil was particularly active in those regions that attempted "to preserve holiness and purity." But he had nonreligious explanations as well. Because laws were so strict regarding sex crimes, they produced a lot of frustration "that it may be in this case as it is with waters when their streams are stopped or dammed up. When they get passage they flow with more violence." The dams of sexual wickedness obviously had broken in New England. On the other hand, Bradford suggested, perhaps contradicting himself, there was no more evil activity in Plymouth than elsewhere, "but they are here more discovered and seen and made public by due search, inquisition and due punishment."[19]

In addition to Bradford's suggestion that sex crimes were rampant, the court records hint at homosexual activity in addition to the three obvious cases described above. One of the earliest historians to study homosexuality in New England claimed that the Plymouth records "show that the prosecution for all sex offenses, between one-fifth and one-fourth were for various homosexual practices."[20] This estimate is very exaggerated. While there are numerous references to "uncleanness" or "unclean practices," the majority of them do make it clear that these were definitely heterosexual. A somewhat hasty count of sexual offenses in Plymouth records produced the following results: there were 129 definite heterosexual offenses including fornication, "licivious going in company of young men," kissing a married woman, adultery, prostitution, and rape; there were 3 definite homosexual offenses; 2 definite buggery cases; one accusation each for sodomy and buggery; and only 15 unspecified cases that might have been either homosexual or heterosexual. Out of a total of 151 sex offenses, then, there were at the most 19 cases of homosexuality, and probably fewer than that. These figures, however, should not in any sense be interpreted as reflecting the percentage of homosexual activity in Plymouth. It was undoubtedly easier, even in such a close knit society, to escape detection for homosexual activity than for heterosexual activity. The most common crime, by far, was fornication, and it was usually detected when pregnancy resulted, a risk obviously absent for homosexuals.

Some of the possible homosexual cases in the Plymouth

records do allow interesting speculation. Most suggestive is the case of Richard Berry and Teage Joanes. In 1649, Berry accused Joanes of sodomy, and both were ordered to attend the next court for trial. Berry also claimed that Joanes committed "unclean practisses" with Sarah Norman, the woman involved in the lesbian case. In the intervening six months between the accusation and the trial, however, Berry changed his mind and testified that he had lied, for which he was sentenced "to be whipte at the poste." If Berry's original intention had been merely to smear Joanes, it is difficult to understand why he would do it in such a way as to implicate himself. It is possible that the two men were lovers. Perhaps they had quarrelled, leading to the accusation, but later reconciled. Berry then decided to suffer the penalty for lying rather than have Joanes suffer the penalty for sodomy. Further evidence for this interpretation stems from a court order three years later when Joanes and Berry "and others with them" were required to "part theire uncivell liveing together." Ten years later, one Richard Beare of Marshfield, a "grossly scandalouse person . . . formerly convicted of filthy, obsceane practises," was disenfranchised. It is possible that this "Beare" is an alternate spelling of Richard Berry.[21] Berry did have a wife, by the way, a rather unsavory woman named Alice. She was accused of several crimes herself. Once she milked someone's cow, another time she stole a "neckcloth," and on another occasion some bacon and eggs.[22]

There are several other cases of "disorderly liveing" or "lude carriage" that suggest the possibility of homosexual activity, but the evidence is far from conclusive. In 1637, for instance, Abraham Pottle, Walter Deuell, Webb Adey, and Thomas Roberts, accused of "disorderly liveing," were required "to give an account how they live." Adey, in particular, got into trouble on several other occasions. He "profaned the Lord's Day" several times by working, for which he was whipped. By 1642, still practicing "his licentious and disorderly manner of liveing," Adey went to jail.[23]

In another case, one John Dunford, "for his slaunders, clamors, lude & evell carriage," was banished from Plymouth. The records are silent as to the exact nature of his "evell carriage," but the rather unusual and severe punishment, especially in light of John Alexander's banishment two years his house, contrary to the court's order.[25] John Emerson was also fined for "entertaining other mens servants," though the sex of the servants is unmentioned.[26] Anthony Bessie was indicted for "liveing alone disorderly, and afterwards for takeing in an inmate [boarder] without order."[27] James Cole was acquitted of the charge of "entertaining townsmen in his house."[28] But Edward Holman was fined for entertaining another man's servant, John Wade, and for taking Wade to Duxbury in his boat.[29]

Other possible homosexual cases include Tristram Hull's, indicated for unspecified "unclean practises." The charge, however, did not keep Hull from being chosen constable of Yarmouth five years later.[30] There was also John Bumpas, whipped for "idle and lasivius behavior."[31] A final possible homosexual case involves Hester Rickard. Convicted of "laciviouse and unaturall practices" in 1661, she was ordered to sit in the stocks, wearing a paper on her hat describing her crime in capital letters. It is likely, however, that her "unnatural practice" was adultery (she was married). On the same day, Joseph Dunham was sentenced to sit in the stocks with a paper on his hat for "divers laciviouse carriages." Dunham was also fined 200 pounds. Though the records do not specifically connect the two, the timing suggests that their cases were related.[32]

The one execution for homosexuality in New England occurred in the colony of New Haven in 1646, when William Plaine of Guilford was convicted of "unclean practices." Though a married man, Plaine reportedly committed sodomy with two men in England before coming to America. Once in Guilford, "he corrupted a great part of the youth . . . by masturbations, which he had committed and provoked others to the like above a hundred times." To make matters worse, this "monster in human shape," as John Winthrop called him, expressed atheistic opinions. Plaine received the death penalty, though it was probably his corruption of youth and his "frustrating the ordinance of marriage" that weighed more heavily on the magistrate than the sodomy.[33]

Though the Puritans nearly always meant homosexuality when they used the term sodomy, one time when it was not used in that context is the exception that proves the rule, while shedding additional light on the practical legal setting for homosexuality itself. In 1641, Massachusetts authorities were horrified to learn that for the previous two years, three men had regularly molested two young girls, beginning when the elder was only seven.[34] The revelations produced outrage and calls for the death penalty, but no one knew exactly how to define the crime. Since the girls apparently consented to the treatment, could it be considered rape? Even if it were rape, at that time there was no specific law against it in Massachusetts, and "there was no express law in the word of God" for a sentence of death. So the authorities tried to stretch the definition of the capital crime of sodomy to fit this case. But this created several legal problems inherent in all accusations for sodomy. English precedent for sodomy and buggery convictions generally required proof of actual penetration. The accused men confessed to molestation, but denied penetration. The magistrates had only the girls' testimony to go on, leading to yet other legal restrictions that provided no man could be compelled to testify against himself, and that two witnesses were needed to any crime that resulted in a death sentence.[35]

In an attempt to solve these problems, the magistrates wrote for advice to other New England colonies, soliciting written opinions from ministers, the nearest equivalent to legal experts.[36] The majority of the respondents concluded that evidence of actual penetration was necessary for the crime to be sodomy. This made the other questions all the more important: could the accused be forced to testify against himself, and, if not, were two witnesses always necessary for a capital conviction? There was disagreement on the former question, though nearly everyone ruled out torture as a means of exacting a confession. As to the number of witnesses, the ministers generally held out for two, except where there was a confession by the accused or "concurrent and concluding circumstances."[37]

Because of the confusion, when the General Court met in May, 1642, they were divided on the sentence. Several magistrates did want the death penalty, but, after much dispute, they finally agreed on a lighter sentence only because the "sin was not capital by any express law of God." The attempt to define it as sodomy had simply not worked. So instead of death, the three were sentenced to severe whippings, confinement to Boston, and in the case of one of them, mutilation of his nostrils and imprisonment.[38]

This whole scandal and the difficulties involved in applying capital punishment are directly related to the whole question of homosexuality. The disagreement over the necessity for penetration, self-accusation, and the number of witnesses applied in those cases as well. A new statutory rape law did nothing to eliminate the legal difficulties in obtaining sodomy convictions. Perhaps the almost rigorous standards of evidence dissuaded authorities from trying to obtain the death penalty for ordinary sodomy cases, falling back instead on more lenient sentences which were possible when the evidence was not totally conclusive.

But if the Puritans were willing to bend over backwards to apply scrupulous legal guarantees to cases involving homosexuality and child molestation—making the imposition of the death penalty practically impossible—they were often willing to forgo these guarantees when prosecuting for buggery. Sodomy and buggery were usually linked together both in the Bible and in Puritan legal codes, but despite the connection between the two crimes, the penalties imposed in

17th-century New England were often quite different. There was little reluctance to impose the death penalty for buggery even though the legal problems were often identical with those inherent in sodomy. Before speculating as to why this discrepancy existed, it might be helpful to describe specific cases and the penalties imposed.

In the same year as the discovery of the mistreatment of the young girls, one William Hackett (or Hatchet) "was found in buggery with a cow, upon the Lord's day." A woman, absent from church because of some illness, "espied him in the very act." When Hackett, a boy of about 18 or 20 years of age, came before the magistrates, he confessed to attempted buggery "and some entrance, but denied the completing of the fact." Many of the same problems came up in this case as in the child molestation case. There was only one witness, and the evidence of penetration was sketchy at best, since the boy denied completing the act. But eventually the court agreed "that his confession of some entrance was sufficient testimony with the woman," and the majority of the magistrates sentenced him to death. Governor Richard Bellingham, who still doubted some of the evidence, refused to pronounce the sentence, but Deputy Governor John Endecott had no such qualms and sentenced the boy to die. After the sentencing, the boy, described as "ignorant and blockish," finally confessed "completing this foul fact, and attempting the like before, with other wickedness." On the day of the execution, the cow was first slain in front of the boy, and then after a prayer by the Rev. Mr. John Wilson of the Boston Church, Hackett, "with a trembling body," was hanged.[39]

A few months later, New Haven executed George Spencer on even flimsier evidence. A sow, previously owned by a man for whom Spencer had worked as a servant, gave birth to a deformed fetus, "a prodigious monster." Unfortunately, some people saw a resemblance between the fetus and poor George Spencer. It seems that Spencer had "butt one eye for use, the other hath (as itt is called) a pearle in itt, is whitish & deformed," like that of the fetus. Furthermore, Spencer was notorious for "a prophane, lying, scoffing and lewd speritt."[40]

Spencer, when examined, first said that he did not think that he had committed buggery with the sow in question. Then he denied it outright, but he was sent to prison because of the "strong possibilities." Spencer continued to deny guilt in prison until visited by one of the magistrates, who reminded him that confessing sins would bring mercy, Spencer then confessed to the crime, though later he claimed he did so merely to please the magistrate. On another occasion, when several other magistrates visited him, Spencer again confessed to that crime as well as several others, such as lying, scoffing at the colony's laws, and profaning the Lord's Day ("calling it the ladyes day"), though he denied other "acts of filthynes, [homosexual?] either with Indians or English." When brought to trial, Spencer denied all that he had formerly confessed, but the court was "aboundantly satisfied in the evidence," even though there were no witnesses and Spencer refused to confess under oath. Despite these legal problems, Spencer, according to the law of Leviticus 20:15, was put to death.[41]

Perhaps the most famous New England buggery trial was that of Thomas Granger, a 16- or 17-year-old youth in Plymouth. In 1642, Granger was indicted for buggery "with a mare, a cow, two goats, five sheep, two calves and a turkey." Somebody saw Granger committing buggery with the mare. Unfortunately, Governor Bradford, who recorded the incident in his history of Plymouth, decided to "forbear particulars." Nevertheless, upon examination, Granger "confessed the fact with that beast at that time, [and] sundry times before and at several times with all the rest of the forenamed in his indictment." The court had some difficulty determining which sheep were involved, so they staged a lineup for Granger, where "he declared which they were

they and which were not." The court then sentenced
Granger to death. The animals were "killed before his face,
according to the law, Leviticus xx.15; and then he himself
was executed."[42]

With some relief, Bradford reported that both Granger
and another man who "had made some sodomitical attempts
upon another"—probably Edward Michell or Edward
Preston—had learned these things in England. But the Governor warned that these cases showed "how one wicked
person may infect many," and cautioned families to choose
their servants wisely.[43]

A few months later, in Massachusetts, the Court of Assistants found Teagu Ocrimi guilty of "a foule, & divilish
attempt to bugger a cow of Mr. Makepeaces." Fortunately
for Ocrimi, his attempt did not succeed. The court ordered
him "to be carried to the place of execution & there to stand
with an halter about his necke, & to be severely whipped."[44]

And in the same colony in 1646, Robert Miller went to
jail, after being accused of buggery. The witnesses disagreed, however, and when the weather turned cold, Miller
was released on bond, and ordered to appear at the next
court. There is no further mention of Miller, however, so
perhaps the charges were dropped for insufficient evidence.[45]

Perhaps the most interesting buggery case occurred in
New Haven in 1647. Again, it involved a sow who bore a
deformed fetus and a man with the thoroughly improbable
name of Thomas Hogg. The fetus "had a faire & white
skinne & head, as Thomas Hoggs is." Hogg, a servant for the
woman who owned the sow, denied guilt. But the case grew
stronger when the court learned that on more than one occasion Hogg had been guilty of indecent exposure: "he said his
breeches were rent, when indead his sperit was rent." Hogg
claimed that "his belly was broke . . . & he wore a steele
trusse, & so it might happen his members might be seene,"
though Goodie Camp testified that she had given him a nee-

dle and thread "to mend his breeches." After imprisoning Hogg for the crimes of bestiality and exposure, the court decided to seek additional evidence. The governor and deputy governor accompanied Hogg to the barnyard and ordered him to fondle ("scratt") the sow in question. The official records tell us that "immedyatly there appeared a working of lust in the sow, insomuch that she powred out seede before them." The magistrates then ordered him to fondle another sow, "but that was not moved at all." If that was not evidence enough, "Lucretia, the governors neagar woeman," testified that she had seen Hogg "act filthiness with his hands by the fier side." Other witnesses testified that he had at various times stolen a dumpling and some cheese. The court decided to consider the buggery charge later on, but in the meantime, for his "filthynesse, lyeing & pilfering," Hogg was severely whipped and sent to prison "with a meane dyet & hard labour, that his lusts may not bee fedd." For some reason, the records do not indicate any further consideration of the bestiality charge. Apparently the charge was dropped, because Hogg was alive and out of jail the following year, when the court warned him for not showing up for watch.[46]

In 1662, another case in New Haven, by then incorporated into Connecticut, suggests the difficulties involved in detecting buggery. In that year, a 60-year-old man named Potter was executed for bestiality, even though "this Wretch, had been for now Twenty years, a member of the Church in that Place, and kept up among the Holy People of God there, a Reputation for Serious Christianity." This pillar of the community (or as Cotton Mather preferred, this "Pillar of Salt"), engaged in such practices on and off for 50 years, since age 10, with a wide variety of animals. The fact that he could do this without detection for half a century suggests that even in a close knit society some discreet individuals could indulge whatever sexual passions they had. Ten years before his execution, Potter's wife discovered him "Confounding himself with a *Bitch*," but he managed to convince her to keep silent. But when his son "saw him hideously conversing with a *Sow*," the story came to light. Apparently the shocked son reported his father. Before his execution, "A *Cow*, Two *Heifers*, Three *Sheep*, and Two *Sowes*, with all of which he had committed his Brutalness," were killed while Potter watched.[47]

These cases indicate that Puritans were less hesitant to punish buggery with death than they were sodomy. Again, since they usually linked the two crimes, the differences in the severity of punishment is puzzling. It is possible that the Puritans suspected that homosexuality was so widespread that a strict application of the law would lead to very unpleasant consequences. Edmund Morgan suggests that this is the reason why the full penalties were generally not applied for heterosexual sex crimes.[48] Bestiality, on the other hand, may have been less common in the 17th century (as in the 20th century), and thus easier to control. Then again, one might speculate that the opposite was the case. In the mid-20th century, Kinsey researchers found that the incidence of bestiality was highest in farming communities—similar to 17th-century New England. Kinsey reported that 40 to 50% of all farm boys had some sort of animal contact. Perhaps, then, Puritan leaders suspected that bestiality was a much more widespread phenomenon than homosexuality and imposed harsher sentences in order to suppress the far more serious of the two crimes.[49]

There is another possibility. The harsh punishments for buggery may reflect a general 17th-century revulsion with animal contacts. The cases mentioned above provide some clues for such an interpretation. The two pig fetus cases indicate that the Puritans believed it was possible for a man to impregnate an animal, an obvious impossibility in sodomy. This possibility may have made buggery even more heinous. The Puritans were not far removed from the middle ages, when reports of man-like creatures were common. Even more relevant were contemporary accounts written by Englishmen visiting Africa, where, they believed, there was a close connection, including sexual intercourse, between Africans and apes.[50] Even more than homosexuality, bestiality dehumanized man. The horror with which the 17th-century Englishman regarded buggery helped them to rationalize racism toward blacks. In New England, it explains why a son would report his own father to the authorities, and why even the man's wife apparently had considered it a few years earlier. The horror may also explain why New Englanders were willing to dispense with some of the rules of evidence to obtain the death penalty for buggery.

But attitudes toward buggery apparently began to soften as the century wore on. The subject still cropped up occasionally in the court records, but convictions decline. In 1666, William Honywell, jailed in Plymouth on suspicion of buggery, was released for insufficient evidence. The same was true in Massachusetts in 1676 and 1677, when juries found insufficient evidence to convict Jack, a black servant, of buggery with a cow and John Lawrence of buggery with a mare.[52]

The last execution for buggery by the Massachusetts Court of Assistants was that of Benjamin Goad in 1673. This youth, accused of buggery with a mare "in the highway or field" in broad daylight, apparently confessed at first, but then denied it at his trial. The jury, confused by the legal technicalities, decided that if Goad's confession when first arrested plus the testimony of one witness were sufficient for conviction, then he was guilty. But if his denial under oath during the trial took precedence, then Goad was guilty only of attempted buggery. The magistrates then declared that Goad was indeed "Capitolly Guilty." The mare was "knockt on ye head," and then Goad was hanged.[53]

This case provides evidence of changing attitudes, since the execution created some controversy. An increasing tolerance for illicit sexual activity of all kinds in the latter decades of the 17th century apparently produced a corresponding decline in the willingness of many citizens to accept strict enforcement of the moral code.[54] The Rev. Samuel Danforth felt compelled to preach and publish a sermon defending Goad's execution. Danforth admitted that some people objected to "making such a *Youth*, a childe of Religious Parents, and that in his tender years, such a Dreadful Example of Divine Vengeance." But while others pitied Goad's youth, Danforth pitied "the holy Law of God." Remember, Danforth told his flock, "Goad gave himself to Self-pollution, and other Sodomitical wickedness. He often attempted Buggery with several Beasts, before God left him to commit it . . . and he continued in the frequent practice thereof for several months."[55]

But the tide was running against those who held Danforth's views. In Plymouth in 1681, Thomas Saddeler was arraigned for buggery with a mare. Though he denied it, the jury found him guilty, but of the lesser charge "of vile, abominable, and presumptuous attempts to buggery with a mare." His punishment was rather severe, but it was not capital as it probably would have been earlier in the century. Saddeler was whipped, forced to sit on the gallows with a rope around his neck, branded in the forehead with the letter "P" (for pollution), and banished from the colony.[56]

Saddeler's is the last buggery case in any of the published records of New England. Just as prosecutions for sodomy ended 30 years earlier, buggery too disappeared from the records. There may be additional cases in the records of countless local courts and these sources must be searched before we will have a more accurate picture of variant sexual activity in colonial America, but for now it seems reasonable to conclude that sexual behavior, of whatever kind, gradually became more a matter of personal conscience and less a concern for the courts. It may be true, as Edmund Morgan suggested, that the "Puritans became inured to sexual offenses, because there were so many."[57] The decline of religious fervor toward the end of the century, the inability of earlier repression—actual or threatened—to stop illicit sex, and the increasing secularization of the state—resulting in less concern for enforcing moral law—combined to make prosecutions for variant sexual activity a thing of the past.[58] Not even the Puritans could prevent men and women from practicing many forms of sexual activity officially regarded as sinful. Perhaps nothing is more symbolic of the failure of the "citty upon a hill" than the history of variant sexual activity in 17th-century New England.

NOTES

[1]See particularly John Demos, *A Little Commonwealth: Family Life in Plymouth Colony* (New York, 1970); Demos, "Families in Colonial Bristol, Rhode Island," *William and Mary Quarterly*, 3rd Ser., XXV (1969), 40–57; Philip J. Greven, Jr., *Four Generations: Population, Land, and Family in Colonial Andover, Massachusetts* (Ithaca and London, 1970); Kenneth A. Lockridge, *A New England Town: The First Hundred Years* (New York, 1970); Robert Higgs and H. Louis Stettler, III, "Colonial New England Demography: A Sampling Approach," *Wm. and Mary Qtly.*, 3rd Ser., XXVII (1970), 282–291.

[2]Edmund S. Morgan, "The Puritans and Sex," *New England Quarterly*, XV (1912), 603.

[3]Geoffrey May, *Social Control of Sex Expression* (New York, 1931), 247.

[4]Two recent pioneering works on the history of homosexuality are Vern L. Bullough, *Sexual Variance in Society and History* (New York, 1976); and Jonathan Katz, *Gay American History: Lesbians and Gay Men in the U.S.A.* (New York, 1976).

[5]Louis Crompton, "Homosexuals and the Death Penalty in Colonial America," *Journal of Homosexuality*, I (1976), 277–278; Katz, *Gay American History*, 24.

[6]Crompton, "Homosexuals and the Death Penalty," 277–281; David H. Flaherty, "Law and the Enforcement of Morals in Early America," in Donald Fleming and Bernard Bailyn, eds., *Perspectives in American History*, V (1971); *Law in American History*, 213.

[7]*Records of the Colony of New Plymouth in New England,* ed. Nathaniel B. Shurtleff and David Pulsifer (Boston, 1855–1861), XI, 12.

[8]Katz, *Gay American History,* 20, 22; Crompton, "Homosexuals and the Death Penalty," 278–279.

[9]For more on the concept of remission, see George L. Haskins, *Law and Authority in Early Massachusetts: A Study in Tradition and Design* (New York, 1960), 204–205; and Jules Zanger, "Crime and Punishment in Early Massachusetts," *Wm. and Mary Qtly.,* 3d Ser., XXII (1965), 473–474. For the death penalty and adultery, see Flaherty, "Law and Morals in Early America," 213–214.

[10]*Records of the Governor and Company of the Massachusetts Bay in New England,* ed. Nathaniel B. Shurtleff (Boston, 1853–1854), 1, 52, 54; "Francis Higginson's Journal," in Stuart Mitchell, ed., *The Founding of Massachusetts* (Boston, 1930), 71.

[11]William Bradford, *Of Plymouth Plantation 1620–1647,* ed. Samuel Eliot Morison (New York, 1970), 204–206.

[12]See B.R. Burg, "Pirate Communities in the Seventeenth Century: A Case Study of Homosexual Society," forthcoming in the *Journal of Homosexuality.* Professor Burg kindly provided me with a manuscript copy of his article.

[13]*Records of Plymouth,* 1, 64.

[14]Crompton, "Homosexuals and the Death Penalty," 290–292: Katz, *Gay American History,* 16–19.

[15]Caroline Bingham, "Seventeenth-Century Attitudes Toward Deviant Sex," *Journal of Interdisciplinary History,* 1 (1971), 447–472. Dutch New Netherland also executed two individuals for sodomy in 1646 and 1658. In 1646, the guilty party (a black man) was sentenced to be choked to death and then burned. In the second case, the man was tied in a sack and thrown into a river to drown; Katz, *Gay American History,* 22–23, 570n.

[16]*Records of Plymouth,* II, 35–36.

[17]See Demos, *A Little Commonwealth,* 157–158, 158n.

[18]*Records of Plymouth,* II, 137, 163.

[19]Bradford, *Of Plymouth Plantation,* 316–317.

[20]May, *Social Control of Sex Expression,* 247.

[21]*Records of Plymouth,* II, 148, 448; III, 37, 177.

[22]*Ibid.*, III, 28, 36, 75, 82.

[23]*Ibid.*, I, 68 to 92, II, 36, 42.

[24]*Ibid.*, I, 128.

[25]*Ibid.*, I, 87.

[26]*Ibid.*, I, 118.

[27]*Ibid.*

[28]*Ibid.*, III, 17.

[29]*Ibid.*, III, 126.

[30]*Ibid.*, II, 36, 115.

[31]*Ibid.*, II, 170.

[32]*Ibid.*, III, 210.

[33]John Winthrop, *The History of New England from 1630 to 1649*, ed. James Savage (Boston, 1853), II, 324; Katz, *Gay American History*, 22.

[34]*Records of Massachusetts Bay*, II, 12–13; Winthrop, *History of New England*, II, 54–58.

[35]*Ibid.*, Bullough, *Sexual Variance*, 437.

[36]Winthrop, *History of New England*, II, 54–58; Bradford, *Of Plymouth Plantation*, Appendix X, 404–413.

[37]Winthrop, *History of New England*, II, 54–58.

[38]*Ibid.*, *Records of Massachusetts Bay*, II, 12–13. On the same day the court handed down these sentences, they adopted several laws to eliminate some, though not all, of the confusion. Developing the concept of statutory rape, the court decreed that any man having "carnall copulation" with any "woman child under ten years ould" would be put to death, regardless of whether or not the girl consented. Rape of a married or engaged woman also carried the death penalty. Rape of an unmarried woman over ten years old could be punished by death, but the judges were given the discretion of applying a lesser penalty. And finally, a man who committed "fornication with any single woman," with her consent, could be punished by forcing them to marry, a fine, corporal punishment or any or all of these at the discretion of the judge. *Records of Massachusetts Bay*, II, 21–22.

[39]Winthrop, *History of New England*, II, 58–60; *Records of Massachusetts Bay*, I, 331.

[40]*Records of the Colony and Plantation of New Haven, from 1638 to 1649*, ed. Charles J. Hoadly (Hartford, 1857), 62–69.

[41]*Ibid.*, Winthrop, *History of New England*, II, 73.

[42]Bradford, *Of Plymouth Plantation*, 320–321; *Records of Plymouth*, II, 44.

[43]Bradford, *Of Plymouth Plantation*, 321.

[44]*Records of the Court of Assistants of the Colony of Massachusetts Bay, 1630–1692* (Boston, 1901–1928), II, 121.

[45]*Records of Massachusetts*, I, 79.

[46]*Records of New Haven*, 295–296.

[47][Cotton Mather], *Pillars of Salt: An History of Some Criminals Executed in this Land, for Capital Crimes, With Some of their Dying Speches* . . . (Boston, 1699), 63–66, Evans No. 877.

[48]Morgan, "The Puritans and Sex," 602.

[49]See Alfred C. Kinsey, Wardell B. Pomeroy, and Clyde E. Martin, *Sexual Behavior in the Human Male* (Philadelphia and London, 1948), 623, 669–670.

[50]Winthrop D. Jordan, *White Over Black: American Attitudes Toward the Negro, 1550–1812* (Chapel Hill, 1968), 28–32.

[51]*Records of Plymouth*, IV, 116.

[52]*Records of Court of Assistants*, I, 74, 87.

[53]*Ibid.*, I, 10–11.

[54]Flaherty, "Law and Morals in Early America," 229.

[55][Samuel Danforth], *The Cry of Sodom Enquired Into: Upon Occasion of the Arraignment and Condemnation of Benjamin Goad. For His Prodigious Villany* . . . (Cambridge, 1674), Evans No. 186.

[56]*Records of Plymouth*, VI, 74–75.

[57]Morgan, "The Puritans and Sex," 595.

[58]Flaherty, "Law and Morals in Early America," 228–233, 244.

chapter 2

Horses and Gentlemen:

The Cultural Significance of Gambling among the Gentry of Virginia

by T. H. Breen

Thorstein Veblen argued that the conspicuous consumption of upper-class women strengthened the social standing of their husbands. Timothy Breen, who has written extensively on the history of colonial Virginia, shows that conspicuous consumption among the gentry of Virginia in the late seventeenth century had much the same purpose. Drawing upon the work of cultural anthropologists, Breen explores the functions that male social rituals served for a society which had almost been torn apart in rebellion a generation earlier.

For readers unfamiliar with this period, colonial Virginia in the 1680s was in turmoil. Men of lower social standing resented the landed gentry, the top five percent of Virginia society. Land-hungry poor white farmers, incensed by political corruption, led the unsuccessful Bacon's Rebellion in 1683. Five years later, mobs of unsuccessful planters, concerned about lower prices for their tobacco crops, marched from plantation to plantation, tearing out tobacco plants as they went. Each victim became a fervent cutter, for once his crop had been destroyed, he sought to ensure that his neighbors would not profit from his loss.

Although Breen's article vividly recaptures the importance of class as a social relationship in colonial Virginia, it fails to recognize that patriarchalism was as much a gentry value as the belief in competitiveness, individualism, or materialism. Patriarchalism allowed gentry men to gamble away the family finances without the consent of their wives; it excluded women from social rituals which were designed to affirm male honor and chivalry. Patriarchalism also structured the competition between men, where the stakes in gambling or horseracing were women and money. But the gentry also tried to avoid blood feuds and duels brought on by losses in this male competition: They did not want to endanger the precious social stability they had so recently achieved.

In the fall of 1686 Durand of Dauphiné, a French Huguenot, visited the capital of colonial Virginia. Durand regularly recorded in a journal what he saw and heard, providing one of the few firsthand accounts of late seventeenth-century Virginia society that has survived to the present day. When he arrived in Jamestown the House of Burgesses was in session. "I saw there fine-looking men," he noted, "sitting in judgment booted and with belted sword." But to Durand's surprise, several of these Virginia gentlemen "started gambling" soon after dinner, and it was not until midnight that one of the players noticed the Frenchman patiently waiting for the contest to end. The Virginian—obviously a veteran of long nights at the gaming table—advised Durand to go to bed. " 'For,' said he, 'it is quite possible that we shall be here all night,' and in truth I found them still playing the next morning."[1]

The event Durand witnessed was not unusual. In late seventeenth- and early eighteenth-century Virginia, gentlemen spent a good deal of time gambling. During this period, in fact, competitive gaming involving high stakes became a distinguishing characteristic of gentry culture. Whenever the great planters congregated, someone inevitably produced a deck of cards, a pair of dice, or a backgammon board; and quarter-horse racing was a regular event throughout the colony. Indeed, these men hazarded money and tobacco on almost any proposition in which there was an element of chance. Robert Beverly, a member of one of Virginia's most

"Horses and Gentlemen: The Cultural Significance of Gambling Among the Gentry of Virginia" by T. H. Breen. Reprinted by permission of the author and publisher from the *William and Mary Quarterly*, 3rd Ser. v. XXXIV, No. 2 (April 1977), 239–257. Copyright © 1978 by T. H. Breen.

Mr. Breen is a member of the Department of History, Northwestern University. Research for this essay was made possible in part by a grant from the Northwestern University Research Committee. The author is indebted to the following people for encouragement as well as criticism: George Dalton, E. P. Thompson, Stephen Foster, Richard R. Beeman, Stephen Innes, Stephen Harper, and Russell R. Menard.

prominent families, made a wager "with the gentlemen of the country" that if he could produce seven hundred gallons of wine on his own plantation, they would pay him the handsome sum of one thousand guineas. Another leading planter offered six-to-one odds that Alexander Spotswood could not procure a commission as the colony's governor. And in 1671 one disgruntled gentleman asked a court of law to award him his winnings from a bet concerning "a Servant maid."[2] The case of this suspect-sounding wager— unfortunately not described in greater detail—dragged on until the colony's highest court ordered the loser to pay the victor a thousand pounds of tobacco.

The great planters' passion for gambling, especially on quarter-horse racing, coincided with a period of far-reaching social change in Virginia.[3] Before the mid-1680s constant political unrest, servant risings both real and threatened, plant-cutting riots, and even a full-scale civil war had plagued the colony.[4] But by the end of the century Virginia had achieved internal peace.[5] General elements contributed to the growth of social tranquility. First, by 1700 the ruling gentry were united as they had never been before. The great planters of the seventeenth century had been for the most part aggressive English immigrants. They fought among themselves for political and social dominance, and during Bacon's Rebellion in 1676 various factions within the gentry atttempted to settle their differences on the battlefield. By the end of the century, however, a sizable percentage of the Virginia gentry, perhaps a majority, had been born in the colony. The members of this native-born elite—one historian calls them a "creole elite"—cooperated more frequently in political affairs than had their immigrant fathers. They found it necessary to unite in resistance against a series of interfering royal governors such as Thomas Lord Culpeper, Francis Nicholson, and Alexander Spotswood. After Bacon's Rebellion the leading planters—the kind of men who Durand watched gamble the night away—successfully consolidated their control over Virginia's civil, military, and ecclesiastical institutions. They monopolized the most important offices; they patented the best lands.[6]

A second and even more far-reaching element in the creation of this remarkable solidarity among the gentry was the shifting racial composition of the plantation labor force. Before the 1680s the planters had relied on large numbers of white indentured servants to cultivate Virginia's sole export crop, tobacco. These impoverished, often desperate servants disputed their masters' authority and on several occasions resisted colonial rulers with force of arms. In part because of their dissatisfaction with the indenture system, and in part because changes in the international slave trade made it easier and cheaper for Virginians to purchase black laborers, the major planters increasingly turned to Africans. The blacks' cultural disorientation made them less difficult to control than the white servants. Large-scale collective violence such as Bacon's Rebellion and the 1682 plant-cutting riots consequently declined markedly. By the beginning of the eighteenth century Virginia had been transformed into a relatively peaceful, biracial society in which a few planters exercised almost unchallenged hegemony over both their slaves and their poorer white neighbors.[7]

The growth of gambling among the great planters during a period of significant social change raises important questions not only about gentry values but also about the social structure of late seventeenth-century Virginia. Why did gambling, involving high stakes, become so popular among the gentlemen at precisely this time? Did it reflect gentry values or have symbolic connotations for the people living in this society? Did this activity serve a social function, contributing in some manner to the maintenance of group cohesion? Why did quarter-horse racing, in particular, become a gentry sport? And finally, did public displays such as this somehow reinforce the great planters' social and political dominance?

In part, of course, gentlemen laid wagers on women and horses simply because they enjoyed the excitement of competition. Gambling was a recreation, like a good meal among friends or a leisurely hunt in the woods—a pleasant pastime when hard-working planters got together. Another equally acceptable explanation of the gentry's fondness for gambling might be the transplanting of English social mores. Certainly, the upper classes in the mother country loved betting for high stakes, and it is possible that the all-night card games and the frequent horse races were staged attempts by a provincial gentry to transform itself into a genuine landed aristocracy.[8] While both views possess merit, neither is entirely satisfactory. The great planters of Virginia presumably could have favored less risky forms of competition. Moreover, even though several planters deliberately emulated English social styles, the widespread popularity of gambling among the gentry indicates that this type of behavior may have had deeper, more complex cultural roots than either of these explanations would suggest.[9]

In many societies competitive gaming is a device by which the participants transform abstract cultural values into observable social behavior. In his now-classic analysis of the Balinese cockfight Clifford Geertz describes contests for extremely high stakes as intense social dramas. These battles not only involve the honor of important villagers and their kin groups but also reflect in symbolic form the entire Balinese social structure. Far from being a simple pastime, betting on cocks turns out to be an expression of the way the Balinese perceive social reality. The rules of the fight, the patterns of wagering, the reactions of winners and losers— all of these elements help us to understand more profoundly the totality of Balinese culture.[10]

The Virginia case is analogous to the Balinese. When the great planter staked his money and tobacco on a favorite horse or spurred a sprinter to victory, he displayed some of the central elements of gentry culture—its competitiveness, individualism, and materialism. In fact, competitive gaming was for many gentlemen a means of translating a particular set of values into action, a mechanism for expressing a loose but deeply felt bundle of ideas and assumptions about the nature of society. The quarter-horse races of Virginia were intense contests involving personal honor, elaborate rules, heavy betting, and wide community interest; and just as the cockfight opens up hidden dimensions of Balinese culture, gentry gambling offers an opportunity to improve our understanding of the complex interplay between cultural values and social behavior in Virginia.

Gambling reflected core elements of late seventeenth- and early eighteenth-century gentry values. From diaries, letters, and travel accounts we discover that despite their occasional cooperation in political affairs, Virginia gentlemen placed extreme emphasis upon personal independence. This concern may in part have been the product of the colony's peculiar settlement patterns. The great planters required immense tracts of fresh land for their tobacco. Often thousands of acres in size, their plantations were scattered over a broad area from the Potomac River to the James. The dispersed planters lived in their "Great Houses" with their families and slaves, and though they saw friends from time to time, they led for the most part isolated, routine lives.[11] An English visitor in 1686 noted with obvious disapproval that "their Plantations run over vast Tracts of Ground . . . whereby the Country is thinly inhabited; the Living solitary and unsociable." Some planters were uncomfortably aware of the problems created by physical isolation.[12] William Fitzhugh, for example, admitted to a correspondent in the mother country, "Society that is good and ingenious is very scarce, and seldom to be come at except in books."[13]

Yet despite such apparent cultural privation, Fitzhugh and his contemporaries refused to alter their life styles in any way that might compromise their freedom of action. They

assumed it their right to give commands, and in the ordering
of daily plantation affairs they rarely tolerated outside interference.[14] Some of the planters even saw themselves as law-
givers out of the Old Testament. In 1726 William Byrd II
explained that "like one of the Patriarchs, I have my Flocks
and my Herds, my Bond-men and Bond-women, and every
Soart of Trade amongst my own Servants, so that I live in a
kind of Independence on every one but Providence."[15]
Perhaps Byrd exaggerated for literary effect, but forty years
earlier Durand had observed, "There are no lords [in Vir-
ginia], but each is sovereign in his own plantation."[16] Whatever the origins of this independent spirit, it bred excessive
individualism in a wide range of social activities. While these
powerful gentlemen sometimes worked together to achieve
specific political and economic ends, they bristled at the least
hint of constraint.[17] Andrew Burnaby later noted that "the
public or political character of the Virginians corresponds
with their private one: they are haughty and jealous of their
liberties, impatient of restraint, and can scarcely bear the
thought of being controuled by any superior power."[18]

The gentry expressed this uncompromising individualism in aggressive competitiveness, engaging in a constant struggle against real and imagined rivals to obtain more
lands, additional patronage, and high tobacco prices. Indeed, competition was a major factor shaping the character
of face-to-face relationships among the colony's gentlemen,
and when the stakes were high the planters were not particular about the methods they employed to gain victory.[19] In
large part, the goal of the competition within the gentry
group was to improve social position by increasing wealth.

Some gentlemen believed that personal honor was at
stake as well. Robert "King" Carter, by all accounts the most
successful planter of his generation, expressed his anxiety
about losing out to another Virginian in a competitive market
situation. "In discourse with Colonel Byrd, Mr. Armistead,
and a great many others," he explained, "I understand you

[an English merchant] had sold their tobaccos in round parcels and at good rates. I cannot allow myself to come from behind any of these gentlemen in the planter's trade."[20] Carter's pain arose not so much from the lower price he had received as from the public knowledge that he had been bested by respected peers. He believed he had lost face. This kind of intense competition was sparked, especially among the less affluent members of the gentry, by a dread of slipping into the ranks of what one eighteenth-century Virginia historian called the "common Planters."[21] Gov. Francis Nicholson, an acerbic English placeman, declared that the "ordinary sort of planters" knew full well "from whence these mighty dons derive their originals."[22] The governor touched a nerve; the efforts of "these mighty dons" to outdo one another were almost certainly motivated by a desire to disguise their "originals," to demonstrate anew through competitive encounters that they could legitimately claim gentility.

Another facet of Virginia gentry culture was materialism. This certainly does not mean that the great planters lacked spiritual concerns. Religion played a vital role in the lives of men like Robert Carter and William Byrd II. Nevertheless, piety was largely a private matter. In public these men determined social standing not by a man's religiosity or philosophic knowledge but by his visible estate—his lands, slaves, buildings, even by the quality of his garments. When John Bartram, one of America's first botanists, set off in 1737 to visit two of Virginia's most influential planters, a London friend advised him to purchase a new set of clothes, "for though I should not esteem thee less, to come to me in what dress thou will,—yet these Virginians are a very gentle, well-dressed people—and look, perhaps, more at a man's outside than his inside."[23] This perception of gentry values was accurate. Fitzhugh's desire to maintain his own outward appearances drove him to collect a stock of monogrammed silver plate and to import at great expense a well-crafted, though not very practical, English carriage.[24] One even finds hints that the difficult of preserving the image of material success weighed heavily upon some planters. When he described local Indian customs in 1705, Robert Beverley noted that native Americans lived an easy, happy existence "without toiling and perplexing their minds for Riches, which other people often trouble themselves to provide for uncertain and ungrateful Heirs."[25]

The gentry were acutely sensitive to the element of chance in human affairs, and this sensitivity influenced their attitudes toward other men and society. Virginians knew from bitter experience that despite the best-laid plans, nothing in their lives was certain. Slaves suddenly sickened and died. English patrons forgot to help their American friends. Tobacco prices fell without warning. Cargo ships sank. Storms and droughts ruined the crops. The list was endless. Fitzhugh warned an English correspondent to think twice about allowing a son to become a Virginia planter, for even "if the best husbandry and the greatest forecast skill were used, yet ill luck at Sea, a fall of a Market, or twenty other accidents may ruin and overthrow the best Industry."[26] Other planters, even those who had risen to the top of colonial society, longed for greater security. "I could wish," declared William Byrd I in 1685, "wee had Some more certain Commodity [than tobacco] to rely on but see no hopes of itt."[27] However desirable such certainty may have appeared, the planters always put their labor and money into tobacco, hoping for a run of luck. One simply learned to live with chance. In 1710 William Byrd II confided in his secret diary, "I dreamed last night . . . that I won a tun full of money and might win more if I had ventured."[28]

Gaming relationships reflected these strands of gentry culture. In fact, gambling in Virginia was a ritual activity. It was a form of repetitive, patterned behavior that not only corresponded closely to the gentry's values and assumptions but also symbolized the realities of everyday planter life.

This congruence between actions and belief, between form and experience, helps to account for the popularity of betting contests. The wager, whether over cards or horses, brought together in a single, focused act the great planters' competitiveness, independence, and materialism, as well as the element of chance.[29] It represented a social agreement in which each individual was free to determine how he would play, and the gentlemen who accepted a challenge risked losing his material possessions as well as his personal honor.[30]

The favorite household or tavern contests during this period included cards, backgammon, billiards, nine-pins, and dice. The great planters preferred card games that demanded skill as well as luck, Put, piquet, and whist provided the necessary challenge, and Virginia gentlemen—Durand's hosts, for example—regularly played these games for small sums of money and tobacco.[31] These activities brought men together, stimulated conversation, and furnished a harmless outlet for aggressive drives. They did not, however, become for the gentry a form of intense, symbolic play such as the cockfight in Bali.[32] William Byrd II once cheated his wife in a game of piquet, something he would never have dared to do among his peers at Williamsburg. By and large, he showed little emotional involvement in these types of household gambling. The exception here proves the rule. After an unusually large loss at the gaming tables of Williamsburg, Byrd drew a pointed finger in the margin of his secret diary and swore a "solemn resolution never at once to lose more than 50 shillings and to spend less time in gaming, and I beg the God Almighty to give me grace to keep so good a resolution. . . ." Byrd's reformation was short-lived, for within a few days he dispassionately noted losing another four pounds at piquet.[33]

Horse racing generated far greater interest among the gentry than did the household games.[34] Indeed, for the great planters and the many others who came to watch, these contests were preeminently a social drama. To appreciate the importance of racing in seventeenth-century Virginia, we must understand the cultural significance of horses. By the turn of the century possession of one of these animals had become a social necessity. Without a horse, a planter felt despised, an object of ridicule. Owning even a slow-footed saddle horse made the common planter more of a man in his own eyes as well as in those of his neighbors; he was reluctant to venture forth on foot for fear of making an adverse impression. As the Rev. Hugh Jones explained in 1724, "almost every ordinary Person keeps a Horse; and I have known some spend the Morning in ranging several Miles in the Woods to find and catch their Horses only to ride two or three Miles to Church, to the Court-House, or to a Horse-Race, where they generally appoint to meet upon Business."[35] Such behavior seems a waste of time and energy only to one who does not comprehend the symbolic importance which the Virginians attached to their horses. A horse was an extension of its owner; indeed, a man was only as good as his horse. Because of the horse's cultural significance, the gentry attempted to set its horsemanship apart from that of the common planters. Gentlemen took better care of their animals, and, according to John Clayton, who visited Virginia in 1688, they developed a distinctive riding style. "They ride pretty sharply," Clayton reported; "a Planter's Pace is a Proverb, which is a good sharp hand-Gallop."[36] A fast-rising cloud of dust far down a Virginia road probably alerted the common planter that he was about to encounter a social superior.

The contest that generated the greatest interest among the gentry was the quarter-horse race, an all-out spring by two horses over a quarter-mile dirt track.[37] The great planters dominated these events. In the records of the county courts—our most important source of information about specific races—we find the names of some of the colony's most prominent planter families—Randolph, Eppes, Jefferson, Swan, Kenner, Hardiman, Parker, Cocke, Batte, Harwick (Hardidge), Youle (Yowell), and Washington. Members of the House of Burgesses, including its powerful speaker, William Randolph, were frequently mentioned in the contests that came before the courts.[38] On at least one occasion the Rev. James Blair, Virginia's most eminent clergyman and a founder of the College of William and Mary, gave testimony in a suit arising from a race run between Capt. William Soane and Robert Napier.[39] The tenacity with which the gentry pursued these cases, almost continuations of the race itself, suggests that victory was no less sweet when it was gained in court.

Many elements contributed to the exclusion of lower social groups from these contests. Because of the sheer size of wagers, poor freeman and common planters could not have participated regularly. Certainly, the members of the Accomack County Court were embarrassed to discover that one Thomas Davis, "a very poore Man," had lost 500 pounds of tobacco or a cow and calf in a horse race with an adolescent named Mr. John Andrews. Recognizing that Davis bore "a great charge of wife and Children," the justices withheld final judgment until the governor had an opportunity to rule on the legality of the wager. The Accomack court noted somewhat gratuitously that if the governor declared the action unlawful, it would fine Davis five days' work on a public bridge.[40] In such cases country justices ordinarily made no comment upon a plaintiff's or defendant's financial condition, assuming, no doubt, that most people involved in racing were capable of meeting their gaming obligations.

The gentry actively enforced its exclusive control over quarter-horse racing. When James Bullocke, a York County tailor, challenged Mr. Mathew Slader to a race in 1674, the county court informed Bullocke that it was "contrary to Law for a Labourer to make a race being a Sport for Gentlemen" and fined the presumptuous tailor two hundred pounds of tobacco and cask.[41] Additional evidence of exclusiveness is found in early eighteenth-century Hanover County. In one of the earliest issues of the colony's first newspaper, the *Virginia Gazette*, an advertisement appeared announcing that "some merry-dispos'd gentlemen" in Hanover planned to celebrate St. Andrew's Day with a race for quarter-milers. The Hanover gentlemen explained in a later, fuller description that "all Persons resorting there are desir'd to behave themselves with Decency and Sobriety, the Subscribers being resolv'd to discountenance all Immorality with the utmost Rigour." The purpose of these contests was to furnish the county's "considerable Number of Gentlemen, Merchants, and credible Planters" an opportunity for "cultivating Friendship."[42] Less affluent persons apparently were welcome to watch the proceedings provided they acted like gentlemen.

In most match races the planter rode his own horse, and the exclusiveness of these contests meant that racing created intensely competitive confrontations. There were two ways to set up a challenge. The first was a regularly scheduled affair usually held on Saturday afternoon. By 1700 there were at least a dozen tracks, important enough to be known by name, scattered through the counties of the Northern Neck and the James River valley. The records are filled with references to contests held at such places as Smith's Field, Coan Race Course, Devil's Field, Yeocomico, and Varina.[43] No doubt, many races also occurred on nameless country roads or convenient pastures. On the appointed day the planter simply appeared at the race track and waited for a likely challenge. We know from a dispute heard before the Westmoreland County Court in 1693 that John Gardner boldly "Challeng'd all the horses then upon the ground to run with any of them for a thousand pounds of Tobo and twenty shillings in money."[44] A second type of contest was a more spontaneous challenge. When gentlemen congregated over a jug of hard cider or peach brandy, the talk frequently turned to horses. The owners presumably bragged about the superior speed of their animals, and if one planter called another's bluff, the men cried out "done, and done," marched to the nearest field, and there discovered whose horse was in fact the swifter.[45]

Regardless of the outcome, quarter-horse races in Virginia were exciting spectacles. The crowds of onlookers seem often to have been fairly large, as common planters, even servants, flocked to the tracks to watch the gentry challenge one another for what must have seemed immense amounts of money and tobacco. One witness before a Westmoreland County Court reported in 1674 that Mr. Stone and Mr. Youle had run a challenge for £10 sterling "in sight of many people."[46] Attendance at race days was sizable enough to support a brisk trade in cider and brandy. In 1714 the Richmond County Court fined several men for peddling liquors "by Retaile in the Race Ground."[47] Judging from the popularity of horses throughout planter society, it seems probable that the people who attended these events dreamed of one day riding a local champion such as Prince or Smoaker.

The magnitude of gentry betting indicates that racing must have deeply involved the planter's self-esteem. Wagering took place on two levels. The contestants themselves made a wager on the outcome, a main bet usually described in a written statement. In addition, side wagers were sometimes negotiated between spectators or between a contestant and spectator.[48] Of the two, the main bet was far the more significant. From accounts of disputed races reaching the county courts we know that gentlemen frequently risked very large sums. The most extravagant contest of the period was a race run between John Baker and John Haynie in Northumberland County in 1693, in which the two men wagered 4000 pounds of tobacco and 40 shillings sterling on the speed of their sprinters, Prince and Smoaker.[49] Some races involved only twenty or thirty shillings, but a substantial number were run for several pounds sterling and hundreds of pounds of tobacco. While few, if any, of the seventeenth-century gentlemen were what we would call gambling addicts, their betting habits seem irrational even by the more prudential standards of their own day: in conducting normal business transactions, for example, they would never have placed so much money in such jeopardy.

To appreciate the large size of these bets we must interpret them within the context of Virginia's economy. Between 1660 and 1720 a planter could anticipate receiving about ten shillings per hundredweight of tobacco. Since the average grower seldom harvested more than 1500 pounds of tobacco a year per man, he probably never enjoyed an annual income from tobacco in excess of eight pounds sterling.[50] For most Virginians the conversion of tobacco into sterling occurred only in the neat columns of account books. They themselves seldom had coins in their pockets. Specie was extremely scarce, and planters ordinarily paid their taxes and conducted business transactions with tobacco notes—written promises to deliver to the bearer a designated amount of tobacco.[51] The great preponderance of seventeenth-century planters were quite poor, and even the great planters estimated their income in hundreds, not thousands, of pounds sterling.[52] Fitzhugh, one of the wealthier men of his generation, described his financial situation in detail. "Thus I have given you some particulars," he wrote in 1686, "which I thus deduce, the yearly Crops of corn and Tobo. together with the surplusage of meat more than will serve the family's use, will amount annually to 60000lb. Tobo wch. at 10 shillings per Ct. is 300£ annum."[53] These facts reveal that the Baker–Haynie bet—to take a notable example—amounted to approximately £22 sterling, more than 7 percent of Fitzhugh's annual cash return. It is therefore not surprising that the common planters seldom took part in quarter-horse racing: this wager alone amounted to approximately three times the income they could expect to receive in a good year. Even a modest wager of a pound or two sterling represented a substantial risk.

Gentlemen sealed these gaming relationships with a formal agreement, either a written statement laying out the terms of the contest or a declaration before a disinterested third party of the nature of the wager. In either case the participants carefully stipulated what rules would be in effect. Sometimes the written agreements were quite elaborate. In 1698, for example, Richard Ward and John Steward, Jr., "Covenanted and agreed" to race at a quarter-mile track in Henrico County known as Ware. Ward's mount was to enjoy a ten-yard handicap, and if it crossed the finish line within five lengths of Steward's horse, Ward would win five pounds sterling; if Steward's obviously superior animal won by a greater distance, Ward promised to pay six pounds sterling.[54] In another contest William Eppes and Stephen Cocke asked William Randolph to witness an agreement for a ten-shilling race: "each horse was to keep his path, they not being to crosse unlesse Stephen Cocke could gett the other Riders Path at the start at two or three Jumps."[55]

Virginia's county courts treated race covenants as binding legal contracts.[56] If a gentlemen failed to fulfill the agreement, the other party had legitimate grounds to sue; and the country justices' first consideration during a trial was whether the planters had properly recorded their agreement.[57] The Henrico court summarily dismissed one gambling suit because "noe Money was stacked down nor Contract in writing made[,] one of wch in such cases is by the law required."[58] Because any race might generate legal proceedings, it was necessary to have a number of people present at the track not only to assist in the running of the contest but also to act as witnesses if anything went wrong. The two riders normally appointed an official starter, several judges, and someone to hold the stakes.

Almost all of the agreements included a promise to ride a fair race. Thus two men in 1698 insisted upon "fair Rideing"; another pair pledged "they would run fair horseman's play."[59] By such agreements the planters waived their customary right to jostle, whip, or knee an opponent, or to attempt to unseat him.[60] During the last decades of the seventeenth century the gentry apparently attempted to substitute riding skill and strategy for physical violence. The demand for "fair Rideing" also suggests that the earliest races in Virginia were wild, no-holds-barred affairs that afforded contestants ample opportunity to vent their aggressions.

The intense desire to win sometimes undermined a gentleman's written promise to run a fair race. When the stakes were large, emotions ran high. One man complained in a York County court that an opponent had interfered with his horse in the middle of the race, "by means whereof the s[ai]d Plaintiff lost the said Race."[61] Joseph Humphrey told a Northumberland County court that he would surely have come in first in a challenge for 1500 pounds of tobacco had not Capt. Rodham Kenner (a future member of the House of Burgesses) "held the defendt horses bridle in running his race."[62] Other riders testified that they had been "Josselled" while the race was in progress. An unusual case of interference grew out of a 1694 race which Rodham Kenner rode against John Hartly for one pound sterling and 575 pounds of tobacco. In a Westmoreland County court Hartly explained that after a fair start and without using "whipp or Spurr" he found himself "a great distance" in front of Kenner. But as Hartly neared the finish line, Kenner's brother, Richard, suddenly jumped onto the track and "did hollow and shout and wave his hat over his head in the plts [plaintiff's] horse's face." The animal panicked, ran outside the posts marking the finish line, and lost the race. After a lengthy trial a Westmoreland jury decided that Richard Kenner "did no foule play in his hollowing and waveing his hatt."[63] What exactly occurred during this race remains a mystery, but since no one denied that Richard acted very strangely, it seems likely that the Kenner brothers were persuasive as well as powerful.

Planters who lost large wagers because an opponent jostled or "hollowed" them off the track were understandably angry. Yet instead of challenging the other party to a duel or allowing gaming relationships to degenerate into blood feuds, the disappointed horsemen invariably took their complaints to the courts.[64] Such behavior indicates not only that the gentlemen trusted the colony's formal legal system—after all, members of their group controlled it—but also that they were willing to place institutional limitations on their own competitiveness. Gentlemen who felt they had been cheated or abused at the track immediately collected witnesses and brought suit before the nearest county court. The legal machinery available to the aggrieved gambler was complex; and no matter how unhappy he may have been with the final verdict, he could rarely claim that the system had denied due process.

The plaintiff brought charges before a group of justices of the peace sitting as a county court; if these men found sufficient grounds for a suit, the parties—in the language of seventeenth-century Virginia—could "put themselves upon the country."[65] In other words, they could ask that a jury of twelve substantial freeholders hear the evidence and decide whether the race had in fact been fairly run. If the sums involved were high enough, either party could appeal a local decision to the colony's general court, a body consisting of the governor and his council. Several men who hotly insisted that they had been wronged followed this path. For example, Joseph Humphrey, loser in a race for 1500 pounds of tobacco, stamped out of a Northumberland County court, demanding a stop to "farther proceedings in the Common Law till a hearing in Chancery."[66] Since most of the General Court records for the seventeenth century were destroyed during the Civil War, it is impossible to follow these cases beyond the county level. It is apparent from the existing documents, however, that all the men involved in these race controversies took their responsibilities seriously, and there is no indication that the gentry regarded the resolution of a gambling dispute as less important than proving a will or punishing a criminal.[67] It seems unlikely that the colony's courts would have adopted such an indulgent attitude toward racing had these contests not in some way served a significant social function for the gentry. . . .

Competitive activities such as quarter-horse racing served social as well as symbolic functions. As we have seen, gambling reflected core elements of the culture of late seventeenth-century Virginia. Indeed, if it had not done so, horse racing would not have become so popular among the colony's gentlemen. These contests also helped the gentry to maintain group cohesion during a period of rapid social change. After 1680 the great planters do not appear to have become significantly less competitive, less individualistic, or less materialistic than their predecessors had been.[68] But while the values persisted, the forms in which they were expressed changed. During the last decades of the century unprecedented external pressures, both political and economic, coupled with a major shift in the composition of the colony's labor force, caused the Virginia gentry to communicate these values in ways that would not lead to deadly physical violence or spark an eruption of blood feuding. The members of the native-born elite, anxious to preserve their autonomy over local affairs, sought to avoid the kinds of divisions within their ranks that had contributed to the outbreak of Bacon's Rebellion. They found it increasingly necessary to cooperate against meddling royal governors. Moreover, such earlier unrest among the colony's plantation workers as Bacon's Rebellion and the plant-cutting riots had impressed upon the great planters the need to present a common face to their dependent laborers, especially to the growing number of black slaves who seemed more and more menacing as the years passed.

Gaming relationships were one of several ways by which the planters, no doubt unconsciously, preserved class cohesion.[69] By wagering on cards and horses they openly expressed their extreme competitiveness, winning temporary emblematic victories over their rivals without thereby threatening the social tranquility of Virginia. These non-lethal competitive devices, similar in form to what social anthropologists have termed "joking relationships," were a kind of functional alliance developed by the participants themselves to reduce dangerous, but often inevitable, social tensions.[70]

Without rigid social stratification racing would have lost much of its significance for the gentry. Participation in these contests publicly identified a person as a member of an elite group. Great planters raced against their social peers. They certainly had no interest in competing with social inferiors, for in this kind of relationship victory carried no positive meaning: the winner gained neither honor nor respect. By the same token, defeat by someone like James Bullocke, the tailor from York, was painful, and to avoid such incidents gentlemen rarely allowed poorer whites to enter their gaming relationships—particularly the heavy betting on quarter horses. The common planters certainly gambled among themselves. Even the slaves may have laid wagers. But when the gentry competed for high stakes, they kept their inferiors at a distance, as spectators but never players.

The exclusiveness of horse racing strengthened the gentry's cultural dominance. By promoting these public displays the great planters legitimized the cultural values which racing symbolized—materialism, individualism, and competitiveness. These colorful, exclusive contests helped persuade subordinate white groups that gentry culture was desirable, something worth emulating; and it is not surprising that people who conceded the superiority of this culture readily accepted the gentry's right to rule. The wild spring down a dirt track served the interests of Virginia's gentlemen better than they imagined.

NOTES

[1][Durand of Dauphine], *A Huguenot Exile in Virginia or Voyages of a Frenchman exiled for his Religion with a Description of Virginia and Maryland*, ed. Gilbert Chinard (New York, 1934 [orig. publ. The Hague, 1687]), 148.

[2]Rev. James Fontaine, *Memoirs of a Huguenot Family* . . ., ed. Ann Maury (Baltimore, 1967 [orig. publ. 1853]), 265–266; John Mercer, cited in Jane Carson, *Colonial Virginians at Play* (Williamsburg, 1965), 49, n. 1; H. R. McIlwaine, ed., *Minutes of the Council and General Court of Colonial Virginia, 1622–1632, 1670–1676* . . . (Richmond, 1924), 252, 281, 285.

[3]Throughout this essay I use the terms gentry, gentlemen, and great planters as synonyms. In each Virginia county a few gentry families dominated civil, ecclesiastical, and military affairs. While the members of these families were substantially wealthier than the great majority of white planters, they were not a class in a narrow economic sense. Their cultural style as well as their financial position set them apart. The great planters and their families probably accounted for less than 2% of the colony's white population. Louis B. Wright, *The First Gentlemen of Virginia: Intellectual Qualities of the Early Colonial Ruling Class* (San Marino, Calif., 1940), 57, estimates their number at "fewer than a hundred families." While entrance into the gentry was not closed to newcomers, upward mobility into that group became increasingly difficult after the 1690s. See Philip A. Bruce, *Social Life of Virginia in the Seventeenth Century* (New York, 1907), 39–100; Aubrey C. Land, "Economic Base and Social Structure: The Northern Chesapeake in the Eighteenth Century," *Journal of Economic History*, XXV (1965), 639–654; Bernard Bailyn, "Politics and Social Structure in Virginia," in James Morton Smith, ed., *Seventeenth-Century America: Essays in Colonial History* (Chapel Hill, N.C., 1959), 90–115; and Jack P. Greene, "Foundations of Political Power in the Virginia House of Burgesses, 1720–1776," *William and Mary Quarterly*, 3d Ser., XVI (1959), 485–506.

[4]These disturbances are described in T. H. Breen, "A Changing Labor Force and Race Relations in Virginia 1660–1710," *Journal of Social History*, VIII (1973), 3–25. The fullest account of Bacon's Rebellion remains Wilcomb E. Washburn, *The Governor and the Rebel: A History of Bacon's Rebellion in Virginia* (Chapel Hill, N.C., 1957).

[5]Several historians have remarked on the unusual political stability of 18th-century Virginia. See, for example, Jack P. Greene, "Changing Interpretations of Early American Politics," in Ray Allen Billington, ed., *The Reinterpretation of Early American History: Essays in Honor of John Edwin Pom-*

fret (San Marino, Calif., 1966), 168–168, and Gordon S. Wood, "Rhetoric and Reality in the American Revolution," *WMQ*, 3d Ser., XXIII (1966), 27–30.

⁶The phrase "creole elite" comes from Carole Shammas, "English-Born and Creole Elites in Turn-of-the-Century Virginia," in Thad W. Tate and David L. Ammerman, eds., *Essays on the Seventeenth-Century Chesapeake* (Chapel Hill, N. C., forthcoming). See also David W. Jordan, "Political Stability and the Emergence of a Native Elite in Maryland, 1660–1715," *ibid.* The process of forming a native-born elite is also discussed in Bailyn, "Politics and Social Structure," in Smith, ed., *Seventeenty-Century America,* 90–115; John C. Rainbolt, "The Alteration of the Relationship between Leadership and Constituents in Virginia, 1660 to 1720," *WMQ*, 3d Ser., XXVIII (1970), 411–434; and Martin H. Quitt, "Virginia House of Burgesses 1660–1706: The Social Educational and Economic Bases of Political Power" (Ph.D. diss., Washington University, 1970).

⁷Breen, "Changing Labor Force," *Jour. Soc. Hist.*, VII (1973), 2–25; Edmund S. Morgan, *American Slavery—American Freedom: The Ordeal of Colonial Virginia* (New York, 1975), 295–362; Rainbolt, "Leadership and Constituents," *WMQ*, 3d Ser., XXVIII (1970), 428–429. On the social attitudes of the small planters see David Alan Williams, "Political Alignments in Colonial Virginia, 1698–1750" (Ph.D. diss., Northwestern University, 1959), chap. 1.

⁸A sudden growth of gambling for high stakes in pre-Civil War England is discussed in Lawrence Stone, *The Crisis of the Aristocracy, 1558–1641* (Oxford, 1965). For the later period see Robert W. Malcolmson, *Popular Recreations in English Society, 1700–1850* (Cambridge, 1973); G. E. Mingay, *English Landed Society in the Eighteenth Century* (London, 1963), 151–153, 249–250; and E. D. Cuming, "Sports and Games," in A. S. Turberville, ed., *Johnson's England: An Account of the Life and Manners of his Age,* I (London, 1933), 362–383.

⁹It is important to stress here that the Virginia gentry did not simply copy English customs. As I argue in this essay, a specific, patterned form of behavior, such as gambling, does not become popular in a society or among the members of a subgroup of that society unless the activity reflects or expresses values indigenous to that culture. In 17th-century Massacusetts Bay, for example, heavy betting did not develop. A small amount of gambling seems to have occurred among the poor, especially among servants, but I can find no incidence of gambling among the colony's social, political, or religious leaders. See Nathaniel B. Shurtleff, ed., *Rec-*

ords of the Governor and Company of the Massachusetts Bay . . . (Boston, 1853–1854), II, 180, III, 201, IV, pt. 1, 366; *Records of the Suffolk County Court, 1671–1680* (Colonial Society of Massachusetts, *Publications* [Boston, 1933]), XXIX, 131, 259, 263, XXX, 1162; and Joseph H. Smith, ed., *Colonial Justice in Western Massachusetts, 1639–1702: The Pynchon Court Record* (Cambridge, Mass., 1961), 109.

[10]Two of Clifford Geertz's essays here helped shape my ideas about Virginia society: "Thick Description: Toward an Interpretive Theory of Culture" and "Deep Play: Notes on the Balinese Cockfight" in Geertz, *The Interpretation of Cultures* (New York, 1973), 3–30, 412–453. Also see Erving Goffman's "Fun in Games" in Goffman, *Encounters: Two Studies in the Sociology of Interaction* (Indianapolis, 1961), 17–81; Raymond Firth, "A Dart Match in Tikopia: A Study in the Sociology of Primitive Sport," *Oceania*, I (1930), 64–96; and H. A. Powell, "Cricket in Kiriwinia," *Listener*, XLVIII (1952), 384–385.

[11]Philip A. Bruce, *Economic History of Virginia in the Seventeenth Century* . . . II (New York, 1935 [orig. publ. 1895]), 151.

[12]"A Letter from Mr. John Clayton Rector of Crofton at Wakefield in Yorkshire, to the Royal Society, May 12, 1688," in Peter Force, ed., *Tracts and Other Papers Relating Principally to the Origin, Settlement, and Progress of the Colonies in North America* . . ., III (Washington, D. C., 1844), no. 12, 21.

[13]Richard Beale Davis, ed., *William Fitzhugh and His Chesapeake World, 1676–1701: The Fitzhugh Letters and Other Documents* (Chapel Hill, N. C., 1963), 15.

[14]On the independence of the Virginia gentry see Gerald W. Mullin, *Flight and Rebellion: Slave Resistance in Eighteenth-Century Virginia* (New York, 1972), chap. 1.

[15]William Byrd II to Charles, earl of Orrery, July 5, 1726, in "Virginia Council Journals, 1726–1753," *Virginia Magazine of History and Biography*, XXXII (1924), 27.

[16][Durand], *A Huguenot Exile*, ed. Chinard, 110.

[17]I discuss this theme in greater detail in a paper entitled "Looking Out For Number One: Cultural Values and Social Behavior in Early Seventeenth-Century Virginia" (paper delivered at the Thirty-Second Conference in Early American History, Nov. 1974).

[18]Rev. Andrew Burnaby, *Travels through the Middle Settlements In North America, In the Years 1759 and 1760: With Observations Upon the State of the Colonies*, in John Pinkerton, ed., *A General Collection of the Best and Most*

Interesting Voyages and Travels in All Ports of the World. . ., XIII (London, 1812), 715.

[19]According to John Rainbolt, the gentry's "striving for land, wealth, and position was intense and, at times ruthless" ("Leadership and Constituents," *WMQ*, 3d Ser., XXVIII [1970], 414). See Carole Shammas, "English-Born and Creole Elites," in Tate and Ammerman, eds., *Seventeenth-Century Chesapeake:* Morgan, *American Slavery—American Freedom*, 288–289; and Rhys Isaac, "Evangelical Revolt: The Nature of the Baptists' Challenge to the Traditional Order in Virginia, 1765 to 1775," *WMQ*, 3d Ser., XXXI (1974), 345–353.

[20]Louis B. Wright, ed., *Letters of Robert Carter, 1720–1727: The Commercial Interests of a Virginia Gentleman* (San Marino, Calif., 1940), 93–94.

[21]Hugh Jones, *The Present State of Virginia Giving a Particular and short Account of the Indian, English, and Negroe Inhabitants of that Colony . . .* (New York, 1865 [orig. publ. 1724]), 48.

[22]Quoted in Thomas Jefferson Wertenbaker, *The Old South: The Founding of American Civilization* (New York, 1942), 19.

[23]Peter Collinson to John Bartram, Feb. 17, 1737, *WMQ*, 2d Ser., VI (1926), 304.

[24]Davis, ed., *Fitzhugh Letters*, 229, 241–242, 244, 246, 249–250, 257–259. For another example of the concern about outward appearances see the will of Robert Cole (1674), in *WMQ*, 3d Ser., XXXI (1974), 139.

[25]Rovert Beverley, *The History and Present State of Virginia*, ed., Louis B. Wright (Chapel Hill, N. C., 1947), 226.

[26]William Fitzhugh to Oliver Luke, Aug. 15, 1690, in Davis, ed., *Fitzhugh Letters*, 280.

[27]William Byrd I to Perry and Lane, July 8, 1686, in "Letters of William Byrd I," *VM HB*, XXV (1917), 132.

[28]Louis B. Wright and Marion Tinling, eds., *The Secret Diary of William Byrd of Westover, 1709–1712* (Richmond, Va., 1941), 223–224.

[29]Gaming was so popular among the gentry, so much an expression of their culture, that it became a common metaphor in their discussion of colonial politics. For example, an unsigned essay entitled "The History of Bacon's and Ingram's Rebellion, 1676" described the relationship between Nathaniel Bacon and Gov. William Berkeley as a card game. Charles M. Andrews, ed., *Narratives of the Insurrections, 1675–1690* (New York, 1915), 57. In another account of Bacon's Rebellion, written in 1705, Thomas

Mathew noted that several members of the House of Burgesses were "not docill enough to Gallop the future Races, that Court seem'd dispos'd to Lead 'em." *Ibid.*, 32. In May 1697 William Fitzhugh explained to Capt. Roger Jones: "your self will see what a hard Game we have to play the contrary party that is our Opposers, having the best Cards and the trumps to boot especially the Honor. Yet would my Lord Fairfax there [in England], take his turn in Shuffling and Dealing the Cards and his Lordship with the rest see that we were not cheated in our game, I question not but we should gain the Sett, tho' the game is so far plaid" (Davis, ed., *Fitzhugh Letters*, 352).

[30]Rhys Isaac provides a provocative analysis of the relationship between games and gentry culture on the eve of the Revolution in "Evangelical Revolt," *WMQ*, 3d Ser., XXXI (1974), 348–353. See also Mark Anthony de Wolfe Howe, ed., "Journal of Josiah Quincy, Junior, 1773," *Massachusetts Historical Society, Proceedings*, XLIX (1915–1916), 467, and William Stith, *The Sinfulness and pernicious Nature of Gaming. A Sermon Preached before the General Assembly of Virginia: At Williamsburg, March 1st 1752* (Williamsburg, 1752), 5–26.

[31]The best discussion of these household games is Carson, *Virginians at Play*, 49–89. See also Charles Cotton, *The Compleat Gamester or Instructions How to Play at Billiards, Trucks, Bowls, and Chess . . .* (1674), in Cyril H. Harmann, ed., *Games and Gamesters of the Restoration: The Compleat Gamester by Charles Cotton, 1674, and Lives of the Gamesters, by Theophilus Lucas, 1714* (London, 1930).

[32]After 1750, however, the gentry's attitude toward household or tavern games seems to have changed. The betting became so heavy that several eminent planters lost fortunes at the gaming tables. A visitor at Williamsburg in 1765 wrote of these men that "they are all professed gamesters, Especially Colonel Burd [William Byrd III], who is never happy but when he has the box and Dices in hand. [T]his Gentleman from a man of the greatest property of any in america has reduced himself to that Degree by gameing, that few or nobody will Credit him for Ever so small a sum of money. [H]e was obliged to sel 400 fine Negroes a few Days before my arival." "Journal of a French Traveler in the Colonies, 1765, I," *American Historical Review*, XXVI (1920–1921), 742. Byrd was not alone. Robert Wormeley Carter and Robert Burwell were excessive gamblers, and as the aging Landon Carter (Robert "King" Carter's son) observed the wagering of the gentry on the eve of the Revolution, he sadly mused, "they play away and play it all away." Jack P. Greene, ed., *The Diary of Colonel Landon Carter of Sabine Hall, 1752–1778*, II (Charlottesville, Va., 1965), 830. On this

generation's addiction to gambling see Emory G. Evans, "The Rise and Decline of the Virginia Aristocracy in the Eighteenth Century: The Nelsons," in Darrett B. Rutman, ed., *The Old Dominion: Essays for Thomas Perkins Abernethy* (Charlottesville, Va., 1964), 68–70.

[33]Wright and Tinling, eds., *Secret Diary*, 75, 442, 449.

[34]Only one mention of cockfighting before 1730 has come to my attention, and that one refers to contests among the "common planters." Jones, *Present State of Virginia*, 48. See Carson, *Virginians at Play*, 151–152.

[35]Jones, *Present State of Virginia*, 48. This observation was repeated in other accounts of Virginia society throughout the 18th century. William Byrd II wrote "my Dear Countrymen have so great a Passion for riding, that they will often walk two miles to catch a Horse, in Order to ride One." William K. Boyd, ed., *William Byrd's Histories of the Dividing Line Betwixt Virginia and North Carolina* (Raleigh, N. C., 1929), 258. See also Carson, *Virginians at Play*, 102–105.

[36]"A Letter From Clayton," in Force, ed., *Tracts and Other Papers*, no. 12, 35.

[37]On the development of racing in Virginia, especially the transition from the quarter-mile straight track to the oval course, see. W. G. Stanard, "Racing in Colonial Virginia," *VM HB*, II (1894–1895), 293–305, and Fairfax Harrison, "The Equine F. F. V.'s: A Study of the Evidence for the English Horses Imported into Virginia before the Revolution," *ibid.*, XXXV (1927), 329–370. I suspect that quarter-horse racing was a sport indigenous to Virginia.

[38]Besides Randolph, there were John Stone, William Hardidge, Thomas Yowell, John Hardiman, Daniel Sullivant, Thomas Chamberlain, Rodham Kenner, Richard Kenner, William Soane, and Alexander Swan.

[39]Aug. 1690, Henrico County, Order Book 1678–1693, 340. All references to manuscript county records are to the photostat copies at the Virginia State Library, Richmond.

[40]Jan. 16, 1666, Accomack Co., Orders, 1666–1670, 9.

[41]Sept. 10, 1674, York Co., Deeds, Orders, Wills, 1672–1694, 85.

[42]*Virginia Gazette*, Nov. 19–26, 1736, Sept. 30–Oct. 7. 1737.

[43]Bruce, *Social Life*, 195–209; Carson, *Virginians at Play*, 108–110.

[44]Apr. 7, 1693, Westmoreland Co., Order Book, 1690–1698, 92; "Racing in Virginia in 1700–05," *VM HB*, X (1902–1903), 320.

[45]Aug. 1683, Henrico Co. Records [Deeds and Wills], 1677–1692, 254.

[46]Oct. 16, 1674, Westmoreland Co., Deeds, Patents, Etc., 1665–1677, 211; Bruce, *Social Life*, 197–198; Carson, *Virginians at Play*, 109.

[47]Beverley Fleet, eds., *Richmond County Records, 1704–1724*, Virginia Colonial Abstracts, XVII (Richmond, Va., 1943), 95–96.

[48]Carson, *Virginians at Play*, 105. See Aug. 29, 1694, Westmoreland Co., Order Book, 1690–1698, 146.

[49]Aug. 22, 1695, Northumberland Co., Order Book, 1678–1698, Pt. 2, 707–708.

[50]Morgan, *American Slavery—American Freedom*, 142, 198, 204

[51]Bruce, *Economic History*, II, 495–512.

[52]Aubrey Land's analysis of the probate records in a tobacco-producing area in nearby Maryland between 1690 and 1699 reveals that 74.6% of the estates there were worth less than £100 sterling. According to Land, the differences between the social structures of Maryland and Virginia at this time were not "very great." Land, "Economic Base and Social Structure," *Jour. Econ. Hist.*, XXV (1965), 641–644.

[53]William Fitzhugh to Dr. Ralph Smith, Apr. 22, 1686, in Davis, ed., *Fitzhugh Letters*, 176.

[54]The full covenant is reproduced in Stanard, "Racing in Colonial Virginia," *VM HB*, II (1894–1895), 296–298.

[55]*Ibid.*, 296.

[56]Virginia law prohibited fraudulent gaming, certain kinds of side bets, and gambling by persons who had "no visible estate, profession, or calling, to maintain themselves." William Waller Hening, ed., *The Statutes at Large; Being a Collection of all the Laws of Virginia . . .*, IV (Richmond, 1820), 214–218; George Webb, *Office and Authority of A Justice of Peace . . .* (Williamsburg, Va., 1736), 165–167. Wagers made between two gainfully employed colonists were legal agreements and enforceable as contracts. The courts of Virginia, both common law and chancery, apparently followed what they believed to be standard English procedure. Whether they were correct is difficult to ascertain. Sir William Holdsworth explains that acts passed by Parliament during the reigns of Charles II and Anne allowed individuals to sue for gaming debts, but he provides no evidence

that English courts regularly settled disputed contests such as horse races. Holdsworth, *A History of English Law* (London, 1966), VI, 404, XI, 539–542.

[57]Not until the 1750s did Virginians begin to discuss gambling as a social vice. See Stith, *The Sinfulness . . . of Gaming;* R. A. Brock, ed., *The Official Records of Robert Dinwiddie,* I (Richmond, Va., 1883), 30–31; Samuel Davies, *Virginia's Danger and Remedy. Two Discourses Occasioned by The Severe Drought . . .* (Williamsburg, 1756).

[58]Oct. 1690, Henrico Co., Order Book, 1678–1693, 351. See also Aug. 28, 1674, Northampton Co., Order Book No. 9, 1664–1674, 269, and Nov. 4, 1674, *ibid.,* No. 10, 1674–1679.

[59]Stanard, "Racing in Colonial Virginia," *VM HB,* II (1894–1895), 267; Henrico Co. Records [Deeds and Wills], 1677–1692, 466.

[60]Carson, *Virginians at Play,* 109–110.

[61]"Some Extracts from the Records of York Co., Virginia," *WMQ,* 1st Ser., IX (1900–1901), 178–179.

[62]Jan. 1694, Northumberland Co., Order Book, 1678–1698, Pt. 2, 643.

[63]Aug. 29, 1694, Westmoreland Co., Order Book, 1690–1698, 146–146a. Also see Oct. 1689, Henrico Co., Order Book, 1678–1693, 313, and Stanard, "Racing in Virginia," *VM HB,* II (1894–1895), 296.

[64]A gentleman could have challenged an opponent to a duel. Seventeenth- and early 18th-century Virginians recognized a code of honor of which dueling was a part, but they did everything possible to avoid such potentially lethal combats. I have found only four cases before 1730 in which dueling was even discussed. County courts fined two of the challengers before they could do any harm. ("A Virginian Challenge in the Seventeenth Century," *VM HB,* II [1894–1895], 96–97; *Lower Norfolk County Antiquarian,* IV [1904], 106.) And two comic-opera challenges that only generated blustery rhetoric are described in William Stevens Perry, ed., *Historical Collections Relating to the American Colonial Church,* I (Hartford, Conn., 1870), 25–28, and Bond, ed., *Byrd's Histories of the Dividing Line,* 173–175. On the court system see Philip A. Bruce, *Institutional History of Virginia in the Seventeenth Century . . .* I (Gloucester, 1910), 484–632, 647–689.

[65]Aug. 29, 1694, Westmoreland Co., Order Book 1690–1698, 146a.

[66]Jan. 1694, Northumberland Co., Order Book 1678–1698, Pt. 2, 643.

[67]Sometimes the courts had an extremely difficult time deciding

exactly what had occurred at a race. A man testified in 1675 that he had served as the official judge for a contest, and that while he knew which horse had finished first, he was "not able to say much less to Sweare that the Horse did Carry his Rider upon his back over the path." Sept. 16, 1675, Surry County, Deeds, Wills and Orders, 1671–1684, 133. For another complex case see Mar. 5, 1685, Rappahannock Co. Orders [no. 1], 1683–1686, 103, 120, 153.

[68]For evidence of the persistence of these values among the gentry in the Revolutionary period see Isaac, "Evangelical Revolt," *WMQ*, 3d Ser., XXXI (1974), 348–353.

[69]The planters' aggressive hospitality may have served a similar function. Hospitality in Virginia should be analyzed to discover its relationship to gentry culture. Robert Beverley makes some suggestive comments about this custom in his *History and Present State of Virginia*, 312–313. An interesting comparison to the Virginia practice is provided in Michael W. Young, *Fighting with Food: Leadership Values and Social Control in a Massim Society* (Cambridge, 1971).

[70]A. R. Radcliffe-Brown, *Structure and Function in Primitive Society: Essays and Addresses* (New York, 1964), chaps. 4, 5.

chapter 3

Eighteenth-Century American Women in Peace and War:

The Case of the Loyalists

by Mary Beth Norton

As many as sixty to eighty thousand colonists from all regions and social ranks fled to Canada and Great Britain during the American Revolution. Mary Beth Norton, who has previously written a book about these "Loyalists" in exile, explores here two themes that not only enlarge on their experience but also furnish a portrait of the divisions between the sexes in colonial society. She examines differences between men's and women's claims to the British government for property confiscated during the Revolution, using as her source 483 claims by American refugee women filed with the British government. She analyzes the language in the claims and the description of household furnishing and family finances supplied by each applicant. Norton finds that men's claims demonstrate detailed knowledge of family finances, but not of missing household items; similarly, women's claims reveal their awareness of lost household goods, but not of missing family properties. Her conclusions challenge the widely held view that in colonial society, marriage was an economic partnership, but that by the early nineteenth century, women's power had diminished as their economic participation in farm and business life declined. She also argues that the experience of the Revolution was far less of a hardship for men than for women during the war itself and in peacetime exile.

In recent years historians have come to recognize the central role of the family in the shaping of American society. Especially in the eighteenth century, when "household" and "family" were synonymous terms, and when household manufactures constituted a major contribution to the economy, the person who ran the household—the wife and mother—occupied a position of crucial significance. Yet those who have studied eighteenth-century women have usually chosen to focus on a few outstanding, perhaps unrepresentative individuals, such as Eliza Lucas Pinckney, Abigail Smith Adams, and Mercy Otis Warren. They have also emphasized the activities of women outside the home and have concentrated on the prescriptive literature of the day. Little has been done to examine in depth the lives actually led by the majority of colonial women or to assess the impact of the Revolution upon them.[1]

Such a study can illuminate a number of important topics. Demographic scholars are beginning to discover the dimensions of eighteenth-century households, but a knowledge of size alone means little without a delineation of roles filled by husband and wife within those households.[2] Historians of nineteenth-century American women have analyzed the ideology which has been termed the "cult of true womanhood" or the "cult of domesticity," but the relationship of these ideas to the lives of women in the preceding century

"Eighteenth-Century American Women in Peace and War: The Case of the Loyalists," by Mary Beth Norton. Reprinted by permission of the author and publisher from the *William and Mary Quarterly*, 3rd Ser. 33 (July 1976), 386–409. Copyright © 1976 by Mary Beth Norton.

Ms. Norton is a member of the Department of History, Cornell University. She wishes to thank Carol Berkin, Carl Kaestle, Pauline Maier, Robert Wells, and Peter Wood for their comments on an earlier version of this article. A portion of it was read at the Second Berkshire Conference on the History of Women, held at Radcliffe College, Oct. 1974.

remains largely unexplored.[3] And although some historians of the Revolution now view the war as a socially disruptive phenomenon, they have not yet applied that insight specifically to the study of the family.[4]

Fortunately, at least one set of documents contains material relevant to an investigation of all these aspects of late eighteenth-century American family life: the 281 volumes of the loyalist claims, housed at the Public Record Office in London. Although these manuscripts have been used extensively for political and economic studies of loyalism, they have only once before been utilized for an examination of colonial society.[5] What makes the loyalist claims uniquely useful is the fact that they contain information not only about the personal wartime experiences of thousands of Americans but also about the modes of life the war disrupted.

Among the 3,225 loyalists who presented claims to the British government after the war were 468 American refugee women. The analysis that follows is based upon an examination of the documents—formal memorials, loss schedules, and private letters—submitted by these women to the loyalist claims commission, and on the commission's nearly verbatim records of the women's personal appearances before them.[6] These women cannot be said to compose a statistically reliable sample of American womanhood. It is entirely possible that loyalist families differed demographically and economically, as well as politically, from their revolutionary neighbors, and it is highly probable that the refugee claimants did not accurately represent even the loyalist population, much less that of the colonies as a whole.[7] Nonetheless, the 468 claimants included white women of all descriptions, from every colony and all social and economic levels: they were educated and illiterate; married, widowed, single, and deserted; rural and urban; wealthy, middling, and poverty stricken. Accordingly, used with care, the loyalist claims can tell us much about the varieties of female experience in America in the third quarter of the eighteenth century.[8]

One aspect of prewar family life that is systematically revealed in the claims documents is the economic relationship of husband and wife within the household. All claimants, male and female alike, had to supply the commission with detailed estimates of property losses. Given the circumstances of the war, documentary evidence such as deeds, bills of sale, and wills was rarely available in complete form, and the commission therefore relied extensively upon the sworn testimony of the claimants and their witnesses in assessing losses. The claimants had nothing to gain by withholding information, because the amount of compensation they received depended in large part on their ability to describe their losses. Consequently, it may be assumed that what the loyalists told the commission, both orally and in writing, represented the full extent of their knowledge of their families' income and property.[9] The women's claims thus make it possible to determine the nature of their participation in the financial affairs of their households.

Strikingly, although male loyalists consistently supplied detailed assessments of the worth of their holdings, many women were unable to place precise valuations on the property for which they claimed compensation. Time after time similar phrases appear in the records of oral testimony before the commission: "She cant say what the Houses cost or what they woud have sold for" (the widow of a Norfolk merchant); "Says she is much a Stranger to the state of Her Husband's Concerns" (the widow of a storekeeper from Ninety-Six, South Carolina); "It was meadow Land, she cannot speak of the Value" (a New Jersey farmer's widow); "Her husband was a Trader and had many Debts owing to him She does not know how much they amounted to" (a widow from Ninety-Six); "She can't speak to the Value of the Stock in Trade" (a Rhode Island merchant's widow); "It was a good Tract but does not know how to value it" (the widow of a Crown Point farmer).[10]

Even when women submitted detailed loss schedules in

writing, they frequently revealed at their oral examinations that they had relied on male relatives or friends, or even on vaguely recalled statements made by their dead husbands, in arriving at the apparently knowledgeable estimates they had initially given to the commission. For example, a New Jersey woman, questioned about her husband's annual income, referred the commissioners to her father and other male witnesses, admitting that she did not know the amount he had earned. Similarly, the widow of a Charleston saddler told the commissioners that "she does not know the Amount of Her husband's Property, but she remembers to have heard him say in the year 1777 that he was worth £2,000 sterling clear of all Debts." Such statements abound in the claims records: "She is unable to speak to the value of the Plantn herself, but refers to Mr. Cassills"; "Says she cannot speak to the Value—the Valuatn was made by Capt McDonald and Major Munro"; "Says her Son in Law Capt Douglas is better acquainted with the particulars of her property than herself and she refers to him for an Account thereof."[11]

Although many female claimants thus lacked specific knowledge of their families' finances, there were substantial variations within the general pattern. The very wealthiest women—like Isabella Logan of Virginia (who could say only that she and her husband had lived in "a new Elegant, large double Brick House with two wings all finish'd in the best taste with Articles from London") and Mrs. Egerton Leigh of South Carolina (who gave it as her opinion that her husband had "a considerable real Estate as well as personal property . . . worth more than £10,000 . . . tho' she cannot herself speak to it with accuracy")—also tended to be the ones most incapable of describing their husbands' business affairs.[12] Yet some wealthy, well-educated women were conversant with nearly every detail of the family finances. For the most part, this latter group was composed of women who had brought the property they described to their husbands at marriage or who had been widowed before the war and had served as executrixes of the estates in question for some time. A case in point is that of Sarah Gould Troutbeck, daughter, executrix, and primary heir of John Gould, a prosperous Boston merchant. Her husband John, an Anglican clergyman, died in 1778, and so she carried the full burden of presenting the family's claim to the commission. Although she deprecatingly described herself to the board as "a poor weak Woman unused to business," she supplied the commissioners with detailed evidence of her losses and unrelentingly pursued her debtors. "Your not hearing from me for so long a time may induce you to think I have relinquished my claim to the interest due on your note," she informed one man in 1788. "If you really entertain any such thoughts I must beg leave to undeceive you." In addition, she did what few loyalists of either sex had the courage to attempt—return to the United States to try to recover her property. When she arrived in 1785, she found her estates "in the greatest confusion" but nevertheless managed within several months to repossess one house and to collect some debts. In the end she apparently won restoration of most of her holdings.[13]

Yet not all the female loyalists who had inherited property in their own right were as familiar with it as was Sarah Troutbeck. Another Massachusetts woman admitted to the commissioners that she did not know the value of the 550 acres left her by a relative, or even how much of the land was cultivated. "Her Brother managed everything for her and gave her what Money she wanted," she explained. In the same vein, a New Yorker was aware that her father had left her some property in his will, but "she does not know what property." A Charleston resident who had owned a house jointly with her brother commented that "it was a good House," but the commission noted, "she does not know the Value of it." And twice-widowed Jane Gibbes, claiming for the farms owned by her back-country South Carolina husbands, told the commission that she had relied on neighbors to assess the worth of the property, for "she can't speak positively to the value of her Lands herself."[14]

But if Jane Gibbes could not precisely evaluate the farms she had lived on, she still knew a good deal about them. She described the total acreage, the amount of land under cultivation, the crops planted, and the livestock that had been lost. In this she was representative of most rural female loyalists with claims that were not complicated by the existence of mortgages or outstanding debts. Although they did not always know the exact value of the land for which they requested reimbursement, they could supply the commission with many important details about the family property: the number of cattle, horses, sheep, and hogs; the types of tools used; the acreage planted, and with what crops; the amounts of grain and other foodstuffs stored for the winter; and the value of such unusual possessions as beehives or a "Covering Horse." It was when they were asked about property on which they had not lived, about debts owed by their husbands, or about details of wills or mortgages that they most often admitted ignorance.[15]

A good example is Mary McAlpin, who had settled with her husband on a farm near Saratoga, New York, in 1767. She did not know what her husband had paid for some unimproved lands, or the acreage of another farm he had purchased, but she was well acquainted with the property on which they had lived. The farm, she told the commissioners, "had been wholly cleared and Improved and was in the most perfect State of Cultivation." There were two "Log Houses plaistered and floored," one for them and one for their hired laborers, and sufficient materials on hand to build" a large and Commodious Brick House." Her husband had planted wheat, rye, peas, oats, barley, corn, turnips, potatoes, and melons; and "the Meadows had been laid down or sown with Clover and Timothy Grass, the two kind of Grass Seeds most Valued in that Country." The McAlpins had had a kitchen garden that produced "in great abundance every Vegitable usually cultivated in that part of America." Moreover, the farm was "well Provided" with such utensils as "a Team waggon, Carts sledges Carwls [sic] Wheels for Waggons, Wheels for Carts, Wheelbarrows, drags for Timber Ploughs, Harrows Hay Sythes Brush Sythes Grubbling Harrows, and all sorts of Carpenters Tools Shoemakers Tools Shovels, Spades, Axes Iron Crow Barrs etc."

After offering all these details, however, Mrs. McAlpin proved unable to assess the value of the property accuracely. She gave the commission a total claim of £6,000, clearly an estimate, and when asked to break down a particular item on her schedule into its component parts she could not do so, saying that "She valued the Whole in the Lump in that Sum." Moreover, she proved ignorant of the terms of her husband's will, confusedly telling the commissioners that he had "left his real personal Estate to his Son—This she supposes was his Lands" (the board's secretary noted carefully, "This is her own Expression"), when in fact she had been left a life interest in the real estate plus half the personal estate.[16] In short, Mary McAlpin typifies the rural female claimant, though her husband's property was substantially larger than average. She knew what he had owned, but she did not know exactly how much it was worth. She was well acquainted with the day-to-day operations of the farm but understood very little about the general family finances. And she knew nothing at all about legal or business terminology.

The pattern for urban dwellers was more varied. In the first place, included in their number were most of the wealthy women mentioned earlier, both those who knew little or nothing about their husbands' estates and those who, like Sarah Troutbeck, were conversant with the family holdings. Secondly, a higher percentage of urban women engaged directly in business. Among the 468 female claimants there were forty-three who declared either that they had earned money on their own or that they had assisted their husbands in some way. Only three of these forty-three can

be described as rural: a tavernkeeper's wife from Ticon-
deroga, a small shopkeeper from Niagara, and the housekeeper for the family of Col. Guy Johnson. All the other
working women came from cities such as Boston, Philadelphia, Charleston, and New York, or from smaller but substantial towns like Williamsburg, Wilmington, N.C., and
Baltimore. The urban women's occupations were as varied as
the urban centers in which they resided. There were ten who
took lodgers, eighteen shopkeepers and merchants of various sorts, five tavernkeepers, four milliners, two mantua
makers, a seamstress, a midwife, an owner of a coffeehouse,
a schoolteacher, a printer, one who did not specify an occupation, and two prostitutes who described themselves as
owners of a small shop and declared that their house had
been "always open" to British officers needing "aid and attention."[17]

As might be expected, the women who had managed
businesses or assisted their husbands (one wrote that she
was "truly his Partner" in a "steady Course of painfull Industry") were best informed about the value of their property. Those who had been grocers or milliners could usually
list in detail the stock they had lost; the midwife had witnesses to support her claim to a high annual income from her
profession; the boardinghouse keepers knew what they had
spent for furniture and supplies; and the printer could readily value her shop's equipment.[18] But even these working
women could not give a full report on all aspects of their
husbands' holdings: the widow of a Boston storekeeper, for
example, could accurately list their stock in trade but admitted ignorance of the value of the property her husband had
inherited from his father, and although the widow of
another Boston merchant had carried on the business after
her husband was wounded at Bunker Hill, she was not familiar with the overall value of their property.[19]

It is therefore not surprising that women claimants on
the average received a smaller return on their claims than did

their male counterparts. Since the commissioners reimbursed only for fully proven losses, the amounts awarded are a crude indicator of the relative ability of individual refugees to describe their losses and to muster written and oral evidence on their own behalf. If women had known as much as their husbands about the family estates, there would have been little or no difference between the average amounts granted to each sex. But of the claims heard in England for which complete information is available, 660 loyalist men received an average return of 39.5 percent, while for 71 women the figure was 34.1 percent. And this calculation does not take into account the large number of women's claims, including some submitted by businesswomen, which were entirely disallowed for lack of proof. [20]

In the absence of data for other time periods and populations, it is difficult to assess the significance of the figures that show that slightly less than 10 percent (9.2 percent, to be exact) of the loyalist refugee women worked outside the home. Historians have tended to stress the widespread participation of colonial women in economic enterprise, usually as a means of distinguishing them from their reputedly more confined nineteenth-century counterparts. [21] The claims documents demonstrate that some women engaged in business, either alone or with their husbands, but 9.2 percent may be either a large or a small proportion of the total female population, depending on how one looks at it. The figures themselves must remain somewhat ambiguous, at least until additional data are obtained. [22] What is not at all ambiguous, however, is the distinctive pattern of the female claimants' knowledge.

For regardless of whether they came from rural or urban areas, and regardless of their background or degree of participation in business, the loyalist women testified almost exclusively on the basis of their knowledge of those parts of the family property with which their own lives brought them into regular contact. What they uniformly lacked were those pieces of information about business matters that could have been supplied only by their husbands. Evidently, late eighteenth-century American men, at least those who became loyalists, did not systematically discuss matters of family finances with their wives. From that fact it may be inferred that the men—and their wives as well, perhaps—accepted the dictum that woman's place was in the home. After all, that was where more than 90 percent of the loyalist women stayed, and their ignorance of the broader aspects of their families' economic circumstances indicates that their interest in such affairs was either minimal or else deliberately thwarted by their husbands.[23]

It would therefore appear that the 9 percent figure for working women is evidence not of a climate favorable to feminine enterprise but rather of the opposite: women were expected to remain largely within the home unless forced by necessity, such as the illness or death of their husbands, to do otherwise. The fact that fewer than one-half (seventeen, to be precise) of the working women enumerated earlier had healthy, living husbands at the time they engaged in business leads toward the same conclusion. The implication is that in mid-eighteenth-century America woman's sphere was rigidly defined at all levels of society, not merely in the wealthy households in which this phenomenon has been recognized.[24]

This tentative conclusion is supported by evidence drawn from another aspect of the claims, for a concomitant of the contention that colonial women often engaged in business endeavors has been the assertion that colonial men, as the theoretical and legal heads of household, frequently assumed a large share of domestic responsibilities.[25] Yet if men had been deeply involved in running their households—in keeping accounts and making purchases, even if not in doing day-to-day chores—they should have described household furnishings in much the same detail as their wives used. But just as female claimants were unable to delineate their husbands' business dealings accurately, so men separated from their wives—regardless of their social status—failed to submit specific lists of lost household items like furniture, dishes, or kitchen utensils. One such refugee observed to the commission in 1788, "As Household Furniture consists of a Variety of Articles, at this distance of time I cannot sufficiently recollect them so as to fix a Value on them to the Satisfaction of my mind."[26] It is impossible to imagine a loyalist woman making a comparable statement. For her, what to a man was simply "a Variety of Articles" resolved itself into such familiar and cherished objects as "1 Compleat set blue and white Tea and Table China," "a Large new Goose feather Bed, bolster Pillows and Bedstead," "a Small painted Book Case and Desk," "1 Japan Tea Board," "2 smoothing Irons," and "1 old brass Coffee Pott." Moreover, although men usually noted losses of clothing in a general way, by listing a single undifferentiated sum, women frequently claimed for specific articles of jewelry and apparel. For example, Mary Swords of Saratoga disclosed that she had lost to rebel plunderers a "Long Scarlet Cloak" and a "Velvet Muff and Tippett," in addition to "One pair of Ear Rings French paste set in Gold," "One small pair of Ear Rings Garnets," and "one Gold Broatch with a small diamond Top."[27]

The significance of such lists lies not only in the fact that they indicate what kinds of property the claimants knew well enough to describe accurately and in detail, but also in the insight they provide into the possessions which claimants thought were sufficiently important to mention individually. For example, a rural New York woman left no doubt about her pride in "a fine large new stove"; a resident of Manhattan carefully noted that one of her lost beds was covered in "Red Damask"; and a Rhode Islander called attention to the closets in her "large new dwelling house."[28] The differentiated contents of men's and women's claims thus take on more importance, since the contrasting lists not only suggest the extent of the claimants' knowledge but also reveal their assessments of the relative importance of their possessions. To men, furniture, dishes, and clothing could easily be lumped together under general headings; to women, such possessions had to be carefully enumerated and described.

In the end, all of the evidence that can be drawn from the loyalist claims points to the conclusion that the lives of the vast majority of women in the Revolutionary era revolved around their immediate households to a notable degree. The economic function of those households in relation to the family property largely determined the extent of their knowledge of that property. In rural areas, where women's household chores included caring for the stock and perhaps occasionally working in the fields, women were conversant with a greater proportion of the family estates than were urban women, whose knowledge was for the most part confined to the furnishings of the houses in which they lived, unless they had been widowed before the war or had worked outside the home. The wealth of the family was thus a less significant determinant of the woman's role than was the nature of the household. To be sure, at the extreme ends of the economic scale, wealth and education, or the lack of them, affected a woman's comprehension of her family's property, but what the women displayed were relative degrees of ignorance. If the loyalist claimants are at all representative, very few married colonial women were familiar with the broader aspects of their families' financial affairs. Regardless of where they lived, they were largely insulated from the agricultural and business worlds in which their husbands engaged daily. As a result, the Revolutionary War, which deprived female loyalists of the households in which they had lived and worked, and which at the same time forced them to confront directly the wider worlds of which they had had little previous knowledge, was for them an undeniably traumatic experience.

At the outbreak of the war, loyalist women expected that "their Sex and the Humanity of a civilized People" would protect them from "disrespectfull Indignities." Most of them soon learned otherwise. Rebel men may have paid lip service to the ideal that women and children should be treated as noncombatants, but in practice they consigned female loyalists to much the same fate as their male relatives. Left behind by their fleeing husbands (either because of the anticipated difficulties of a journey to the British lines or in the hope that the family property might thereby be preserved), loyalist wives, with their children, frequently found themselves "stripped of every Thing" by American troops who, as one woman put it, "not contented with possessing themselves of her property were disposed to visit severity upon her person and Those of her friends."[29] Female loyalists were often verbally abused, imprisoned, and threatened with bodily harm even when they had not taken an active role in opposing the rebel cause.[30]

When they had assisted the British—and many aided prisoners or gathered intelligence—their fate was far worse. For example, the New Yorker Lorenda Holmes, who carried letters through the lines in 1776, was stripped by an angry band of committeemen and dragged "to the Drawing Room Window . . . exposing her to many Thousands of People Naked." On this occasion Mrs. Holmes admitted that she "received no wounds or bruises from them only shame and horror of the Mind," but a few months later, after she had shown some refugees the way to the British camp, an American officer came to her house and held her "right foot upon the Coals until he had burnt it in a most shocking manner," telling her "he would learn her to carry off Loyalists to the British Army."[31]

As can readily be imagined, the women did not come

through such experiences emotionally unscathed. One Massachusetts mother reported that her twelve-year-old daughter suffered from "nervous Fits" as a result of "the usage she met with from the Mobs"; and another New England woman, the wife of a merchant who was an early target of the local committee because he resisted the nonimportation movement, described to a female friend her reaction to a threatening letter they had received: "I have never injoyed one hours real Sattisfaction since the receipt of that Dreadfull Letter my mind is in continual agitation and the very rustling of the Trees alarms me." Some time later the same woman was unfortunate enough to be abused by a rebel militiaman. After that incident, she reported, "I did not recover from my fright for several days. The sound of drum or the sight of a gun put me into such a tremor that I could not command myself."[32] It was only natural for these women to look forward with longing to the day when they could escape to Canada or, better still, to England, "a land of peace, liberty and plenty." It seemed to them that their troubles would end when they finally left America. But, as one wrote later with the benefit of hindsight, their "severest trials were just begun."[33]

Male and female refugees alike confronted difficult problems in England and Canada—finding housing, obtaining financial support, settling into a new environment. For women, especially widows with families, the difficulties were compounded. The Bostonian Hannah Winslow found the right words: it was a "cruell" truth, she told her sister-in-law, that "when a woman with a family, and Particularly a large one, looses her Husband and Protector People are afraid to keep up the Acquaintance least they may ask favrs."[34] Many of the men quickly reestablished their American friendship networks through the coffeehouses and refugee organizations; the women were deprived not only of the companionship such associations provided but also of the information about pensions and claims that was transmitted along the male networks. As a result, a higher proportion of female than male loyalists made errors in their applications for government assistance, by directing the memorials to the wrong officials and failing to meet deadlines, often because they learned too late about compensation programs. Their standard excuses—that they "had nobody to advise with" and that they "did not know how to do it"—were greeted with skepticism by the claims commission, but they were undoubtedly true.[35]

On the whole, female loyalists appear to have fared worse in England than their male counterparts, and for two major reasons. In the first place, the commissioners usually gave women annual pensions that were from £10 to £20 lower than those received by men, apparently because they believed that the women had fewer expenses, but also because in most cases the women could not claim the extra merit of having actively served the royal cause.[36] Second, fewer women than men found work to supplement the sums they received from the government. To the wealthier female refugees work seemed so automatically foreclosed as an option that only a small number thought it necessary to explain to the commission why they could not contribute to their own support. Mary Serjeant, the widow of a Massachusetts clergyman, even regarded her former affluence as a sufficient reason in itself for her failure to seek employment. In 1782 she told the commissioners, "Educated as a Gentlewoman myself and brought up to no business I submit it to your [torn], Gentlemen, how very scanty must be the Subsistence which my Own Industry [can] procure us." Those who did try to earn additional income (many of whom had also worked outside the home in America) usually took in needlework or hired out as servants or housekeepers, but even they had trouble making ends meet. One orphaned young woman reported, "I can support myself with my needle: but not my two Sisters and infant Brother"; and another, who had learned the trade of mantua making, commented, "I

now got Work for my selef [sic]—but being oblidged to give
long credit and haveing no Money of my one [sic] to go on
with, I lived Cheifly upon tea which with night working
brought me almost into the last stadge of a Consumtion so
that when I rec'd my Money for work it went almost [all] to
dockters."[37]

Many of the loyalist women displayed a good deal of
resilience. Some managed to support themselves, among
them the Wells sisters of Charleston, who in 1789 opened a
London boardinghouse for young ladies whose parents
wished them to have a "suitable" introduction to society.
Others survived what might seem an overwhelming series of
setbacks—for example, Susannah Marshall of Maryland,
who, after running taverns in Baltimore and Head of Elk and
trying but failing to join Lord Dunmore off Norfolk in 1776,
finally left the United States by sea the following year, only
to have her chartered ship captured first by the Americans
and then by the British. In the process she lost all the goods
she had managed to salvage from her earlier moves, and
when she arrived in England she not only learned of her
husband's death but was unsuccessful in her application for
a subsistence pension. Refusing to give up, she went to work
as a nurse to support her children, and although she described herself to the commission in 1785 as "very Old and
feeble," she lived long enough to be granted a permanent
annual allowance of £20 in 1789.[38]

Susannah Marshall, though, had years of experience as
a tavernkeeper behind her and was thus more capable of
coping with her myriad difficulties than were women whose
prewar experience had been restricted to their households.
Such women recognized that they were "less able than many
who never knew happier days to bear hardships and struggle with adversity." These women, especially those who had
been, as one of them put it, *"born to better expectations"* in
America, spoke despairingly of encounters with "difficultys
of which she had no experience in her former life," of "Ad-
versities which not many years before she scarcely thought it

possible, that in any situation, she should ever experience."[39]

For women like these, exile in England or Canada was one long nightmare. Their relief requests have a desperate, supplicating tone that is largely absent from those submitted by men. One bewailed the impending birth of her third child, asking, "What can I do in my Condishtion deprived of helth with out Friends or mony with a helpless family to suffer with me?" Another begged the commission's secretary for assistance "with all humility" because "the merciless man I lodge with, threatens to sell the two or three trifling articles I have and put a Padlock on the Room unless I pay him the Rent amounting to near a Pound." By contrast, when a man prepared a memorial for the exceptionally distressed Mrs. Sarah Baker, he coolly told the commissioners that they should assist her because her children "as Soldiers or Sailors in his Majesty's Service may in future compensate the present Expence of saving them."[40]

The straits to which some of the female refugees were driven were dramatically illustrated in early 1783 when a South Carolina woman appeared before the commission "in Rags," explaining that she had been "obliged to pawn her Goods." It was but the first incident of many. Time and again women revealed that they had sold or pawned their clothes—which were usually their most valuable possessions—to buy food for themselves and their children. One was literally "reduced to the last shift" when she testified before the commission; another, the New Yorker Alicia Young, pawned so much that "the want of our apparel made our situation very deplorable" until friends helped her to redeem some of her possessions. Strikingly, no man ever told the commission stories like these. Either male refugees were able to find alternatives to pawning their clothes, or, if they did not, they were too ashamed to admit it.[41]

Such hardships took a terrible mental as well as physical toll. Evidence of extreme mental stress permeates the female loyalists' petitions and letters, while it is largely absent from

the memorials of male exiles. The women speak constantly
of their "Fear, Fatigue and Anxiety of Mind," their "lowness
of Spirit," their "inexpressable" distress, their "accumulated
anguish." They repeatedly describe themselves as "desolate
and distressed," as "disconsolate, Distressed and helpless . . . with a broken Spirit Ruined health and Constitution," as "Oppressed in body and distressed in mind."[42] "I
am overwhelm'd with misfortunes," wrote one. Poverty
"distracts and terrifies me," said another; and a third begged
"that she may not be left a Prey to Poverty, and her constant
companons [sic], Calamity and Sorrow." "My pen is unable
to describe the horrors of My Mind—or the deploreable Situation of Myself and Infant family," Alica Young told a
member of the commission. "Judge then Dr Sir what is to
become of me, or what we are to exist upon—I have no kind
of resource . . . oh Sir the horrors of my Situation is almost
too much for me to bear." Most revealing of all was the wife
of a Connecticut refugee: "Nature it self languishes," Mary
Taylor wrote, "the hours that I should rest, I awake in such
an aggitation of mind, as though I had to suffer for sins, that
I neaver committed, I allmost shudder when I approache the
Doone [doom?]—as every thing appears to be conspired
against me, the Baker, and Bucher, seams to be weary of
serving me oh porvity what is its Crime, may some have
Compassion on those who feeals its power—for I can doo
nothing—but baith my infant with my tears—while seeing
my Husbands sinking under the waight of his misfortuens,
unable to afford me any release."[43]

Even taking into account the likelihood that it was more
socially acceptable for women to reveal their emotions, the
divergence between men's and women's memorials is too
marked to be explained by that factor alone. It is necessary to
probe more deeply and to examine men's and women's varying uses of language in order to delineate the full dimensions
of the difference.[44] As C. Wright Mills pointed out in an
influential article some years ago, actions or motives and the

vocabularies utilized to describe them cannot be wholly separated, and commonly used adjectives can therefore reveal the limitations placed on one's actions by one's social role. Mills asserted that "the 'Real Attitude or Motive' is not something different in kind from the verbalization or the 'opinion,' " and that "the long acting out of a role, with its appropriate motives, will often induce a man [or, one is compelled to add, a woman] to become what at first he merely sought to appear." Furthermore, Mills noted, people perceive situations in terms of specific, "delimited" vocabularies, and thus adjectives can themselves promote or deter certain actions. When adjectives are "typical and relatively unquestioned accompaniments of typical situations," he concluded, "such words often function as directives and incentives by virtue of their being the judgements of others as anticipated by the actor."[45]

In this theoretical context the specific words used by female loyalists may be analyzed as a means of understanding the ways in which they perceived themselves and their circumstances. Their very phraseology—and the manner in which it differs from that of their male counterparts—can provide insights into the matrix of attitudes that helped to shape the way they thought and acted. If Mills is correct, the question whether the women were deliberately telling the commission what they thought it wanted to hear becomes irrelevant: it is enough to say that they were acting in accordance with a prescribed role, and that that role helped to determine how they acted.[46]

With these observations in mind, the fact that the women refugees displayed an intense awareness of their own femininity assumes a crucial significance. The phrases permeate the pages of the petitions from rich and poor alike: "Though a Woman"; "perhaps no Woman in America in equal Circumstances"; "being done by a Woman"; "being a poor lame and infirm Woman." In short, in the female loyalists' minds their actions and abilities were to a certain extent defined by their sex. Femininity was the constant point of reference in measuring their achievements and making their self-assessments. Moreover, the fact of their womanhood was used in a deprecating sense. In their own eyes, they gained merit by not acting like women. Her services were "allmost Matchless, (being done by a Woman)," wrote one; "tho a Woman, she was the first that went out of the Gates to welcome the Royal Army," declared another. Femininity also provided a ready and plausible excuse for failures of action or of knowledge. A South Carolinian said she had not signed the address to the king in Charleston in 1780 because "it was not posable for a woman to come near the office." A Pennsylvanian apologized for any errors in her loss estimate with the comment, "as far as a Woman can know, she believes the contents to be true." A Nova Scotian said she had not submitted a claim by the deadline because of "being a lone Woman in her Husband's Absence and not having any person to Advise with." A Vermonter made the ultimate argument: "had she been a man, Instead, of a poor helpless woman—should not have faild of being in the British Servace.' [47]

The pervasive implication is one of perceived inferiority, and this implication is enhanced by the word women used most often to describe themselves: "helpless." "Being a Poor helpless Widow"; "she is left a helpless Widow"; "a helpless woman advanced in life"; "being a helpless woman": such phrases appear again and again in the claims memorials.[48] Male loyalists might term themselves "very unhappy," "wretched," "extremely distressed," or "exceedingly embarrassed," but *never* were they "helpless." For them, the most characteristic self-description was "unfortunate," a word that carried entirely different, even contrary, connotations.[49] Male loyalists can be said to have seen their circumstances as not of their own making, as even being reversible with luck. The condition of women, however, was inherent in themselves; nothing they could do could change their circumstances. By definition, indeed, they were incapable of helping themselves.

It should be stressed here that, although women commonly described themselves as "helpless," their use of that word did not necessarily mean that they were in fact helpless. It indicates rather that they perceived themselves thus, and that that perception in turn perhaps affected the way they acted (for example, in seeking charitable support instead of looking for work). Similarly, the fact that men failed to utilize the adjective "helpless" to refer to themselves does not mean that they were not helpless, for some of them surely were; it merely shows that—however incorrectly— they did think that they could change their circumstances. These two words, with all their connotations, encapsulate much of the divergence between male and female self-perceptions in late eighteenth-century America, even if they do not necessarily indicate much about the realities of male– female relationships in the colonies.[50]

There was, of course, more to the difference in sex roles than the sex-related ways in which colonial Americans looked at themselves. The claims documents also suggest that women and men placed varying emphases on familial ties. For women, such relationships seemed to take on special order of magnitude. Specifically, men never said, as several women did, that after their spouses' deaths they were so "inconsolable" that they were unable to function. One woman declared that after her husband's execution by the rebels she was "bereft of her reason for near three months," and another described herself as "rendered almost totally incapable of Even writing my own Name or any assistance in any Shape that Could have the least Tendency to getting my Bread."[51] Furthermore, although loyalist men expressed concern over the plight of the children they could not support adequately, women were much more emotionally involved in the fate of their offspring. "Your goodness will easily conceive, what I must feel for My *Children*," Alice

Young told a claims commissioner; "for myself—I care not—Misfortunes in the World but *Them*—they have no provision—no provider—no protector—but God—and me." Women noted that their "Sorrows" were increased by the knowledge that their children were "Partners in this Scene of Indigence." Margaret Draper, widow of a Boston printer, explained that although she had been ill and suffering from a "disorderd Mind," "what adds to my affliction is, my fears for my Daughter, who may soon be left a Stranger and friendless." In the same vein, a New Jersey woman commented that she had "the inexpressible mortification of seeing my Children in want of many necessaries and conveniences . . . and what still more distresses me, is to think that I am obliged by partaking of it, to lessen even the small portion they have."[52]

The women's emphasis on their families is entirely compatible with the earlier observation concerning the importance of their households in their lives. If their menfolk were preoccupied with the monetary consequences of adhering to the crown, the women were more aware of the human tragedy brought about by the war. They saw their plight and that of their children in much more personal terms than did their husbands. Likewise, they personalized the fact of their exile in a way that male loyalists did not, by almost invariably commenting that they were "left friendless in a strange Country." Refugee men, though they might call themselves "strangers," rarely noted a lack of friends, perhaps because of the coffeehouse networks. To women, by contrast, the fact that they were not surrounded by friends and neighbors seemed calamitous. "I am without Friends or Money," declared one; I am "a friendless, forlorn Woman . . . a Stranger to this Country, and surrounded by evils," said another. She is "far from her native Country, and numerous Friends and Relations where she formerly lived, much respected," wrote a third of her own condition.[53]

When the female refugees talked of settling elsewhere or

of returning to the United States, they spoke chiefly of the friends and relatives they would find at their intended destinations. Indeed, it appears from the claims that at least six women went into exile solely because their friends and relatives did. A loyalist woman who remained in the United States after the war explained that she did so because she chose "to reside near my relations [rather] than to carry my family to a strange Country where in case of my death they would be at the mercy of strangers." And Mary Serjeant's description of her situation in America as it would have been had her husband not been a loyalist carried the implication that she wished she too had stayed at home: "His poor Children and disconsolate Widow would now have had a House of their own and some Land adjoining to it And instead of being almost destitute in a Land of Strangers would have remained among some Relatives."[54]

In sum, evidence drawn from the loyalist claims strongly suggests that late eighteenth-century women had fully internalized the roles laid out for them in the polite literature of the day. Their experience was largely confined to their households, either because they chose that course or because they were forced into it. They perceived themselves as "helpless"—even if at times their actions showed that they were not—and they strongly valued ties with family and friends. When the Revolution tore them from the familiar patterns of their lives in America, they felt abandoned and adrift, far more so than did their male relatives, for whom the human contacts cherished by the women seemed to mean less or at least were more easily replaced by those friendships that persisted into exile.

The picture of the late-eighteenth-century woman that emerges from the loyalist claims, therefore, is of one who was almost wholly domestic, in the sense that that word would be used in the nineteenth-century United States. But at the same time the colonial woman's image of herself lacked the positive attributes with which her nineteenth-century counterpart could presumably console herself. The eighteenth-century American woman was primarily a wife and a mother, but America had not yet developed an ideology that would proclaim the social value of motherhood. That was to come with republicanism—and loyalist women, by a final irony, were excluded by their political allegiance from that republican assurance.[55]

NOTES

[1]See, for example, such works as Mary Sumner Benson, *Women in Eighteenth-Century America: A Study of Opinion and Social Usage* (New York, 1935); Elisabeth Anthony Dexter, *Colonial Women of Affairs*, 2d. ed. (New York, 1931); and Joan Hoff Wilson, "Dancing Dogs of the Colonial Period: Women Scientists," *Early American Literature*, VII (1973), 225–235. Notable exceptions are Julia Cherry Spruill, *Women's Life and Work in the Southern Colonies* (Chapel Hill, N.C., 1938), and Eugenie Andruss Leonard, *The Dear-Bought Heritage* (Philadelphia, 1965). On the importance of the early American family see David Rothman, "A Note on the Study of the Colonial Family," *William and Mary Quarterly*, 3d Ser., XXIII (1966), 627–634.

[2]Two recent works that deal with family size, among other topics, are Robert V. Wells," Household Size and Composition in the British Colonies in America, 1675–1775." *Journal of Interdisciplinary History*, IV (1974), 543–570, and Daniel Scott Smith, "Population, Family and Society in Hingham, Massachusetts, 1635–1880" (Ph. D. diss., University of California, Berkeley, 1973). Internal household relationships in 17th-century New England have been analyzed by Edmund S. Morgan, *The Puritan Family: Religion & Domestic Relations in Seventeenth-Century New England* (Boston, 1944), and John Demos, *A Little Commonwealth: Family Life in Plymouth Colony* (New York, 1970).

[3]Barbara Welter, "The Cult of True Womanhood, 1820–1860," *American Quarterly*, XVII (1966), 151–174, was the first to outline the dimensions of this ideology. For writings dealing with some of the implications of the "cult of domesticity" see Carroll Smith-Rosenberg, "The Hysterical Woman: Sex Roles and Role Conflict in 19th-Century America," *Social Research*, XXXIX (1972), 652–678; Ann Douglas Wood. "Mrs. Sigourney

and the Sensibility of the Inner Space." *New England Quarterly*, XLV (1972), 163–181; Kathyryn Kish Sklar, *Catharine Beecher: A Study in American Domesticity* (New Haven, Conn., 1973); and Nancy Falik Cott, "In the Bonds of Womanhood: Perspectives on Female Experience and Consciousness in New England, 1780–1830" (Ph.D. diss., Brandeis University, 1974), esp. chap. 6 An explicit assertion that women were better off in 18th-century America than they were later is found in Dexter, *Colonial Women of Affairs*, vii, 189–192, and in Page Smith, *Daughters of the Promised Land* (Boston, 1970), 37–76. But two European historians have appropriately warned that it may be dangerous to assume the existence of a "golden, preindustrial age" for women, noting that the "goldenness is seen almost exclusively in terms of women's work and its presumed relationship to family power, not in terms of other vital aspects of their lives, including the physical burdens of work and child bearing." Patricia Branca and Peter N. Stearns, "On the History of Modern Women, a Research Note," *AHA Newsletter*, XII (Sept. 1974), 6.

[4]For example, John Shy, "The American Revolution: The Military Conflict Considered as a Revolutionary War," in Stephen G. Kurtz and James H. Hutson, eds., *Essays on the American Revolution* (Chapel Hill, N.C., 1973), 121–156; John Shy, "The Loyalist Problem in the Lower Hudson Valley: The British Perspective," in Robert A. East and Jacob Judd, eds., *The Loyalist Americans: A Focus on Greater New York* (Tarrytown, N.Y., 1975), 3–13; and Ronald Hoffman, *A Spirit of Dissension: Economics, Politics, and the Revolution in Maryland* (Baltimore, 1973), esp. chaps. 6, 8.

[5]Catherine S. Crary, "The Humble Immigrant and the American Dream: Some Case Histories, 1746–1776," *Mississippi Valley Historical Review*, XLVI (1959), 46–66.

[6]For a detailed examination of the claims process see Mary Beth Norton, *The British-Americans: The Loyalist Exiles in England, 1774–1789* (Boston, 1972), 185–222. More than 468 women appear in the claims documents; excluded from the sample selected for this article are all female children, all English women who never lived in America (but who were eligible for compensation as heirs of loyalists), and all American women who did not personally pursue a claim (that is, whose husbands took the entire responsibility for presenting the family's claims). In addition to those requesting reimbursement for property losses, the sample includes a number of women—mostly the very poor, who had lost only a small amount of property, if any—who applied solely for the subsistence pensions which were also awarded by the claims commissioners. On the allowance system see *ibid.*, 52–61, 111–121, and 225–229.

[7]On the statistical biases of the loyalist claims see Eugene Fingerhut, "Uses and Abuses of the American Loyalists' Claims: A Critique of Quantitative Analyses," *WMQ*, 3d Ser., XXV (1968), 245–258.

[8]This approach to women in the Revolutionary era differs from the traditional focus on their public contributions to the war effort. See, for example, Elizabeth F. Ellet, *The Women of the American Revolution* (New York, 1848–1850); Walter Hart Blumenthal, *Women Camp Followers of the American Revolution* (Philadelphia, 1952); Elizabeth Cometti, "Women in the American Revolution," *NEQ*, XX (1947), 329–346; and Linda Grant DePauw, *Four Traditions: Women of New York during the American Revolution* (Albany, 1974).

[9]Only if they intended to commit fraud could loyalists gain by withholding information from the commission; two refugees, for example, requested compensation for property they had already sold during the war. But the commissioners found deliberately fraudulent only 10 of the claims submitted to them, and although they disallowed others for "gross prevarication," none of the claims falling into either category were submitted by women. See Norton, *British-Americans*, 217–219, on the incidence of fraud, and 203–205, 216–217, on the importance of accurate testimony.

[10]Joyce Dawson, testimony, May 5, 1787, A.O. 12/56, 330, Public Record Office; Isabella McLaurin, testimony, Nov. 27, 1784, A.O. 12/47, 233; Margaret Hutchinson, testimony, Aug. 10, 1786, A.O. 12/16, 34; Margaret Reynolds, testimony, Dec. 9, 1783, A.O. 12/46, 168; case of Mrs. Bowers, Feb. 24, 1783, A.O. 12/99, 48; Elizabeth Campbell, testimony, n.d., A.O. 12/26, 267. For other similar statements see A.O. 12/10, 254, A.O. 12/48, 233, A.O. 12/50, 390–391, and A.O. 13/68, pt. 1, 183.

[11]Frances Dongan, testimony, Dec. 6, 1784, A.O. 12/13, 267–272; case of Charlotte Pollock, June 27, 1783, A.O. 12/99, 336; Mary Ann Balfour, testimony, Mar. 13, 1786, A.O. 12/48, 242; Janet Murchison, testimony, July 26, 1786, A.O. 12/34, 405; Mary Kearsley, testimony, Apr. 28, 1785, A.O. 12/38, 282. Cf. Mrs. Kearsley's testimony with her written memorial. A.O. 13/102, 324–329. And see, for other examples, A.O. 12/4, 220, A.O. 12/14, 265, A.O. 12/47, 239, A.O. 13/63, 342, and A.O. 13/94, 318–326.

[12]Isabella Logan, loss schedule, Feb. 17, 1784, A.O. 13/32, 129; case of Lady Leigh, July 1, 1783, A.O. 12/99, 313. See also, the claim of Mary Auchmuty, A.O. 12/24, 114–117, 264–266, and A.O. 13–63, 133–140.

[13]Sarah Troutbeck to commissioners, June 5, 1787, A.O. 13/49, pt. 2, 565; Troutbeck to Samuel Peters, May 22, 1788, Peters Papers, III, fol. 83 (microfilm), New York Historical Society, New York City; Troutbeck to commissioners, Jan. 3, 1785, A.O. 13/137, 609. Her total claim covers fols.

539–590 in A.O. 13/49, pt. 2, and fols. 726–740 in A.O. 13/74. On the recovery of her property see A.O. 12/81, 47. For other examples of well-to-do women with a good knowledge of the family property see A.O. 13/134, 571–574, and A.O. 12/54, 61–71 (Mary Rothery), A.O. 13/64, 81–99, and A.O. 13/97, 344–348 (Henrietta Colden), and A.O. 12/13, 311–314 (Mary Poynton). Mary Winslow knew her own property in detail but was not so familiar with her husband's (A.O. 13/79, 757–758).

[14]Case of Mrs. Dumaresq, Mar. 31, 1783, A.O. 12/99, 134; case of Margaret Smithies, Nov. 13, 1783, A.O. 12/100, 66; case of Barbara Mergath, May 8, 1783, A.O. 12/99, 234; Jane Gibbes, testimony, Dec. 15, 1783, A.O. 12/46, 245–247.

[15]Jane Gibbes, testimony, Dec. 16, 1783, A.O. 12/46, 247–249; Widow Boyce, loss schedule, Oct. 16, 1783, A.O. 13/90, 181; Elizabeth Hogal, loss schedule, n.d., A.O. 12/27, 37. Typical examples of claims submitted by rural women may be found in A.O. 13/56, 91–93, A.O. 13/138, 475, A.O. 12/4, 72–74, A.O. 12/20, 270–271, A.O. 12/26, 14–16, and A.O. 12/29, 79. Cf. claims from rural men in A.O. 13/79, 73–77, 211–216. For a claim involving property owned elsewhere see that of Elinor Maybee, A.O. 12/28, 343–346, and A.O. 12/64, 1; for one involving both a mortgage and a misread will see that of Margaret Hutchinson, A.O. 12/16, 33–37, and A.O. 12/63, 61.

[16]Mary McAlpin, loss schedule, n.d., A.O. 13/131, 10–11, and testimony, Nov. 14, 1785, A.O. 12/21, 51–65.

[17]The list totals more than 40 because some women listed two enterprises. The women divided as follows: 10 each from New York City and Charleston, 7 each from Boston and Philadelphia, 2 from Baltimore, and 1 each from Savannah, Williamsburg, Wilmington, N.C., and St. Augustine. Twenty-eight were long-time widows or single, or were married but operated businesses independently of their husbands; 8 assisted their husbands; and 7 took over businesses after the death or incapacitation of their husbands.

[18]The quotation is from Rachel Wetmore, claims memorial, Mar. 25, 1786, A.O. 13/16, 271. For a milliner's claim see Margaret Hutchinson's, A.O. 13/96, 601–602; for a grocer and boardinghouse keeper's see Sarah Simpson's A.O. 12/25, 25–28. The midwife, Janet Cumming, claimed to have made £400 sterling annually, and her witnesses confirmed that estimate (A.O. 12/50, 347–348). See also Margaret Draper's original and revised loss estimates, A.O. 13/44, 342–344, 387, and Mary Airey's schedule, A.O. 12/24, 79.

[19]Hannah Pollard, claims memorial and testimony, A.O. 13/49, pt. 1, 158–159, 166; testimony re: claim of Mary Campbell, Oct. 24, 1786, A.O.

12/50, 103–105. The detailed schedule presented by the tavernkeeper Rachel Brain had been prepared by her husband before his death; see A.O. 12/26, 308–310.

[20]For a general discussion of claims receipts see Norton, *British-Americans*, 216–220. Property claims submitted by 10 of the businesswomen were disallowed, and at least another 10 of them apparently did not pursue a claim for lost property. (Because of the destruction and disappearance of some of the claims records it is impossible to be more precise.)

[21]This emphasis appears to have resulted from the influence of Dexter's *Colonial Women of Affairs*. Although she was careful to explain that she had searched only for examples of women who worked outside the home, and although she did not attempt to estimate the percentage of such women in the female population as a whole, historians who draw upon her book invariably stress the wide-ranging economic interests of colonial women. See, for example, Gerda Lerner, *The Woman in American History* (Reading, Mass., 1971), 15–19, and Carol Ruth Berkin, *Within the Conjuror's Circle: Women in Colonial America* (Morristown, N.J., 1974), 8–10.

[22]If anything, the loyalist claimants tended to be more urban than other loyalists and the rest of the American population, and therefore would presumably overrepresent working women. See the analysis in Norton, *British-Americans*, 37–39, and Fingerhut, "Uses and Abuses of Loyalists' Claims," *WMQ*, 3d Ser., XXV (1968), 245–258. Further, the method of choosing the sample—including only those women who themselves submitted claims and pension applications—would also tend to bias the result in favor of working women, since they would be the most likely to act on their own.

[23]The failure of 18th-century men to discuss finances with their wives is also revealed in such letters as that of Jane Robbins to her daughter Hannah Gilman, Sept. 1799, Gilman Papers, Massachusetts Historical Society, Boston. Mrs. Robbins declared that, although her husband had made his will some years before, "I never saw it till after his death." Further, she informed her daughter, on his deathbed he told her, "I should have many debts to pay that I knew nothing about."

[24]Berkin, *Conjuror's Circle*, 12–14, and Nancy F. Cott, ed., *Root of Bitterness: Documents of the Social History of American Women* (New York, 1972), 8–10, link sex role differentiation specifically to the upper classes that were emerging in the process which has been called "Europeanization" or "Anglicization."

25See, for example, Spruill, *Women's Life and Work*, 78–79.

26David Ingersoll to commissioners, July 30, 1788, A.O. 13/74, 288. For rare cases of men who did list household furnishings see A.O. 13/98, 431–432, and A.O. 13/73, 140–155.

27Martha Leslie, loss schedule, Mar. 25, 1784, A.O. 13/91, 2–3; Frances Dongan, inventory [Nov. 1, 1783], A.O. 13/109, 45; Catherine Bowles, loss schedule, May 10, 1783, A.O. 13/90. 175–176; Mary Swords, "Things Plundered from me by the Rebels," n.d., A.O. 13/67, 311.

28Mary Gibbins, loss schedule, n.d., A.O. 13/80, 167; "Estimate of Losses sustained at New York by Hannah Foy in the year 1775" [1782]. A.O. 13/54, 431; Elizabeth Bowers, loss schedule, n.d., A.O. 13/68, pt. 1, 64.

29Sarah Stuart, memorial to Lords of Treasury, Jan. 22, 1786, A.O. 13/135, 702; Elizabeth Phillips, affidavit, Oct. 9, 1788, A.O. 13/67, 303; Phebe Stevens, claims memorial, Mar. 23, 1784, A.O. 13/83, 580. For accounts of rebel looting see, for example, A.O. 12/56, 326–327, A.O. 13/73, 485, A.O. 13/91, 190, A.O. 13/93, 556, A.O. 13/102, 1278, A.O. 13/109, 43, A.O. 13/121, 478, and A.O. 13/126, 589.

30See, for example, A.O. 12/21, 53–54, A.O. 13/110, 351, A.O. 13/112, 55, A.O. 13/123, 240–241, A.O. 13/128, 7, and A.O. 13/135, 698. Two women said they suffered miscarriages as a result of scuffles with Revolutionary troops (A.O. 13/81, 59, and A.O. 13/64, 76–77), and a third was raped by a rebel soldier. The latter incident is discussed in Thomas Goldthwait to his daughter Catherine, Aug. 20, 1779, J. M. Robbins Papers, Mass. Hist. Soc.

31Lorenda Holmes, claims memorial, n.d., A.O. 13/65, 529–530. Similar though less graphic tales were recounted by other women whose assistance to the British was also discovered by the Revolutionaries. See A.O. 12/49, 56–58, A.O. 12/102, 80, A.O. 13/45, 530, A.O. 13/67, 192, A.O. 13/68, 125, A.O. 13/96, 263, and A.O. 13/102, 1107.

32Mary Serjeant, loss schedule, Feb. 19, 1783, A.O. 13/49, 285; Christian Barnes to Elizabeth Smith, July 13–28, 1770, Christian Barnes Letterbook, Library of Congress; Barnes to Elizabeth Smith Inman, Apr. [2]9, [1775], in Nina Moore Tiffany, ed., *Letters of James Murray, Loyalist* (Boston, 1901), 187–188.

33Louisa Susannah Wells Aikman, *The Journal of a Voyage from Charlestown, S.C., to London undertaken during the American Revolution* . . . (New

York, 1906), 52; Catherine Goldthwait to Elizabeth [Inman], Mar. 27, 1780, Robbins, Papers, Mass. Hist. Soc. For a discussion of the loyalists initial optimism and subsequent disillusionment see Mary Beth Norton, "The Loyalists' Image of England: Ideal and Reality," *Albion*, III (1971), 62–71.

[34]Hannah Winslow to [a sister-in-law], June 27, 1779, Winslow Papers, Mass. Hist. Soc. See also Rebecca Dolbeare to John Dolbeare, Aug. 30, 1780, Dolbeare Papers, Mass. Hist. Soc., Polly Dibblee to William Jarvis, Nov. 1787, A.O. 13/41, 248. For a general discussion of the exiles' financial problems see Norton, *British-Americans*, 49–61. For another similar observation by a single woman see Louisa Oliver to Andrew Spooner, Mar. 1, 1788, Hutchinson–Oliver Papers, Mass. Hist. Soc.

[35]The quotation is from the case of Mary Hind, Feb. 1783, A.O. 12/99, 35. For examples of other women who claimed ignorance of proper forms and application procedures see A.O. 12/46, 165, A.O. 12/99, 238, A.O. 13/24, 284, A.O. 13/26, 63, 199, 282, 360, A.O. 13/113, 88, A.O. 13/131, 65, and A.O. 13/137, 150. Of course, a few men also made similar claims; see, for example, A.O. 12/43, 322–325, 328–331, and A.O. 12/46, 63. On the male networks see Norton, *British-Americans*, 63–79, 162–164, 186–196, 206–216. The memorials submitted by women were not only more prone to error but also more informal, less likely to be written in the third person, less likely to contain the sorts of ritualistic phrases and arguments used by the men, and consequently more likely to be personally revealing.

[36]Norton, *British-Americans*, 52–61, 111–121, discusses the bases for pension decisions. It was standard practice for the commission to lower a family's allotment immediately after the death of the husband, regardless of the fact that the widow usually had to meet medical and funeral expenses at exactly that time. The pension records (A.O. 12/99–105, and T. 50/11ff, Public Record Office) show that women's pensions were normally smaller than men's. In addition, T. 50/11 reveals a clear case of discrimination: in 1789 the Charleston midwife Janet Cumming (see note 18 above) was, under the commission's rules, entitled to an annual pension of £200 for loss of profession (she was the only woman to qualify for one in her own right); instead, she was granted only a £50 widow's allowance.

[37]Mary Serjeant to John Wilmot and Daniel P. Coke, Dec. 1, 1782, A.O. 13/49, pt. 1, 283; Ann Asby to commissioners, Apr. 14, 1788, A.O. 13/43, 147; Susanna Sandys, memorial, n.d., A.O. 13/84, 613. (Sandys was English, though the daughter of a refugee, and is quoted here because of the detailed nature of her comments.) For a statement similar to Mrs. Serjeant's see Margaret Smythies to Lords of Treasury, Jan. 23, 1782, A.O. 13/67, 230. For two women who did explain why they could not work see

A.O. 13/75, 627, and A.O. 13/53, 193. Information about nearly all the loyalist women who worked in England may be located in the following documents: A.O. 12/30, 230, A.O. 12/99, 50, 244, 264, A.O. 12/101, 137, A.O. 12/102, 87, 136, 164, 165, 175, 187, A.O. 13/43, 661, A.O. 13/44, 427, A.O. 13/71, 156, and A.O. 13/131, 359.

[38]On the Wells sisters' enterprise see Steuart Papers, 5041, fol. 123, National Library of Scotland, Edinburgh; Ann Elmsley to James Parker [1789?], Parker Papers, Pt. IV, no. 15, Liverpool Record Office, England; and Aikman, *Journal of a Voyage*, 71. Susannah Marshall's story may be traced in A.O. 13/62, 4, 7, A.O. 12/6, 257–263, and A.O. 12/99, 244.

[39]Harriet, Mary, Sarah, and Elizabeth Dawson and Ann Dawson Murray to commissioners, n.d., A.O. 13/113, 195; Mary Muirson to Lords of Treasury, May 28, 1784, A.O. 13/56, 342; Isabella Logan, claims memorial, Feb. 17, 1784, A.O. 13/32, 126; Patience Johnston, claims memorial, Dec. 21, 1785, A.O. 13/26, 196. For similar statements see A.O. 13/40, 93, A.O. 13/75, 354, 603, A.O. 13/132, 257, and A.O. 13/134, 504.

[40]Mary Lowry to [Samuel Remnant], n.d., A.O. 13/31, 202; Mary Curtain to Charles Monro, July 7, 7, 1789, A.O. 13/137, 98; Samuel Peters to Daniel P. Coke, Nov. 20, 1784, A.O. 13/43, 352. Cf. the statements in the text with those of men; for example, Samuel Porter to Lords of Treasury, Feb. 23, 1776, T. 1/520, 27; Thomas Banks to Lords of Treasury, Feb. 9, 1779, T. 1/552, 3; John Saunders to Lords of Treasury, Mar. 31, 1785, F.O. 4/1, 248, Public Record Office.

[41]Case of Margaret Reynolds, Mar. 26, 1783, A.O. 12/99, 116; Charlotte Mayne to—[Aug. 1783], H.O. 42/3, Public Record Office; Alicia Young to Robert Mackenzie, June 3, 1789, A.O. 13/67, 641. Mrs. Young gave the commissioners a detailed list of the items she had pawned (A.O. 13/67, 646). For other similar accounts of women pawning or selling their goods see A.O. 12/99, 13, 56, 60, A.O. 12/101, 196, 364, A.O. 13/43, 350, A.O. 13/64, 76, and A.O. 13/135, 81, 426.

[42]"Mrs Derbage's Narrative," Mar. 1789, A.O. 13/34, 298; Penelope Nicoll, deposition, July 6, 1787, A.O. 13/68, 267; Mary Broadhead to commissioners, Nov. 12, 1788, A.O. 13/125, 626; Margaret Draper to John Robinson, June 27, 1777, A.O. 13/44, 345; Rose Brailsford to Lords of Treasury, Dec. 29, 1779, A.O. 13/125, 580; Joyce Dawson to Lord Dunmore, July 24, 1781, A.O. 13/28, 220; Charlotte Pollock to Lords of Treasury, n.d., A.O. 13/133, 442.

[43]Lucy Necks to Lady North, Aug. 14, 1781, A.O. 13/32, 155; Elizabeth Barkesdale to commissioners, Nov. 24, 1786, A.O. 13/125, 402;

Lydia Doty to Lords of Treasury, May 8, 1782, A.O. 13/113, 328; Alicia Young to Robert Mackenzie, June 6, 1789, A.O. 13/67, 643; Mary Taylor to commissioners, Apr. 12, 1783, A.O. 13/42, 590. In sharp contrast to such statements, Andrew Allen, a male refugee, wrote in Feb, 1783, "Notwithstanding what has happened I have the Satisfaction to feel my Spirits unbroken and my Mind prepared to look forwards without Despondency." Allen to James Hamilton, Feb. 3, 1783, Dreer Collection, Historical Society of Pennsylvania, Philadelphia.

[44]Recent articles by linguists raise provocative questions about sex differences in speech. Most of them are concerned with 20th-century oral expression, however, and it is difficult to determine how accurately they apply to 18th-century documents. Among the most interesting are Nancy Faires Conklin, "Toward a Feminist Analysis of Linguistic Behavior," *University of Michigan Papers in Women's Studies*, I (1974), 51–73; Mary Ritchie Key, "Linguistic Behavior of Male and Female," *Linguistics: An International Review*, LXXXVIII (1972), 15–31; Cheris Kramer, "Women's Speech: Separate but Unequal?" *The Quarterly Journal of Speech*, LX (1974), 14–24; and Robin Lakoff, "Language and Woman's Place," *Language in Society*, II (1974), 45–79.

[45]C. Wright Mills, "Situated Actions and Vocabularies of Motive," *American Sociological Review*, V (1940), 904–913, esp. 906–909.

[46]The only woman claimant who appears to have manipulatively assumed a "feminine" role was Sarah Troutbeck. It is also difficult to determine, first, what it was that the commission "wanted" to hear from female loyalists and, second, how the women would know what the commission wanted, given their isolation from the male information networks. It could perhaps be argued that every 18th-century woman "knew" what every 18th-century man expected of her, but the fact is that the women claimants had a great deal to gain by displaying a very "unfeminine" knowledge of their husband's estates and by demonstrating their competence to the commission. See, for example, A.O. 12/101, 186, A.O. 12/40, 40–44, and A.O. 12/66, 6.

[47]The long quotations: Margaret Hutchinson, claims memorial, Feb. 23, 1784, A.O. 13/96, 601, Eleanor Lestor, claims memorial, n.d., A.O. 12/48, 359; Elizabeth Thompson to John Forster, Dec. 21, 1785, A.O. 13/136, 8; Mary Kearsley, testimony, Apr. 28, 1785, A.O. 12/38, 282; Mary Williams, affidavit, Dec. 21, 1785, A.O. 13/26, 535; Catherine Chilsom, claims memorial, Mar. 11, 1786, A.O. 13/24, 90. The shorter phrases: A.O. 13/16, 271, A.O. 13/24, 357, A.O. 13/26, 357.

[48]A.O. 13/118, 488, A.O. 13/67, 234, A.O. 13/73, 586, A.O. 13/81, 59. Men also described women in the same terms; for examples see A.O. 13/28, 215, and A.O. 12/101, 235. The widows of Revolutionary soldiers also called themselves "helpless"; see, for example, Papers of the Continental Congress, V, 16 (M-41), Roll 50, V, 37, 122 (M-42), Roll 55, National Archives.

[49]T. 1/612, 157, A.O. 13/53, 62, A.O. 13/137, 574, A.O. 12/8, 124. For a few "unfortunate" men see A.O. 12/46, 104, A.O. 12/51, 208, A.O. 12/13, 188, and A.O. 12/42, 132.

[50]The women who were most definitely not helpless (for example, Susannah Marshall, Janet Cumming, and Sarah Troutbeck) did not use that word to describe themselves. Consequently, it appears that the term was not simply a formulaic one utilized by all women indiscriminately, but rather that it represented a real self-perception of those who did use it. At least one 18th-century woman recognized the sex-typed usage of the word "helpless." In her book of essays, Judith Sargent Murray noted that she hoped that "the term, *helpless widow*, might be rendered as unfrequent and inapplicable as that of *helpless widower*." See Judith Sargent Murray, *The Gleaner*, III (Boston, 1789), 223.

[51]Isabella Logan, claims memorial, Feb. 17, 1784, A.O. 13/32, 126; Jane Hilding, claims memorial, July 30, 1788, A.O. 13/46, 315; Joyce Dawson to Lord Dunmore, July 24, 1781, A.O. 13/28, 220. Also of interest is Jane Constable to Lords of Treasury, n.d., A.O. 13/73, 374.

[52]Alicia Young to Robert Mackenzie, June 6, 1789, A.O. 13/67, 643; Jane Roberts, claims memorial, Mar. 17, 1784, A.O. 13/71, 245; Margaret Draper to Lord————, Oct. 15, 1782, A.O. 13/44, 349; Elizabeth Skinner to commissioners, Aug. 28, 1786, A.O. 13/112, 61. Mrs. Draper lived to see her daughter well married (Margaret Draper to the Misses Byles, June 21, 1784, Byles Papers, I, 134, Mass. Hist. Soc.) Cf. men's attitudes toward their children and other dependents in A.O. 13/75, 556, A.O. 12/105, 115, A.O. 13/131, 399, and A.O. 13/137, 2.

[53]Elizabeth Putnam to Thomas Dundas, Nov. 7, 1789, A.O. 13/75, 309; Elizabeth Dumaresq to Lord Shelburne, Sept. 14, 1782, A.O. 13/44, 429; Elizabeth Barkesdale to commissioners, Nov. 24, 1786, A.O. 13/125, 402, Rachel Wetmore, claims memorial, Mar. 25, 1786, A.O. 13/16, 272. Other comments on neighbors and relatives may be found in A.O. 12/3, 231, A.O. 12/56, 339, A.O. 13/25, 275, A.O. 13/32, 595, A.O. 13/44, 345, A.O. 13/75, 544, 641, and A.O. 13/107, 271. Mr. and Mrs. James Parker had

an interesting exchange of letters on the subject of whether she would join him in England, in which her ties to her American friends figured strongly. "Tho I would not hesitate one moment to go with you my Dearest friend to any place on earth, yet I cannot think of parting forever with my Dear and valuable friends on this side the atlantick, without many a heart felt sigh," she wrote on July 24, 1783. His response (Mar. 5, 1784) recognized her concern: "I realy sympathize with you on this trying scene of leaving of your Country and all our friends." Parker Papers, Pt. VIII, nos. 26, 31, Liverpool Record Office.

[54]Elizabeth Macnair to John Hamilton, Dec. 27, 1789, A.O. 13/131, 400; Mary Serjeant to John Wilmot and Daniel P. Coke, Dec. 1, 1782, A.O. 13/49, pt. 1, 283. See also A.O. 13/34, 471, and A.O. 13/70B, 145, on resettlement. For women who followed friends and relatives into exile see A.O. 13/116, 468, A.O. 13/114, 662, A.O. 12/102, 24, and A.O. 13/37, 3.

[55]On the development of republican ideology pertaining to women see Linda K. Kerber, "Daughters of Columbia: Educating Women for the Republic, 1787–1805," in Stanley Elkins and Eric McKitrick, eds., *The Hofstadter Aegis* (New York, 1974), 36–59.

period

II

(1820-1860)

The
Commercial
Age

chapter 4

The Ideal Husband as Depicted in the Nineteenth-Century Marriage Manual

by Michael Gordon

Ministers and then doctors furnished the social prescriptions for middle-class husbands in the nineteenth century. In the selection reprinted here, sociologist Michael Gordon analyzes these ideals as found in forty marriage manuals published between 1832 and 1892. Of course, the expectation for each sex was complemented by that for the other: The husband was supposed to be dominant, the wife submissive; the husband was asked to provide for his family, his wife was called upon to care for the home and children. But Victorian ideals such as these offer no insight into actual behavior. The wealth of pornography, the frequency of visits to brothels, and the high rates of venereal disease in the nineteenth century testify to behavior much at variance with the ideals. But the ideals are doubly important as the standard to which many men held themselves, and as the standard by which deviance was defined.

Much research in the field of marriage and the family is hamstrung by a lack of accurate information on 19th-century patterns. Studies that purport to evaluate and discuss changes over time in the American family often use as a basis for comparison what William Goode has called "the classical family of Western Nostalgia," (Goode, 1956, p. 3). While it is true that some important historical studies do exist (e.g., Monahan, 1951), for the most part studies of this type have relied on source materials which permit only limited generalizations. This seems to be changing to the extent that both historians and sociologists are turning to the study of family life in this country in the 18th and 19th centuries. Moreover, they are doing this with a rigor and concern for methodology that has often been lacking in older studies. The present study hopes to make a contribution to this emerging tradition.

In view of what has been argued above, one might ask why choose to study marriage manuals? Surely they do not have much to tell us about what marriage and family life were like in the 19th century. To some extent this is true: admittedly, marriage manuals, like-training manuals, do not offer us information about actual behavior at the time they were published, or in the years that follow. They do, however, provide us with a picture or what "experts" felt to be desirable patterns at a particular time. This is significant on

"The Ideal Husband as Depicted in the Nineteenth-Century Marriage Manual" by Michael Gordon. Reprinted by permission of the author and publisher from the *Family Coordinator*, 19 (July 1969), 226–231. Copyright © 1969 by the National Council on Family Relations.

Michael Gordon is Assistant Professor of Sociology, University of Conn., Storrs, Conn. 06268.

A revised version of a paper presented at the 1968 Annual Meeting of the National Council of Family Relations, New Orleans, Louisiana. The study was supported by a Temple University Faculty Grant. The author would like to thank Charles Bernstein and Roslyn Strokoff for their assistance in this study.

three counts: to begin with, by looking at trends in the advice given, we may be in the position to see, in cases where alternative forms of data are available, whether the writers of this literature are heralds of future patterns or defenders of the *status quo;* secondly, from the perspective of intellectual history, we may be able to ascertain how the ideas presented in the manuals relate to broader currents in the society at large, e.g., do Darwinian notions enter into 19th-century discussions of mate selection; thirdly, and finally, we can establish when particular conceptions of ideal marriage patterns were first promulgated, e.g., the acceptance of female sexuality.

Before going on to describe the methods used in this study, a brief comment on the history of the marriage manual is in order. The fundamental writings of almost all faiths deal, to some degree, with the question of how domestic life should be conducted and thus have something of the marriage manual about them. In the West, as one might expect, early books dealing with marriage had a strongly religious flavor. They were the so-called domestic conduct books, the forerunners of the marriage manual as we know it today. Chilton Powell, in his *English Domestic Relations 1487–1653* (1917), tells us that one of the first books *printed* in England was a domestic conduct book, Caxton's *Book of Good Manners* (1487). Powell says of these books:

> *In its most complete form, a book of this type contained four principal subjects: (1) discussion of the marriage state from religious and secular standpoints, (2) the legal elements involved in contracting matrimony, (3) the mutual relations of husband and wife, (4) the government of the family, including housekeeping, the upbringing of children, the management of children, the management of servants, and general household economics. The ultimate sources of all these books were the New Testament (especially the teaching of St. Paul), the classics, and the church fathers (Powell, 1917, pp. 101–102).*

From the 15th through the 19th centuries books of this type were published in England, and there is no reason to believe that books of this type were not brought to this country by early settlers, as well as imported throughout the Colonial period. While the question of whether or not domestic conduct books were produced in this country cannot definitely be answered, the available bibliographic sources suggest that few books of this type were published here. Some of the 19th-century manuals included in this study have the flavor of domestic conduct books about them, but they do not conform precisely to the model Powell presents. The important shift in the 19th century is from the collection of sermons—which is what many of the 19th-century manuals are—to the book written specifically to guide people through the perils of domestic life. This shift is reflected in the increasing frequency with which secular individuals are found as authors.

METHODS

The foremost problem faced in attempting to carry out a study of this kind was coming up with a representative group of titles. For the years prior to 1876, there are some bibliographic sources of American titles available, but in the words of an eminent reference librarian "they are far from complete and often inaccurate" (Winchell, 1967, pp. AA 38). Although the author is considering undertaking a study of early manuals in this country using these sources, at the time the present study was undertaken the decision was made to rely on the *American Catalog of Books* (henceforth referred to as the *ABC*) as the primary source of titles—with supplementary titles added from other sources. The *ABC* is known to be comprehensive and reliable, and thus allows one to refer to titles taken from it as representative of the period it covers. While the *ABC* began publication in 1876, the first volume covers all books in print at that time; this enables one to pick up relevant titles published earlier in the century, but still in print. Actually 23 of the forty books ultimately included in the study were first published before 1876.

The forty books used in this study were chosen in the following manner. All titles listed in the *ABC* under the headings of "marriage" or "sex" were considered candidates for inclusion in the study; initially, the only books excluded were those whose titles clearly suggested they had little relevance for the present study, e.g., anthropological, historical, and legal works. An attempt was made to locate copies of all the remaining books, some 115 in all. Of these 85 were ultimately located. The remaining 30 titles (many of which were pamphlets) were not listed by the National Union Catalog as being in the collection of any library in the United States. Forty of the 85 titles located met the criteria for inclusion in the study.

A book was considered appropriate for inclusion in the study if it contained advice with regard to courting, marriage, and family life. With a few exceptions the books used in the study are completely devoted to one or all of these topics, but in some cases a book was used which contained one or more relevant chapters (e.g., a phrenological work which devoted sections to a discussion of how phrenology could be used to select a mate).

The contents of the forty books were coded into a number of categories and relevant and illustrative quotations were taken down as well. Since this article focuses, for the most part, on the way in which males, or more specifically husbands, are presented, it will not be necessary to discuss the coding categories. What follows will be limited to those findings specifically related to the manner in which the husband and potential husband are depicted in these manuals.

FINDINGS

No clear and definite trends emerged from the analysis of the 19th-century manuals. Quite surprisingly, in view of the prevailing stereotypes, a great deal of variation was discovered. While it is true that certain concerns were more salient than others during this period, the ways in which they were approached indicate a diversity of outlook which has not often been attributed to our Victorian ancestors. Nevertheless, those areas that show the greatest amount of agreement shall be discussed below.

Perhaps the most suitable place to begin a discussion of the findings is the topic of mate choice or more specifically, the selection of a husband. A majority of the books (25/40) contained a discussion of this point. In general, the criteria suggested for the selection of a husband can be subsumed under three categories: 1. religious considerations; 2. moral or character considerations; and 3. physical or constitutional considerations. It should be noted that these are not meant to be mutually exclusive categories.

With respect to religious considerations, the topic of "intermarriage" was often found in the 19th-century manuals; however, the intermarriage referred to was seldom, if ever, of the inter-racial or inter-religious variety. The term was used to refer to marriages involving Christian believers and nonbelievers, and to a lesser extent to those of members of different denominations. Marriages of this variety, particularly those involving a nonbeliever, were viewed in a very serious light and they were described in terms as "forbidden alliances" and "sinful marriages." The rationale for this position was as follows. Religion was seen as being important, if not the most important, element in family life and as such the family was endangered when one of the pair was a nonbeliever or a member of a different denomination. From the perspective of the couple's adjustment alone such a marriage was held to be unwise.

> The duties of the conjugal relation cannot be fully discharged without the aids of Christianity. *The parties must be* CHRISTIANS *in order to possess such a spirit as well as ensure peace and joy until they are separated by death (Thayer, 1854, p. 45).*

Marriages of this type were believed to be foredoomed to failure, though one of the authors saw the relationship as being salvageable if a nonbeliever was willing to respect his mate's religiosity (Wise, 1850).

The next most frequently encountered admonition centers around what have been called moral or character considerations. This usually took the form of discussions of a trait or traits which were a sure sign of a potentially poor husband. As all-encompassing a list of things to avoid as is to be had in any of the manuals is the following one.

> . . . *idleness, intemperate use of intoxicating drinks, smoking, chewing, snuffing tobacco, the taking of opium, licentiousness in every form, gambling, swearing and the keeping* [sic] *late hours at night (L. N. Fowler, 1855, p. 131).*

Drinking and to a lesser extent smoking were often presented as indicators of an unwise choice. Other authors went beyond this and warned their readers not to "unite in marriage with a man of bad habits, with the idea of reforming him" (Talmage, 1886, p. 5). In general, on this point, a woman was advised to seek a man with good habits, a man who valued homelife, and who was neat and frugal as well. A man who met these requirements would, it was assured, assume his parental duties, spend his evenings at home rather than in the tavern and in all respects make a good husband.

The final element that appears with any observable frequency is what has been referred to as physical considerations, though as shall be shown below, this involves more than this label suggests. During the 19th century both Social Darwinism and phrenology had their heydays and this was reflected, to a limited degree, in some of the manuals. The title of the following manual exemplifies the eugenic approach:

> Intermarriage *or the mode in which, and the causes why beauty, health and intellect, result from certain unions and deformity, disease and insanity from others: demonstrated by delineations of the structure and forms and descriptions of the functions and capacities which each parent, in every pair bestows on children—in conformity with certain natural laws and by account of corresponding effects in the breeding of animals* (Walker, 1839, title page).

Phrenology was presented in several of the study's books as a key to avoiding a bad choice. One author advised:

> *Phrenology makes us acquainted with the faculties of the mind and their manifestations, the combinations which produce harmony between the parties united, and the means of adapting the exercise of each faculty in one individual to that of another, besides informing us in relation to the nature and adaptation of those faculties which are connected with our social and domestic relations.*
>
> *It informs us that they should be exercised in harmony with the other faculties of the mind, in order to secure all the designs connected with their existence, and also that the evils of domestic life are almost always the result of a clashing of these social qualities* (Fowler, 1855, p. 72).

This quotation is fairly representative of the type of statements found in books written by devotees of the phrenological point of view.

The three criteria discussed above represent those most frequently found in the manuals; one other criterion mentioned was not included in the previous discussion because it is difficult to separate from discussions of the husband's role. The criterion in question is "love." Romantic love in the "cardio-vascular sense" is seldom, if ever, discussed in the manuals. Actually only one manual, Moses Hull's *That Terrible Question* (1872) contains anything that even approaches it. Hull argued that love "should be the guiding star" in mate choice. "True marriage, as we have before intimated, is a union of spirits. Where the spirits are truly united, there is marriage; nowhere else" (Hull, 1872, p. 17). He even went on to argue that true marriage did not exist when this spiritual union is lacking, even though the couple may have been legally wed.

As has already been indicated, Hull's position was an unusual one. For the most part, the authors of these manuals argued that love should be an important element in marriage; however, this love took the form of a strongly reciprocated affection rather than a fierce flame compelling the couple to unite. The following quotation was contained in one of the manuals:

> *True love is founded on esteem, and esteem is the result of intimate acquaintance and confidential intercourse. (Ryan, 1873)*

That is to say, a married couple should feel love for each other, but the love should grow out of the relationship rather than being the cause of it.

Before going on to summarize the general tone of the advice given on husband selection it is necessary to comment on one final point, *viz.* money. Marrying expressly for money was frowned upon in all the manuals that discussed this. The following quotation typifies the sentiment of the period.

> *My advice is, marry a man who is a fortune in himself. Houses, lands, and large inheritance are well enough, but the wheel of fortune turns so rapidly that through some investment, all these in a few years may be gone (Talmage, 1882, p. 25).*

The thing to note here is that marrying for money was not presented so much as an evil thing as it was an unwise one.

All in all, the nature of the recommendations given with regard to choosing a husband might be classified as highly rationalistic. The ideal husband was a religious man, of good character and in excellent health. Clearly a highly conventional and idealized picture.

Having looked at the characteristics deemed desirable in a prospective husband the next thing to be considered is what was expected of a male once he assumed this role. Here, as was the case with the selection criteria, there is a great deal of variation; nonetheless, two considerations are more frequently encountered than any others: 1. the husband as the dominant partner; and 2. the husband as provider.

About 25 percent of the manuals contain some mention of the importance of the husband assuming a dominant role in the marriage. This was often expressed with a scriptural reference. One quoted St. Paul approvingly:

> *Wives, submit yourselves unto your husband as unto the Lord. For the husband is the head of the wife, even as Christ is the head of the Church. (Bean, 1832, pp. 59–60)*

The author, a minister, in his own words, went on to qualify this by saying that the submission should not resemble that of a slave to its master but rather

> . . . *a reasonable and advantageous submission such as a man of good sense knows it becomes him to receive, and an affectionate wife will yield with pleasure (Bean, 1832, p. 61).*

Another minister who also quoted St. Paul moderated this in the following way:

> *Husbands should remember that in order to have the submission of their wives they must temper their authority with love, prudence and wisdom (Brandt, 1892, p. 121).*

These arguments for submission and reverence would seem to confirm the patriarchal image of the 19th-century family, particularly since they were found in some manuals published throughout the study period. The point that should be kept in mind, however, is that this view does not characterize all the manuals, or even a majority of them.

The only other theme related to the role of the husband that was present in more than an isolated instance or two is that of the importance of his being able to provide for his family in at least a modest fashion. None of the manuals that contain this point argue that he should strive for great riches, or at least this way was not to be seen as an all-consuming goal. Generally, it was felt that while a man should try to make the most of himself, he could only be asked to provide to the best of his abilities.

These two aspects of the husband role are the only ones that appear with any notable frequency. Several others are mentioned here and there but not in enough manuals to warrant discussion.

CONCLUSION

In the way of a summary it can be said that the three most salient criteria recommended for the selection of a husband provide us with a picture of a man who is a practicing Christian, in good health, with no immoral habits. Marrying for money was frowned upon not so much because of ethical considerations as practical ones. Love, if it entered the picture, was of the marital rather than the romantic variety, i.e., it grew out of the marriage rather than being the cause of it. Once married the man was to assume the dominant role in the relationship, but without being a tyrant. Finally, the main responsibilities of the husband were seen as lying in his role as provider.

It should be emphasized that what has been said above was not found in the majority of manuals but rather is based on those ideas that appeared with the greatest frequency in the manuals; a great deal of diversity was found in the group as a whole.

The findings reported in this article are taken from a study which will encompass 20th-century as well as 19th-century marriage manuals. When completed, this study will be able to provide scholars and practitioners in the marriage and family field with comparative material of a kind that has not previously been available. It is hoped that this study will encourage researchers to look at other adult education media in an historical perspective to see if they present a picture of ideal patterns of courtship, marriage and family life, which are in variance or agreement with the one found in the marriage manuals.

REFERENCES

Bean, James. *The Christian Minister's Affectionate Advice to a New Married Couple.* Boston: Christian Register Office, 1832.

Brandt, John. *Marriage and the Home.* Chicago: Laird and Lee, 1892.

Fowler, L. N. *Marriage Its History and Ceremonies.* New York: S. R. Wells, n.d., first edition with date listed in Library of Congress, 1855.

Goode, William J. *After Divorce.* New York: The Free Press, 1956.

Hull, Moses. *That Terrible Question.* Boston: Colby and Rich, 1874.

Monahan, Thomas P. *The Pattern of Age at Marriage in the United States.* Philadelphia: privately printed, 1951.

Powell, Chilton Latham. *English Domestic Relations, 1487–1653.* New York: Columbia University Press, 1917.

Ryan, Michael. *The Philosophy of Marriage.* Philadelphia: Lindsay and Blakiston, 1873.

Talmage, T. DeWitt. *Marriage Ring.* New York: Fund and Wagnalls, 1886.

Thayer, William M. *Pastor's Wedding Gift.* Boston: John P. Jewett, 1854.

Walker, Alexander. *Intermarriage.* New York: J. and H. G. Langley, 1839.

Wells, S. R. *Wedlock.* New York: Samuel R. Wells, 1869.

Wise, Daniel. *Bridal Greetings.* New York: Lane and Scott, 1850.

chapter 5

The Mountain Man
as Western Hero:

Kit Carson

by Henry Nash Smith

In contemporary society, television and radio convey popular images of masculinity; a century ago, cheap popular fiction served much the same function. Henry Nash Smith's The Virgin Land, *published in 1950, assessed the impact of the American frontier on the national consciousness. In this chapter from his classic work, Smith analyzes the changing literary presentation of the frontiersman (whom he terms "the sons of Leatherstocking") in American popular literature. In the 1830s, the frontiersman was seen as an anarchic figure, fleeing the civilized world of women and families to join the trappers and Indians; several decades later, he was presented as a representative of that civilization, blazing the trails for families of settlers moving west. It is interesting to match this new image with Gordon's description of the ideals for the Victorian husband. It appears that the writers of American dime novels were looking at the frontiersman through the prism of middle-class social ideals of masculinity.*

The first generation of fictional Wild Western heroes after
Cooper—the sons of Leatherstocking—were primarily symbols of anarchic freedom. The notion that men who ranged
the wilderness had fled from the restraints of civilization—
for better or for worse, according to the social philosophy of
the observer—had been greatly strengthened during the
1830's by the spectacular development of the Rocky Mountain fur trade. The fur trapper, or Mountain Man, was much
more clearly uncivilized than Daniel Boone had been. The
prime theater of his activities lay hundreds of miles distant
from the frontier beyond the Great American Desert, and
was not a region that invited agricultural settlement. He had
adopted many more Indian ways than had the typical
pioneers of the area east of the Mississippi. His costume, his
speech, his outlook on life, often enough his Indian squaw,
gave him a decidedly savage aspect. Yet the trappers dominated the exploration of the trans-Mississippi region, and
the successor of Boone and Leatherstocking in the role of
typical Wild Western hero was certain to be a mountain man.
Cooper had acknowledged this fact in *The Prairie* by trans-
porting Leatherstocking beyond the Mississippi and trying
halfheartedly to make him over into a trapper. But Leatherstocking did not really belong in the Far West—a region
about which his creator knew next to nothing. Besides, the
old hunter considered the vocation of a trapper somewhat
beneath his dignity.

This low opinion of the fur trade was shared by Timothy
Flint, whose *The Shoshonee Valley*, published in 1830, is the
first novel in which mountain men figure as characters. It is
true that Flint divides his trappers into two classes. A few,

potentially virtuous, experience in the presence of mountain landscapes "a certain half chill sensation of the awful and sublime" which will be recognized as evidence of at least rudimentary ethical nobility. But by far the greater number of the trappers are as insensitive as deer to the charms of the scenery, and therefore by implication vulgar or wicked.[1] These "strange, fearless, and adamantine men," Flint says,

> *renouncing society, casting off fear, and all the common impulses and affections of our nature . . . finding in their own ingenuity, their knife, gun and traps, all the Divinity, of which their stern nature and condition taught them the necessity . . . became almost as inaccessible to passions and wants, and as sufficient to themselves, as the trees, or the rocks with which they were conversant.* [2]

Such an existence satisfied man's baser impulses. Few who have tasted its dangerous joys can return with pleasure to the tedious routine of the settlements. Life in the mountains is especially attractive because of its unrestricted love and licensed polygamy. All the trappers have

> *an instinctive fondness for the reckless savage life, alternately indolent and laborious, full and fasting, occupied in hunting, fighting, feasting, intriguing, and amours, interdicted by no laws, or difficult morals, or any restraints, but the invisible ones of Indian habit and opinion.* [3]

Charles Sealsfield, although he was not committed to the essentially theocratic social theory of the New Englander Flint, was equally certain that the Western trapper was a monster, peculiar to America, produced by the absolute freedom of wilderness life. He asserts that the fur trade is carried on by men to whose intractable minds even the rational liberty of the settled portions of the United States seemed an intolerable constraint.[4] Having fled to the wilderness to escape the control of law, the trappers come to regard a wild freedom as the one absolute necessity of existence. In this situation, every man must rely upon his own physical prowess. Warlike skills, practical cunning, and sheer ferocity are developed to the highest degree. The true trapper hates mankind and kills any rival with "a real fiendish joy."[5]

The picture of the mountain man presented in David H. Coyner's fictionalized narrative *The Lost Trappers* (1847) is in substantial agreement with Sealsfield's, although it has less of his overstraining and love of hyperbole. Coyner asserts that the mountain man rejects civilized life deliberately because he despises its

> *dull uniformity and monotony . . . when compared in his mind with the stirring scenes of wild western adventure. The security and protection of the laws have no attraction for him; for he wants no other means of defence than his rifle, which is his daily companion. He is impatient of the formalities and the galling restrictions of well organized society, and prefers the latitude and liberty of a life in the woods.*[6]

Emerson Bennett, whose novel *The Prairie Flower* may have been based upon a narrative composed by an actual traveler on the Oregon Trail, introduces a few passages of remarkably accurate dialogue in the scenes dealing with the four trappers who figure in the story; one of them tells tall tales which belong to the authentic tradition of Davy Crockett.[7] But Bennett has nothing to contribute to the interpretation of the mountain man's character. He merely reshuffles the standard themes—the trapper's love of freedom, his indifference to hardship and danger, his hatred of the dull life of settled communities.[8] The novelist is noncommittal concerning the ethical character of the trapper, mingling hints of primitivistic approval with contradictory suggestions of moral condemnation, and concludes tamely that the mountain man is "a strange compound of odds and ends—of inexplicable incongruities—of good and evil."[9] As a straw in the wind pointing to the future development of the Wild Western hero we may note that Bennett's trappers, to the horror of the genteel hero Frank Leighton, delight in scalping Indians.[10] Leatherstocking, who always insisted that the white man and the Indian had different "gifts," had never condoned scalping by whites. As the literary Western hero moves beyond the Mississippi he is becoming more and r .ore fully assimilated to the mores of the Indian.

At the same time, he is conceived as more and more completely autonomous, isolated, and self-contained. This is in accord with factual reporting by firsthand observers in the mountains. Lewis H. Garrard's autobiographical narrative *Wah-To-Yah*, for example, places great emphasis upon the mountain men's anarchic freedom and self-sufficiency. In the trappers' camps Garrard experienced "a grand sensation of liberty and a total absence of fear." There was no one to say what he should do; no "conventional rules of society constrained him to any particular form of dress, manner, or speech." It is true that Garrard was a youngster on his first vacation away from home, but he reports other attitudes than his own. He quotes the kindly advice of an old mountaineer:

> *If you see a man's mule running off, do n't stop it—let it go to the devil; it is n't yourn. If his possible sack falls off, do n't tell him of it; he'll find it out. At camp, help cook—get wood an' water—make yourself active—get your pipe, an' smoke it—do n't ask too many questions, an' you'll pass!"*[11]

The dissolution of the bonds that tie man to man in society could hardly be carried farther than this.

The best known mountain man was Kit Carson, who owed his fame to Jessie Benton Frémont's skillful editing of her husband's reports on his exploring expeditions in the early 1840's.[12] Although these narratives had been widely read before 1846, the Mexican War created an even greater audience for them by bringing to bear on everything related to the winning of the West the yeasty nationalism aroused by the conflict. The momentary effect was to make of the fur trapper and mountain man just such a pioneer of empire as the glorifiers of Kentucky had tried to make of Boone in earlier decades. This in turn implied that Carson must be depicted according to canons of progress and civilization and even gentility that had not previously been invoked in discussion of the mountain man. Carson, like Boone, had now to be transformed into

> *one of the best of those noble and original characters that have from time to time sprung up on and beyond our frontier, retreating with it to the west, and drawing from association with uncultivated nature, not the rudeness and sensualism of the savage, but genuine simplicity and truthfulness of disposition, and generosity, bravery, and single heartedness to a degree rarely found in society.*

Barbaric life in the wilderness held grave dangers for the ethical purity considered obligatory in national heroes. But if the typical Wild Westerner was, as the contemporary journalist just quoted was forced to admit, "uncurbed," a prey to his own base passions, still an unassailable formula could be found for Carson: "In the school of men thus formed by hardships, exposure, peril, and temptation, our hero acquired all their virtues, and escaped their vices."[13] This almost exactly reproduces Timothy Flint's characterization of Boone and Cooper's characterization of Leatherstocking.

The pure and noble Carson was developed in later years by a series of biographers. The first of these, DeWitt C. Peters, was an army surgeon who had been stationed near the famous scout's home in New Mexico during the 1850's, and who made use of an autobiographical narrative dictated by the hero. The Peters biography appeared in 1858 before Kit's death and established the genteel interpretation of his character. Kit himself complained that Peters "laid it on a leetle too thick."[14] One instance will illustrate the doctor's method. Commenting upon the return of a trapping expedition under command of Ewing Young to Santa Fé in 1831, Peters confronts the fact that according to Carson's own account the mountain men went on a long spree. But this will never do. The biographer therefore commits the following extravaganza:

> *Young Kit, at this period of his life, imitated the example set by his elders, for he wished to be considered by them as an equal and a friend. He, however, passed through this terrible ordeal, which most frequently ruins its votary, and eventually came out brighter, clearer and more noble for the conscience-polish which he received. He contracted no bad habits, but learned the usefulness and happiness of resisting temptation, and became so well schooled that he was able, by the caution and advice of wisdom, founded on experience, to prevent many a promising and skillful hand from grasping ruin in the same vortex.*[15]

Two subsequent biographies of Carson, one by an obscure novelist named Charles Burdett in 1862, and one by the famous popularizer of history, John S. C. Abbott, in 1873, are based on Peters and the Frémont reports, with various flourishes on the theme of the mountain man's spectacular refinement. Burdett implies that Carson never touched liquor, and emphasizes his extreme frugality amid men who loved to spend a year's earnings in a single splurge.[16] Abbott, accepting these positions as established, goes to the further extreme of maintaining that no oath ever passed Carson's lips. As Abbott remarks, "Even the rude and profane trappers around him could appreciate the superior dignity of such a character."[17] The historian also invoked the outworn theme of communion with nature (in this instance, in the Yellowstone country) as the source of his hero's virtue:

> *Men of little book culture, and with but slight acquaintance with the elegancies of polished life, have often a high appreciation of the beauties and the sublimities of nature. Think of such a man as Kit Carson, with his native delicacy of mind; a delicacy which never allowed him to use a profane word, to indulge in intoxicating drinks, to be guilty of an impure action; a man who enjoyed, above all things else, the communings of his own spirit with the silence, the solitude, the grandeur, with which God has invested the illimitable wilderness; think of such a man in the midst of such scenes as we are now describing.* [18]

This sort of thing could lead only to more and more acute distress in the reader. The future belonged to a different Kit Carson who had been developed entirely apart from the genteel conception—the Indian fighter, the daredevil horseman, the slayer of grizzly bears, the ancestor of the hundreds of two-gun men who came in later decades to people the Beadle dime novels. The rip-roaring Kit Carson made a brief appearance in Emerson Bennett's *The Prairie Flower* in 1849,[19] and came fully into his own in a thriller called *Kit Carson, The Prince of the Gold Hunters,* by one Charles Averill. This is probably the book dealing with his exploits that Kit found in October of that year amid the plunder taken by Apaches from a wagon train they had stampeded. He was decently embarrassed by it.[20]

Averill's novel was one of the consequences of a literary trend that had almost as much to do with Kit's rise to fame as did his association with Frémont. The subliterary story of adventure deliberately contrived for a mass audience, called "steam literature" because it was printed on the newly introduced rotary steam presses, was developed by editors of the weekly story papers established in imitation of the penny daily newspaper in the late 1830's and early 1840's. The earliest of these weeklies were the Boston *Notion* and *New World*, and *Brother Jonathan* of New York. At first the story papers relied heavily on pirated British fiction. Thus in 1842 both the *New World* and *Brother Jonathan* brought out Bulwer-Lytton's *Zanoni* at a "shilling," that is 12½¢.[21] In 1844 Maturin M. Ballou, then twenty-five years old, Boston-born son of the noted Universalist minister Hosea Ballou, joined forces with another young writer named Frederick Gleason in publishing three sea stories that Ballou had written under the pseudonym "Lieutenant Murray." The tales were highly successful—the first, *Fanny Campbell*, sold 80,000 copies within a few months—and the two young partners immediately expanded their publishing venture by hiring writers to grind out novelettes for them, including a few, such as Mrs. Ann S. Stephens, who later found steady employment on Beadle's staff. The Ballou-Gleason series of tales, selling at a shilling, was the ancestor of the many comparable series published during the second half of the century by Beadle and his competitors. Gleason and Ballou also pioneered the development of a national system of distribution by maintaining agents in nine cities, including Samuel French of New York.[22]

In 1846 Gleason and Ballou established a weekly story paper, *The Flag of Our Union*, which soon outstripped the Boston *Notion* and its other competitors to dominate the field. After holding the lead for five years it yielded in turn to the *New York Ledger*, which Robert Bonner bought in 1851 and publicized by the most sensational methods.[23] But Ballou had plenty of energy left. In 1854 he forced Gleason to sell out to him, and after various experiments, in 1857 inaugurated a series called *The Weekly Novelette*, selling for four cents. Each issue carried one-fifth of a story, so that the whole story cost twenty cents.[24] In that year Ballou's publications included *The Flag of Our Union*, a story weekly with a circulation of 80,000; *The Dollar Magazine*, a monthly with a circulation of 100,000; and *Ballou's Pictorial*, an illustrated weekly with a circulation of 140,000. To provide fiction for these various periodicals Ballou had enlarged his staff. Several of the newly added writers also went over to Beadle, later, including Dr. John Hovey Robinson, A. J. H. Duganne, and the veteran E. Z. C. Judson ("Ned Buntline"). Ballou himself was the author of at least two stories published later by Beadle. Under Ballou's guidance these writers, by the late 1850's, had developed the standard procedures of the popular adventure story.[25] They could turn with ease from pseudo-Gothic tales of knights in armor to yarns about pirates in the Caribbean; but popular demand brought most of them back in the end to the standard subjects of the American past: the Revolution, Kentucky, and, with increasing frequency, the Far West. Bennett's and Averill's stories belong to this class.[26]

The cast of characters in Averill's *Kit Carson* is substantially that standardized by Cooper—a genteel hero, a heroine, assorted villains, and the faithful guide—but the pattern has undergone a significant evolution. The logic of the Far Western materials has begun to make itself felt. Although the upper-class Eastern hero is still present, he has sunk into insignificance, and is hardly more than a vestigial remnant beside the gigantic figure of Carson. Furthermore, Kit is presented without any mystical or genteel mummery; he is notable for his prowess and his courage alone. He is introduced to both the official hero and the reader by the device of a miniature, described with a quaint hagiological charm which is only increased by the contrast between subject and medium. The painting depicts

> *a man on horseback, in the dress of a western hunter, equipped like a trapper of the prairies; his tall and strongly knit frame*

drawn up, erect and lithe as the pine tree of his own forests; his broad, sun-burnt face developing a countenance, on which a life of danger and hardship had set its weather-beaten seal, and placed in boldest relief the unerring signs of a nature which for reckless daring and most indomitable hardihood, could know scarce a human superior.

Far in the background of the painting, rolled the waving grass of a boundless prairie; amid the silent wilderness of which, towered the noble figure of the hunter-horseman, half Indian, half whiteman in appearance, with rifle, horse and dog for his sole companions, in all that dreary waste; though to the right a yelling pack of wolves were seen upon his track, and on his left the thick, black smoke, in curling wreaths, proclaimed the prairie fire, while in the clear, gray eye that looked from the thrilling picture forth, there seemed to glance a look of proud indifference to all, and the conscious confidence of ennobling self-reliance. [27]

This figure, which the reader will recognize has little physical resemblance to the actual Kit Carson, is the Leatherstocking of *The Prairie*, made younger, mounted on a horse, and given an appreciably greater degree of self-assurance. Gone is the humility of the former servant, but gone also is the power to commune with nature. The Wild Western here has been secularized—if the term may be employed in this connection—and magnified. He no longer looks to God through nature, for nature is no longer benign: its symbols are the wolves and the prairie fire. The scene has been shifted from the deep fertile forests east of the Mississippi to the barren plains. The landscape within which the Western here operates has become, in Averill's words, a "dreary waste." It throws the hero back in upon himself and accentuates his terrible and sublime isolation. He is an anarchic and self-contained atom—hardly even a monad—alone in a hostile, or at best a neutral, universe.

NOTES

[1]*The Shoshonee Valley; A Romance*, 2 vols. (Cincinnati, 1830), 1, 21.— The substance of Chapters VIII, IX, and X appeared in the *Southwest Review* (XXVIII, 164–189, Winter, 1943; XXXIII, 276–284, 378–384, Summer, Autumn, 1948; XXXIV, 182–188, Spring, 1949). I wish to thank the editor of that magazine for permission to reprint the material here.

[2]*Ibid.*, 1, 20.

[3]*Ibid.*, 1, 21–22.

[4]Charles Sealsfield (pseud. of Karl Anton Postl), *Life in the New World; or, Sketches of American Society*, first published in 1835–1837, in German; Eng. trans. Gustavus C. Hebbe and James Mackay (New York, 1844), p. 42.

[5]*Ibid.*, p. 43.

[6]David H. Coyner, *The Lost Trappers; A Collection of Interesting Scenes and Events in the Rocky Mountains* (New York, 1847), pp. xii–xiii.

[7]*The Prairie Flower; or, Adventures in the Far West* (Cincinnati, 1849), p. 31. Harold A. Blaine has noted extensive plagiarism from George F. Ruxton's *Adventures in Mexico and Life in the Far West* in *The Prairie Flower* ("The Frontiersman in American Prose Fiction: 1800–1860," unpublished doctor's thesis, Western Reserve University, 1936, pp. 239–240).

[8]*Ibid.*, p. 29; *Leni-Leoti; or, Adventures in the Far West* (Cincinnati, 1849), p. 38.

[9]*The Prairie Flower*, p. 29.

[10]*Idem*.

[11]Lewis H. Garrard, *Wah-To-Yah, and the Taos Trail; or, Prairie Travel and Scalp Dances, with a Look at Los Rancheros from Muleback and the Rocky Mountain Campfire* (Cincinnati, 1850), pp. 270–271.

[12]The publicizing of Carson through Frémont's reports is pointed out by James Madison Cutts, *The Conquest of California and New Mexico* (Philadelphia, 1847), pp. 166–167; and by Charles E. Averill, *Kit Carson, The Prince of the Gold Hunters; or, The Adventurers of the Sacramento* (Boston, 1849), p. 58.

[13]Cutts, *Conquest of California*, pp. 165–167. This anonymous account of Carson was also reprinted in *The Rough and Ready Annual; or Military Souvenir* (New York, 1848), pp. 153–168.

[14]Edwin L. Sabin, *Kit Carson Days: 1809–1868* (Chicago, 1914), p. 506.

[15]DeWitt C. Peters, *The Life and Adventures of Kit Carson, the Nestor of the Rocky Mountains, from Facts Narrated by Himself* (New York, 1858), p. 50.

[16]Charles Burdett, *Life of Kit Carson: The Great Western Hunter and Guide* (Philadelphia, 1862), pp. 83–84, 367, 369.

[17]John S. C. Abbott, *Christopher Carson. Familiarly Known as Kit Carson* (New York, 1873), p. 70.

[18]*Ibid.*, pp. 183–184.

[19]*The Prairie Flower*, pp. 58–60.

[20]*Kit Carson's Autobiography*, ed. Milo M. Quaife (Chicago, 1935), p. 135. Later Wild Western heroes sometimes took it for granted that they would be described in the newspapers and books down in the clearings (Oregon Sol in Edward S. Ellis, *Nathan Toddi; or, the Fate of the Sioux' Captive.* Beadle's Dime Novels, No. 18, 1860, p. 64).

[21]Frederic Hudson, *Journalism in the United States, from 1690 to 1872* (New York, 1873), pp. 587–589.

[22]Ralph Admari, "Ballou, the Father of the Dime Novel," *American Book Collector*, IV, 121–122 (September–October, 1933).

[23]Ralph Admari, "Bonner and 'The Ledger,' " *ibid.*, VI, 176–181 (May–June, 1935).

[24]*Ibid.*, IV, 123; Hudson, *Journalism in the United States*, p. 647.

[25]Admari, "Ballou," *American Book Collector*, IV, 124.

[26]Bennett's early novels were published by various firms in Cincinnati (including J. A. & U. P. James) and subsequently by T. B. Peterson of Philadelphia: these publishing centers were feeling the same impulses that were motivating Ballou and Gleason in Boston, and Bonner in New York. In 1856 Bonner hired Bennett to write for the *New York Ledger*, and in 1867 Bennett became a contributor to Street & Smith's *New York Weekly* (with "Sol Slocum; or, The Maid of the Juniata. A Tale of the Frontier," beginning on December 26 in Vol. XXIII, No. 6, p. 4).

[27]*Kit Carson, The Prince of the Gold Hunters*, pp. 57–58.

[28]Carson appears occasionally in the Beadle stories, as for example in James F. C. Adam's *The Fighting Trapper; or Kit Carson to the Rescue*. Beadle's New York Dime Library, No. 1045 (1901, reprint of original ed. 1879).

The story contains an old trapper, Vic Vannoven, "rough but generous," toward whom the heroine feels as she would toward her father, so that we recognize him as a legitimate descendant of Leatherstocking. Kit Carson, young and agile, "the most renowned Indian fighter the world ever produced," appears briefly toward the end of the story to rescue the heroine and her party. He preserves the elusive, almost elfish quality he had had in Emerson Bennett's *The Prairie Flower*. Adams, incidentally, was not so violent a prohibitionist as the genteel biographers were. After the fight Kit offers brandy to the party, and he consumes "quiet draughts" during his turn on guarding during the night (p. 26).

chapter 6

Husbands
and Fathers

by Eugene D. Genovese

The usual view is that slavery weakened the slave father's ties to his wife and children; in effect, that slavery emasculated him. It is well known that slaves were not legally permitted to marry; slave men did not have the right to vote, sign contracts, or own property. Because a slave husband could not provide for his family or protect his children or wife from being sold or abused, it has been claimed that he lost respect in the eyes of his wife and children. The slave man, it has been believed, slept with many women on the plantation but honored few family responsibilities to any of them. The final blow to any sense of male obligation was the frequency of slave sale, which permanently separated men from their families.

In his prize-winning study of plantation slavery, Roll, Jordan, Roll: The World the Slaves Made, *Eugene D. Genovese agrees with some of these generalizations. He finds evidence of slave women being violated by their masters and of slave sale, but with lower frequency than has been commonly thought. But he also overturns many of the familiar arguments about slave men as husbands and fathers by exploring the reasons why masters sought to encourage slave masculinity. Southern planters sought to shore up the slave nuclear family and the traditional division of labor between the sexes: They wanted a relatively satisfied labor force, and they wanted to live in accordance with their ideology, a paternalist ethic which defined a doctrine of reciprocal obligations between a planter and his slaves. The slave man seized upon this paternalist ideology to assert a nation of slave rights, thereby establishing certain limits on the master's power and allowing himself some possibility for personal dignity and self-respect.*

Usually men, not women, plowed on the large plantations, but when the minority of plantation women who did plow are added to those on smaller units who had to work alongside their men or even alone, it would appear that the rigors of plowing engaged the efforts of a substantial minority of southern slave women.[1] On many plantations the women proved superior to the men in picking cotton; in general, men and women did about equally well. Not unusually a woman would rate as the most valuable field hand on the place or as the single most physically powerful individual. Some excelled in such exacting roles as logrollers and even lumberjacks.[2] And if the men often helped their wives to keep up with their tasks, the roles could be reversed. "My daddy was a field hand," recalled Pierce Harper, who had been a slave in North Carolina, "and my mother worked in the field, too, right 'longside my daddy, so she could keep him lined up." Her mother had a reputation as the best field hand on the place and her father as the worst. "My mother," she explained, "used to say he was chilesome. . . ."[3]

Slave men provided for their families to a greater extent than has been appreciated. The overwhelming majority of the masters gave their slaves enough to eat but did not err on the side of generosity; and the fare was coarse and monotonous. The slaves would have suffered much more than many in fact did from malnutrition and the hidden hungers of nutritional deficiencies if the men had not taken the initiative to hunt and trap animals. "My old daddy," recalled Louisa Adams of North Carolina, "partly raised his chilluns on game. He caught rabbits, coons an' possums. He would work all day and hunt at night."[4] Mothers sang to their babies:

From Roll, Jordan, Roll: The World the Slaves Made by Eugene D. Genovese. Reprinted by permission of Pantheon Books, a Division of Random House, Inc. Copyright © 1972, 1974 by Eugene D. Genovese.

Bye baby buntin'
Daddy's gone a-huntin'
Ter fetch a little rabbit skin
Ter wrap de baby buntin' in. [5]

The men took pride in their effort. Edgar Bendy of Texas boasted, "I used to be plumb give up to be de best hunter in Tyler and in de whole country. I kilt more deer dan any other man in de country. . . ." And the boys took pride in their fathers, grandfathers, and uncles. A half century later John Glover of South Carolina remembered his grandfather as "a great 'possum hunter."[6] The men had some justification for their boasting. Trapping wild turkeys, for example, required considerable skill; not everyone could construct a "rabbit gum" equal to the guile of the rabbits; and running down the quick, battling raccoon took pluck.[7] For a boy growing up, the moment when his father thought him ready to join in the hunting and to learn to trap was a much-sought recognition of his own manhood.

For the slaves, fishing was much more than the lazy pastime of white plantation romance. They varied monotonous and inadequate diets by catching fish, crabs, and gathering oysters, clams, conchs, turtles, terrapins, shrimp, and prawns, and anything else available. The coastal lowlands of Maryland, Virginia, South Carolina, and Georgia as well as the bayou country of Louisiana offered special opportunities, but most regions had some kind of stream with something worth catching. According to Mrs. Schoolcraft, every black man on the South Carolina coast made his own canoe "by burning the inside, and then scraping out a great oaken log, some ten or twelve feet long."[8]

The archaeological excavation of a slave cabin in Georgia by Robert Ascher and Charles H. Fairbanks turned up evidence of a wide assortment of animals, birds, and fish. "The animals," they write, "were young, old, and in-between, suggesting that their pursuer took whatever he could find."

Their study supports the insistence of ex-slaves and antebellum travelers that the men put much effort into supplementing their families' diet. As they conclude: "In sum, through excavation, we have learned that the people in one cabin managed to add considerable protein to their diet, apparently through their own efforts."[9]

Many slaves had Saturday afternoons free for hunting and trapping, but many more had to find time after a long day's work during the week. A free afternoon did not always avail anyway since opossum and raccoon, the slaves' great favorites, run at night. When the masters frowned on this activity, they had to go singly or in pairs and risk punishment. Although few masters wanted their slaves to run about at night instead of resting for the next day's work, most saw the advantage in allowing the slaves to get some of their own food, and the masters also needed these efforts to help control the ravages of raccoons, squirrels, and crows in their fields.[10]

The slaves' great allies in hunting opossum and raccoon were their dogs. The dogs treed the prey and fought them when the slaves had shaken them down. The slaves took particular pride in their dogs and insisted that a first-class 'possum dog should not be confused with a first-class 'coon dog. To each dog his own work.[11] The slaves' dogs created many problems for the slaveholders and for the neighborhood generally. They sometimes killed domestic animals; they barked too much; they ran around filthy and constituted a nuisance. In 1752, Virginia's House of Burgesses gravely debated a proposal for destroying the slaves' dogs. During the nineteenth century Alabama outlawed them but could not enforce the law. The slaves everywhere had their way. "Our greatest trial," wrote Elizabeth Hyde Botume, "was the dogs. No colored man considered himself safe, or even respectable, without one or more miserable-looking curs."[12]

Many plantations had at least one slave who used a gun

for hunting on a larger scale. Some masters simply allowed one or two reliable men to carry a gun in order to bring in large game for the quarters; others designated one or two slaves as plantation specialists who worked for the Big House table as well or even exclusively. In some cases the hunting guns had been given to slaves assigned to guard the plantation.[13] The states generally outlawed the practice of giving slaves guns, although localities often made room for exceptions. With or without legal sanction, masters did as they pleased, and the sight of slaves hunting with guns rarely raised eyebrows.[14]

The big all-plantation hunts came during the winter, which by happy coincidence combined an easier work pace with a great abundance of opossum and raccoon. White and black men turned the opportunity into a holiday.

Possum up de gum stump,
Raccoon in de hollow—
Git him down and twist him out,
And I'll give you a dollar.[15]

As in corn shuckings, the accompanying camaraderie strengthened paternalist ties, especially since the masters so clearly played the leading organizational role while the slaves did most of the work and provided the marvelous stories and gaiety that made the subsequent bonfires so memorable. At the same time, the slave men accumulated a supply of their favorite foods for their families and gave their women the wherewithal and the occasion to demonstrate their culinary skills.

Sensible masters actually encouraged a limited sexual division of labor among their slaves and saw some advantage in strengthening the power of the male in the household. Many planters identified slave women by their husbands' names: Tom's Sue or Joe's Mary. A strong man who kept his wife and children in line contributed to social peace and good order. William Ervin of Lowndes County, Mississippi, laid down the following as the second point in his Rules for the Plantation:

> *2nd. Each family to live in their own house. The husband to provide fire wood and see that they are all provided for and wait on his wife. The wife to cook & wash for the husband and her children and attend to the mending of clothes. Failure on either part when proven shall and must be corrected by words first but if not reformed to be corrected by the Whip.*[16]

Hugh Davis, whose scrupulous biographer considers him typical of the bigger planters of the Alabama Black Belt, included among his rules:

> *Men alone are required to feed and perform all lot work [animal care] at the close of every day. The women are required, when work is done in the field, to sweep their houses and yards and receive their supper [communally prepared] at the call of the cook, after which they may sew or knit but not leave their houses otherwise.*[17]

On the large plantations, which displayed a greater division of labor than the small plantations and farms, men did heavy work on rainy days or in slack periods while the women sewed, cleaned up the grounds, and did assorted lighter tasks. Even then, the foreman of the women's crew was often a man.[18]

This division of labor and the strengthened male role within it, which so many planters encouraged, helped shape the kind of men who might prove more independent than slaves were supposed to be. The slaveholders, therefore, here as elsewhere, had to live with a contradiction: dispirited slave men could not keep the good order necessary for efficiency and, besides, might become troublesome in their very irresponsibility; spirited slaves with a sense of being men would help keep good order and render the plantation more efficient, but they too, in different ways, might become troublesome in their very responsibility. Slaves remained a troublesome property.

Meanwhile, in ways wholesome and not so wholesome, the men asserted themselves. If Nancy William's mother spent extra hours in making quilts for the family, her father built the shelves and closets to house them. If Mary Ann Lipscomb's mother had to weave when tired from a day's labor, her father did his best to help. Other men asserted themselves at the expense of their wives by contemptuously refusing to do "women's work."[19]

The struggle to become and to remain men, not the "boys" their masters called them, included some unattractive manifestations of male aggression. The freedmen, Miss Botume noted, spoke affectionately of their wives but in such a way as to suggest that they were property, virtually slaves, helpless children who had to be taught everything.[20] Almost everywhere in the South the freedmen demanded wages high enough to allow them to support their families. They wanted their women home with the children, and the women supported the demand vigorously. Many women may have preferred housekeeping to the rigors of farm work and thought they were choosing an easier life, but most seem to have felt a great need to give their children a full-time mother. In any case, these tough women, who so often proved militant during the political struggles of Reconstruction, displayed not merely a willingless but a desire to defer to their husbands both at home and in the new political world they were entering together. For all the deformations introduced by slavery, they knew that many of their men were strong and dependable and wanted the others to become so.

NOTES

[1]For general surveys see Bonner, *Georgia Agriculture*, p. 87; J. B. Sellers, *Slavery in Alabama*, p. 66; J. G. Taylor, *Negro Slavery in Louisiana*, p. 62; Phillips and Glunt, eds., *Florida Plantation Records*, p. 515; and Myers, ed., *Children of Pride*, passim. For the recollections of ex-slaves see Jeremiah W. Loguen, *Reverend J. W. Loguen as a Slave and as a Freeman* (New York, 1970 [1859]), p. 18; Rawick, ed., *S.C. Narr.*, II (2), 80; III (4), 36; *Texas Narr.*, IV (1), 223; *Miss. Narr.*, VII (2), 158, 165; *Mo. Narr.*, XI, 130, 261; *Ga. Narr.*, XII (1), 113; XII (2), 250, 269, 322; XIII (4), 217; *N. C. Narr.*, XIV (1), 93, 180, 215, 312, 313; XV (2), 57, 130, 149, 159. Fogel and Engerman doubt that many women plowed, but I fear that they have been misled by the records of the larger plantations, which exhibited a greater sexual division of labor; see *Time on the Cross*, p. 141.

[2]Sydnor, *Slavery In Mississippi*, p. 96; Bonner, ed., "Plantation Experiences of a New York Woman," *NCHR*, XXXIII (July, 1956), 400; *Life and Times of Frederick Douglass*, p. 142; Rawick, ed., *Ala. Narr.*, VI (1), 46, 338; Fisk University, *Unwritten History of Slavery*, p. 13; Northup, *Twelve Years a Slave*, pp. 155–156; Yetman, ed., *Life Under the "Peculiar Institution,"* p. 252.

[3]Rawick, ed., *Texas Narr.*, IV (2), 109.

[4]Rawick, ed., *N. C. Narr.*, XIV (1), 3; also *S. C. Narr.*, III (3), 193. I have found only one reference to hunting by women; see *Ark. Narr.*, IX (4), 6.

[5]Puckett, *Folk Beliefs*, p. 75.

[6]Rawick, ed., *Texas Narr.*, IV (1), 67; *S. C. Narr.*, II (2), 138.

[7]Dick, *Dixie Frontier*, p. 35; Hundley, *Social Relations*, p. 343; Rawick, ed., *S. C. Narr.*, II (2), 215.

[8]Schoolcraft, *Plantation Life*, pp. 42–43; House, ed., "Deterioration of a Georgia Rice Plantation During Four Years of Civil War," *JSH*, IX (Feb., 1943), 108; G. G. Johnson, *Social History of the Sea Islands*, pp. 85–86; Sydnor, *Slavery in Mississippi*, p. 34, n. 58; Wall, "Founding of Pettigrew Plantations," *NCHR*, XXVII (Oct., 1950), 409; Fisk University, *Unwritten History of Slavery*, p. 136; Hundley, *Social Relations*, pp. 343–344.

[9]Ascher and Fairbanks, "Excavation of a Slave Cabin," *Historical Archeology* (1971), pp. 3–17. See also Dick, *Dixie Frontier*, p. 96; Lyell, *Second Visit*, II, 17; Northup, *Twelve Years a Slave*, p. 200; Saxon *et al.*, *Gumbo Ya-Ya*, p. 238; Yetman, ed., *Life Under the "Peculiar Institution,"* pp. 61, 268,

331; Fisk University, *Unwritten History of Slavery*, p. 44; Rawick, ed., *S. C. Narr.*, III (3), 56; *N. C. Narr.*, XIV (1), 105.

¹⁰See, e.g., the correspondence between Joseph Bieller of Louisiana and his father, Jacob, in the Snyder Papers.

¹¹J. G. Williams, *"De Ole Plantation,"* pp. 62–63.

¹²Greene, ed., *Diary of Col. Landon Carter*, I, 72–73, 75, 335; C. S. Davis, *Cotton Kingdom in Alabama*, p. 93; Botume, *First Days Amongst the Contrabands*, p. 95.

¹³Heyward, *Seed from Madagascar*, pp. 124, 127; D. E. Huger Smith, "Plantation Boyhood," in A. R. Huger Smith, *Carolina Rice Plantation of the Fifties*, p. 67; F. L. Riley, ed., "Diary of a Mississippi Planter," *Publications of the Mississippi Historical Society*, X (1909), 434; Olmsted, *Seaboard*, p. 447; Catterall, ed., *Judicial Cases*, II, 219; V, 305; Yetman, ed., *Life Under the "Peculiar Institution,"* p. 73; Rawick, ed., *N. C. Narr.*, XV (2), 418; J. G. Taylor, *Negro Slavery in Louisiana*, pp. 126, 180.

¹⁴Mooney, *Slavery in Tennessee*, p. 13; J. B. Sellers, *Slavery in Alabama*, p. 235; Louisiana, Ascension Parish, Police Jury Minutes, I, 36 (1837–1856); Leak Diary, March 21, 1853.

¹⁵Rawick, ed., *Texas Narr.*, IV (2), 234; also G. W. Cable, "Creole Slave Songs," in Katz, ed., *Social Implications of Early Negro Music*, pp. 62–63. For descriptions of these festive hunts see B. F. Jones, "A Cultural Middle Passage," unpubl. Ph.D. dissertation, University of North Carolina, 1965, pp. 125ff.; Phillips, *American Negro Slavery*, p. 314; J. G. Williams, *"De Ole Plantation,"* p. 61; D. Maitland Armstrong, *Day Before Yesterday: Reminiscences of a Varied Life* (New York, 1920), pp. 76–77.

¹⁶Ervin Journal, p. 46.

¹⁷W. T. Jordan, *Hugh Davis*, p. 95.

¹⁸F. L. Riley, ed., "Diary of a Mississippi Planter," pp. 343–344; Seale Diary, March 7, 1857; Monette Day Book and Diary, *passim*; LeBlanc Record Book, 1859–1866.

¹⁹WPA, *Negro in Virginia*, pp. 88–89; Rawick, ed., *S. C. Narr.*, III (3), 104; Scott, *Southern Lady*, p. 30.

²⁰Botume, *First Days Amongst the Contrabands*, pp. 221, 226.

chapter 7

"A Partnership of Equals":
Feminist Marriages in 19th-Century America

by Blanche Glassman Hersh

The feminist movement, it is often argued, failed to go far enough in offering a sharp critique of family relations. The women's movement emphasized the suffrage question to the exclusion of other issues closer to home, the unequal division of labor between husbands and wives and the sexual double standard. The most notable personal example usually cited is the marriage of Angelina Grimké and Theodore Weld, two antebellum abolitionists and feminists. After the wedding, Grimké virtually retired from public speaking on behalf of the women's movement, while Weld continued a public career of reform activities. In The Slavery of Sex: Feminist-Abolitionists in Nineteenth-Century America, *Blanche Glassman Hersh considers and revises this interpretation. In the article reprinted here, she paints a group portrait of thirty-eight antebellum feminist marriages and shows that Grimké–Weld were the exception rather than the rule. Most husbands of feminists supported their wives public lives and were committed to the ideal of sexual equality.*

In seeking to understand these couples on their own terms, Hersh reveals their idea of sexual equality to be far different from our own. They accepted the man's role as breadwinner and believed in women's natural qualities as wives and mothers. Far from championing nonmonogamous marriage, their goal was to raise the husband to a purer sexual standard, one much closer to his wife's. Because the dominant ideology of the era defined women's sphere in terms of the home, an attack on that ideology was understood as women's right to break out of that sphere. In their equal partnerships, these feminists sought female as well as male participation in public reform work.

The first generation of American feminists, whose roots were in the radical antislavery movement of the antebellum period, are generally credited with bringing into public debate the question of woman's equality and making important legal gains. Beginning with their demand that women be permitted to speak publicly against slavery and other evils, they went on to campaign for equal educational and work opportunities, the right of married women to own property and have guardianship of their children, and the right of all women to vote and participate in government.

These early feminists failed, however, to achieve their broader goal of abolishing the customs and prejudices that assigned women to an inferior role and enslaved them in a narrow social sphere.[1] Some historians have seen the institutions of marriage and family as the prime obstacles to woman's emancipation, and attributed the failure of the movement to the feminists' inability to radically restructure these institutions. William O'Neill, for example, has asserted that "feminism was born out of a revolt against stifling domesticity, and nurtured in the understanding that for women to be really free the entire fabric of their lives had to be rewoven. . . " Ellen DuBois has also argued that the traditional nuclear family stood in the way of women's emancipation.[2]

On the basis of my research, I will argue first, that the feminists who organized the first women's rights movement did not reject domesticity but only demanded that women not be limited to the domestic role. Second, a closer look at their lives reveals that they shaped their own marriages and families into new patterns that permitted them personal emancipation. Though they valued the family as the central

"A Partnership of Equals: Feminist Marriages in 19th-Century America" by Blanche Glassman Hersh. Reprinted by permission of the author and the publisher from *University of Michigan Papers in Women's Studies*, v. 2, No. 3 (1977), pp. 39–62. Copyright © 1975 by Blanche Glassman Hersh.

institution and the moral bulwark of society, they did indeed see the need for new roles and new arrangements within this traditional framework. An impressive number of these women chose to marry men who were also feminists, and created egalitarian relationships based on autonomy and shared responsibilities that would still be radical today. The rejection by both husbands and wives of the conventional view of "woman's proper sphere" was the key innovation in these feminist families. The equality they achieved, though imperfect, permitted the women to play the dual role of wife-mother and reformer, and freed them to work for the radical causes of the day. It was the closest they came to a practical solution to the classic female dilemma of balancing home and work.

This first generation of feminists, then, combined the conservative goal of strengthening the home with the radical demand that women gain equality within the family and freedom, like men, to work in the world outside the family. This was as true of the "conservative" leaders like Lucy Stone and Mary A. Livermore as it was of the more radical women like Elizabeth Cady Stanton—they were all in agreement on the need for marriage reform but differed in their willingness to openly challenge their society on this most controversial of questions. Though the women failed to achieve this reform in their society, probably a politically impossible goal in the nineteenth century, they did provide important models for the future. These models represented a pivotal reform in the movement as a whole, one that has gone virtually unnoticed by historians. The example of these feminist families stands today as a reminder of important directions not taken.

This paper seeks to explore this neglected aspect of the woman's movement and offer tentative answers to some important historical questions: What kind of men became feminists and married women reformers? What was the nature of marriages that afforded women freedom to become important leaders? How did such marriages in practice compare with feminism in principle?

The broader study of which this paper is a part is concerned with a group of fifty-one women whom I call feminist-abolitionists because they began their reform careers in the 1830's and 1840's by defending the right of women to play an equal role with men in the antislavery movement. They called the first woman's rights conventions of the 1850's and 1860's and many of these long-lived women continued active in the postwar suffrage movement.[3] Thirty-seven of these fifty-one women married and, of these, a full twenty-eight had the complete support of their husbands for their feminist activities.[4] That so many of these women married at all[5] can only be explained by the fact that most were able to marry men who shared their reform commitment and complied with their desire for independence after marriage.[6]

The importance of the husband's attitude is confirmed by the fact that the four women in this group who married men with more conventional views were unable to maintain both marriage and reform work—one or the other was sacrificed.[7] Even their middle-class status and the servants it provided were insufficient to ensure the freedom they required. In the nineteenth century, the acquiescence of her husband was necessary if a wife wished to work outside of the home. This was a woman's problem which cut across class lines. Women in many states in the antebellum period were still legally totally subservient to their husbands, unable to own property, keep their own wages, or obtain guardianship over their children. They were everywhere expected to stay in the domestic sphere and remain submissive to their husbands' demands. The feminist-abolitionists regularly proclaimed in their speeches that marriage was a state of slavery for women and compared the "inferior and degraded and helpless" position of the wife to that of the slave on the Southern plantation.[8]

The radical egalitarianism of the feminist marriages is especially intriguing because it was combined with a conservative morality and conventional views of sexuality that often appeared as an aggressive Victorianism. The goal of the feminists was to reform and elevate marriage, not to avoid or abolish it. They rejected the few radicals who questioned legal marriage and advocated free love, and kept them at a safe distance from the woman's movement.[9] Instead of suggesting that women replace family duties with carriers, or marriage with a less conventional arrangement (as many feminists today are urging), the nineteenth-century feminists—both women and men—attempted to broaden woman's sphere to include both family *and* whatever else she was desirous and capable of doing. The women saw no contradiction in glorifying domesticity while spending a great deal of their own time away from home because they saw their reform work as an *extension* of their home duties, not a substitute for them.

Considering this shared commitment to reform, it is not surprising to find that the feminist husbands as a group were extraordinarily like their wives in background and world view. Both women and men came from old New England families whose Yankee Puritanism bred in them a compulsion to duty and a profound belief in the Christian Republic. The majority of the husbands were urban and middle-class: businessmen, lawyers, teachers, writers and editors, ministers; a large minority were farmers and artisans.[10] All but three of the twenty-eight men who supported their wives' reform careers were active reformers themselves, although only a handful worked at it full time. They shared with their wives a religious commitment to eradicate evil and a fervent desire to help make the world better by emancipating and elevating the human family. Their perfectionist world view enabled them to transcend their society's sex roles and sex stereotypes. Like their wives, they fit badly into conventional molds. Many displayed the "moral sensibilities" and romantic fervor generally associated with the female sex. Henry and Sam Blackwell, who married Lucy Stone and Antoinette Brown, were, typically, businessmen-reformers who also wrote poetry and dreamed of the better world to come.

Like their wives, a disproportionate number of husbands grew up in religious faiths like Quakerism which taught the spiritual equality of the sexes and permitted women greater independence. Others gravitated towards liberal sects like Unitarianism and Universalism.[11] The orthodox churches were anathema to both women and men because of their antifeminism and antiabolitionism as well as their pessimistic view of human nature. While they retained the evangelical zeal of the period of religious revivalism in which they were raised, the feminist-abolitionists rejected the Calvinistic belief in damnation and original sin and moved to more optimistic and rationalistic faiths which provided a theology more congenial to their reform beliefs. They all placed a higher value on Christian morality than on ritual and dogma.

Though the men did not in their youth experience rejection first-hand as their wives had, they nevertheless became sensitive to injustice against women in the same way they responded to the plight of the slave, and for the same reasons. They were men who took the principle of human rights seriously and were moved by moral considerations to protest violation of these rights. Like their wives, they often came from families sympathetic to reform. Several had mothers who were notable for their independence and feminism. The mother of Daniel Livermore, for example, was a "woman's rights woman" who brought up her sons and daughters to share equally in household tasks. The mother of Henry and Sam Blackwell was also strongly for woman's rights and voted with Lucy Stone in 1868 in defiance of the law.[12]

Family backgrounds and liberal religious beliefs were probably contributing influences but do not explain why most of their siblings were not reformers. The men, like their wives, were unusual people, distinguished from their contemporaries by the ability to envision a world in which evil and injustice would be eliminated, and by the determination to pursue their vision. Their choice of strong-minded wives was not unrelated to their faith in reform. For both women and men, choosing the right mate was a reform in itself, a reflection of their belief in equality but also a step toward self-improvement and the perfection of society. Like their wives, the men were strengthened by their religious faith to face the ridicule heaped upon them as the husbands of nonconforming women.

Probably the most common charge hurled against them was that they were "hen-pecked husbands" who "ought to wear petticoats."[13] The evidence contradicts this charge. The large majority of the feminist husbands left private correspondence and other records behind that indicate vigor and independence of thought rather than weak-kneed submissiveness. All of them were vocal about their belief in woman's equality and a few wrote and lectured on the subject. William Stevens Robinson, husband of Harriet Robinson, was typical. A nationally known political writer, his Free Soil newspaper in the 1850's ran strong statements on woman's rights. In one of many editorials, he argued for woman's right to vote and hold office and concluded: "Who set up any man as a judge of what is woman's sphere, or what the Almighty Maker designed her to be?" The cause of woman, he wrote on another occasion, was "the movement of civilization itself."[14]

Though a few of the husbands, like Robinson, were nationally prominent reformers, most were not and therefore faced the uncommon male dilemma of being eclipsed by their wives' fame (or notoriety). Most of them seemed to accept this with good grace and took pride in their wives' successes. They were able to do this partly because they shared their wives' cause. They were also exceptional men, apparently secure in their masculinity and not easily threatened. David Lee Child, husband of Lydia Maria Child, accepted the need for his wife to leave their home for long periods of time to edit the newspaper of the American Anti-Slavery Society, and later to support him with her writing. He could do this because he was engaged in a cause he knew was right though unprofitable, and because he considered her an equal, independent person. Mrs. Child noted to a friend that David "despised the idea of any distinction in the appropriate spheres of human beings. . . ."[15]

Stephen Symonds Foster, husband of Abby Kelley Foster, was another example of a man faced with the fact that his wife was more successful in her reform efforts than he (although both worked at it as their main occupation). Because she was more in demand as a speaker, he often stayed home to work the farm and care for their daughter while she traveled on extensive tours to lecture on antislavery and woman's rights. When the child became seriously ill, he was her chief nurse. His letters to Abby reveal careful attention to his daughter's needs and education. He also dealt with the question of their respective careers. In a letter in 1850, five years after their marriage, he congratulated her on a good tour and noted that her achievement threw him "entirely into the shade." Her "great success" might awaken his envy, he admitted, "if it were not, after all, *my own*. . . ." As it was, he went on, he could only congratulate himself on "the good fortune which placed such a *prize* within my grasp."[16]

The Fosters' marriage thrived in spite of their unconventional lifestyle. Abby, who had postponed their marriage for several years for fear that it would interfere with her work, regretted this later and was delighted with their arrangement. Their friends noted the independence each had managed to retain. Thomas Wentworth Higginson, writer and reformer, described them as "two of the very strongest individualities united in one absolutely independent and perfectly harmonious union." Lucy Stone, whose standards for marriage were very high, wrote of the Fosters' home: *"There* was seen the beauty and the possibility of a permanent partnership of equals."[17]

Lucretia and James Mott, the eldest and most revered among the feminist-abolitionists, also achieved a "permanent partnership of equals." Theirs was considered a "true marriage" and he an ideal husband, the model of a capable, independent-minded reformer who fully appreciated his wife's superior talents and complemented her with his own quiet strength. Known for his warmth and generosity, he was also reserved and shy. It seemed natural to him that his more vivacious and energetic wife should be the one to express the views they both shared. There is no evidence in the many letters available that James Mott resented or felt eclipsed by his more famous spouse. On the contrary, he did everything possible to support her, and accompanied her on extensive preaching and lecturing tours. Their lives were so intertwined that their granddaughter, preparing to write about Lucretia Mott, found it "difficult to write of one without the other." In an eloquent statement of the role played by husbands in the woman's movement, she wrote that it was impossible to contemplate the lives of these two "without realizing that *his* life made *hers* a possibility."[18] In the Motts' ideal society, women would be free to develop their capabilities without first receiving permission from their husbands. In the imperfect world in which they lived, a wife was dependent to a large degree on the will and whim of her husband. For this reason, her long career as Quaker minister, abolitionist, and woman's rights leader was indeed made possible by her husband's enlightened view of woman's sphere.

Lucretia and James Mott provided an important model of egalitarian marriage for younger feminists to emulate. Lucy Stone, agonizing over the prospect of marriage because of her "horror of being a legal wife," was impressed with the success of their marriage and strongly influenced by James Mott's advice to her to follow their happy example. This example was also used in propaganda to further the woman's cause. Higginson pointed to James Mott when he praised the role of "Women's Husbands" in an article in the *Woman's Journal*. "In the existing state of prejudice," he argued, "it may sometimes require moral courage in a man to recognize frankly the greater ability or fame of his wife." Mott, he recalled, had never made a speech, "but in his sphere of quiet sense and justice he was as self-relying and as strong as she in hers. . . ."[19]

Other men also displayed James Mott's kind of quiet strength and were admired for the ungrudging encouragement they gave their wives. Charles Dudley Miller, a lawyer from a prominent New York family and husband of Elizabeth Smith Miller, joined his wife in signing the call to the first national woman's rights convention and supported all her feminist endeavors, including her work for the radical journal, the *Revolution*. He was especially praised in the movement for accompanying his wife while she wore the bloomer dress (which she originated), enduring the ensuing ridicule with what Elizabeth Cady Stanton described as "coolness and dogged determination." Stanton said he had "done more to raise the women in his circle of acquaintance to self-respect, courage, thought and action" than any one man she knew.[20]

Samuel Blackwell, less well-known than his more prominent brother Henry, was also an unusual and much-admired man among the feminists. He married Antoinette Brown shortly after she became the first woman ordained as a minister in an orthodox church (she later converted to Unitarianism). As a young theology student at Oberlin, she had not expected to find a man who would sympathize with her feelings and acquiesce in her plans to continue writing and working. Noting in a letter written in 1850 that it would "take a miracle to find a man of talent and heart to do this," she had resigned herself to not marrying. Five years later she was still determined that "nothing but an unsought all absorbing affection can make me feel it right to waver in my plan for an untiring life-work of isolation." The following year, having found this miracle and this affection, she married, and enjoyed one of the happiest and closest marriages on record. She would later admit happily that her marriage had been a help not a hindrance to her public service because of her husband's "sustaining sympathy."[21] She managed to raise five children and also continue a long career of writing, preaching, and reform work.

These examples are typical of the larger group and strongly suggest that, given their feminist commitment, these men were able to support their wives in equal marriages of strong partners without any loss of personal dignity or self-respect. It should be noted as a counter-argument that few of the men were challenged in their role as primary breadwinner in the family, a central feature of "man's sphere."[22] Most of these wives either volunteered their efforts or received only small incomes from lecturing and writing, although several were employed full-time as doctors and teachers. The fame and talent of all of them, however, was a substantial challenge to their husbands' sense of importance.

The day-to-day lives of the feminist husbands and wives also suggested the possibility that marriage could be framework of the conventional social system. The models they created were uniquely based on equality and autonomy but they were neither perfect nor free from tensions. Their concept of "equality," while radical, needs to be qualified and interpreted within the context of their nineteenth-century beliefs. The husbands were unusual in encouraging their wives to be active outside the home and in helping with family responsibilities, especially child-rearing. Both women and men clearly rejected the nineteenth-century doctrine that assigned the sexes to separate spheres. In their view, the spheres of men and women were overlapping, each sharing responsibility both in the home and in the community. In this sense, they modified the prevailing beliefs in a significant way.[23] The spheres were not seen as identical, however. The rights and duties of women as citizens and as spiritual beings were viewed as the same as those of men, but in their social roles as wives and mothers, women were assigned special moral and domestic responsibilities[24] based on inherent sex differences.[25] Woman's primary duty was to the home, man's to his work outside the home.

On a daily basis, therefore, most of the women still bore the major part of the responsibility for the home and family. In spite of their travels and speaking engagements, a good part of their time was spent supervising servants, doing chores themselves, and caring for their children. All but four of the women who married had children, and many had large families (the average number of children was just under four). They were conscientious mothers who felt it important to supervise the education and moral upbringing of their children, especially the younger ones. They also put a high value on good housekeeping. They tended to be efficient and well-organized because they had important things to do with the time saved. The order and regularity of Lucretia Mott's household, for example, was legendary, even at the height of her reform activities and with a constant stream of visitors to look after. Mrs. Mott explained that she was able to accomplish so much by performing only necessary housekeeping duties and skipping the non-essentials, "the self-imposed labors under which so many women struggled." She did no fancy sewing or light reading, and all entertainment was kept simple. Many of the reformers who dined at the Motts while attending a convention recalled in their reminiscences that Mrs. Mott would bring a cedar tub of hot water and a snowy cloth to the table after each meal, and wash the silver and china without any interruption in her brilliant conversation.[26]

Their sometimes extraordinary efforts to excel at housekeeping were partly good tactical strategy—the feminist journals were filled with stories proving that strong-minded women could be good wives and mothers, and lengthy descriptions of their well-ordered homes and well-mannered children. They also had a need to compensate for not devoting themselves exclusively to their families, although their guilt was diminished by the worthiness of their cause. Basically, though, they believed that both jobs were important, and saw one as an extension of the other. Elizabeth Smith Miller saw no contradiction in writing for the *Revolution* and also publishing a popular book with recipes and advice on entertaining graciously.

In spite of the emphasis on domesticity, the feminists did enjoy an equality in marriage that was cherished by them and unique in nineteenth-century society. Many couples began life together by omitting the customary "obey" from the marriage vows. Several went on record, like Lucy Stone and Henry Blackwell, to protest the legal slavery of marriage and establish their own rules. In their protest, published at the time of their marriage in 1855, he renounced all the privileges which the law conferred on the husband, and the whole system by which "the legal existence of the wife is suspended during marriage." Personal independence and equal human rights, they declared, could never be forfeited.[27] Henry Blackwell kept all the promises he made at the time of their marriage and devoted a good part of his life to the woman's movement. Their protest stood for a long time as an inspiration to budding feminists.

Others also made marriage contracts and issued declarations of mutual obligation. Angelina Grimké and Theodore Weld were married in a simple Quaker ceremony in which each spoke spontaneously of their love and devotion, and Weld took the opportunity to denounce the laws giving men control over their wives' property. Abby Kelley and Stephen Foster married in a similar manner and agreed that they would retain their independence and could withdraw whenever they chose. In accordance with their principles, the farm they subsequently purchased was deeded to them jointly. Antoinette Brown and Sam Blackwell also contracted at the time of their marriage to be "joint owners of all properties, real estate and moneys."[28]

Behind the legal pronouncements in all of these cases, there was a genuine commitment to what Antoinette Brown described as "independent thought and keen feeling for justice between men and women." Lucretia Mott also spoke often of the key to these "true marriage relationships": the independence of the husband and wife was equal, their dependence mutual, and their obligations reciprocal. She proselytized throughout her life for changing the customary "man and wife" in the wedding ceremony to "husband and wife" because the former implied that the wife was "a mere appendage." Marriage "left a man still a man, and a woman still a woman," she declared, only now they stood in a *"new* relation to each other."[29]

The feminist marriages were also characterized by sharing of activities, responsibilities, and decision-making. Not only did the husbands help with home duties and woman's rights campaigns, the wives often shared in their husbands' work as well. Harriet and William Robinson, for example, worked closely together in a long reform career. She assisted with his antislavery paper in the 1850's and her diary in those years recorded her happily combining proofreading chores with housework, sewing, and child care. In the postwar years he helped her with suffrage activities and she edited a book of his writings. Amelia Bloomer, in the early years of their marriage, served as deputy to her husband in his job as postmaster and wrote articles for his newspaper. He later helped her start her own journal, the *Lily*, and shared the facilities of his paper with her. They continued to collaborate on a multitude of reform projects in their happy fifty-four year marriage, and raised two adopted children in the same spirit of cooperation. He took faithful care of her letters and speeches and published her *Life and Writings*.[30]

Clarina Howard Nichols similarly edited the newspaper in Vermont which her husband published and, in fact, took over its complete management when he became seriously ill shortly after their marriage. She managed the paper for six years before this fact was announced publicly. Though her husband was against this deception, she explained, she felt it necessary to labor "under my husband's hat" in order to establish her competence and lay a better foundation for requesting support for the reforms they advocated. He also encouraged her to leave home for lecture tours, and his sympathy and support, she later recalled, gave her the courage to engage in what was then an unheard-of activity for a woman. He had come to value his own rights, she observed, and wished to have women gain them also.[31]

The marriage of Mary A. Livermore and her husband Daniel, a Universalist minister, was still another example of a close, collaborative partnership. She contributed to his books and preached at his pulpits; he helped her with her lectures and preserved the notes and letters she would later use for her autobiography. Like so many of the feminists, she first served as co-editor and reporter for his newspaper and later established her own, the *Agitator*, with his help. In his book *Woman Suffrage Defended*, he argued that "the responsibilities of the home need not conflict with the duties one owes to humanity, to society and the State." Privately he practiced what he preached, and urged his wife to use her talents outside the home. When she had qualms about leaving for her first lecture tour, he declared that it was preposterous for her to continue doing housework when "work of a better and higher order" was waiting for her. While they had servants and relatives to care for the house and children so that her absences were not burdensome to him, he was nevertheless expressing a most atypical attitude.[32] Furthermore, in what must have been an unusual move even in this group, Daniel Livermore gave up his paper and his pastorate in Chicago in 1870 and moved the family back to the Boston area so that she could merge her paper with the new *Woman's Journal* and take over the editorship.[33] Like all the feminist husbands, he obviously considered his wife's work important and respected her rights as an individual. He apparently accepted her greater fame without feeling personally threatened or resentful. His attitude explains much of the harmony in their unconventional relationship.[34]

The record of these and other feminist marriages leads one to the inescapable conclusion that their shared commitment to reform was a strengthening force in their relationships, in spite of financial problems and other difficulties that it may have caused. It was not only the shared belief in woman's equality, but the common sense of a broader mission which reinforced their initial attraction to one another and provided a continuing source of inner strength and mutual respect. Their reform work also provided them with a focus for family activities and a circle of close friends who shared their cause, both adding to the stability of the marriage.

A chief source of pride among the feminist-abolitionists was the fact that these strong-minded women were able to marry and continue their work without loss of either domestic virtue or reform commitment. This was true in all but one of the twenty-eight feminist marriages in this group. One of the most compatible and dedicated couples proved to be the exception to the rule. It was ironic that Angelina Grimké and Theodore Weld, because they married in 1838 in the midst of the controversy over her public speaking, were the ones who most consciously saw their union as an experiment. The bride, because she had dared to defy the customs of the day by speaking before mixed audiences, was viewed as a "notorious" woman who had been utterly "spoiled" for domestic life. Because even some of Weld's friends held this opinion, the couple decided their marriage would be proof that a woman could be both an abolitionist and a good wife, as well as a test of their belief in equality.[35] Both expected that she would continue to write, and lecture occasionally. Though they achieved personal equality in their marriage, and shared much of the household and child-rearing tasks, it was virtually the end of the Grimkés' public career. Both Angelina and Sarah, who lived with them most of her life, became bogged down in child care, financial difficulties, and Angelina's health problems, and were able to participate only occasionally in reform work.

The Grimkés have been cited by at least one historian as symbols of the failure of the woman's movement to see the institutions of marriage and family as the chief obstacles to woman's equality.[36] The conventional nineteenth-century marriage was certainly incompatible with equality because most men, and many women, expected that wives would play a subservient role. What is most striking about the feminists, however, is how many were able to solve woman's dilemma at least for themselves by molding their marriages into new shapes. The Grimkés were exceptions rather than the norm. Most of their colleagues in the movement not only retained their independence in spite of marriage, they achieved it *because* of the kinds of marriages they made. (The financial help they received from their husbands in addition to psychological support for their work was also not inconsequential.) The Grimkés were also atypical in that Weld, too, was preoccupied with family needs and was able to do only a little more for reform than the women. Theirs was not solely a female dilemma.[37]

Even the more successful feminist marriages were faced with some conflicts. Both husbands and wives were constantly torn between public duties and private needs and obligations. The women especially often suffered guilt, either because they felt they were neglecting their home and children, or because they were devoting less time to their reform work than they felt they should.[38]

The tensions in feminist marriages did not arise from a conflict in ideology, but from the difficulty most true in the area of sexuality. Though much is known of their rhetoric and little of their practices, one can infer that sexual feelings were often at war with the high moral standards they preached, and represented a continuing source of tension. Ironically, their Victorianism was as consistent with their world view as their belief in equality: subordinating physical passion to spiritual and intellectual concerns was still another means of emancipating the human family; bringing men up to the same level of purity and self-control as women was necessary to elevate the race to a higher stage of civilization.

Women were clearly seen as more virtuous and more in tune with spiritual values, but not necessarily lacking in sexual desires.[39] Publicly the feminists emphasized women's moral superiority over men, but privately they acknowledged, however delicately, that women had a capacity for sexual enjoyment. There is also evidence in their letters of strong sexual feelings, whether acknowledged or not. Abby Kelley, accepting Stephen's proposal of marriage, wrote that as the thirsty traveler in the desert longs for the cool spring, "so does my heart pant to stand before the world the *wife* of Stephen S. Foster." "My arm of flesh," she went on, "is eager to follow the promptings of the spirit. . . ." Antoinette Brown Blackwell's warm and loving letters to her husband were typical. Writing from a lecture tour several years after their marriage, she confessed: "The truth is I fall in love with you anew every time we separate." "There is only one luxury that I long for," she wrote, "and that is yourself . . . even the babes are not wanted here." With a slight tinge of guilt, she added: "I always think of you and very little of them."[40]

All the feminists, however, believed the sex drive to be far greater in men (which helped to explain why women were better able to control their carnal desires).[41] All were repelled by "excessive" sexuality and felt it desirable to subordinate physical passion to the force of reason. This prudishness and sexual inhibition had its origins in their Puritan upbringing and flourished in the period of religious revivalism in which they grew up. Though the feminists renounced the evangelical churches, their cultural roots remained a strong influence in their lives. As children they had been taught that salvation was endangered by placing carnal pleasure before spiritual love, and that men were distinguished from beasts only by their ability to control their passion and ascend to the heights of heavenly love. This was the ideal to strive for.

With self-control as the highest goal, there was inevitable torment about feelings that were physical, not spiritual. Theodore Weld, courting Angelina Grimké, expressed the constant fear that he would lose the self-restraint he prized so highly and spoke of "warring against nature." His stormy feelings, he wrote her, were kept in subjection "only by the rod of iron in the strong hand of conscience and reason and never laid aside for a moment with safety." Angelina on her part was obsessed with guilt about her sexual feelings and fear that she was putting her beloved in the place of Jesus.[42] It is safe to assume that this tension was a continuing one since sexual restraint was as highly valued after marriage as before.

Henry Blackwell's courtship letters to Lucy Stone also reveal this conflict between physical and spiritual drives. Attempting to overcome her reluctance to marry, he argued that "any philosophy which commands us to suppress our natural instincts is false." So that he would not be misunderstood as displaying an excessive interest in the "lower passions," he also assured her constantly that they would live a "pure and rational life." Lucy, with a strong repugnance for things sexual, was probably more persuaded by the latter argument than the former. After she finally accepted him, they vowed in a series of impassioned letters to live a life dedicated to "noble aims" and "self-improvement."[43]

The rhetoric of the feminists also stressed the need to

subordinate passion to reason and self-control. They counseled women in lectures, articles, and books against too frequent sexual intercourse in marriage and for moderation in all things. Impressionistic evidence indicates very little difference in the attitudes of women and men feminists. These attitudes, and their attempts to impose their moral standards on others, placed them in the vanguard of the nineteenth-century movement toward greater repression of sexuality and increased prudishness.[44]

The feminists differed in important ways, though, from other elements of Victorian America. They did not join in the prevailing "conspiracy of silence" about sexual matters. Instead they campaigned for sex education and public discussion of morality, and insisted that women be given information about their anatomy and physiology. More important, their morality was functional within the context of nineteenth-century society, and a response to the reality of woman's physical and psychological needs. Their tendency toward sexual repression at least partly reflected a feminist concern that married women, legally subject to their husbands, were vulnerable to "sexual abuse" (a term which, like "excessive," they never defined but which presumably meant sexual practices or frequency that were unacceptable to the wife). Their call for sexual restraint was at least partly a response to the suffering caused by frequent pregnancies and sexual exploitation of women both inside and outside of marriage.

The efforts of the feminist women and men to elevate spiritual intercourse in marriage over physical union were consistent with their demand for woman's sexual autonomy. This was played down in public rhetoric, especially in the conservative postwar period when efforts at marriage reform virtually ended. Privately, though, all of the first generation of feminists, including the "conservative" leaders like Lucy Stone, felt that "the right of a wife to her own person," i.e., the right to refuse to have sexual intercourse with her husband, was at the heart of woman's emancipation.[45] They agreed with Elizabeth Cady Stanton's view that the "false marriage relation" endured by so many women was "nothing more nor less than legalized prostitution."[46] Any means, then, of limiting the exposure of women to their husbands' "brutal lusts," and reducing the frequency of their pregnancies, was a path to "personal freedom." To this end they preached late marriage and "moral restraint" within marriage. These were the only means of birth control they could accept. Contraceptive devices, when they became available in the 1840's and 1850's, were considered unnatural and associated with non-marital sex and prostitution. The movement for birth control was conducted outside of the suffrage movement and unrelated to it. Woman's emancipation would yield freedom *from* sex, not for it.[47]

The sexual restraint preached by the feminists was not only functional in its intent to protect and emancipate women, it was also consistent with their vision of improving and elevating the human family. Like many nineteenth-century people, they believed in the conservation of sexual energy: by exercising self-control, they could divert excess sexual energy into higher pursuits. Even more important, they believed that sexual expression that was limited to procreation would produce a "nobler type of human kind." They held a romantic belief in "love babies"—superior children who were the products of love not "passional indulgence."[48] The perfection of the race provided still another argument for fewer and more carefully chosen sexual encounters within marriage. Self-control and freedom for self-development were both cornerstones of the feminists' program to "make the world better" and their ideal of marriage incorporated both concepts. One can only speculate about the difficulties they encountered in putting their beliefs into practice.

To sum up, then, the idealism of the feminists may have produced marital tensions, but their shared commitment to reform served as a source of strength and stability. On the whole, they came remarkably close to their ideal "partnership of equals." The autonomy and freedom enjoyed by the wives were highly unusual, especially when compared with conventional nineteenth-century marriages. The support of their husbands for this independence was equally striking. The new models of marriage they created represented an important contribution to nineteenth-century feminism and are still of interest today.

NOTES

[1]As radical abolitionists, they similarly contributed to legal emancipation but failed in their broader goal of abolishing racial prejudices.

[2]William L. O'Neill, *Everyone Was Brave; The Rise and Fall of Feminism in America* (Chicago: Quadrangle Books, 1969), pp. 33–34; Ellen DuBois, "Struggling Into Existence: The Feminism of Sarah and Angelina Grimké," *Women: A Journal of Liberation* (Spring 1970); reprinted as pamphlet by New England Free Press, Boston.

[3]See Appendix for list of 51 women; data on all of them can be found in *Notable American Women, 1607–1950, A Biographical Dictionary*, 3 vols., ed. Edward T. James (Cambridge: Harvard University Press, 1971). For the broader study, see Blanche Glassman Hersh, " 'The Slavery of Sex': Feminist-Abolitionists in Nineteenth Century America" (Ph.D. Dissertation, University of Illinois, 1975); an adaptation of this will be published by the University of Illinois Press.

[4]Of the remaining nine, four married men who opposed their work; the attitude of five husbands is not known. Seven of the group married twice, but in compiling statistics I have arbitrarily decided to count only the second marriage because in every case it was the longer and more significant one. There were three divorces in the group, none in marriages to feminist men.

[5]Roughly 72% of the group married. This is not out of line with available statistics for the general population. (See Yasukichi Yasuba, *Birth Rates of the White Population in the United States, 1800–1860* [Baltimore: Johns Hopkins Press, 1962], p. 114.) It is surprisingly high, however, considering the strong feminism of all the women and their desire to work for reform.

[6]I am not equating "equality" and "support" with that elusive quality called happiness, but evidence indicates that 18 of the 28 feminist

marriages were unusually compatible; only five are known to have had some conflicts or periods of separation; information is too scant on five others to draw even tentative conclusions. All four of the women who married antifeminist husbands gave evidence of strong dissatisfaction.

[7]Three of the women—Prudence Crandall, Abby Hutchinson, and Julia Ward Howe—were forced to give up their reform careers; the fourth, Jane Grey Swisshelm, deserted her husband and was later divorced by him.

[8]From a speech by Abby Kelley, quoted in Jane H. Pease, "The Freshness of Fanaticism; Abby Kelley Foster: An Essay in Reform" (Ph.D. Dissertation, University of Rochester, 1969), p. 86. For other typical descriptions of marriage as slavery, see a speech by Lucy Stone in *Una*, April 1854, by Amelia Bloomer in 1853, in D. C. Bloomer, ed., *Life and Writings of Amelia Bloomer* (Boston: Arena Pub. Co., 1895), p. 105, and by Antoinette Brown in 1853, in *History of Woman Suffrage*, 6 vols., first 3 vols. ed. by E. C. Stanton, S. B. Anthony, and M. J. Gage (New York: Fowler & Wells, 1881–1922), 1:580. (Hereafter cited as H.W.S.)

[9]Linda Gordon has pointed out that, given the repressive climate of the late 19th century, even the Free Lovers tended in practice to lead "faithful, monogamous legally-married lives"; see her "Voluntary Motherhood: The Beginnings of Feminist Birth Control Ideas in the United States," *Feminist Studies* 1 (Winter–Spring 1973): 5–22; quotation on p. 16.

[10]The 37 husbands included 10 businessmen, 7 lawyers, 4 writers or editors, 3 ministers, 1 doctor, 1 teacher, and 10 farmers or artisans; the occupation of 1 is not known. Five of the men were primarily reformers who also worked at farming, trades, or teaching to help support their families.

[11]Eight husbands were Quakers, 11 were either Unitarian or Universalist or unaffiliated with organized religion. The affiliation of 9 is not known but was probably liberal because of their compatibility with their wives, who all moved away from the orthodox church.

[12]See Mary A. Livermore, *The Story of My Life* (Hartford, Conn.: A. D. Worthington & Co., 1899) and Elinor Rice Hays, *Those Extraordinary Blackwells* (New York: Harcourt, Brace & World, 1967).

[13]The *New York Herald*, 12 Sept. 1852, describing the men attending the national woman's rights convention; H.W.S., 1:854.

[14]Harriet H. Robinson, ed., *"Warrington" Pen-Portraits* (Boston: By the Editor, 1877), pp. 547, 562.

[15]Lydia Maria Child to Angelina Grimké Weld, 2 Oct. 1838, in *Letters of Theodore Dwight Weld, Angelina Grimké Weld and Sarah Grimké, 1822–1844*, 2 vols., ed. Gilbert H. Barnes and Dwight L. Dumond (New York: D. Appleton-Century Co. for the American Historical Association, 1934), 2:702. (Hereafter cited as *Weld-Grimké Letters.*)

[16]For the daughter's illness in 1858–59, see Pease, "The Freshness . . ."; Stephen Foster to Abby Kelly Foster, 11 Sept. 1850, Kelley-Foster Papers, American Antiquarian Society. (Hereafter cited as A.A.S.)

[17]For Abby Kelley's views, see Pease, p. 83; Higginson is quoted on p. 84. Lucy Stone is quoted in a newsclipping on Stephen Foster's death, in Harriet Robinson Scrapbook, Schlesinger Library, Radcliffe College. (Hereafter cited as S.L.) For another admiring opinion on their marriage, see Aaron M. Powell, *Personal Reminiscences* (New York: Caulon Press, 1899), pp. 8, 10.

[18]Anna Davis Hallowell, ed., *James and Lucretia Mott, Life and Letters* (Boston: Houghton, Mifflin & Co., 1884), preface and p. 89; her description of their contrasting personalities is on pp. 89, 271, and *passim*; testimonial from friends about their marriage is on p. 400. See also Paulina Wright Davis's description of the Motts in *Revolution*, 4 Aug. 1870.

[19]Lucy Stone to H. B. Blackwell, 1854?; James Mott to Lucy Stone, 29 June 1853, both in Blackwell Family Papers, Library of Congress, Manuscript Division. (Hereafter cited as Blackwell Papers, L.C.) Thomas Wentworth Higginson, "Women's Husbands," *Woman's Journal*, 27 Sept. 1873.

[20]Elizabeth Cady Stanton, *Eighty Years and More: Reminiscences 1815–1897* (European Pub. Co., 1898; reprint ed., New York: Schocken Books, 1971), p. 202; *Revolution*, 4 Aug. 1870. Elizabeth Smith Miller was Stanton's cousin and the daughter of Gerrit Smith, well-known abolitionist and feminist.

[21]Antoinette Brown to Lucy Stone, "1850" and to Samuel Blackwell, 1855?, Antoinette Brown Blackwell Reminiscences, Blackwell Family Papers, S.L.; see also Hays, *Extraordinary Blackwells*.

[22]Lydia Maria Child, an atypical feminist-abolitionist in other ways as well, was the only woman in this group who was the primary breadwinner for all of her married life.

[23]Ellen DuBois has argued that the central significance of the suffrage movement rested in the fact that it attempted to introduce women into the public sphere without challenging their subordinate position at home

("The Radicalism of the Woman Suffrage Movement: Notes Toward the Reconstruction of Nineteenth-Century Feminism," *Feminist Studies* 3 [Fall 1975]: 63–71.) Since most of this first generation continued active in suffragism through the 1880's, 1890's, and even later, their modification of the doctrine of separate spheres is worth noting.

[24]The two most eloquent defenses of this position were made at the beginning and at the end of the 19th-century movement. Sarah Grimké used the argument in *Letters on the Equality of the Sexes, and the Condition of Woman* (Boston, 1838; reprint ed., New York: Source Book Press, 1970); Angelina Grimké further developed the concept of special roles in a letter to Amos A. Phelps, 2 Sept. 1837, Phelps Papers, Boston Public Library. Elizabeth Cady Stanton discussed the different roles of women in her speech "The Solitude of Self" in 1892, Stanton Papers, L.C.

[25]Only rarely did any feminists question the effect of cultural conditioning on woman's character and behavior. See, for example, Lydia Maria Child in *National Anti-Slavery Standard*, 30 Oct. 1869, and in *Letters of Lydia Maria Child* (Boston: Houghton, Mifflin & Co., 1883), pp. 243–44; see also T. W. Higginson in *Woman's Journal*, 2 May 1870, and Susan B. Anthony 1854 speech on "Woman's Rights," Anthony Papers, S.L. All of them, however, firmly believed that there were innate and unchangeable psychological differences between the sexes.

[26]Lucretia Mott is quoted in Hallowell, *James and Lucretia* . . . , p. 251; see Ida Husted Harper, *Life and Work of Susan B. Anthony*, 3 vols. (Indianapolis: Bowen-Merrill Co., 1898–1908), 1:122, for a description of the cedar tub ritual; Antoinette Brown Blackwell, in her Reminiscences, S.L., said everything in the Mott household moved "in a kind of associated harmony."

[27]Henry Blackwell reaffirmed the protest after Lucy's death, and declared in a letter to his sister Elizabeth, 11 Sept. 1895, that their marriage had been "a noble and life-long partnership of equals"; this and the protest, with his endorsement in 1897, are in Blackwell Papers, L.C.

[28]For the Weld-Grimké marriage, see *Weld-Grimké Letters*, 2:678–99; the Fosters' public declaration at the time of their marriage in 1845 is in Kelley–Foster Papers, Worcester Historical Society; Brown discussed the proposed contract in a letter to Samuel Blackwell, 14 Dec. 1855, Blackwell Papers, S.L.

[29]Antoinette Brown to Samuel Blackwell, 14 Dec. 1855, Blackwell Papers, S.L.; Mott is quoted in *Elizabeth Cady Stanton As Revealed in Her Letters, Diary and Reminiscences*, 2 vols., ed. Theodore Stanton and Harriot

Stanton Blatch (New York: Harper & Bros., 1922; reprint ed., New York: Arno Press, 1969), 2:178. Her views on the marriage ceremony are in Hallowell, *James and Lucretia* . . . p. 350.

[30]See Diary of William Stevens and Harriet Hanson Robinson, her entries, 1852, 1856, 1855, Harriet Robinson Papers, S.L.; D. C. Bloomer, *Life and Writings* . . . *passim.*

[31]Clarina H. Nichols to Susan B. Anthony, 24 Mar. 1852, and to Editor of *Herald of Freedom*, 14 April 1856; both in Joseph G. Gambone, ed., "The Forgotten Feminist of Kansas: The Papers of Clarina I. H. Nichols, 1854–1885," *Kansas Historical Quarterly* 39 (Spring and Summer 1973): 14, note 8; 246–47. See also her Reminiscences in H.W.S., 1:171–200.

[32]D. P. Livermore, *Woman Suffrage Defended* (Boston: Lee & Shepard, 1885), p. 75; M. A. Livermore, *Story of My Life*, p. 486.

[33]Henry Blackwell similarly put his wife's work before his own. In 1870 he was temporarily out of business and wrote his sister Elizabeth (3 May 1870, Blackwell Papers, L.C.) that he was reluctant to start a new business because it meant separation from Lucy and less opportunity to help in her work. He ultimately became an associate editor and later editor of the *Woman's Journal* and devoted the rest of his life to the woman's movement.

[34]A writer who interviewed the Livermores in 1871 found him "a proud and happy husband." (Virginia Townsend, "A Night At the Home of Mary A. Livermore," *Melrose Journal*, 11 Nov. 1871, in Melrose [Mass.] Public Library). Their granddaughter recalled that he "always stood behind her and urged her on," and often stayed home to look after household matters so that she could go out and lecture. (Interview with Mrs. M. D. Barrows, 10 Feb. 1916, in Livermore Scrapbook, Melrose Public Library.)

[35]T. Weld to A. Grimké, 15 April 1838, and A. Grimké to T. Weld, 29 April 1838, in *Weld-Grimké Letters*, 2:638, 649.

[36]DuBois, "Struggling Into Existence. . . ."

[37]Alice S. Rossi uses the Weld-Grimké marriage as an example to make the point that the private lives of men as well as women often influence the course of their public careers, although conventional histories and biographies usually fail to make this connection. Weld himself, she points out, typically was reluctant to admit that Angelina's health problems (probably linked to her pregnancies and "female" difficulties)

prevented her, and him to a lesser extent, from pursuing their careers. See her "Feminist History in Perspective: Sociological Contributions to Biographic Analysis" in *A Sampler of Women's Studies*, ed. Dorothy Gies McGuigan (Ann Arbor, Mich.: Center for Continuing Education of Women, 1973), pp. 85–108.

[38]A few of the feminist couples, like the Childs and the Annekes, suffered conflicts and disappointments that were not directly related to the career-versus-home dilemma. These are outside of the scope of this brief paper but are discussed in Hersh, "The Slavery of Sex . . . ," chap. 8.

[39]My conclusions support Carl Degler's argument that the prevalent view of 19th-century woman's lack of sexuality is a reflection of the prescriptive literature of the time rather than of the reality. The feminists were among those who perpetuated this view, but the evidence indicates that they themselves did not conform to the ideal. See his "What Ought To Be and What Was: Women's Sexuality in the Nineteenth Century," *American Historical Review* 79 (December 1974): 1467–90.

[40]Abby Kelley to Stephen Foster, 30 July 1843, Kelley–Foster Papers, A.A.S.; Antoinette Brown Blackwell to Samuel Blackwell, undated, Blackwell Papers, S.L.

[41]Even Elizabeth Cady Stanton, who in later years spoke of "woman's natural passion," argued in a temperance speech in 1852 that economic independence would keep women from entering into prostitution because "thank God, the true woman in her organization is too refined and spiritual, to be the victim of an overpowering passion"; *Lily*, May 1852.

[42]*Weld-Grimké Letters*, 2:555, 560, 566, 625.

[43]H. B. Blackwell to Lucy Stone, 22 Jan. 1854, 22 Dec. 1854; Lucy Stone to H. B. Blackwell, 26 April 1856, Blackwell Papers, L.C.

[44]For a discussion of the general trend, see Charles E. Rosenberg, "Sexuality, Class and Role in 19th-Century America," *American Quarterly* 25 (May 1973): 131–54.

[45]In a letter to Elizabeth Cady Stanton, 14 Aug. 1853, Stanton Papers, L.C., Lucy Stone noted that sexual abuse in marriage was "perfectly appalling" and agreed that "the truth lies there." To Antoinette Brown, 11 July 1855, Blackwell Papers, L.C., she wrote that the "real question" that "underlies the whole movement" was: "Has woman a right to herself?" She also expressed uncertainty about whether the "time was right" to do justice to the issue, a timidity that later would contribute to the rift in the movement.

[46]Elizabeth Cady Stanton is quoted in Stanton and Blatch, *Elizabeth Cady Stanton . . .* , 2: 70.

[47]The opposition of the feminists was not absolute. Occasionally in private correspondence one finds the wish that some acceptable means could be found to control conception. See Emily Blackwell in Hays, *Extraordinary Blackwells*, p. 100, and Stanton in Alma Lutz, *Created Equal. A Biography of Elizabeth Cady Stanton, 1815–1902* (New York: John Day Co., 1940), p. 44. Dr. Elizabeth Blackwell reluctantly advised that, when necessary, the "safe period" (based on miscalculations at this time) could be resorted to; she also recommended douching with tepid water and coitus interruptus, probably the most widely used means of birth control in the 19th century; Peter Fryer, *The Birth Controllers* (New York: Stein & Day, 1966), p. 180.

[48]See, for example, Harriot K. Hunt, *Glances and Glimpses* (Boston, 1856; reprint ed., New York: Source Book Press, 1970), p. 183, and Henry C. Wright, *Marriage and Parentage*, 5th ed. (Boston: B. Marsh, 1866). Elizabeth Cady Stanton, in a speech on divorce, spoke of "those holy instincts of the women to bear no children but those of love"; H.W.S., 1:720.

BIBLIOGRAPHY

Manuscript Collections

American Antiquarian Society. Papers of Abby Kelley Foster and Stephen S. Foster.

Boston Public Library. Manuscript Division. Antislavery Collection. Lydia Maria Child and David Lee Child Papers. Amos A. Phelps Papers. Weston Family Papers.

Library of Congress. Manuscript Division. Susan B. Anthony Papers. Blackwell Family Papers. Elizabeth Cady Stanton Papers.

Melrose (Mass.). Public Library. Manuscript Division. Mary A. Livermore Collection.

Schlesinger Library on the History of Women in America. Radcliffe College. Susan B. Anthony Papers. Blackwell Family Papers. Harriet Hanson Robinson Papers.

Worcester Historical Society. Papers of Abby Kelley Foster and Stephen S. Foster.

Unpublished Ph.D. Dissertations
(available from University Microfilms)

Hersh, Blanche Glassman. " 'The Slavery of Sex': Feminist-Abolitionists in Nineteenth-Century America." University of Illinois, 1975.

Pease, Jane H. "The Freshness of Fanaticism; Abby Kelley Foster: An Essay in Reform." University of Rochester, 1969.

Taylor, Lloyd C., Jr. "To Make Men Free; An Interpretative Study of Lydia Maria Child." Lehigh University, 1956.

Warbasse, Elizabeth. "The Changing Legal Rights of Married Women, 1800–1861." Radcliffe College, 1960.

Books and Articles

Blackwell, Alice Stone. *Lucy Stone, Pioneer of Woman's Rights.* Boston: Little, Brown, & Co., 1930.

Blackwell, Antoinette Brown. *The Sexes Throughout Nature.* New York: G. P. Putnam's Sons, 1875.

Bloomer, D. C., ed. *Life and Writings of Amelia Bloomer.* Boston: Arena Pub. Co., 1895.

Child, Lydia Maria. *Letters of Lydia Maria Child, with Biographical Introduction by John G. Whittier and Appendix by Wendell Phillips.* Boston: Houghton, Mifflin & Co., 1883.

Cromwell, Otelia. *Lucretia Mott.* Cambridge: Harvard University Press, 1958.

Degler, Carl N. "What Ought to Be and What Was: Women's Sexuality in the Nineteenth Century." *American Historical Review* 79 (December 1974): 1467–90.

DuBois, Ellen. "Struggling Into Existence: The Feminism of Sarah and Angelina Grimké." *Women: A Journal of Liberation* (Spring 1970); reprinted as pamphlet by New England Free Press, Boston.

Fryer, Peter. *The Birth Controllers.* New York: Stein & Day, 1966.

Gambone, Joseph G., ed. "The Forgotten Feminist of Kansas: The Papers of Clarina I. H. Nichols, 1854–1885." 8 installments. *Kansas Historical Quarterly* 39–40 (Spring 1973–Winter 1974).

Gordon, Linda. "Voluntary Motherhood: The Beginnings of Feminist Birth Control Ideas in the United States." *Feminist Studies* 1 (Winter–Spring 1973): 5–22.

Gordon, Michael and Bernstein, M. Charles. "Mate Choice and Domestic Life in the 19th Century Marriage Manual." *Journal of Marriage and the Family* 32 (November 1970): 665–74.

Grimké, Sarah M. *Letters on the Equality of the Sexes, and the Condition of Woman*. Boston: Isaac Knapp, 1838; reprint ed., New York: Source Book Press, 1970.

Hallowell, Anna Davis, ed. *James and Lucretia Mott. Life and Letters*. Boston: Houghton, Mifflin & Co., 1884.

Harper, Ida Husted. *Life and Work of Susan B. Anthony*. 3 vols. Indianapolis: Bowen-Merrill Co., 1898–1908.

Hays, Elinor Rice. *Morning Star; A Biography and Lucy Stone, 1818–1893*. New York: Harcourt, Brace & World, 1961.

Hays, Elinor Rice. *Those Extraordinary Blackwells*. New York: Harcourt, Brace & World, 1967.

History of Woman Suffrage. 6 vols. Vols. 1–3 ed. Elizabeth Cady Stanton, Susan B. Anthony, Matilda Joslyn Gage. New York: Fowler & Wells, 1881–1887. Vol. 4 ed. S. B. Anthony and Ida Husted Harper. Rochester, 1902. Vols. 5–6 ed. I. H. Harper. New York: by National American Woman Suffrage Assoc., 1922.

Hunt, Harriot K. *Glances and Glimpses*. Boston: John P. Jewett & Co., 1856; reprint ed., New York: Source Book Press, 1970.

Jeffrey, Kirk. "Marriage, Career, and Feminine Ideology in Nineteenth-Century America: Reconstructing the Marital Experience of Lydia Maria Child, 1828–1874." *Feminist Studies* 2, No. 2/3 (1975): 113–30.

Lerner, Gerda. *The Grimké Sisters from South Carolina*. Boston: Houghton Mifflin Co., 1967; New York: Schocken Books, 1971.

Livermore, Daniel Parker. *Woman Suffrage Defended*. Boston: Lee & Shepard, 1885.

Livermore, Mary A. *The Story of My Life*. Hartford, Conn.: A. D. Worthington & Co., 1899.

Lutz, Alma. *Created Equal, A Biography of Elizabeth Cady Stanton, 1815–1902*. New York: John Day Co., 1940.

Notable American Women, 1607–1950, A Biographical Dictionary. 3 vols. Edited by Edward T. James. Cambridge: Harvard University Press, 1971.

O'Neill, William L. *Everyone Was Brave; The Rise and Fall of Feminism in America*. Chicago: Quadrangle Books, 1969.

Powell, Aaron M. *Personal Reminiscences*. New York: Caulon Press, 1899.

Robinson, Harriet H., ed. *"Warrington" Pen-Portraits*. Boston: By the Editor, 1877.

Rosenberg, Charles E. "Sexuality, Class and Role in 19th-Century America." *American Quarterly* 25 (May 1973): 131–154.

Rossi, Alice S. "Feminist History in Perspective: Sociological Contributions to Biographic Analysis." *A Sampler of Women's Studies*. Edited by Dorothy Gies McGuigan. Ann Arbor, Mich.: Center for Continuing Education of Women, 1973, pp. 85–108.

Rossi, Alice S., ed. *The Feminist Papers*. New York: Columbia University Press, 1973; Bantam Books, 1974.

Rugoff, Milton. *Prudery and Passion; Sexuality in Victorian America*. New York: G. P. Putnam's Sons, 1971.

Sklar, Kathryn Kish. *Catherine Beecher, A Study in American Domesticity*. New Haven: Yale University Press, 1973.

Smith, Daniel Scott. "Family Limitation, Sexual Control, and Domestic Feminism in Victorian America." *Feminist Studies* 1 (Winter-Spring 1973): 40–57.

Smith-Rosenberg, Carroll. "The Female Animal: Medical and Biological Views of Woman and Her Role in Nineteenth-Century America." *Journal of American History* 60 (September 1973): 332–56.

Smith-Rosenberg, Carroll. "The Hysterical Woman: Sex Roles and Role Conflict in 19th-Century America." *Social Research* 39 (Winter 1972): 652–78.

Stanton, Elizabeth Cady. *Eighty Years and More: Reminiscences 1815–1897*. European Publ. Co., 1898; reprint ed., with new introduction by Gail Parker, New York: Schocken Books, 1971.

Stanton, Elizabeth Cady. *Elizabeth Cady Stanton As Revealed in Her Letters, Diary and Reminiscences*. 2 vols. Edited by Theodore Stanton and Harriot Stanton Blatch. New York: Harper & Bros., 1922; reprint ed., New York: Arno Press, 1969.

Swisshelm, Jane Grey. *Crusader and Feminist; Letters of Jane Grey Swisshelm, 1858–1865.* Edited by Arthur J. Larsen. St. Paul: Minnesota Historical Society, 1934.

Swisshelm, Jane Grey. *Half A Century.* 2d ed. Chicago: Jansen, McClurg & Co., 1880.

Walters, Ronald G., ed. *Primers for Prudery: Sexual Advice to Victorian America.* New Jersey: Prentice-Hall, 1974.

Weld, Theodore Dwight. *Letters of Theodore Dwight Weld, Angelina Grimké Weld and Sarah Grimké, 1822—1844.* 2 vols. Edited by Gilbert H. Barnes and Dwight L. Dumond. New York: D. Appleton-Century Co. for the American Historical Association, 1934.

Wright, Henry C. *Marriage and Parentage.* 5th ed. Boston: B. Marsh, 1866.

Yasuba, Yasukichi. *Birth Rates of the White Population in the United States, 1800–1860.* Baltimore: Johns Hopkins Press, 1962.

period

III

(1861-1919)

The Strenuous Life

chapter 8

Sexuality, Class and Role in 19th-Century America

by Charles E. Rosenberg

No culture has been considered more sexually repressive for women and men than the Victorian; none is more misunderstood by sexual moderns, applying Freudian-influenced views of sexuality. In reinterpreting Victorian sexual ideology from the vantage point of that culture rather than from our own, the work of Charles Rosenberg and Carroll Smith-Rosenberg has been exemplary. They have sought to understand the social context in which Victorian sexual ideology emerged and the social functions it served. Applying this framework to men's history, they have identified the contribution of evangelical religion in shaping an ideology of male self-denial and sexual continence and have examined the effect of this ideology on middle-class notions of male respectability and self-discipline.

The article by Charles Rosenberg reprinted here is noteworthy as well for its application of social-psychological concepts to history. Rosenberg describes the middle-class male "sex role" he finds in Victorian medical literature and marriage manuals. He then specu-

lates about some of the "strains" or conflicts which developed for middle-class men in living up to the role. One kind of strain, he suggests, emerges from conflicts between expectations for men as members of a class and as members of a sex; men are expected to be sexually aggressive, but the middle class is also expected to be self-disciplined and self-denying. Another kind of strain arises from the conflict between male and female roles, when, instead of complementing each other, the roles conflict because women are failing to act in the harmonious way men expect. The first type of role strain arises out of conflicts within *the norms that men confront, the second from conflict* between the norms for each sex.

Any historical consideration of sexuality necessarily involves a problem in method. Most would-be students are concerned with behavior, but must satisfy themselves with the materials of myth and ideology; such scholars must somehow extrapolate a relationship between the content of this ideology and the behavior it, presumably, reflected and legitimated.

This difficulty manifests itself in a particularly intractable form to those attempting to understand the 19th century.[1] Historians and social scientists still tend to see mid-and-late-19th century sexuality as peculiar; Victorian is still a synonym for repressive. The few social historians concerned with sexuality have written in emotional and intellectual consistency with immediately post-Victorian reformers of sexual behavior who perpetuated the vision of a "neurotic"— or, perhaps more accurately, pathogenic—19th century (at least for the middle class), a period in which the sexual impulse was systematically repressed and deformed.

Such diagnoses are necessarily suspect. One cannot solve problems of historical interpretation by describing a whole society, or a major class grouping within it, as though it were some poorly adjusted individual. We may find many mid-and-late-19th-century attitudes toward human sexuality both alien and alienating; but it is quite another matter to characterize these ideas as simply and inevitably dysfunctional.[2]

But perhaps this is not quite accurate; for on one level, that of the total society, historians have begun to assume that this repressive ideology was indeed functional. They have, that is, argued that sexual repression (and impulse deferral

"Sexuality, Class and Role in 19th-Century America" by Charles E. Rosenberg. Reprinted by permission of the author and publisher from *American Quarterly* (published by the University of Pennsylvania), v. 35, No. 2 (May 1973), pp. 131–153. Copyright, 1973, Trustees of the University of Pennsylvania.

in general) served the needs of an increasingly bureaucratized society by helping to create a social discipline appropriate to a middle class of managers, professionals and small entrepreneurs. But such views simply reinforce a traditional irony; for on the individual level, we still tend to see these ideological justifications for repression as dysfunctional, indeed pathogenic in their stifling of basic human needs.[3]

Should one simply assume this irony and elaborate a chastening discontinuity between the needs of society and those of the individuals who make it up? I think not, if only because it is too simple; one must distrust any approach which fails to recognize that human beings, in any culture, come in assorted psychological shapes and sizes. No analytical strategy which assumes that the behavior of groups can be explained by considering them as undifferentiated individuals writ large can provide intellectually satisfactory. (Especially when our understanding of individual psychodynamics is far from definitive, and our understanding of the relationship between individual and group processes more tenuous still.)

The discussion of sexuality which follows is based on the assumption that all individuals have peculiar needs and "choose" particular configurations of roles appropriate to these needs. Though all individuals must play a number of such roles simultaneously, all are necessarily interrelated—with each other and with each individual's pattern of sexual behavior. The paper begins with an evaluation of one element relatively discernible in historical materials: formal prescriptions of sex and gender roles. A second and more tentative portion of the argument suggests some of the ways in which these roles may have related to the actual expression of sexuality.

To delineate role prescriptions is, of course, not to describe behavior; no particular individual need have lived his or her life in accordance with these projected values. On the other hand, one never escapes them entirely; every member of a particular generation has somehow to find an individual accommodation with respect to these ideal prescriptions. Even those who reject a life entirely consistent with such ideals cannot elude them completely—for they constitute a parameter which helps define the nature and content of their deviance. In the series of choices which can be said to describe growth, options rejected as well as those accepted form a part of one's self-image, become an element in the configuration of emotional resonance which ultimately defines individuality.[4]

A recent critic has suggested that the fundamental literary reflections of Victorian sexuality were "pornography and expurgation."[5] This may indeed be true of belles lettres. There do exist, however, a class of materials that attempt to explain, rationalize, somehow come to terms with the sexual impulse. Most are medical and the pages which follow are based upon such writings.

The medical and biological literature relating to sexuality in 19th-century America is a mixed and surprisingly abundant lot, ranging from earnest marriage manuals to the insinuating treatises of quacks advertising their ability to treat venereal disease or procure abortion. It includes careful academic monographs and cheaply printed paperback guides to midwifery and domestic medicine. It is a genre complex, disparate and ambiguous.[6] And as such it reflects the needs and attitudes of almost all elements among those who could, or hoped to, consider themselves middle class, that is from the educated and economically secure to the shopkeepers, skilled workers and clerks who sought this secure identity.

Yet one can, I think, identify a number of characteristic aspects. The first is a tone of increasing repressiveness which marks much of the material written in the two generations after the 1830s; by the 1870s this emphasis had moved from the level of individual exhortation to that of organized efforts to enforce chastity upon the unwilling.[7] Closely related to this theme of repressiveness is a virtual obsession with masturbation; the tract on "secret vice" became a well-defined genre in this period.[8] Not surprisingly, sexual activity in youth and adolsecence was explicitly and emphatically discountenanced. Almost every one of these themes was expressed before the 1830s; it is clear, nevertheless, that they were intoned with increasing intensity and frequency after this period.

A second general trait is that of ambivalance and inconsistency; not only within the genre as a whole, but within the same article or treatise—even within a single paragraph—facts casually assumed are directly contradicted. A third theme, one not unrelated to the second, is the persistence of an older, male-oriented antirepressive behavioral ethos. Though the evidence is less explicit, the existence of this variant norm is undeniable. A final quality of these arguments is their employment of a common vocabulary and store of images, a kind of lingua franca of scientific authority and metaphor doing service as scientific fact. Let me briefly elaborate each of these tendencies and then attempt to explain some of their peculiar characteristics in terms of contemporary class and gender roles.

The trend toward repressiveness, not surprisingly, correlates in time with the activist millennialism of the generation following the Second Great Awakening, that is, the decades following the 1830s. Authorities of the 18th and early 19th centuries routinely indicated "sexual excess"; yet their injunctions have a calm, even bland tone. These writers accepted sexual activity after puberty as both normal and necessary; though all assumed that an intrinsically limited quantity of vital force might be depleted through excess, all assumed as well that physiological functions unfulfilled could be pathogenic. Thus the not infrequent advice that marriage might cure hysteria, that masturbation could be cured only through sexual intercourse, that maidenhood and celibate bachelorhood were unnatural and potentially disease-producing states.

Beginning with the 1830s, however, the ritualized prudence of these traditional admonitions became sharpened and applied far more frequently, while for some authors sexuality began to assume an absolutely negative tone.[9] Thus, for example, the dangers of sexual intercourse within marriage became, for the first time, a subject of widespread censure. Such warnings applied, moreover, to both sexes: only the need for propagating the species, some authors contended, could justify so dangerous an indulgence. Even if the female did not suffer the physical "drain" that ejaculation constituted for the male, she suffered an inevitable loss of nervous energy. "With the male, excessive indulgence frequently causes general debility, weakness, and lameness of the back, dyspepsia, impotency, and predisposition to almost innumerable diseases, by rendering the system susceptible to the action of other causes of disease. In the female, such excesses frequently cause uterine inflammation, and ulceration, leucorrhoea, deranged menstruation, miscarriage, barrenness as well as debility, hysteria, and an endless train of nervous and other diseases."[10] A generally wary attitude toward the dangers of sexual activity can also be seen in advice suggesting the proper frequency of intercourse. A month's interval was probably the most common injunction, though some more flexible writers conceded that even weekly "indulgence" might not be harmful to a "healthy laboringman." Almost all such authorities strongly opposed sexual intercouse during gestation and lactation—periods, it was argued, when nervous excitement would divert vital energies needed for the fullest development of the fetus or nursling.[11]

Logically related to the increasing prevalence of repressive attitudes was a growing concern with masturbation. It was, according to scores of writers both lay and medical, the "master vice" of the period, the source of a variety of ills ranging from tuberculosis to myopia. Many of the tracts dedicated to combating this evil were, of course, cynical appeals to fear and guilt by business-seeking quacks.[12] Yet the concern demonstrated by would-be health reformers and phrenologists, as well as the more specifically evangelical indicates a depth of anxiety transcending the individual and the cynically exploitive. Such widespread concern can only be interpreted as reflecting a more general emotional consensus; even the calculating arguments of quack physicians can be presumed to reflect a not unsophisticated evaluation of where emotional appeals might most profitably be made. Perhaps most alarming to contemporaries was the universality of the practice. "This polluting stream flows through all grades of society, . . . and even the shepherd and shepherdess, who have been surrounded by every thing that could inspire the heart with sentiments of virtue and purity, have desecrated the scene, where Heaven has displayed in rich profusion, the evidences of its love and power, by indulgence in a vice, in view of which angels, if possible, weep, and creation sighs."[13] Not even the youngest child could be presumed immune; one physician noted that even infants of eighteen months had been taught the "horrid practice."[14] Perhaps the instances of "furious masturbation" which had been observed in such infants demonstrated the power of this instinct; but the very strength of this animal attribute only underlined the need for controlling it.

Control was the basic building block of personality. To allow the passions—among which sexuality was only one—to act themselves out, was to destroy any hope of creating a truly Christian personality. "Self-respect" was impossible if mind could not control emotion. Sexual health lay fundmentally in the ability to "restore the calm equilibrium of mind and senses; put down the terrible mastery of passion." One could not relax even momentarily, for such emotions intruded themselves "upon the attention of all alike, with more or less power of impertinent distraction."[15] This was, of course, in many ways a traditional view: the ability to deal with such "impertinent distractions" lay at the emotional center of a time-hallowed male ideal of Christian stoicism. But as the 19th century progressed, it was expressed with an intensity alien to the tradition of gentlemanly virtue through prudent moderation. It was, moreover, oriented increasingly toward sexuality as such; earlier guides to the good life had always discussed the insidious effects of the "passions," but in such tracts the dangers of gluttony, anger or envy figured as prominently as those posed by sexuality.

Consistent with the need for self-control was a parallel emphasis upon the need to repress childhood and adolescent sexuality. Physicians warned with increasing sharpness as the century progressed, that marriage contracted before the attainment of full maturity resulted inevitably in the stunting of both husband and wife; any children they might conceive would embody this constitutional weakness. Elizabeth Blackwell, for example, argued that both sexes— and especially males—should remain continent until 25. Puberty was assumed to be crucially important in both psychic and physical development; and thus sexual activity during this labile period was particularly dangerous. It was never too early, health reformers warned, to train children in respect for the Seventh Commandment. "In the unformed immature condition of the physical system, at the date of the first evolution of the reproductive instinct, an unbridled indulgence could not fail to prove destructive to the perfection of the bodily powers, as well as highly detrimental to the moral and mental development."[16] So generally unquestioned was this view that a physician undertaking a gynecological survey of the Oneida Community, where sexual activity in youth was accepted, expressed surprise that the women of the Community seemed no different from other American females: "However repugnant it may be to our sense of manhood, we cannot resist the conclusion that sexual intercourse at this tender age does not arrest the steady tendency to a fine and robust womanhood."[17] Consistently enough, traditional admonitions that women marry early so as to avoid sexual frustration and its consequent psychic dangers began to disappear by the generation of the Civil War. Newer hygienic ideals urged mental discipline and physical exercise as appropriate modes for the discharge of nervous energy.[18] The need in an increasingly urban and bureaucratized middle class to create ideological sanctions justifying postponement of the normal age for marriage is obvious enough. Not surprisingly, this trend coincides both with statistical evidence that urban family size was decreasing and with a growing and acrimonious debate over birth control and abortion.

Another general characteristic of this medical and biological literature is its remarkable inconsistency. Sex was natural, yet unnatural. Children were innocent, yet always at risk because of their ever recurring sexual appetite. Most strikingly, female sexuality was surrounded by an ambivalence so massive as to constitute one of the central analytical dilemmas in the understanding of 19th-century social history. One popular writer, for example, warned that women were "not affected so much by over indulgence as by Masturbation. Delicacy not allowing an ardent woman to tell her husband of her needs, she is apt to relieve herself by this unnatural practice. There are, however, but few women who crave sexual intercourse. The excess is generally on the part of the man." H. Newell Martin, first professor of biology at Johns Hopkins, was able in a widely used text on the *Human Body* to cite on one page the opinion that few women of the more luxurious classes regarded sexual congress as anything more than a nuisance after the age of 22 or 23, and on the next page quote an even more authoritative opinion noting that orgasm is necessary for the health of both sexes, but especially for women.[19] Similarly, laymen believed that woman could not conceive unless she felt sexual pleasure;

and some wives, indeed, sought to suppress sexual excitement—consciously at least—as a mode of birth control. [20] Women, on the one hand, were warned that excessive sexuality might cause illness—and, at the same time, that sickness, physical unattractiveness and lack of sexual responsiveness might well lead to the loss of their husbands' affection to "other women." Most men seem to have desired sexually responsive wives, yet feared that "excessive" sexuality might lead either to infidelity, or less consciously, to dangerous and demanding impositions upon their abilities to perform adequately. As the century progressed, the term nymphomania was applied to degrees of sexual expression which would be considered quite normal today. H. R. Storer, for example, a prominent Boston physician, could refer casually to the case of a "virgin nymphomaniac." [21]

As if in response to the mixed emotional cues implicit in these inconsistent ideals of sexual behavior, middle-class Americans began to elaborate a synthetic role, that of the Christian gentleman. The Christian gentleman was an athlete of continence, not coitus, continuously testing his manliness in the fire of self-denial. This paradigmatic figure eschewed excess in all things and most important, allowed his wife to dictate the nature of their sexual interaction. A pious father should instruct his son "as to a gentleman's duty of self-control in the marital relations." [22] Too frequent intercourse was physically draining and led to a striving after ever greater sensation, to a "constitutional irritability" which required ever more frequent and diverse stimulation; this "sick irritability" had clearly to be distinguished, publicists argued, from the healthy and sparing strength of true manliness. Continence implied strength, not weakness. [23] "Reserve is the grand secret of power everywhere." "Be noble, generous, just, self-sacrificing, continent, manly in all things—and no woman worthy of you can help loving you, in the best sense of the word." Yet the majority of men, most mid-century evangelically oriented authors had to confess, were still slaves of the "love of domination, ungoverned passion, grossness," and "filthiness of habit."[24] Continence and manliness were still far from synonymous.

Which suggests our third major theme: the implacable persistence of an older male-oriented behavioral ethos, one which placed a premium on aggressive masculinity. "I regret," a self-consciously horrified physician recorded in the early 1880s, "to say that I have known some fathers to tickle the genital organs of their infant boys until a complete erection of the little penis ensued, which effect pleases the father as an evidence of a robust boy."[25] Obviously, of course, premarital chastity and marital fidelity hardly serve as an inclusive description of mid-19th century behavior. The prostitution, the venereal disease rate, the double standard itself all document the gap between admonition and reality. Equally striking evidence is to be found in male fears of weakness, impotence and premature ejaculation—widespread anxieties to which the century's abundance of quack specialists in "secret diseases" appealed. Insofar, moreover, as particular males internalized the transcendent behavioral prescriptions embodied in the idea of the Christian Gentleman and thus avoided premarital activity they would necessarily experience increased anxieties as to their ultimate sexual capacity. Thus the often brutal and impulsive behavior of husbands on honeymoons (a universal complaint of the would-be defenders of woman's marital rights) is most plausibly explained by the husband's fear of inadequacy (in addition to possible ambivalence toward the act itself). The marriage night was an institutionalized trauma for the pure of both sexes. [26]

This traditional masculine ethos had *its* ideological justification as well; most prominent among these justifications, as we have suggested, was the idea that sexual energies had somehow to be discharged if health was to be maintained after puberty. As late as 1891, a regretful physician complained that such beliefs were still frequently used to justify the double standard: "There are those among the males of our generation, who attribute to men an inherent natural need to gratify passions, claiming that the weaker sex understand it to be necessary to man's nature, and willingly tolerate lustful ante-nuptial and post-nuptial practices."[27] Evangelicals still accused physicians of backslapping recommendations of fornication as cure for masturbation and other ills; to more "realistic" and worldly physicians—perhaps individually more committed to the masculine ethos—masturbation was a normal, if not indeed whimsical, symptom of adolescence, to be cured by the application of copulation in required doses. Fathers still proudly sent their sons off to bawdy houses to establish their masculinity. Perhaps most pervasive were warnings that men be assertive and avoid the slightest hint of femininity; as one physician phrenologist explained, "a woman admires in man true *manliness*, and is repelled by weakness and effeminacy. A womanish man awakens either the pity or the contempt of the fair sex."[28]

A final characteristic of 19th-century American and English writings on sexuality is of a general kind, and relates not so much to content as to formal structure. All these books, pamphlets and articles, no matter what their particular orientation, spoke in the same vocabulary, used the same images, made the same appeal to such standard expository modes as that of argument from design. Even more generally, all these authors used disease sanctions as their basic framework for exposition and admonition; their hypothetical etiologies served, of course, to shape and sanction particular life-styles. Almost all these accepted modes of argument were, moreover, so open-ended that appeals of the most varying kind could employ the same figures and analogies. Both sides, for example, employed arguments drawn from design; liberals emphasized that the function implicit in the secretion of semen implied expulsion and use; the more repressive argued that woman's menstrual cycle implied the maximum frequency for sexual intercourse. The more evangelically oriented similarly emphasized that copulation in lower animals took place infrequently, only at the initiative of the female, and only for the purpose of reproduction. These practices were thus "natural"—that is, more primitive—and man's comparatively frenetic sexuality a sign of civilized degeneracy. Lack of control, on the other hand, was always seen as animal, as characteristic of a brutal, less highly organized being. Like any alphabet, these traditionally accepted modules of image and assumption could be manipulated into vastly different configurations.[29]

At this point a word of caution is indicated. We have, thus far, perhaps emphasized the repressive, even the antisexual. Yet most physicians who expressed their attitudes in regard to such questions endorsed a rather more moderate position. They assumed, that is, that the sexual powers had necessarily to be exercised—but that morality and social policy demanded that they be limited until marriage. "Although function is the natural destiny of organs," as the editor of the *British Medical Journal* noted blandly in 1882, "considerations, both of morality and expedience, and even of health, concur in the advice that it is better to hold over the formation of a certain habit until the bodily frame is thoroughly consolidated and the practice can be indulged in a legitimate manner."[30] Such stolidly nontranscendent prudence was as close as the majority of physicians ever came to endorsing wholeheartedly the evangelical attitude toward sexuality. Few, however, were willing to publicly challenge the more intensely repressive formulations routinely offered the public by their more evangelically inclined colleagues. Significantly, however, even the handful of physicians explicitly hostile to the evangelical view of sexuality were convinced that "intellect" must always dominate, that no passion must ever escape conscious control.[31]

These, very briefly and schematically, are the most obvious characteristics of medical and biological attitudes toward sexuality in 19th-century America. I should now like to suggest some of the ways in which class and gender roles helped shape and are in turn reflected in this literature.

But first a minor caveat. For the purposes of this discussion we must very largely limit our remarks to those Americans who considered themselves part of the "respectable" middle class—for it is they who produced the sources upon which we must depend, and whose needs and anxieties these sources mirror. Yet, it might be objected, class status is an extraordinarily difficult commodity for the sociologist, let alone the historian, to measure objectively. Vocation, income, religion, birth, all play a role, but in particular configurations not always amenable to orderly historical reconstition. At the same time, however, consciousness of class identity is a primary emotional reality, especially when such identity is marginal or ill-defined. And status definitions in 19th-century. America were, contemporaries and historians have agreed, particularly labile and would thus have tended to make class identification particularly stressful and problematic. A good many Americans must, it follows, have been all the more anxious in their internalization of those aspects of life-style which seemed to embody and assure class status. And contemporaries clearly regarded overt sexuality, especially in women, as part of a life-style demeaning to middle-class status. Virtue and self-denial, like evangelical religion itself, could be embraced by any man who so willed—and thus serve as transcendent and therefore emotionally reassuring tools in the forging of a life-style appropriate to assuaging, on the one hand, the expected scorn of established wealth and breeding, and, on the other, anxieties of economic insecurity symbolized by the ominous existence of the poor.

In the symbolic categories employed by 19th-century writers on sexuality, the "immoral" rich and debauched poor equally embodied "depravity" and license. It was assumed, for example, that domestic servants were a source of moral contagion, that they took particular pleasure in teaching masturbation and salaciousness generally to the innocents placed in their charge. "It seems," one physician wailed, "as if this class took special delight in poisoning the minds of the young and innocent and initiating them into habits of vice." For every case, another physician charged, in which precocious sexuality was aroused through idiopathic causes, "three to five" were incited by servants. Such views continued almost unchanged into the opening years of the present century; in 1910, for example, a well-meaning female physician warned against servants playing a role in the sexual education of children, for their "point of view can hardly fail to be coarse and may be really vicious."[32]

Servants, it must be recalled, were a part of every household with any pretension to respectability; as such they represented an intrusive emotional reality. The widespread hostility toward domestics to which we refer might well have mirrored middle-class repression of the sexuality which the lower orders were presumed to enjoy. However, it may have reflected as well at least some measure of reality. The social and psychological meaning of such behavior— whether real or fantasied—is not at all clear. Servants may in "seducing" their youthful charges have been simply acting out an older sexual ethos, one still normal in the lower and rural classes. Such seductions could also have been used to express hostility and rage toward their employers. The biological mother might also have projected this hostility-shaded image as one mode of expressing rivalry and ambivalence toward the woman who actually cared for her children. It may also conceivably have mirrored the unwillingness of particular individuals to accept the role of *their* own parents in the inevitable sexual contacts between child and child-rearer. This almost whimsically complex catalogue demonstrates clearly the difficulties of interpretation in this area; there are simply no easy or one-dimensional explanations.

Public health advocates assumed that sexual license was characteristic of slum life and, like drink, one of those traits which kept the poor poor. The rich too were, consolingly, seen in these mythic categories as victims of sensuality, of a chronic moral decay. In the United States, perhaps even more than in England, the ideal type of the Christian Gentleman served as one mode of legitimating the lives which so many Americans had necessarily to lead: lives of economic virtue, sexual prudence, of a chronic need to evaluate and reassert appropriate life-styles. [33]

I have, thus far, emphasized the repressive—and in their intensity and pervasiveness novel—aspects of 19th-century American attitudes toward sexuality. Yet a great deal of evidence points to 19th-century patterns of sexuality not so much absolutely repressive as sharply variant. No critical observer has failed to note the inconsistency between a growing ideological discountenance of sexuality, an increasing and reciprocal emphasis upon the ideal of domesticity— and a behavioral reality which included widespread prostitution, illegitimacy, birth control and abortion.

The key, I feel, to this apparent paradox lies in the nature of existing gender roles. For a primary reality to men and women was precisely their ability to act out their socially prescribed roles as men and women; and 19th-century gender roles embodied and implied conflict, conflict not only with those characteristics assigned the opposite sex, but with other components of contemporary social values (including prescriptions of class-appropriate behavior). To be more specific: despite a superfluity of evangelical exhortation, the primary role model with which men had to come to terms was that which articulated the archaic male ethos—one in which physical vigor, and particularly aggressive sexual behavior was a central component. There is, as we have argued, an abundance of evidence supporting the emotional relevance of this masculine ethos, as well as of its prescribing and informing behavior.

Consistently enough, the most hated target of mid-19th-century feminist advocates of moral reform was the double standard which recognized and, in a sense, legiti-mated the male ethos. And gradually, as we have seen, male and female writers extended the area of conflict and control to include sexuality within marriage: until woman controlled access to her own body, she could not enjoy true freedom—or physical and mental health. For the husband came to mar-riage as one woman physician put, it, "imbued with the belief—an iron-clad tradition of the ages that marriage gives him a special license, and under this license often he puts to shame the prostitution of the brothel."[34] Moral reformers not only demanded that men conform to the same standards of sexual morality as women, but taught that the best means of achieving this goal was through woman's control of the male child's moral education and the ending of sexual segregation in childhood. Such reformers warned again and again that the polarization of male and female traits perpetuated in this segregation guaranteed that true sexual morality would never be established. [35]

The depth and significance of the conflict which charac-terized this polarization of gender role traits is particularly well illustrated in the 19th-century's masturbation literature—not only in its very existence, but even more clearly in its internal themes. That of the need for control is self-evident; but an equally prominent theme is the fear of sexual failure. Was masturbation, after all, not an ultimate confession of male sexual inadequacy? Such tracts warned melodramatically of its demeaning and emasculating conse-quences. The confirmed onanist's genitals might, for exam-ple, "shrink and become withered, and cases have been known, in which, faded and entirely decayed, the little re-mains of them disappeared into the abdomen." Finally he would become impotent, unable to "penetrate the finest woman in the world." These threatened consequences, indi-cate, moreover, the emotional centrality of a particular indi-vidual's consciousness of male–female orientation. Thus warnings against the consequences of prolonged masturbation tended to incorporate personality traits associated with the female role stereotype. "All the intellectual faculties are weakened. The man becomes a coward; sighs and weeps like a hysterical woman. He loses all decision and dignity of character."[36] The intonation of such symptom catalogues assumes a ritual character and to some individuals presumably an expiatory one. The ideological emphasis on secret vice and its consequences served, that is, not only to exacerbate guilt in those seeking a plausible structure in which to place their need to feel such guilt, but as well to ritually express and thus perhaps allay a subconscious ambivalence in regard to masculine identification. Only the transcendent categories of Christian commitment could serve as an adequate counter to the reality of such behavioral demands. Thus the need to impart the intensity of millennial zeal to that ritual of self-denial which underwrote the social logic of the Christian Gentleman.

Significantly, the masturbator's alleged characteristics also served to project the vision of a figure emotionally and socially isolated: "They drivel away their existence on the outskirts of society: . . . they are at once a dead weight, a sluggish, inert mass in the paths of this busy, blustering life, having neither the will nor the capacity to take a part in the general matters of life." The demand for economic achievement, in other words, served in synergistic parallel with that for sexual achievement; and just as many men were not prepared to live in terms of the ideals demanded by the masculine ethos, so many were uncomfortable with those characteristics which tended in reality to make the self-made man.[37]

Admonitions proscribing female masturbation are, not surprisingly, quite different in content. Perhaps most obviously, disease sanctions varied in emphasis; failure or inadequacy in childbearing played an extraordinarily prominent role, though cancer, insanity and tuberculosis were also frequently cited consequences of female addiction to "solitary abuse."[38] Even more significantly, male authors express a pervasive disquiet in the presence of female sexuality. A central issue, of course, is still control, but in this context it is not self-control, but control of women's sexuality.[39] Masturbation is, as a few of our 20th-century contemporaries have argued, the ultimate in female autonomy; to mid-19th-century physicians, perhaps not coincidentally, it threatened to result either in frigidity or nymphomania—both modalites through which the husband might be humiliated (either in reality or fantasy).[40] Evidence indicating male anxieties in regard to female sexuality are as old as history itself and have attracted an elaborate, if dissonant, body of discussion: whatever metapsychological interpretation one places upon this phenomenon, its existence seems undeniable. And it is hardly surprising that in the 19th century, when gender roles were particularly rigid and polarized, when social change may be presumed to have created structural strain such roles that the ideological sanctions which helped define and enforce gender roles should have been intoned with particular vehemence. And it is, as a matter of fact, no difficult matter to locate a goup of mid-and-late-19th-century authorities on sexuality whose moral admonitions would document a monolithic antisexuality.[41]

It was, such zealots charged, the individual physician's moral responsibility to denounce casual and "excessive" marital sex. "All excess in that direction he will discountenance. . . . Unmastered importunity and too submissive an affection must be met by separate beds, by uncommunicating rooms, and if need be, by strong expostulation."[42] Significantly, all emphasized the need for limiting, and ideally for absolutely eschewing, all sexual activity during pregnancy and lactation. William Alcott, for example, warned that intercourse during gestation was particularly dangerous, especially if the mother should experience orgasm. "The nervous orgasm," he explained, "is too much for the young germ."[43] Procreation was the purpose of sexual intercourse; once the child had been conceived, every energy should be bent toward nurturing the young life. The male child's oedipal anxieties and fear of female sexuality would appear to be thus neatly expressed in Alcott's intellectual ideogram—the mother dramatically betraying the child within her in succumbing to the father's sexuality.

The specific emphases and emotional tone of these authors fall into a pattern so consistent that one is tempted to suggest a common psychic function for their ideological commitment. All, for example, tended to deny the intensity of female sexual needs; all tended to see sexual relationships as normally exploitive; all tended to identify woman with a higher moral calling. This strong identification with woman—assuming that she exhibited the appropriate passive, asexual and nurturant qualities—suggests not only the possible roots of the author's own needs, but the ways in which the several dimensions of behavior had come to be seen as rigidly male or female. They suggest a family milieu in which power and autonomy, emotional loyalty, and identification were constantly—and in some cases dysfunctionally—defined in terms of either/or, father or mother, male or female. (A family pattern, it might be suggested, in which new economic functions and ecological realities had created new patterns of emotional identification.) These writers consistently associated woman's sexual innocence with her maternal function: Dio Lewis, a popular advocate of temperance and health reform "liked," for example, "to think that the strong passion of my mother was the maternal." Men, Lewis continued, "can hardly understand the childlike innocence in which the pure woman considers this whole class of subjects." [44]

Beginning with the second third of the 19th century, moreover, a new sanction became increasingly—and I feel revealingly—plausible; that of the primacy of the mother in determining heredity and the need, therefore, to grant her dominion in the structuring of sexual relations. "DESTINY

IS DETERMINED BY ORGANIZATION," as abolitionist Henry C. Wright put it, "ORGANIZATION IS DETERMINED BY MATERNAL CONDITIONS."[45]

We have become accustomed to thinking of such formulae as in some sense ultimately dysfunctional; we assume as well that such ideological sets may have encouraged aggression or other inappropriate—deflected—modes of response. Yet, this is at best a partialistic way of approaching a most complex problem; for such generalizations are based not only on a transparently monolithic view of actual behavior patterns, but upon an equally schematic view of human psychodynamics. In the first place, many Americans simply paid no attention to these pious injunctions.[46] Some men ignored them at no particular psychic cost, others only at great cost. But to others, it may be argued, these seemingly unreal and absolutely dysfunctional views were functional indeed. For some men at least, the glorification of denial, with its transcendent justification in the categories of evangelical Christianity, could well have served as an ideological defense against the ever present demands of the masculine ethos, demands which some men at least could not meet (demands, moreover, in conflict with other social norms and values).

In Victorian England and America, moreover, the repression of sexuality could mean security, the ability to predict economic and social reality—in short, autonomy and social respectability. In a period when the urban lower and lower-middle classes had few enough areas for the establishment of ego function, the very process of deferring pleasure—with its ideological sanction in the evangelical world-view and social sanction in its organic relationship to status definition—provided one mode through which individuals of marginal social status might begin to find security and dignity.[47] Others, as I have suggested, incapable for individual reasons of living an assertive sexual life, could find in this ideology of denial a sanction for their particular disability. Hardly ideal perhaps, but any option is better than none, and in terms of social reality the uncontrolled expression of sexuality was—and presumably is—hardly an option consistent with ego development in many individuals. In terms of individual psychodynamics (since members of a particular generation fall into varied categories of potential behavior) it is not clear that all, or even most, Americans would have found the freedom to act out some fundamental sexual need a healing ordinance. Even in the self-consciously liberated 1970s, when the expression of sexuality is sometimes seen as a moral imperative, we seem not to have produced a generation of psychically fulfilled and sexually adequate citizens.

American society in the past century offered, in other words, a variety of behavioral options in the area of sexuality. And if some individuals suffered as a result of the conflict implied by the emotional inconsistencies embodied in these options, other Americans presumably benefited from the availability of varied behavioral options. Let me be a bit more specific. For some individuals, the expression of aggressive sexuality would have an important relationship to ego function generally; those males, that is, able to live out the imperatives of the masculine ethos would find in this virility a source of strength generalizable to other areas of personality development. (Some women, similarly, could find achievement within the traditional role of nurturant wife and mother; others would find only tension and ambiguity.) To certain other American men, internalization of the pieties implicit in the Christian Gentleman ideal (combined with a measure of worldly success) provided a viable framework for personality adjustment, despite a stressful ambivalence in regard to the imperatives of the masculine ethos. For still other men, of course, neither of these options provided usable solutions; indeed, the particular neurotic needs of some could well have found an ideal focus in the very structure of ambiguity which so characterized available gender roles. One might argue that it was not so much repression as such which characterized Victorian sexuality, but rather a peculiar and in some ways irreconcilable conflict between the imperatives of the Masculine Achiever and the Christian Gentleman. Few males were completely immune from the emotional reality of both.

Woman had also to create an appropriate emotional balance between two conflicting roles; she could retreat to passivity and purity (often in the form of maternity) and reject the male's proffered sexuality, but only at the expense of failing within the even more traditional role of female as giving and nurturant; for true nurturance implied sexual warmth and availability.

These gender roles must be understood, moreover, as a basic variable in the emotional structuring of particular marriages. The need of the male to achieve sexually, to act out his frustrations and insecurities in the form of aggressive sexuality in conjunction with the female's socially legitimate "spirituality" provided the wife with a natural emotional leverage. The power to reject was the power to control—and one of the few avenues to such power and autonomy available to women within the Victorian family. It was, as well, a power now sanctioned in the newly forged categories of the female-oriented evangelical view of sexuality. Woman's characteristically ambivalent sexual role must, that is, have helped structure—if not indeed occasion—intramarital conflict. Both husband and wife were in this sense prisoners of the same ritual pattern.

Sexual adjustment within the urban middle-class family would, moreover, naturally reflect any stress peculiar to the changing social environment of mid-19th-century America. Economic or career tensions affecting the husband, role anxieties in the wife would all have had to find some expression if not resolution in the marriage bed, that potential context of reassurance or rejection. Such realities can be illustrated concretely by the conflict surrounding birth control, a demographic fact for many 19th-century urban families. One dimension of family decisions to practice birth control (or abortion) was economic. But this was only one aspect of an inevitably complex and ambiguous situation. Many husbands, for example, must have experienced deep ambivalence, desiring on the one hand, a small family to ease economic burdens, yet regretting the loss of male status symbolized by abundant fatherhood—not to mention the control of his wife implied by the existence of numerous children. Whether decisions to limit family size actually affected sexual intercourse per se depended, of course, on the means employed, the confidence of the woman in such means, and the personality needs of husband and wife.[48]

There is another aspect of 19th-century sexual prescriptions which I have, thus far, avoided discussing systematically. This is the ideological function of these formulae, their relationship, that is, to the maintenance of a particular social order. In examining the ideological content of the scientific intonations and disease sanctions we have been describing, there are some obvious points of structural reference. Most apparent is the emotional centrality of a fundamental expository metaphor, one which might be called "mercantilist." The body is visualized in this metaphor as a closed energy system, one which could be either weakened through the discharge of energy or strengthened through its prudent husbanding.

These omnipresent images of control and physiological penury lend credibility to interpretations which emphasize the parallelism between those modes of behavior implied by the needs of a developing capitalism and the rationalization and ordering of sexual energies to this purpose. "The gospel of continence," in the words of Peter Cominos, the most forthright recent advocate of this position, "reveals its meaning when it is related to the dynamic quality inherent in the structure and functioning of the Respectable Economic System, the compulsion to accumulate and reinvest capital."[49] This ideology of sexual penury would thus be as functional to the Western European bourgeoisie as its equivalents in those non-Western cultures where ecological realities demand that reproduction be curtailed: one would normally expect in such a culture to find a well-articulated ideology of taboo, ritual, mythic constructs, and disease sanctions enforcing and legitimating the logic of sexual frugality.

All well, and possibly even good. But the interpretive problem is a good deal more complex. We are dealing with a world of ideology and behavior more fragmented, more obviously inconsistent than that characteristic of most traditional cultures. The attempt, moreover, to associate repression of sexuality with the creation of an ethos appropriate to capitalism presents grave chronological problems. Why, for example, should mid-19th-century see the efflorescence of this doctrine? Efforts by the new bourgeoisie to forge an appropriate life-style had been in process since at least the 16th century: one must, that is, in attempting to employ this line of argument, relate this peculiarly repressive ideology not simply to "capitalism," but with a particular stage in its development—the crystallization of industrialism and its structural implications in the shape of urbanization, bureaucratization, a declining birth rate and the like. Even so, the connection between these themes and images and the supposed needs of this society cannot simply be assumed. Thus, for example, similar ideas concerning the drain of sexual expenditure upon bodily health—especially in the case of semen—has a long and astonishingly mixed cultural history; Taoism, for example, in which such ideas figured prominently, would seem at first glance—and perhaps the second as well—to have little in common with the social and intellectual world of 19th-century England and America.

The preceding pages have attempted to suggest *one* possible perspective through which to view sexuality as it was perceived and acted out by 19th-century Americans: the effect of two basic social roles, class and gender, in shaping sexual behavior. Using expressions of ideology as indices to more fundamental change, I have sought primarily to describe and then to suggest possible forms of interaction, and thus areas for further investigation. What, for example, was the relationship between evangelicalism and the peculiarly structured role characteristics we have described? What were the effects of an urban bureaucratized life upon the emotional structure of the family? There are no simple answers to such profound questions, and only recently have historians become aware that these were, indeed, questions. In point of fact, we do not now possess a generally agreed upon model appropriate to explaining the precise relationships between structural change—economic, demographic and techno logical—and the micro-system of the family and the individual.

There is, on the other hand, a plausible framework in which to place the intellectual and emotional phenomena we have sought to describe. The pervasive emphasis upon control, the temporal correlation between these repressive formulae and a parallel commitment to the transcending reassurance of evangelical religion can be seen as acculturation phenomena—mechanisms facilitating adjustment to a new social discipline.

Yet even were this interpretation "correct"—in the limited sense that so general a formulation can be termed correct—it must remain schematic, useful only in a heuristic sense. Almost every element in this complex, and largely implicit, model remains still to be explored, to be made explicit.[50] The present paper has sought, in a thus necessarily tentative way, to contribute to this discussion, to examine some of the ways in which available role prescriptions may have functioned in the particular configuration of emotional and structural reality which faced Americans in the latter half of the 19th century.

I have sought, moreover, to avoid the use of certain now-traditional psychodynamic categories, especially the tendency to interpret sexual behavior in terms of a value laden and one-dimensional polarity of expression versus repression. I have assumed, on the contrary, that individuals vary, that most manage somehow to grow and differentiate, and that the social and sexual values of the mid-and-late 19th century were probably no more inimical to human potential than those of any other period. Or that if they were, it remains still to be demonstrated. Granting that certain Victorian attitudes toward sexuality and the types of ideal behavior these ideas legitimated may have imposed costs—to particular individuals perhaps tragic and irreparable costs—does not compromise the essential logic of this position.

NOTES

[1]Among the more important, and characteristically diverse, recent attempts to deal with this general problem are: Peter T. Cominos, "Late-Victorian Sexual Respectability and the Social System," *International Review of Social History*, 8 (1963), 18–48, 216–50; Steven Marcus, *The Other Victorians. A Study of Sexuality and Pornography in Mid-Nineteenth-Century England* (New York: Basic Books, 1966); Stephen Nissenbaum, "Careful Love: Sylvester Graham and the Emergence of Victorian Sexual Theory in America, 1830–1840," Diss. University of Wisconsin 1968; Graham Barker-Benfield, "The Horrors of the Half Known Life: Aspects of the Exploitation of Women by Men," Diss. University of California, Los Angeles, 1968; Nathan G. Hale Jr., "American 'Civilized' Morality, 1870–1912," in *Freud and the Americans. The Beginnings of Psychoanalysis in the United States, 1876–1917* (New York: Oxford Univ. Press, 1971), pp. 24–46; David M. Kennedy, "The Nineteenth-Century Heritage: The Family, Feminism, and Sex," in *Birth Control in America. The Career of Margaret Sanger* (New Haven: Yale Univ. Press, 1970), pp. 36–71. I have been particularly influenced by the work and suggestions of my wife, Carroll Smith-Rosenberg, who has shared research and ideas at every stage in the gestation of this paper. The following pages will emphasize male attitudes and problems; she is completing a parallel essay on female sexuality in 19th century America. Her emphasis on gender role and role conflict as an

appropriate analytic mode has been particularly important to me. See, for example, her articles, "Beauty, the Beast and the Militant Woman: A Case Study in Sex Roles and Social Stress in Jacksonian America," *American Quarterly*, 22 (1971), 562–84; "The Hysterical Woman: Sex Roles and Role Conflict in 19th Century America," *Social Research*, 39 (1972), 652–78; C.S. and Charles E. Rosenberg, "The New Woman and the Troubled Man: Medical and Biological Views of Woman's Role in Nineteenth-Century America," *Journal of American History* (Sept. 1973).

[2]We have come to think is such terms as result of our tendency to impose individual psychodynamic models upon a total culture, thus allowing the convenient "diagnoses" of its modal ills. For an early criticism of this position, see Erwin H. Ackerknecht, "Psychopathology, Primitive Medicine and Primitive Culture," *Bulletin of the History of Medicine*, 14 (1943), 30–67, reprinted in Ackerknecht, *Medicine and Ethnology Selected Essays* (Baltimore: Johns Hopkins Press, 1971).

[3]An important question, both for historical method on the one hand and psychiatric theory on the other, relates to whether such discontinuities between the content of a particular ideological set and certain irreducible human needs can be explicitly and absolutely pathogenic, or whether it is simply the immediate occasion for conflict in individuals otherwise predisposed. At the moment, analysis in this area hinges inevitably on questions of value.

[4]The strategy of examining role options in terms of their emotional meaning to the individuals who choose to embrace them, is, of course, not limited to sex and gender roles. It is even more easily applied to certain adult roles; the present author, for example, recently completed a collective biographical examination of a number of American scientists who studied in Germany in the mid-19th century in an effort to explain the emotional logic which led these men to embrace so "deviant" a social role. Charles Rosenberg, "Science and Social Values in Nineteenth-Century America. A Case Study of the Growth of Scientific Instutitions," in Everett Mendelsohn and Arnold Thackray, eds. *Science and Values*, (in press).

[5]The phrase is from a review by Robert Ackerman in *Victorian Studies*, 14 (1970), 108.

[6]Many of these materials are rare. I have used the excellent collections at the National Library of Medicine, Bethesda, College of Physicians of Philadelphia, and the Countway Library of Medicine, Boston and would like to thank John B. Blake. L.M. Holloway and Richard Wolfe of these institutions for their aid and courtesy. There is no adequate bibliographical

guide to such writings, with the exception of the appropriate subject categories in the *Index-Catalogue of the Library of the Surgeon-General's Office* (Washington: G.P.O., 1879–). The bibliographies in Nissenbaum, "Careful Love," and Norman Himes, *Medical History of Contraception* (Baltimore: Williams & Wilkins, 1936), provide valuable supplementary materials.

[7]As personified in the career of Anthony Comstock most conspicuously and in the social purity movement more generally. For an important description of this moral reform, see David J. Pivar, "The New Abolitionism: The Quest for Social Purity. 1876–1900," Diss. University of Pennsylvania 1965.

[8]A recent student has emphasized the 18th century origin of this subgenre, but the mid-19th century saw a proliferation of such tracts and pamphlets so distinct as to constitute a more than quantitative change. Robert H. MacDonald, "The Frightful Consequences of Onanism: Notes on the History of a Delusion," *Journal of the History of Ideas*, 28 (1967), 423–31. S.A. Tissot's (1728–97) widely read and influential tract on onanism was, significantly, not reprinted in the United States until 1832, almost a half century after its original publication. The anonymous English pamphlet "Onania" was, so far as is known, reprinted only once (1724) before 1820 and apparently in a relatively small edition, since a single copy only is known to survive. See entry 1435, Robert B. Austin, *Early American Medical Imprints. . . . 1668–1820* (Washington, D.C.: G.P.O., 1961), p. 152. English books dealing with masturbation, however, almost certainly did circulate in the early national period. Probably the most widely read was Samuel Solomon's *A Guide to Health; Or, Advice to Both Sexes, in Nervous and Consumptive Complaints . . .* (n.p., n.d.). The imprints on this famous quackish tract are all deliberately vague, but one copy at the Countway Library of medicine is inscribed with the date 1804 in a contemporary hand. In regard to Solomon, see also R.S.H. Foster to James Jackson, Sept. 21, 1838, Jackson Papers, Countway Library.

[9]As in parallel fashion, the rationalistic and pragmatic temperance reform of the late 18th century had been metamorphosed in the same period into an uncompromising crusade for teetotalism. The connection of both instances of activist—even punitive—moralism with the pietistic energies of the Second Great Awakening which immediately preceded it seems clear enough, but difficult to specify in terms of precise relationships. The tendency toward such repressiveness was nowhere as clearly marked during the years of the Second Great Awakening itself. One possible explanation for the tone of intrusive moralism which marked the generations after the 1830s centers on the possibility that childhood

socialization was altered during the years of the Awakening so as to create a peculiar collective experience for many of those brought up in these years, and later to become prominent in social and moral reform movements. Certainly the attitude toward childhood sexuality might, for example, be seen in this content: such an explanation would also help explain the sudden concern with masturbation in mid-century and succeeding decades. But such suggestions are, of course, speculative; that the cooling ardors of pietism were succeeded by a more rigid and formal moralism is, however, unquestionable.

[10]John Ellis, *Marriage and its Violations. Licentiousness and Vice* (New York: The author, 1860), p. 21. Cf. Nissenbaum, "Careful Love," p. 4.

[11]Three years might thus intervene between conception and weaning, a period during which no sexual intercourse was to be tolerated. This taboo is relatively common in non-Western cultures and its latent function is generally presumed to be that of population control. Impressionistic evidence indicates that few mid-19th century Americans obeyed this injunction; in those who urged it most strongly, its function must be sought in the area of individual psychodynamics.

[12]Their tone of conscious manipulativeness indicates that at least some individuals in the culture did not share these phobic attitudes.

[13]John Fondey, *A Brief and Intelligible View of the Nature, Origin and Cure of Tubercular or Scrofulous Disease* . . . (Philadelphia: W.C.&J. Neff, 1860), p. 45.

[14]Parents were warned again and again that it was their responsibility to "repress the premature development of the passions," "natural instincts" though they may have been. W.S. Chipley, *A Warning to Fathers, Teachers and Young Men, in Relation to a Fruitful Cause of Insanity* . . . (Louisville, KY.: L.A. Civill & Wood, 1861), pp. 169, 174.

[15]These phrases, typical of many scores of others, are from Walter Preston, *The Sufferer's Manual. A Book of Advice and Instruction for Young Men* . . . (Chicago: n.p., 1879), p. 37; William Capp, *The Daughter Her Health, Education and Wedlock Homely Suggestions for Mothers and Daughers* (Philadelphia: F.A. Davis, 1891, p. 72.

[16]*An Hour's Conference with Fathers and Sons, in Relation to a Common and Fatal Indulgence of Youth* (Boston: Whipple & Damrell, 1840), p. 26; Elizabeth Blackwell, *Counsel to Parents on the Moral Education of their Children* (New York: Brentano's, 1880), pp. 94–95. Cf. L.N. Fowler, *The Princi-*

ples of Phrenology and Physiology Applied to Man's Social Relations (Boston: L.N.&O. Fowler, 1842), p. 18.

[17]Ely Van De Warker, "A Gynecological Study of the Oneida Community," Rep. from *American Journal of Obstetrics*, 17(1884), 11.

[18]As hereditarian ideas became increasingly plausible in the second half of the century, they were naturally made to underwrite this argument; the sanction of individual sin was reinforced by that of potential race degeneration.

[19]James Ashton, *The Book of Nature; Containing Information for Young People who think of Getting Married* (New York: Wallis & Ashton, 1861), p. 45; Martin, *The Human Body*, 2nd ed., rev. (New York: Holt, 1881), appendix, pp. 20–21.

[20]Though physicians tried to scout the idea throughout the century, it seems, significantly, to have had a tenacious hold on the popular mind. Cf. Alice Stockham, *Tokology, A Book for Every Woman* (Chicago: Sanitary, 1887), p. 326; Frederick Hollick, *The Marriage Guide, or Natural History of Generation* . . . (New York: T.W. Strong, c. 1860), p. 339; T.S. Verdi, *Maternity. A Popular Treatise for Young Wives and Mothers* (New York: J.B. Ford, 1870), p. 25; M.K. Hard, *Woman's Medical Guide* (Mt Vernon, Ohio: W.H. Cochran, 1848), p. 51.

[21]*Causation, Course, and Treatment of Reflex Insanity in Woman* (Boston: Lee & Shepard, 1871), pp. 211–12; Robert T. Wakely, *Woman and her Secret Passions* (New York: n.p., c. 1846), p. 92; M. Larmont, *Medical Adviser and Marriage Guide* . . . (New York: E. Warner, 1861), pp. 320–22.

[22]M. L. Holbrook, *Parturition without Pain: A Code of Directions for Escaping from the Primal Curse* (New York: M. L. Holbrook, 1882), p. 36.

[23]William Alcott, for example, was never able to escape the ambiguity inherent in these contradictory orientations. Sex itself he always praised as a gift of God, a necessity for the preservation of the species, and sexual vigor he admired as a sign of health. Thus the emotional logic inherent in his plaintive distinction between sexual "power," which he could only characterize as healthy and admirable, and "excitability," which he saw as "pathological," as tainted by loss of control. Cf. Charles E. Rosenberg, Introduction, Alcott, *Physiology of Marriage* (1866; rpt. New York: Arno, 1972).

[24]A.E. Newton, *The Better Way: An Appeal to Men in Behalf of Human Culture through Wiser Parentage* (New York: M.L. Holbrook, 1890), p. 29.

[25]Henry N. Guernsey, *Plain Talks on Avoided Subjects* (Philadelphia: F.A. Davis, 1899), p. 25.

[26]The reality of masculine expectation was unavoidable; William Acton, for example, probably the most widely quoted English advocate of a chaste sex life, warned that only a careful moral indoctrination in secondary schools could avert the well nigh universal social pressure on young men to experiment sexually. "Supported by such a public opinion [the young man] need not blush when tempted or jeered by the licentious. Innocence, or even ignorance of vice, will no longer be a dishonor or a jest . . ." cited in Cominos, "Late-Victorian Respectability," p. 40. Acton and like-thinking Americans frequently made this point.

[27]Paul Paquin, *The Supreme Passions of Man; Or the Origin, Causes, and Tendencies of the Passions of the Flesh* (Battle Creek, Mich.: Little Blue Book, 1891), p. 71; Cf. Elizabeth Blackwell, *The Human Elements in Sex . . .* 3rd ed. (London: J.&A. Churchill, 1884), p. 28.

[28]S.R. Wells, *Wedlock, Or the Right Relations of the Sexes . . .* (New York. The author, 1869), p. 44.

[29]Significantly, even in writers most explicitly evangelical in their orientation, purely religious arguments were employed infrequently and only in an ancillary capacity; the way in which scientific in form, and dependent for their legitimacy upon the status of scientific knowledge, dominate debate even in this culturally sensitive area implies a great deal about the progress of secularization in 19th-century America. For a more explicit discussion of this problem, see C.E. Rosenberg, "Science and American Social Thought," in David Van Tassel & Michael Hall, eds., *Science and American Society* (Homewood, Ill.: Dorsey, 1966), pp. 135–62.

[30]"A Grave Social Problem," *British Medical Journal*, 1 (Jan. 14, 1882), 56.

[31]A few radicals did assume an openly critical stance; all talk of absolutely interdicting adolescent sexuality and limiting it severely in marriage was, in the words of one such author, mere "child's talk." For nature, he explained, "is a tyrant"; the sexual impulse could never be suppressed completely. Misguided attempts to reach this end would result inevitably in mental and physical illness. J. Soule, *Science of Reproduction and Reproductive Control. The Necessity of some Abstaining from Having Children—The Duty of All to Limit their Families According to their Circumstances Demonstrated* (n.p., c. 1856), pp. 21, 32–34.

[32]Sydney Elliot, *Aedology. A Treatise on Generative Life*, rev. ed. (New

York: St. Clair, 1892), p. 181; C.A. Greene, *Build Well. The Basis of Individual, Home and National Elevation . . .* Boston: Lothrop, c. 1885), pp. 149–50; Caroline Latimer, *Girl and Woman. Book for Mothers and Daughters* (New York: D. Appleton, 1910), p. 141.

[33]This discussion is not, of course, meant to imply that the sexual life of the "lower orders" in mid-19th century was necessarily less repressed than that of the would-be members of the middle class. Contemporary data would indicate that lower-class membership need not imply greater freedom of expression in matters sexual. Cf. Lee Rainwater, *And the Poor Get Children* (Chicago: Quadrangle, 1960).

[34]Alice Stockham, *Karezza. Ethics of Marriage* (Chicago: Alice B. Stockham, 1896), p. 77.

[35]Male and female, they seemed to sense, were serving as ever more emotionally charged polarities, organizing about themselves an increasingly inclusive assortment of personality traits and behaviors. Every aspect of high culture, even Christianity itself, was shaped by this polarization. "Man," as one mid-century feminist put it, "must be regenerated by true and deep religious experiences. (Religion is feminine), or by the love and influence of Woman. . . ." Eliza Farnham, *Woman and her Era* (New York: A.J. Davis, 1864), 11:44.

[36]The first quotation is from John B. Newman, *The Philosophy of Generation. . . .* (New York: John C. Wells, 1849), p. 63, the phrase concerning impotence from Drs. Jordan and Beck, *Happiness or Misery? Being Four Lectures on the Functions and Disorders of the Nervous System and Reproductive Organs* (New York: Barton & Son, c. 1861), p. 18, the final quotation from R.J. Culverwell, *Self Preservation, Manhood, Causes of its Premature Decline. . . .* (New York: n.p., [1830]), p. 28. (The last passage, significantly, is also to be found—plagiarized—in Wesley Grindle, *New Medical Revelations, Being a Popular Work on the Reproductive System, Its Debility and Diseases* (Philadelphia: n.p., 1857), p. 90. Emphasis on the "mortification" of the impotent groom on his wedding-night was also standard. Cf. A.H. Hayes, *The Science of Life; Or Self-Preservation. . . .* (Boston: Peabody Medical Institute, c. 1868), pp. 180–81.

[37]Jordan & Beck, *Happiness or Misery?*, p. 39. A recent psychiatric historian has suggested that the archetypical symptoms of 19th-century masturbatory insanity resemble those of the schizoid personality. If true in particular cases, this interpretation would not be inconsistent with the argument we have tried to suggest. E.H. Hare, "Masturbatory Insanity: The History of an Idea," *Journal of Mental Science*, 108 (1962), 9. A word of

caution: despite our tendency to see this masturbation literature as characteristic of Anglo-Saxon Protestantism, the three most quoted authorities in the late 1830s and 40s were French-speaking: S.A. Tissot, Leopold Deslandes and C.F. Lallemand.

[38]This sanction illustrates clearly a characteristic 19th-century emotional polarity, that between sexuality and maternity. It should also be noted that although virtually all 19th-century writers on masturbation noted that its devotees included females as well as males, this generally conceded observation never seemed to suggest the naturalness of sexuality in women.

[39]A few, clearly atypical, medical authors were so dominated by particular anxieties that their formulations starkly underline emotional themes normally presented in terms more indirect and ambivalent. A few, for example, warned that artifical phalli employed by female masturbators would create needs which no husband could ever satisfy. J. DuBois, *Marriage Physiologically Considered*. 2nd ed. (New York: Printed for the Booksellers, 1839), pp. 26–27. (One Scotch physician even suggested the use of a kind of chastity belt to guard against this possibility. John Moodie, *A Medical Treatise: with Principles and Observations, to Preserve Chastity and Morality* [Edinburgh: Stevenson, 1848]). A related procedure was that of clitoridectomy as a radical cure for hysteria, nymphomania and allied complaints. Cf. John Duffy, "Masturbation and Clitoridectomy. A Nineteenth-Century View," *Journal of the American Medical Association*, 186 (Oct. 19, 1963), 246–48; Guy Nichol. "The Clitoris Martyr," *World Medicine* (May 6, 1969), 59–65; Isaac Baker Brown, *On the Curability of Certain Forms of Insanity, Epilepsy, Catalepsy, and Hysteria in Females* (London: Robert Hardwicke, 1866). This procedure was never widely practiced. Isaac Baker Brown, the London gynecologist who sought to popularize clitoridectomy, enjoyed little success and was, indeed, formally condemned by the Obstetrical Society of London as a result of his enthusiasm.

[40]For representative examples of the persistence of such anxieties, see C.S. Eldridge, *Self-Enervation Its Consequences and Treatment* (Chicago: C.S. Halsey, 1869), pp. 15–17, 25; J. E. Ralph, *Senunalia*. . . . (New York: Warner, 1865), p. 81; E. Becklard, *Physiological Mysteries and Revelation, in Love, Courtship, and Marriage* (New York: Holland & Glover, 1844), pp. 100–1; Joseph W. Howe, *Excessive Venery, Masturbation and Continence* . . . (New York: Bermingham, 1883), p. 41. Thomas L. Nichols, *Esoteric Anthropology* . . . (London: Nichols, n.d.), p. 84.

[41]The English physician William Acton was probably the best known among such evangelically oriented authors (Steven Marcus' *Other Victo-*

rians contains a chapter analyzing Acton's writings. Marcus is, however, rather arbitrary, in his interpretations.) In the United States, such enthusiasts as John Cowan, Dio Lewis, and, to an extent, William Alcott, exemplify the position of those similarly fearful of the perils implicit in the expression of sexuality.

[42]W. Goodell, *Lessons in Gynecology* (Philadelphia: D.G. Brinton, 1879), p. 366.

[43]Alcott, *Physiology of Marriage*, p. 153.

[44]Dio Lewis, *Chastity; Or, Our Secret Sins* (New York: Fowler & Wells, 1894 c. 1874), pp. 117, 13.

[45]Henry C. Wright, *The Empire of the Mother over the Character and Destiny of the Race*, 2nd ed. (Boston: Bela Marsh, 1866), p. 67.

[46]One thinks of the Americans who consumed the oceans of whiskey and brandy distilled in 19th-century America despite the zealous admonitions of temperace advocates.

[47]In what is probably the strongest passage in Steven Marcus' *Other Victorians*, the author underlines the tragedy inherent in the need of the urban poor to repress sexuality as prerequisite to the achievement of a minimum human dignity (pp. 147–50).

[48]For additional discussion of the relationship between role conflict and birth control in mid-century, see Carroll Smith-Rosenberg and Charles Rosenberg, "The New Woman and Troubled Man."

[49]Cominos, "Late-Victorian Sexual Respectability," p. 216.

[50]We must, for example, define the appropriate demographic and economic realities—and this implies the evaluation of such factors as change in occupation and family size, age at first marriage and patterns of internal migration. The precise defintion of such factors as change in occupation and family size, age at first marriage and patterns of internal migration. The precise defintion of such parameters must precede any final evaluation of the relationship between these structural realities and the ideological formulations which help shape the formal and emotional perceptions of individuals in a particular generation.

chapter 9

The "Poor Man's Club":
Social Functions of the Urban Working-Class Saloon

by Jon M. Kingsdale

Despite the intimacy of contact between the sexes, they have often inhabited separate emotional and physical worlds. No part of the man's public world has been more visible than the corner saloon. As Jon Kingsdale indicates in the article reprinted here, working-class men in the late nineteenth and early twentieth centuries sought to escape from their wives and children in companionship with other men and with prostitutes. In saloons they sang about "A Flower from My Angel Mother's Grave" and harmonized to "A Boy's Best Friend is his Mother," a tuneful sentimentality toward motherhood quite consistent with their desire to socialize with other men.

As a distinct men's subculture, the saloon was to many Americans a symbol of wickedness. It was not simply that the antisaloon leagues, led by native-born middle-class men and women, were unable to tolerate European beer halls and foreign customs of social drinking. It was also that reformers, especially women's temperance advocates, attacked male prerogatives: The drunken husband was often seen as failing to provide for his wife and children. Whether his actual expenditure at the saloon imposed a real hardship on his wife and children or simply represented an accepted sexual division in social worlds is hard to say, even from the evidence Kingsdale presents. Nonetheless, it can be recognized that the saloon was more than a social institution within the working-class neighborhood: It was also a cultural symbol in the ongoing tensions between social groups and between the sexes.

Historical studies of the period 1890 to 1920 generally refer to the saloon in connection with urban machine politics or Temperance, yet often ignore the saloon's social and cultural functions. But an analysis of the urban saloon is important to an understanding of working-class social history in this period. Saloons seem to have exercised a significant influence upon the values and behavior of the urban working class; certainly they were central to the workingman's leisure-time activities. The saloon provided him a variety of services and played three significant roles in a growing urban industrial environment: it was a neighborhood center, an all-male establishment and a transmitter of working-class and immigrant cultures.

In the middle of the 19th century, as American's cities were experiencing the first shocks of industrialization and "new-stock" immigration, the saloon came to replace colonial taverns and corner grocers as the urban liquor dispensary, par excellence. The saloon became an increasingly popular institution: by 1897 licensed liquor dealers in the United States numbered over 215,000, and unlicensed "blind pigs" or "blind tigers" represented an estimated 50,000 additional outlets.[1] Most brewers—the brewing industry being highly competitive at the close of the 19th century—sponsored as many outlets as possible, as exclusive retailers of their own beer, thus saturating cities with saloons. In Chicago, for instance, saloons were as numerous as groceries, meat markets and dry goods stores counted together.[2] Cities without effective restrictions were deluged with saloons: in 1915 New York had over 10,000 licensed saloons, or one for every 515 persons; Chicago had one

"The 'Poor Man's Club': Social Functions of the Urban Working-Class Saloon" by Jon M. Kingsdale. Reprinted by permission of the author and the publisher from *American Quarterly* (published by the University of Pennsylvania), Vol. 25, December 1973, pp. 472–489.

The author wishes to thank Dr. Robert Sklar for both his criticisms and encouragement.

licensed saloon for every 335 residents; Houston had one for every 298 persons; San Francisco had a saloon for every 218 persons.[3] The skewed distribution of saloons within cities and the large number of unlicensed retailers meant that many an urban working-class district had at least one saloon for every 50 adult males (fifteen years of age and older). Reflecting both the growing popularity of saloons and a switch from distilled spirits to beer, alcoholic beverage consumption increased steadily after 1850. While consumption of distilled spirits fell by half, adult per capita consumption of beer rose from 2.7 gallons at mid-century to 29.53 gallons per year in the period 1911–15.[4]

Of the saloon's popularity there can be little doubt: in one day half the population of a city might visit its saloons. A survey of Chicago found that on an average day the number of saloon customers equaled half the city's total population.[5] In Boston, with a total population of less than half a million in 1895—including women and children, most of whom did not frequent saloons—a police count numbered 227,000 persons entering the city's saloons.[6] Many of those counted were suburban commuters not included in the city's population, as well as customers entering for a second or third time that day; nevertheless, considering the size of Boston's adult male population, the count is surprisingly high.

Part, but not all, of the saloon's attraction was alcoholic. Certainly the liquor was an integral and necessary element, as the failure of most temperance substitutes in America proved. But saloons did a great deal more than simply dispense liquor. The alcoholic "stimulation"—the neurological effects of alcohol are actually depressant, producing a diminution of inhibitions and thus a reduction in reserve and distance in social gatherings[7]—cannot readily be distinguished from the social aspects of the saloon. The bartender, as "host" in his saloon, knew as well as the middle-class hostess of today that alcohol is an excellent icebreaker. As Raymond Calkins concluded after an extensive survey, the saloon, with its absence of time limit and its stimulus to self-expression and fellowship, was a natural social center.[8]

Despite city ordinances regulating location and levying high license fees, it was relatively easy to open a saloon. With $200 to start, one could easily find a brewer willing to provide financial backing and find a location. The brewer paid the rent, the license fee, a bond if necessary, and supplied the fixtures and the beer. The saloon-keeper agreed to sell no other brand of beer and reimbursed his brewer by means of a special tax added on to the normal price of each barrel of beer. Four-fifths of Chicago's saloons were estimated to be under such an arrangement with brewers in 1907, as were 80 to 85 per cent of New York's saloons in 1908.[9]

Although an appealing and easily accessible occupation, saloon keeping was often an unprofitable business enterprise. The competition was tremendous; many saloons closed after only a few months in operation. In the lean years, 1897–1901, a third of Chicago's saloons closed down or sold out—in one and a half blocks of Chicago's 17th ward eighteen saloons opened and closed in as many months.[10] Some saloons flourished as fancy establishments or well-known hangouts for politicians, athletes and other notables. But many saloons failed, and of those which stayed on, most merely continued to do a steady quiet business with neighborhood regulars.

Urban saloons of the late 19th and early 20th centuries did not conform to a single pattern. Saloons varied greatly in appearance, atmosphere and character of the clientele they served. Yet a majority of urban saloons may be subsumed under a single prototypic description. Usually situated on a corner for maximum visibility, the typical workingman's saloon was readily recognizable by its swinging shuttered doors and wrought iron windows cluttered with potted ferns, posters and bottles of colored water. Inside was a counter running almost the length of the room, paralleled by

a brass footrail. The floor was covered with sawdust. Across
from the bar were perhaps a few tables and chairs backed up
by a piano, pool table or rear stalls. Behind the bar and over
an assortment of lemons, glasses and unopened magnums of
muscatel, port and champagne hung a large plate-glass mirror. The other walls would sport a number of murals, posters, photographs and brewer's advertisements. As common
as the plate-glass mirror was the presence of at least one
chromo reproduction of a disrobed siren reclining on a
couch. The posters and photographs were often of sports
heroes: about 1890 a picture of John L. Sullivan would have
been found in most saloons. A few men might be leaning
over the bar, clustered about the saloon-keeper—in his white
starched coat or vest, moustache and well-oiled hair; a few
more might be playing pool or sitting at tables talking over a
beer, reading or playing cards. Beer for five cents and whiskey for ten or fifteen were the staples. The whiskey was
drunk straight—to do otherwise would be considered
effeminate—followed by a chaser of water or milk to put out
the fire.

The typical workingman's saloon experienced rather
slow business through the day until about seven or eight
o'clock, except on weekends when it was generally crowded
from Saturday noon to early Monday morning. The morning
in most saloons began at about five or six o'clock and was
spent mostly in cleaning up and preparing the free lunch for
the noontime crowd and teamsters who would drop in
throughout the afternoon. But in the evenings things picked
up as workingmen gathered in saloons to enjoy each other's
company.

Though by far the most common, the working-class saloon described above was not the only type of urban saloon.
There were suburban beer gardens, downtown businessmen's saloons, and waterfront dives and barrelhouses
serving sailors, tramps, petty criminals and the very poor.
Jacob Riis, in *How the Other Half Lives*,[11] described the lowest

of the low in a New York tenement slum: in a dark clammy hovel were grouped ten or fifteen tramps and petty criminals seated on crates and broken chairs around a keg of stale beer. The dregs from used beer barrels lying out on the sidewalk awaiting the brewer's cart were drained off and doctored up to be served in old tomato cans to the less than distinguished clientele. But this was an extreme case. William Cole and Kellog Darland of the South End House in Boston described a typical waterfront dive as small, dirty and inhospitable.[12] It was lighted by unshaded flickering gas jets revealing a gaudy mirror, foul beer-soaked sawdust on the floor, and no tables, chairs or inviting free lunch to encourage patrons to linger at their ease.

At the other end of the spectrum, the business districts contained a large number of well-appointed saloons catering to professionals, businessmen and the middle and upper classes in general. Here the bars were of mahogany, the pictorial art of a better class, and some even had orchestras. These saloons were often used as meeting places for business purposes, especially by sales representatives and buyers who might complete a transaction over a beer in an oak table alcove. In the suburbs could be found old homes of solid decor, converted to roadhouses for the use of travelers and suburban residents. Also in the suburbs as well as in town were German-model beer gardens providing good food and open spaces in which to relax while listening to a symphony orchestra.

With this perspective in mind, let us turn to an analysis of the social functions of the working-class urban saloon. The workingman's saloon was a leisure-time institution playing a large part in the social, political, even the economic, aspects of his life. It performed a variety of functions, major and minor: furnishing the cities' only public toilets, providing teamsters with watering troughs, cashing checks and lending money to customers, in addition to serving as the political and recreational focus of the workingman.

In its most encompassing function the saloon served many workingmen as a second home. If the middle-class male retired to his living room after dinner to relax, the workingman retired to the corner saloon to meet his friends, relax and maybe play a game of cards or billiards. Many workingmen thought of and treated the corner saloon as their own private club rather than as a public institution. They used it as a mailing address; leaving and picking up messages, and meeting friends there; depositing money with, or borrowing from the saloon-keeper. Workingmen played cards, musical instruments and games, ate, sang and even slept there. Even today, "home territory" bars are characterized by a familiarity among patrons and hostility or suspicion toward newcomers.[13]

For slum residents, especially in immigrant ghetto and tenement districts, the neighboring saloons were inevitably more attractive than their own overcrowded, dirty, noisy, ugly, poorly lighted and ventilated flats. For many immigrants their new homes in America were merely places to sleep and eat—life moved out of the flats into the streets and saloons.[14] Large numbers of lodging-house boarders adopted saloons as surrogate homes, their own quarters being cramped, filthy and dull.[15] Compared to cheap boarding houses that slept men dormitory style in long rows of bunks, the corner saloon was by far the more hospitable place to spend the evenings. Some saloon habitués even slept there—a place on the floor at night cost five cents.

Saloons also functioned as food suppliers. The "free lunch" fed thousands of men in each city. There was usually something on hand in saloons to munch on at any time, but from about eleven o'clock in the morning to three in the afternoon a special buffet lunch was served free to customers—who were, of course, expected to buy at least one beer. If a saloon did not serve a free lunch it often served a "businessman's lunch," which for ten to twenty-five cents was better than most restaurants could offer. The accent in the free lunch was on salty and spiced foods to provoke thirst, but for five cents the workingman got a better lunch than most ten cent restaurants served, plus a beer and more attractive surroundings in which to enjoy it. Saloons could afford the free lunch because the brewer supplied the food at cost, having purchased it cheaply in quantity.

Saloons that sold lunches and some large saloons that offered free lunches provided quite a feast. One saloon in the 17th ward of Chicago, a working-class district, offered in its free lunch a choice of frankfurters, clams, egg sandwiches, potatoes, vegetables, cheeses, bread, and several varieties of hot and cold meats. Employing five men at the lunch counter, it gave away between thirty and forty dollars' worth of food a day: 150 to 200 pounds of meat, 1 to 2 bushels of potatoes, 50 loaves of bread, 35 pounds of beans, 10 dozen ears of corn and $2 worth of other vegetables.[16] This was not the typical fare in a workingman's saloon, but even the average free lunch in an Eastern city—the free lunches in the East were usually less generous than those of the West and South, due perhaps to higher food prices and less competition among saloons of the East—was sufficient for noontime needs. In Boston, New York, Philadelphia or Baltimore a typical free lunch would consist of bread or crackers, bologna or weinerwurst, sliced tomatoes, salad, pickles, onions, radishes and perhaps soup or a hot meat stew.[17] But even this, considering that cheap restaurants in Boston charged five cents for a sandwich, a piece of pie, two doughnuts, or a glass of milk, ten cents for a meat pie and twenty-five cents for a full dinner, was a bargain.[18]

The free lunch fed a large portion of the working class and the middle class. Probably half or more of the cities' saloons offered a free lunch. In some cities, such as Boston, saloons were required by law to offer free food, if not exactly a meal, though in others, Atlanta for instance, they were forbidden by law to offer food. In Chicago, at the end of the 19th century, 92 of the 157 saloons in the 19th ward, and 11 of the 163 saloons in the 17th ward, both working-class districts, offered a free lunch.[19] Along a distance of four miles on Madison Street, which ran through working-class residential and business districts of Chicago, 115 saloons offered a free lunch, compared to three restaurants offering a 5¢ lunch, five 10¢ restaurants, twenty 15¢ restaurants and twenty-five restaurants charging 20¢ to 35¢.[20]

Saloons were also the most important source of recreation and amusement for the urban working class. They provided both recreational facilities and a general atmosphere which encouraged informal, spontaneous group activities. They catered to a larger clientele in a greater variety of ways than any other leisure-time institution, until athletics, films, the automobile and radio achieved a dominant position in recreational activities in the 1920s. In Boston,[21] to take one example, the relatively extensive system of outdoor swimming facilities drew an attendance of just over 2 million in 1899—an attendance which Boston's saloons surpassed in nine days. Poolrooms in Boston drew a daily attendance one-tenth as large as the saloons attracted; coffee rooms did less well than poolrooms; and reading rooms in Boston drew a daily attendance less than one-twentieth of the saloon's patronage. While there was always a saloon just down the street or around the corner, city parks were usually located at such a distance from working-class residential districts that they were of little value to workers except on Sundays and holidays. In Boston the parks nearest working-class areas were far beyond walking distance.[22] In Manhattan parks were conspicuous by their absence from tenement areas.[23] Chicago's fine system of parks was located primarily in the suburbs.[24] Public and private athletic facilities, reading rooms, clubs, labor union recreational halls, etc., were not plentiful at the turn of the century, nor were they desired by the working class nearly so much as saloons. They often catered to the values of a sponsoring philanthropist, whereas saloons tried to give the workingman exactly what he wanted.

Saloons offered a variety of amusements and recreational facilities, such as newspapers, cards, movies, a gramophone or live entertainment—usually a violinist, singer or vaudeville show—billiards, bowling, and sporting news relayed by ticker tape. Tables and chairs, cards and billiards were the most common and widely used facilities, though for an evening's entertainment at least one saloon offering a burlesque show was usually within easy reach of any working-class neighborhood.[25]

The quality and quantity of amusements varied from one city to the next, and from one section of the country to another. In the East facilities were often limited due to strict government regulations which either explicitly prohibited certain forms of recreation in saloons, or kept the number of saloons in a city low enough that there was little competitive incentive to sponsor amusements in order to attract customers. In Boston, for example, pool tables in saloons were permitted only in rare instances; tables, chairs and cards were rare; prostitution and gambling were totally divorced from the saloons.[26] Gambling machines, billiards, bowling and similar games were prohibited in Philadelphia's saloons.[27] Recreational facilities were more plentiful in the West. The great majority of saloons in St. Louis had tables, chairs and cards; many had billiard tables, and some had pianos.[28] Tables, chairs, cards, billiards, gambling machines and games, and prostitution were common in the saloons of San Francisco.[29] In Chicago, of the 320 saloons in the 17th and 19th ward, 183 had tables and chairs, 209 provided newspapers, 102 had pool tables and several saloons ran small gymnasiums, provided handball courts, music halls and/or gambling.[30]

More important than the actual facilities was the air of relaxed, informal sociability which pervaded saloons. Saloon names like "The Fred," "Ed and Frank's," "The Club" and "The Poor Man's Retreat" promised a warm, friendly atmosphere.[31] Patrons of a saloon often had something in common with each other—neighborhood ties, similar interests or a common occupation or ethnic background—to stimulate group feelings and camaraderie. Neighborhood ties and a common ethnic background most often united the group. Sometimes formal groups patronized saloons: singing societies, lodge chapters and neighborhood committees often met in saloons or adjoining rooms.[32] Boxers and other athletes opened saloons which attracted fellow sportsmen and spectators. Saloons such as the "Milkmen's Exchange" and the "Mechanic's Exchange" attracted workingmen of the same occupation.[33]

Alcohol, by virtue of its inhibition-releasing effect, stimulated feelings of social familiarity, group identification and solidarity and was, itself, a focus of group activity. The custom of treating was nearly universal: each man treated the group to a round of drinks, and was expected to stay long enough to be treated in turn by the rest of the group—which made for much happy backslapping, sloppy singing and drunken exuberance. If things were going slowly the saloon-keeper might treat the house to a round in order to stimulate fellowship and, hopefully, a few more paying rounds. The saloon-keeper often played the part of a host, keeping the "guests" happy—and somewhat orderly—and keeping the "party" going.

Singing seems to have been fairly common, both by groups and arising spontaneously.[34] The songs, like the conversation, were often highly sentimental, lamenting the fallen girl or the drunk, idolizing motherhood, patriotism, the nobility of the workingman, the righteousness of working-class causes, or almost any other highly emotional subject. Such songs as "A Boy's Best Friend is His Mother," "Always Take Mother's Advice" and "A Flower From My Angel Mother's Grave" typify the sentimentality of saloon singing.[35] But the saloon could be subdued and relaxed as well as loud and exuberant. Men might sit over a single beer for hours in earnest conversation, quietly playing cards or discussing politics.

Being central to the workingman's leisure-time activities, saloons came into contact with almost all aspects of his life; they touched the life of the cities at many points, from crime and poverty to politics and work. Crime, poverty, prostitution and machine graft flourished in the city and fed off saloons. Though the causes of these evils were deep-rooted and complex, the saloon was often pictured—in an overly simplified view—as the sole or main force responsible for the cities' problems. The saloon symbolized that threat which the lower-class immigrant, caught up in the harsh urban-industrial explosion after the Civil War, posed to traditional American morality.

Evils were ascribed all too simply to saloons, and the evils manifest in saloons were often exaggerated. As E. C. Moore, professor of sociology and social worker at Hull House, testified, saloons generally did not stand for intemperance and vice.[36] In two hundred visits to saloons in Chicago's working-class districts he saw only three drunken men. Only 2 of the 157 saloons in Chicago's 19th ward were known to police as hangouts for thieves; one was known as a house of assignation. In Boston and Philadelphia gambling and prostitution were completely divorced from the saloons. But in many cities the connection did exist. The Raines Law in New York, prohibiting all liquor retailers except hotels from opening on Sunday, the biggest day of business, turned hundreds of saloons into brothels, or so-called Raines Law hotels. In certain well-defined sections of Chicago, St. Louis, San Francisco, Denver, Buffalo, Baltimore and many more cities prostitution and gambling were rife in the saloons.[37] Chicago's Vice Commission of 1911 found saloons to have been the most conspicuous and important element in connection with prostitution aside from the brothels themselves.[38] Prostitutes were tolerated by some saloon-keepers for the added business they were expected to attract. Sometimes the proprietor contracted with the girls to pay them a commission on drinks bought for them—a commission the saloon could well afford since it charged twenty-five cents for a beer in the rear stalls, and often served the girls soft drinks when they ordered distilled liquor. Sometimes waiters were expected when they took a job to bring their own prostitutes or bar girls with them to solicit drinks. Most saloons in almost every city were also guilty of consistently breaking laws regulating their closing hours and forbidding sales on Sunday. The fighting and drunkenness endemic to slum life was found as much in the saloons as on the streets and in tenements—perhaps more so, despite the fact that more saloon-keepers refused to serve drunks and tried to maintain order in their saloons, out of self-interest if for no other reason.

In assessing the relationship of crime, poverty and insanity to saloons, one is handicapped not so much by a lack of information as by a plethora of contradictory statistics, reflecting the bias of the surveyor as well as the reluctance of subjects to be completely frank. When data do seem reliable and statistical correlations are strong and positive, still, nothing is revealed of the causal relationship. Nevertheless, for what it is worth, the correlation of intemperance with pauperism, crime and insanity seems to have been very high.[39] What this says about saloons is unclear since intemperance was not dependent solely upon saloons, nor did it disappear with Prohibition. As for the allegation, commonly made by temperance advocates, that the liquor bill was a drain on the family budget, it would seem to have been the cause, in itself, of very few cases of poverty. Liquor consumption averaged not more than 5 per cent of a workingman's family budget.[40]

Saloons became involved even in the occupational concerns of the working class. Men of the same occupation would gather at certain saloons, and unemployed co-workers would go there for news of job openings and perhaps some relief. Employers in need of laborers might apply to the saloon-keeper. Prior to the existence of the International Longshoremen's Association dockworkers were usually hired by saloon-keepers—and sometimes forced to spend their wages in the contractor's saloon.[41]

The unions had mixed feelings about saloons. Though union members were overwhelmingly anti-prohibitionist, union organizers and officers often feared the dulling effect of alcohol on working-class consciousness. Thus, although locals of the Union Bakers and Confectioners met in saloons before the establishment of a national office, an officer of the national union states his opposition to saloons, "especially when a 'Baker's Home' is connected therewith. When possible we establish employment offices ourselves, to give work free of charge to our members."[42] The Knights of Labor and the Brotherhood of Locomotive Firemen refused membership to saloon-keepers. The United Garment Workers, the Journeymen Tailors and the The United Garment Workers, to name only a few, tried whenever possible not to hold meetings in halls connected with saloons. But saloons welcomed unions and offered their rooms at prices below market level for chapter meetings, at a time when many unions were hard pressed to find any halls open to them. At the turn of the century half or more of the United Brewery Workers, the Wood Carvers' Association, the Amalgamated Wood Workers, and the Brotherhood of Boiler Makers and Iron Shipbuilders met in saloons or halls connected with them.[43] In Buffalo, at the turn of the century, 63 of the city's 69 labor organizations held their meetings in halls connected with saloons, and in many other cities the dependence on saloons was nearly as great.[44]

In politics, too, saloons played a major role. The liquor industry as a whole was thoroughly involved in politics, and saloons in particular were often associated with urban machine politics. Saloons provided politicians a means to contact and organize workingmen, and the political machine sold favors to saloons. In the former case, saloons were especially useful at the ward level. The ward leader was the backbone of the political machine, his club the bastion of political power in the ward. He built his following out of the ward club, called them together at the club for special occasions and kept them happy there. The club was a pleasant place where leaders and followers could find relaxation at a billiard table or a bar, and chew the political fat. It served as a social institution, a center for recreation and camaraderie, and a refuge from wife and family. The ward leader needed to be friendly, generous and thoroughly knowledgeable about his neighborhood. Saloons fitted the needs of the machine politician perfectly. Saloons could, and did, easily double as ward clubs, and the type and extent of the saloon-keeper's contact with his neighborhood was a valuable political asset. Being a working-class social center, the saloon provided a natural stage for politicians and an excellent base for organizing the vote. Plus, saloons were a good source of bums, drunks, petty criminals, hoboes and anyone else who might sell his vote for a few dollars in cash or in liquor. Half the Democratic captains of Chicago's first ward at the beginning of the 20th century were saloon proprietors.[45] One-third of Milwaukee's 46 city councilmen in 1902 were saloon-keepers, as were about a third of Detroit's aldermen at the end of the 19th century.[46] Tweed's "Boodle Board" of aldermen was composed in half of saloon-keepers or ex-saloon-keepers; in 1884 nearly two-thirds of the political conventions and primaries in New York City were held in saloons; and in 1890 eleven of New York City's 24 aldermen were saloon-keepers.[47]

If the saloon was a natural center for political activity and a boon to the machine politician, the combination of early-hour closing laws and strong competition among saloons made the crooked politician and his favors indispensable to saloon-keepers. Proprietors were forced to pay the police and the political machine in order to stay open late at night, as well as for prostitution and gambling. In Chicago's first ward the annual Democratic Club Ball cost every saloon-keeper fifteen to twenty-five dollars in fifty-cent tickets, not to mention the routine monthly payments.[48] Thus was cemented the bond between saloon and politician. The saloon was as often the victim as it was the springboard of the machine politician—in either case the relationship was intimate.

Not surprisingly, the saloon was itself a major, perhaps the major, issue in urban politics and reform. Sunday closing laws and their enforcement were a perennial, often highly emotional and important, campaign issue, which elicited from saloons an active and organized response. For instance, the Keep Your Mouth Shut Organization, centered in Detroit, supported, out of assessments on its member saloons, political candidates favorable to the liquor interests. The Detroit Liquor Dealers Protective Association was founded in 1880 with the intention of challenging "unfair" liquor legislation in the courts and aiding any of its 400 members charged with violations of the closing laws. At the end of the 19th century both retailers and brewers organized fraternal orders to promote their interests and protect themselves from temperance legislation. The Royal Ark organized Detroit's saloons into wards, each with a captain to look after the interests of the saloons in his ward. It also distributed to its members a list of endorsed candidates who would not enforce Sunday, holiday and early-hour closing laws. This was known at the "Saloon Slate."[49]

If, then, the saloon affected the workingman's life in a variety of ways, what significant role did it play for the working class? The urban workingman's saloon served three major functions. First, saloons served as a major social focus of the neighborhood. The saloon was a local institution in an economy well on its way to production and consumption en masse. It was a neighborhood center in an urban environment which denied its residents that sense of community and stability inherent in an earlier, small-town America. Although some working-class saloons clustered about industrial enterprises, feeding off factory workers during the day, or depended on nightly entertainment and prostitution to draw patrons from a wide radius, these types were common only in certain slum, business and industrial areas of a city. Most saloons in residential districts—urban and suburban—drew a steady crowd of neighborhood regulars. And most city blocks had at least one "neighborhood" saloon. Indeed, the corner saloon may have been the most neighborly institution in the city. While children played in the street and women talked on tenement stoops, the men went to a saloon.

The saloon-keeper, himself, was often an important figure in the neighborhood and claimed a large place in the hearts of his regular customers. If a new saloon opened or an old one changed management the whole neighborhood would know of it in a matter of hours and come in to size up the new proprietor.[50] The saloon-keeper often fostered community ties, for commercial reasons or otherwise. He might open connecting rooms for the entertainment of a local boys' club, or provide them with a club room for a small price.[51] He might be the favorite local "pharmacist," prescribing stale beer for a gaseous stomach, a sloe gin fizz for clearing morning-after headaches, and other mixtures for chest colds, cramps, etc.

Saloons mirrored the character of the surrounding neighborhood, helped to shape it and tried to serve it. One could speak of the typical Jewish saloon on the lower East Side where the signs and conversation were all in Yiddish, of an Italian café-style saloon, the Irish-American stand-up saloon, or the German beer garden which attracted not only neighboring males, but their families as well.[52] Whatever the ethnic background, saloons offered their services to the community. In a survey of Chicago's saloons they were noted to offer furnished rooms free or for a small charge to local men's clubs, musical societies, fraternal orders, small wedding parties and neighborhood meetings. As the surveyor stated, "The saloon is, in short, the clearing house for the common intelligence—the social and intellectual center of the neighborhood."[53]

In a second aspect of its role, the saloon was a male institution in a culture still predominantly male-oriented, but loosing ground quickly to the concept of female emancipation and equality. Although some women drank in restaurants and beer gardens, the social and legal injunction against women drinking in, or even entering, working-class saloons was generally observed, except by prostitutes.[54] The saloon was a thoroughly male institution with the appropriate atmosphere, from the sawdust on the floor to the pictures of athletes on the walls to the prostitutes in the backroom stalls. The saloon supported and reinforced a stereotypically masculine character and a self-sufficient all male culture separate from the prissy world of women and the constraints of family. Judging from barroom conversation and behavior, women were valued primarily as sexual objects. Otherwise they were pictured as a nuisance, superfluous at best, downright troublesome at worst. The ideal as represented in the decor and personified by the saloonkeeper was the strong male, unfettered by domestic chains and enjoying the camaraderie of his fellows with a carefree sociability. As children often gathered at saloon doorways, excited by the noisy scene within, the saloon probably played a part in the process by which many boys formed their values as American males. That happy, boisterous, uninhibited scene was a powerful model for the American male. As Jack London put it: "In the saloons life was different. Men talked with great voices, laughed great laughs, and there was an atmosphere of greatness. . . . Terrible they might be, but then that only meant they were terribly wonderful, and it is the terribly wonderful that a boy desires to know."[55] Drink was the badge of manhood, the brass rail "a symbol of masculinity emancipate."[56]

It seems likely that some sort of bachelor subculture existed prior to Prohibition and has since waned. The proportion of singles among the male population has declined significantly since the end of the 19th century: of males aged fifteen and over, the proportion single declined from 42% in 1890 to 33% in 1940, and to less than 25% in 1950.[57] The thousands of men in any large city who lived in lodging houses, spending their days at work and their evenings in saloons and pool halls, had little real contact with women other than prostitutes. The saloon was particularly important as a social center for this group of workingmen. Many saloon-goers were, of course, married, but in some saloons the patrons were noted to be mostly over thirty and single.[58] Clark Warburton, in his study of the effects of Prohibition, estimated that more than half of working-class drinking was done by single men.[59] Certainly many of the heavy drinkers, saloon regulars, were bachelors: although only 45% of Boston's male population aged fourteen or over was single, 60% of a study sample of arrested drunks in Boston in 1909 were unmarried.[60]

For married men the saloon was an escape from wife and family. The workingmen at McSorley's—of John Sloan's painting, "McSorley's Saloon"—looked "as if they never thought of a woman. They were maturely reflecting in purely male ways and solemnly discoursing, untroubled by skirts or domesticity."[61] For married men, free for only a few hours, as well as for young "stags" and older bachelors, the saloon was an escape, a bastion of male fellowship and independence.

Abstainers, too, seem to have understood the self-sufficient masculine character of saloons. Saloons were often pictured by Prohibitionists and middle-class women as competitors to home and family.[62] Feminists heartily supported the Temperance movement. The Women's Christian Temperance Union was a leading temperance organization, also strongly committed to female suffrage and feminism. The Anti-Saloon League, though it tried to stay clear of all causes other than Temperance, apparently felt that the link between prohibition and woman suffrage was so strong that the League could hardly afford to ignore the latter. For the Temperance movement was in part a reflection of a public desire, especially strong among women, to curb the self-assertive, boisterous masculinity of the saloon, to support and protect the family, and to return the husband—immigrant workingmen in particular—to the home. Even moderate temperance advocates felt that the nation needed and Prohibition might start "a new awakening to the values of the home . . . broadened into a contagion that shall cover the country."[63]

Third, the saloon was symbolically and functionally alien to that traditional American ethic rooted in a largely Anglo-Saxon, Protestant population heavily influenced by its Puritan antecedents. The Yiddish saloon on the lower East Side, as much as the intoxicated "nigger" in the South, was perceived as a threat to the traditional culture and social fabric. The saloon was not only the symbol of a predominantly urban, new-immigrant, working-class life-style alien to the traditional American ascetic ethic of work, frugality, self-control, discipline and sobriety; it served as an alternative, a competitor, to the traditional pattern. Content to waste his time and money in saloons and take his sodden pleasures in near absolute leisure, the urban immigrant worker lacked the ability and incentive to boot-strap himself up into the middle class. In the eyes of the temperance advocate, it was the saloon that kept him down, thus impeding the process of cultural assimilation and slowing down America's march to material bliss.

Rather than aid immigrant groups to assimilate, rather than encourage the working class to adopt middle-class manners and aspirations, the workingman's saloon tended to conserve and reinforce ethnic and class ties. Saloons in immigrant districts usually attracted and catered to a single ethnic group, according to the character of the neighborhood and the nationality of the saloon-keeper. As a highly adaptive local institution, the saloon tended to reflect and serve the character of its clientele: drinking habits, games, newspapers, language—all reflected the ethnic milieu. Immigrants also used their saloons for ethnic group meeting halls and for the celebration of their national occasions. Moreover, the saloon provided immigrants, Eastern and Southern Europeans especially, the kind of informal, relaxed, slow moving social setting many had been accustomed to in the old country. As for class ties, the workingman's saloon was oriented toward relief from work and toward the weekend binge: the absence of time limits, the stimulus to uninhibited self-expression, the lack of any goal-oriented activity in saloons made them a purely nonproductive leisurely institution, reflecting working-class values in general and a lower-class tendency to divorce work and enjoyment in particular.

The ethnic and class orientation of saloons was clear. They were most dense in immigrant neighborhoods and most frequented by the working class. The working-class saloon was central to a way of life engendered by large-scale immigration and a growing urbanism and industrialism, and appropriate to a relatively newly formed proletariat. Providing ample opportunity for relaxation, supporting immigrant groups in their efforts to retain ethnic identity, harboring vice, gambling, criminals and machine politicians, the saloon was alien to Puritan America and efficiency minded Progressives alike.

The saloon, then, was a community center tending to give some coherence to neighborhoods by focusing the attention of male residents upon the people and events of the area. It was a male institution reinforcing stereotypically masculine qualities and catering to the social needs of that large segment of men who remained bachelors. It was a form of amusement that encouraged the working class, immigrants especially, in the retention of their cultural identity and retarded the movement to assimilation into the American middle class.

The character of the urban workingman's saloon as depicted above suggests some interesting questions, the answers to which lie beyond the scope of my own research. An understanding of the role of saloons suggests that Temperance may have been a practical politically goal-oriented movement. Temperance sentiment in the late 19th and early 20th centuries is often ascribed to an excess of reactionary populism or status-group concern for symbolic cultural victories. Rarely is it viewed today as a practical measure designed primarily to achieve tangible results.[64] But if the saloon itself was not merely a liquor dispensary—if, as I have claimed, it actually played a significant role in the life of workingmen, immigrants especially—then why should the Temperance movement, which was in part a battle against saloons per se, be seen primarily as a symbolic issue? If the saloon functioned as an institutional support of working-class and ethnic values, an obstacle to assimilation, and a competitor or alternative to the traditional ideal of family, then perhaps Prohibition was a logical measure in line with immigration restriction to preserve the Anglo-Saxon Protestant character of America, and in line with child labor laws to preserve and protect the family. Perhaps we ought to ask what effect Prohibition actually had on family structure and working-class values.

The saloon study also raises some questions about the concept of community in 20th century America. If saloons imparted a focus and some meaning to working-class neighborhoods, did they also give male residents a real sense of community? Can we look to corner saloons and pool halls, neighborhood theaters and local chapters of labor unions, women's clubs and fraternal organizations for at least a watered down sense of belonging and identity? What other local institutions may have contributed in a similar manner to a sense of community? And what was the effect of the waning of neighborhood recreational institutions in the 1920s? Social historians might profitably look to the neighborhood, as well as to the city, for a basic social unit.

Finally, the social functions of urban working-class saloons suggest some interesting questions concerning the existence and nature of a male ethic and a bachelor subculture. If a special image of the American male shaped his values and behavior, what exactly was that image, what were its effects and what other institutions besides the saloon were intimately tied to it? Perhaps labor unions, amateur athletics, family structure and other organizations and activities should be looked at with reference to the needs and motives arising out of a male ethic. Certainly the existence of a bachelor subculture should be of interest to social historians. Census statistics indicate that there was a substantially larger proportion of single men before World War II than at present—due perhaps to an inordinately large number of single males among first-generation immigrants. The only reference I have found to this phenomenon is in one of a series of sociological sketches by Ned Polsky, which ascribes the decline of pool halls since the 1920s to the disappearance of a subculture of professional bachelors.[65] Polsky is referring to lower-class bachelors for the most part: hustlers, petty gamblers and criminals, saloon-keepers and probably a good number of workingmen. With urban modernization, growing national wealth and an increased tendency among men to marry, this component of the urban scene has waned. We might ask if this was actually a subculture with a distinctive value set and a measure of continuiy. If so, what institutions besides saloons, pool halls and lodging houses were intimately connected with it? What has happened to them and to the subculture itself? It is, I think, the proper vocation of the social historian to delve into these subtler aspects of history in order to comprehend the texture of life in the past.

NOTES

[1]U.S., Congress, House, *Twelfth Annual Report of the Commissioner of Labor*, House Doc. 564, 55th Cong., 2d sess., 1897, p. 41: Andrew Sinclair, *Prohibition, the Era of Excess* (Boston: Little, Brown, 1962), p. 77.

[2]Francis G. Peabody, ed., *The Liquor Problem: a Summary of Investigations Conducted by the Committee of Fifty* (Boston: Houghton Mifflin, 1905), p. 147. The reports of the Committee of Fifty, as well as a number of other sources on which I relied heavily, reflect the progressive reformer's point of view. By and large, the members of the Committee were academics, clergymen and other professionals who proposed to dispel the confusion caused by a welter of contradictory claims put out by wet and dry propagandists. They concluded that what was needed were saloon substitutes rather than the all too simple solution of legislative prohibition. Recognizing that saloons were attractive because they performed necessary services, the Committee of Fifty suggested that those services be taken over by temperate enterprises. Their accounts represent the honest and, on the whole, successful effort of socially concerned and well-educated men to comprehend the dynamics of a difficult problem.

[3]U.S., Department of Commerce, Bureau of the Census, *General Statistics of the Cities: 1915*, p, 37.

[4]E.M. Jellinek, "Recent Trends in Alcoholism and Alcohol Consumption," *Quarterly Journal of Studies on Alcohol*, 8 (June 1947), 2.

[5]Peabody, ed., *The Liquor Problem*, p. 147.

[6]Francis G. Peabody, "Substitutes for the Saloon," *Forum*, 21 (1896), 598.

[7]J.N. Cross, *Guide to the Community Control of Alcoholism* (New York: American Public Health Assoc., 1968), pp. 21–24.

[8]Raymond Calkins, *Substitutes for the Saloon* (Boston: Houghton Mifflin, 1901), pp. 2–5.

[9]George K. Turner, "The City of Chicago," *McClure's Magazine*, Apr. 1907, p. 577; Arthur H. Gleason, "The New York Saloon," *Collier's Weekly*, Apr. 25, 1908, p. 16.

[10]Turner, "Chicago," p. 579.

[11]Jacob Riis, *How the Other Half Lives* (1890; rpr. Cambridge: Harvard Univ. Press, 1970), p. 139.

[12]William I. Cole and Kellog Darland, "Substitutes for the Saloon in

Boston," in *Substitutes for the Saloon* ed. by Raymond Calkins (Boston: Houghton Mifflin, 1901), p. 321.

[13]Sherri Cavan, *Liquor License, an Ethnography of Bar Behavior* (Chicago: Aldine, 1966), pp. 211–13.

[14]Robert W. DeForest and Lawrence Veiller, eds., *The Tenement House Problem* (New York: MacMillan, 1903), Vol. 1; Oscar Handlin, *The Uprooted* (Boston: Little, Brown, 1951), pp. 153–62.

[15]Royal L. Melendy, "The Saloon in Chicago, II," *American Journal of Sociology*, Jan. 1901, pp. 450–54.

[16]Melendy, "The Saloon in Chicago, I," *American Journal of Sociology*, Nov. 1900, p. 295.

[17]Calkins, *Saloon Substitutes*, pp. 15–18: "The Experiences and Observations of a New York Saloon-Keeper as Told by Himself," *McClure's Magazine*, Jan. 1909, p. 305.

[18]Cole and Darland, "Saloon Substitutes in Boston," in *Saloon Substitutes*, ed. Calkins, p. 329.

[19]E.C. Moore, Chap. 8, in *Economic Aspects of the Liquor Problem*, ed. John Koren (Boston: Houghton Mifflin, 1899), p. 219.

[20]Melendy, "Saloon in Chicago, II," p. 455.

[21]Peabody, "Saloon Substitutes," p. 598.

[22]"Saloon Substitutes in Boston," in *Saloon Substitutes*, ed. Calkins, p. 333.

[23]DeForest and Veiller, *Tenement Problem*, Vol. 2, chap. 1.

[24]Melendy, "Saloon in Chicago, II," p. 448.

[25]Melendy, "Saloon in Chicago, I," p. 298.

[26]Chicago Commission on the Liquor Problem, Chicago City Council, *Preliminary Report to the Mayor and Aldermen*, 1916.

[27]U.S. Brewer's Association, *Proceedings of the 49th Annual Convention* (Atlantic City, N.J., 1909), p. 121.

[28]Frederic H. Wines and John Koren, *The Liquor Problem in Its Legislative Aspects* (Boston: Houghton Mifflin, 1898), p. 329.

[29]*Economic Aspects*, ed. Koren, chap. 8. p. 233; Calkins, *Saloon Substitutes*, p. 381.

[30]*Economic Aspects,* ed. Koren, chap. 8. p. 214; Melendy, "Saloon in Chicago, I." p. 293.

[31]Calkins, *Saloon Substitutes,* pp. 8, 9.

[32]Melendy, "Saloon in Chicago, II," pp. 435, 437.

[33]Calkins, *Saloon Substitutes,* pp. 8, 9.

[34]George Ade, *The Old-Time Saloon, Not Wet–Not Dry, Just History* (New York: R. Long & R.R. Smith, 1931), pp. 126–29.

[35]Ibid.

[36]*Economic Aspects,* ed. Koren, chap. 8, p. 213.

[37]Melendy, "Saloon in Chicago, I," p. 303; Calkins, *Saloon Substitutes,* Appendix IV.

[38]The Vice Commission of Chicago, *The Social Evil in Chicago* (Chicago: Gunthorp-Warren, 1911)

[39]For some reliable studies done before Prohibition on crime, poverty, and insanity in connection with alcohol and intemperance in America, see: Koran, ed., *Economic Aspects;* U.S., Department of Commerce and Labor, *Bulletin of the Bureau of Labor,* S.E. Forman, "Charity Relief and Wage Earnings" (Washington, D.C.: GPO, 1908); Mass., Bureau of Statistics of Labor, *The Twenty-Sixth Annual Report,* by Horace G. Wadlin (Boston: Wright & Potter, 1896).

[40]Robert C. Chapin, "The Standard of Living Among Workingmen's Families in New York City" (New York, 1909), quoted in Clark Warburton, *The Economic Results of Prohibition* New York: Columbia Univ. Press, 1932), p. 138.

[41]James H. Timberlake, *Prohibition and the Progressive Movement, 1900–1920* (Cambridge: Harvard Univ. Press, 1963), p. 83.

[42]Edward M. Bemis, appendix, "Attitude of Trade Unions," in *Substitutes for the Saloon,* ed. Raymond Calkins (Boston: Houghton Mifflin, 1901). p. 304.

[43]Ibid., pp. 307–13.

[44]Calkins, *Saloon Substitutes,* p. 61.

[45]Turner, "Chicago," p. 584.

[46]John M. Barker, *The Saloon Problems and Social Reform* (Boston:

Everett Press, 1905), p. 32; Lawrence D. Engelmann, "O, Whiskey: The History of Prohibition in Michigan," Diss. University of Michigan 1971, p. 78.

[47]Peter Odegard, *Pressure Politics* (New York: Columbia Univ. Press, 1928), p. 247.

[48]Turner, "Chicago," p. 587.

[49]Engelman, *O, Whiskey*, pp. 71–75.

[50]"Experiences of a Saloon-Keeper," p. 310.

[51]Calkins, *Saloon Substitutes*, pp. 1, 52.

[52]Robert A. Stevenson, "Saloons," *Scribner's Magazine*, May 1901, pp. 573–75.

[53]Melendy, "Saloon in Chicago, I," p. 295.

[54]U.S., Department of Commerce, *Cities: 1915*, p. 35.

[55]*John Barleycorn* (New York: Century, 1913), pp. 30, 31.

[56]Travis Hoke, "The Corner Saloon," *American Mercury*, Mar. 1931, p. 311.

[57]Paul H. and Pauline F. Jacobson, *American Marriage and Divorce* (New York: Rinehart, 1959), p. 35.

[58]*Economic Aspects*, ed. Koren, p. 219.

[59]*The Economic Results of Prohibition* (New York: Columbia Univ. Press, 1932), p. 138.

[60]Maurice F. Parmelee, *Inebriety in Boston* (New York: Columbia Univ. Press, 1909), pp. 25–41.

[61]Hutchins Hapgood, "McSorley's Saloon," *Harper's Weekly*, Oct. 25, 1913, p. 15.

[62]Typical of temperance propaganda pitting the saloon against family and home is a cartoon in the Anti-Saloon League's weekly newspaper, *American Issue*, Jan. 17, 1914, p. 1, in which the saloon-keeper is portrayed as battling the housewife for the workingman's paycheck. The caption reads, "Which Needs It Most?"

[63]The Rev. Robert A. Woods, "A New Synthesis After the Saloon," in *Substitutes for the Saloon*, ed. Francis G. Peabody, 2nd ed., rev. (Boston: Houghton Mifflin, 1919), p. 325.

[64]Typical of today's critical perspective on Temperance and Prohibition are: Joseph R. Gusfield, *Symbolic Crusade: Status Politics and the American Temperance Movement* (Urbana: Univ. of Illinois Press, 1963); Andrew Sinclair, *Prohibition, the Era of Excess* (Boston: Little, Brown, 1962). For a sympathetic modern interpretation of Prohibition as a Progressive reform which, at least initially, advanced the status and living conditions of the American working class, see: J.C. Burnham, "New Perspectives on the Prohibition 'Experiment' of the 1920's," *Journal of Social History*, 2 (Fall 1968), 51–68.

[65]*Hustlers, Beats, and Others* (Chicago: Aldine, 1967).

chapter 10

The Boy Scouts
and the Validation of
Masculinity

by Jeffrey P. Hantover

The Boy Scouts of America, founded in 1910, was the largest and most prominent male youth organization in the twentieth century. As a cultural phenomenon, the Scouts are interesting because they represent the organization of adolescent boys in institutions designed and led by adult men. The problem in need of an explanation is this new interest on the part of adult males in shaping the behavior and beliefs of male adolescents. Jeffrey Hantover, a sociologist, argues that scouting arose from the tensions surrounding the male sphere of work around the turn of the century. Middle-class men were no longer finding validation for their masculinity in work: The jobs were becoming increasingly bureaucratized and sedentary, and with the entry of a larger proportion of women into such work, these jobs took on an increasingly feminine aura. Hantover believes that scouting offered middle-class men the opportunity to validate their masculinity outside their work, and he finds his proof in an intriguing source, the applications to become scout-masters of 575 Chicago men. In making this correlation between men's work and the beginning of scouting, Hantover starts with the view of masculinity as a cultural rather than a biological construct, a social ideal which men try to achieve by marshalling personal and social resources. As the ability to reach these goals is blocked in one area, men seek validation elsewhere.

The Boy Scouts of America was formally incorporated in 1910 and by 1916 had received a federal charter, absorbed most of the organizations which had claimed the Scouting name, and was an accepted community institution. The President of the United States was the organization's honorary president, and Scouting courses were offered in major universities. At the end of its first decade, the Boy Scouts was the largest male youth organization in American history with 358,573 scouts and 15,117 scoutmasters.

The Boy Scouts' rapid national acceptance reflected turn-of-the-century concern over the perpetuation and validation of American masculinity. The widespread and unplanned adoption of the Scout program prior to 1916 suggests that Scouting's message, unadorned by organizational sophistication, spoke to major adult concerns, one of which was the future of traditional conceptions of American masculinity.

This paper will argue that the Boy Scouts served the needs of adult men as well as adolescent boys. The supporters of the Scout movement, those who gave their time, money, and public approval, believed that charges in work, the family, and adolescent life threatened the development of manliness among boys and its expression among men. They perceived and promoted Scouting as an agent for the perpetuation of manliness among adolescents; the Boy Scouts provided an environment in which boys could become "red blooded" virile men. Less explicitly, Scouting

"The Boy Scouts and the Validation of Masculinity" by Jeffrey P. Hantover. Reprinted by permission of the author and the Society for the Psychological Study of Social Issues from *Journal of Social Issues*, Vol. 34, No. 1 (1978), pp. 184–195. Copyright © 1978 by the Society for the Psychological Study of Social Issues.

The author wishes to thank Joseph Pleck and Mayer Zald for their constructive comments. Correspondence regarding this article may be addressed to J. Hantover, 225 E. 70th, New York, NY 10021.

provided men an opportunity to counteract the perceived feminizing forces of their lives and to act according to the traditional masculine script.

THE OPPORTUNITY TO BE A MAN: RESTRICTION AND ITS CONSEQUENCES

Masculinity is a cultural construct and adult men need the opportunity to perform normatively appropriate male behaviors. Masculinity is not affirmed once and for all by somatic change; physical development is but a means for the performance of culturally ascribed behaviors. American masculinity is continually affirmed through ongoing action. What acts a man performs and how well he does them truly make a male a man.

However, the availability of opportunities is not constant. Anxiety about the integrity and persistence of the male role can result from a restriction of opportunities experienced by the individual and the groups with which he identifies. Adult experiences produce adult anxieties. Masculine anxiety can arise when adult men know the script and wish to perform according to cultural directions but are denied the opportunity to act: The fault lies in social structuring of opportunities and not in individual capabilities and motivations.

The anxiety men increasingly exhibited about the naturalness and substance of manliness in the period of 1880 to World War I flowed from changes in institutional spheres traditionally supportive of masculine definitional affirmation. Feminism as a political movement did raise fears of feminization but, as Filene (1975) suggests, in relation to preexistent anxiety about the meaning of manliness. Changes in the sphere of work, the central institutional anchorage of masculinity, undercut essential elements in the definition of manliness. Men believed they faced diminishing opportunities for masculine validation and that adolescents faced barriers to the very development of masculinity.

Masculine anxiety at the turn of the century was expressed in the accentuation of the physical and assertive side of the male ideal and in the enhanced salience of gender in social life. The enthronement of "muscularity" is evident in leisure activities, literary tastes, and cultural heroes. In the early nineteenth century, running and jumping were not exercises befitting a gentleman (Rudolph, 1962), but now men took to the playing fields, gyms, and wilderness in increasing numbers. Football, baseball, hiking, and camping became popular and were defended for their contribution to the development of traditional masculine character. Popular magazine biographies of male heroes in the period 1894 to 1913 shifted from an earlier idealization of passive traits such as piety, thrift, and industry to an emphasis on vigor, forcefulness, and mastery (Greene, 1970). Literary masculinization extended beyond mortals like Teddy Roosevelt to Christ who was portrayed as "the supremely manly man": attractive to women, individualistic, athletic, self-controlled, and aggressive when need be—"he was no Prince of Peace-at-any-price" (Conant, 1915, p. 117).

Sex-role distinctions became increasingly salient and rigid. The birth control issue became enmeshed in the debate over women's proper role; diatribes against expanded roles for women accompanied attacks on family limitation. The increased insistence on sexual purity in fiction and real life was a demand for women to accept the traditional attributes of purity, passivity, and domesticity. The emphasis on the chivalric motif in turn-of-the-century youth organizations (Knights of King Arthur, Order of Sir Galahad, Knights of the Holy Grail) can be interpreted as an expression of the desire to preserve male superordination in gender relations.

PERCEIVED FORCES OF FEMINIZATION

Men in the period 1880 to World War I believed that opportunities for the development and expression of masculinity were being limited. They saw forces of feminization in the worlds of adults and adolescents. I will concentrate on changes in the adult opportunity structure. However, the forces of feminization that adolescents were thought to face at home and school should be mentioned, for they contributed to the anxiety of men worried about the present and wary of the future.

For the expanding urban middle class, the professionalization and sanctification of motherhood, the smaller family size, the decline in the number of servants who could serve as buffers between mother and son, and the absence of busy fathers from the home made the mother–son relationship appear threatening to proper masculine socialization. The expansion of the public high school took sons out of the home but did not allay fears of feminization. Female students outnumbered males, the percentage of female staff rose steadily between 1880 and World War I, and the requirements of learning demanded "feminine" passivity and sedentariness. Education would weaken a boy's body and direct his mind along the "psychic lines" of his female instructors. Finally, let me suggest that G. Stanley Hall's concept of adolescence may have generated sex-role anxiety by extending and legitimating dependency as a natural stage in the developmental cycle. A cohort of men who had reached social maturity before the use and public acceptance of adolescence as an age category, who had experienced the rural transition to manhood at an early age, and who had fought as teenagers in the Civil War or knew those who had were confronted with a generation of boys whose major characteristics were dependency and inactivity.

Changes in the nature of work and in the composition of the labor force from 1880 to World War I profoundly affected masculine self-identity. From 1870 to 1910 the number of clerical workers, salespeople, government employees, technicians, and salaried professionals increased from 756 thousand to 5.6 million (Hays, 1957). The dependency, sedentariness, and even security of these middle-class positions clashed with the active mastery, independence, self-reliance, competitiveness, creativity, and risk-taking central to the traditional male ideal (Mills, 1951). In pre-Civil War America, there were opportunities to approach that ideal: It is estimated that over 88% of Americans were farmers or self-employed businessmen (Mills, 1951). They owned the property they worked; they produced tangible goods; and they were not enmeshed in hierarchical systems of "command and obedience."

Industrialization and bureaucratization reduced opportunities to own one's business, to take risks, exercise independence, compete, and master men and nature. The new expanded middle class depended on others for time, place, and often pace of work. The growth of chain stores crowded out independent proprietors, made small business ventures shortlived, and reduced the income of merchants frequently below the level of day laborers (Anderson & Davidson, 1940). Clerical positions were no longer certain stepping stones to ownership; and clerical wages were neither high enough to meet standards of male success nor appreciably greater than those of less prestigious occupations (Filene, 1975; Douglas, 1930).

This changed occupational landscape did not go unnoticed. College graduates were told not to expect a challenging future:

> *The world is steadily moving toward the position in which the individual is to contribute faithfully and duly his quota of productive or protective social effort, and to receive in return a modest, certain, not greatly variable stipend. He will adjust his needs and expenses to his income, guard the future by insurance or some analogous method, and find margin of leisure and opportunity sufficient to give large play to individual tastes and preferences. (Shaw, 1907, p. 3)*

Interestingly for this paper's thesis, these graduates were to seek fulfillment in activities outside work.

The increased entry of women into the labor force raised the specter of feminization as did the changed character of work. In terms of masculine anxiety, the impact was two-fold: the mere fact of women working outside the home in larger numbers and their increased participation in jobs which demanded nonmasculine attributes. From 1870 to 1920, there was a substantial increase in the percentage of women aged 16 and over in nonagricultural occupations—from 11.8% to 21.3% (Hill, 1929). Men expressed concern over the entrance of women into a previously exclusive domain of masculine affirmation. (Women's occupations were not enumerated in the federal census until 1860.) Magazine and newspaper cartoons showed women in suits, smoking cigars, and talking business while aproned men were washing dishes, sweeping floors, and feeding babies (Smuts, 1959). Sex-role definition, not simple income, was at stake. Only one-third of employed men in 1910 worked in occupations where women constituted more than 5% of the work force (Hill, 1929). The actual threat posed by working women was more cultural than economic. Women doing what men did disconfirmed the naturalness and facticity of sex-role dichotomization.

Imposed on this general concern was the anxiety of men in white-collar positions. It was into these "nonmasculine" jobs that women entered in large numbers. Women were only 3% of the clerical work force in 1870, but 35% in 1910 (U.S. Department of Commerce, 1870; Hill, 1929). The increase for specific occupations between 1910 and 1920 is even more dramatic, especially for native white women of native parentage: female clerks increased 318%; bookkeepers, accountants, and cashiers, 257%; stenographers and typists, 121%; and sales personnel, 66% (Hill, 1929). It is to be argued that men in these occupations, feminine in character and composition, sought nonoccupational means of masculine validation, one of which was being a scoutmaster.

SCOUTING AND THE CONSTRUCTION OF MANLINESS

The Boy Scouts of America responded explicitly to adult sex-role concerns. It provided concerned men the opportunity to support "an organized effort to make big men of little boys . . . to aid in the development of that master creation, high principled, clean and clear thinking, independent manhood" (Burgess, 1914, p. 12). At the turn of the century, manliness was no longer considered the inevitable product of daily life; urbanization appeared to have removed the conditions for the natural production of manliness. Scouting advertised itself as an environmental surrogate for the farm and frontier:

> *The Wilderness is gone, the Buckskin Man is gone, the painted Indian has hit the trail over the Great Divide, the hardships and privations of pioneer life which did so much to develop sterling manhood are now but a legend in history, and we must depend upon the Boy Scout Movement to produce the MEN of the future. (Daniel Carter Beard in Boy Scouts of America, 1914, p. 109)*

Scouting's program and structure would counter the forces of feminization and maintain traditional manhood. Following the dictates of Hall's genetic psychology, boys were sexually segregated in a primary group under the leadership of an adult male. The gang instinct, like all adolescent instincts, was not to be repressed but constructively channeled in the service of manhood. By nature boys would form gangs, and the Boy Scouts turned the gang into a Scout patrol. The gang bred virility, did not tolerate sissies, and would make a boy good but not a goody-goody; in short, he would "be a real boy, not too much like his sister" (Puffer, 1912, p. 157; also see Page, 1919).

The rhetoric and content of Scouting spoke to masculine fears of passivity and dependence. Action was the warp and woof of Scouting, as it was the foundation of traditional American masculinity. After-school and summer idleness led to and was itself a moral danger, and scouts were urged to do "anything rather than continue in dependent, and enfeebling, and demoralizing idleness" (Russell, 1914, p. 163). "Spectatoritis" was turning "robust, manly, self-reliant boyhood into a lot of flat-chested cigarette smokers with shaky nerves and doubtful vitality" (Seton, 1910, p. xi). So Scout activities involved all members, and advancement required each boy to compete against himself and nature. Scouting stands apart from most nineteenth-century youth organizations by its level of support for play and its full acceptance of outdoor activities as healthy for boys.

The Scout code, embodied in the Scout Oath, Law, Motto, and requirements for advancement, was a code for conduct, not moral contemplation. It was "the code of red blooded, moral, manly men" (Beard, Note 1, p. 9). The action required by the code, not one's uniform or badges, made a boy scout and differentiated a scout from a nonscout. The British made a promise to act, but the Americans made a more definite commitment to action: they took an oath. More than the British, Americans emphasized that theirs was a "definite code of personal purposes," whose principles would shape the boy's total character and behavior.

The Scout code would produce that ideal man who was master of himself and nature. The American addition to the Scout oath, "To keep myself physically strong, mentally awake, and morally straight," was a condition for such mastery. In pre-Civil War America, "be prepared" meant being prepared to die, having one's moral house in order (Cran-

dall, 1957). The Scout motto meant being prepared to meet
and master dangers, from runaway horses to theater fires
and factory explosions. In emergencies, it was the scout who
"stood firm, quieted those who were panic stricken and un-
obtrusively and efficiently helped to control the crowds"
(Murray, 1937, p. 492). American Scouting added the tenth
law: "A Scout is Brave." Bravery meant self-mastery and
inner direction, having the courage "to stand up for the right
against the coaxing of friends or the jeers or threats of
enemies."

The linchpin of the Scout code was the good deed. Boys
active in community service reassured males that the
younger generation would become manly men. To Scout
supporters, the movement provided a character building
"moral equivalent to war." The phrase was used by William
James in 1910 to suggest a kind of Job Corps for gilded
youths. They would wash windows, build roads, work on
fishing boats, and engage in all types of manual labor. This
work would knock the childishness out of the youth of the
luxurious classes and would produce the hardiness, discipline, and manliness that previously only war had done
(James, 1971). As a result, young men would walk with their
heads higher, would be esteemed by women, and be better
fathers and teachers of the next generation. Scouts would
not accept payment for their good deeds. To take a tip was
un-American, un-masculine, and made one a "bit of a boot
lick" (Eaton, 1918, p. 38). Adherence to the Scout code
would produce traditional manliness in boys' clothing:

*The REAL Boy Scout is not a "sissy." He is not a hothouse
plant, like little Lord Fauntleroy. There is nothing "milk and
water" about him; he is not afraid of the dark. He does not do
bad things because he is afraid of being decent. Instead of being
a puny, dull, or bookish lad, who dreams and does nothing, he
is full of life, energy, enthusiasm, bubbling over with fun, full
of ideas as to what he wants to do and knows how he wants to*

*do it. He has many ideals and many heroes. He is not hitched
to his mother's apronstrings. While he adores his mother, and
would do anything to save her from suffering or discomfort, he
is self-reliant, sturdy and full of vim. (West, 1912, p. 448)*

THE SCOUTMASTER
AND MASCULINE VALIDATION

Scouting assuaged adult masculine anxiety not only by training boys in the masculine virtues. The movement provided
adult men a sphere of masculine validation. Given the
character and composition of their occupations and the centrality of occupation to the male sex role, young men in
white-collar positions were especially concerned about their
masculine identity. They were receptive to an organization
which provided adult men the opportunity to be men as traditionally defined.

At the core of the image of the ideal scoutmaster was
assertive manliness. Scoutmasters were "manly" patriots
with common sense and moral character who sacrificially
served America's youth (Boy Scouts of America, 1920).
Scouting wanted "REAL, live men—red blooded and right-
hearted men—BIG men"; "No Miss Nancy need apply" (Boy
Scouts of America, n.d., p. 9). Scoutmasters by the force of
their characters, not by their formal positions (as in a bureaucracy), would evoke respect. They were portrayed as men of
executive ability who took decisive action over a wide range
of problems and were adroit handlers of men and boys. An
analysis of the social characterisics and motivation of all the
Chicago scoutmasters for whom there are records—original
applications—through 1919 ($N = 575$) raises questions about
the veracity of this portrayal (Hantover, 1976).

The first scoutmasters were men of education, occupational, and ethnic status, but they did not serve solely from a
sense of *noblesse oblige* and a disinterested commitment to all

boys. They were more concerned about saving middle-class boys from the effeminizing forces of modern society than with "civilizing" the sons of the lower classes. Only four scoutmasters singled out the lower class for special mention; just 8% of the over 700 experiences with youth listed by scoutmasters were with lower-class youth. The typical Chicago scoutmaster was white, under 30, native born, Protestant, college educated, and in a white-collar or professional/semi-professional occupation. Scoutmasters were more Protestant, better educated, and in higher prestige occupations than the adult male population of Chicago. Many teachers, clergymen, and boys' workers were scoutmasters because Scouting was part of their job, was good training for it, or at least was congruent with their vocational ideology. If we exclude those men drawn to Scouting by the requirements of their occupations, Scouting disproportionately attracted men who had borne longer the "feminine" environment of the schools and now were in occupations whose sedentariness and dependence did not fit the traditional image of American manliness.

Though the motivational data extracted from the original scoutmaster applications are limited, there does emerge from the number and quality of responses a sense that clerical workers were concerned about the development of masculinity among adolescents and its expression by adults. Clerical workers were more concerned than other occupations unrelated to youth and service about training boys for manhood, filling a boy's time with constructive activities so he would not engage in activities detrimental to the development of manhood, and about the sexual and moral dangers of adolescence.

It is not simply chance, I believe, that clerical workers gave elaborate and individualistic responses which evince a sense of life's restrictedness and danger. A 26-year-old stenographer, "always having lived in Chicago and working indoors," felt Scouting was a way to get outdoors for himself, not the scouts. A 21-year-old clerk, implying that his career had reached its apogee, praised Scouting for its development of initiative and resourcefulness and admitted that lack of these qualities had handicapped him greatly. A draftsman, only 27, thought "association with the boys will certainly keep one from getting that old and retired feeling." Another young clerk evokes a similar sense of life's restrictedness when he writes that Scouting "affords me an opportunity to exercise control over a set of young men. I learn to realize the value of myself as a force and as a personality."

The masculine anxiety that clerical workers felt may not have been generated by their occupation alone. They brought to the job achievements and attributes which at the turn of the century could have exacerbated that anxiety. Clerical workers had the highest percentage of high school educated scoutmasters of any occupational group. They were subject to the perceived feminine forces of high school without the status compensation of a college education and a professional position. With education controlled, Protestants and native Americans were more likely to be clerical workers. It was the virility and reproductive powers of the native American stock which was being questioned after the Civil War. Women in the better classes (native and Protestant) denied men the opportunity to prove their masculinity through paternity. Albion Small complained, "In some of the best middle-class social strata in the United States a young wife becomes a subject of surprised comment among her acquaintances if she accepts the burden of maternity! This is a commonplace" (Small, 1915, p. 661). The fecundity and alleged sexuality of the immigrants raised turn-of-the-century fears about the continued dominance of the native Protestant stock. The experiences of key reference groups as well as one's own individual experiences were factors contributing to a sense of endangered masculinity.

CONCLUSION

Adult sex-role anxiety is rooted in the social structure; and groups of men are differentially affected, depending on their location in the social system and the opportunity structure they face. Critics of men's supposed nature can be dismissed as misguided by medical and religious defenders. But when the opportunity structure underlying masculinity begins to restrict, questioning may arise from the ranks of the men themselves. When taken-for-granted constructs become the objects of examination, anxiety may arise because elements in a culture system are defended as natural, if not transcendent, rather than convenient or utilitarian. Under the disconfirming impact of social change, men may at first be more likely to reassert the validity of traditional ends and seek new avenues for their accomplishment than to redefine their ends.

"Men not only define themselves, but they actualize these definitions in real experience—*they live them*" (Berger, Berger, & Kellner, 1974, p. 92). Social identities generate the needs for self-confirming action. The young men in the scoutmaster ranks were the first generation to face full force the discontinuity between the realities of the modern bureaucratic world and the image of masculine autonomy and mastery and the rhetoric of Horatio Alger. They found in the Boy Scouts of America an institutional sphere for the validation of masculinity previously generated by the flow of daily social life and affirmed in one's work.

NOTES

[1]Beard, D.C. Untitled article submitted to *Youth Companion*. Unpublished manuscript, Daniel Carter Beard Collection, Library of Congress, 1914.

REFERENCES

Anderson, H. D., & Davidson, P. E. *Occupational trends in the United States.* Stanford: Stanford University Press, 1940.

Berger, P., Berger, B., & Kellner, H. *The homeless mind.* New York: Vintage Press, 1974.

Boy Scouts of America. Fourth annual report. *Scouting,* 1914, *1.*

Boy Scouts of America. *Handbook for scoutmasters* (2nd ed.). New York: Boy Scouts of America, 1920.

Boy Scouts of America. *The scoutmaster and his troop.* New York: Boy Scouts of America, no date.

Burgess, T. W. Making men of them. *Good Housekeeping Magazine,* 1914, *59,* 3–12.

Conant, R. W. *The virility of Christ.* Chicago: no publisher, 1915.

Crandall, J. C., Jr. *Images and ideals for young Americans: A study of American juvenile literature, 1825–1860.* Unpublished doctoral dissertation, Universtiy of Rochester, 1957.

Douglas, P. *Real wages in the United States, 1890–1926.* New York: Houghton Mifflin, 1930.

Eaton, W. P. *Boy scouts in Glacier Park.* Boston: W. A. Wilde, 1918.

Filine, P. G. *Him, her, self: Sex roles in modern America.* New York: Harcourt Brace Jovanovich, 1975.

Greene, T. P. *America's heroes: The changing models of success in American magazines.* New York: Oxford University Press, 1970.

Hantover, J. P. *Sex role, sexuality, and social status: The early years of the Boy Scouts of America.* Unpublished doctoral dissertation, University of Chicago, 1976.

Hays, S. P. *The response to industrialism: 1885–1914.* Chicago: University of Chicago Press, 1957.

Hill, J. A. *Women in gainful occupations 1870 to 1920* (Census Monograph No. 9, U.S. Bureau of the Census). Washington, D.C.: U.S. Government Printing Office, 1929.

James, W. The moral equivalent of war. In J. K. Roth (Ed.), *The moral equivalent and other essays.* New York: Harper Torchbook, 1971.

Mills, C. W. *White collar.* New York: Oxford University Press, 1951.

Murray, W. D. *The history of the boy scouts of America.* New York: Boy Scouts of America, 1937.

Page, J. F. *Socializing for the new order of education values of the juvenile organization.* Rock Island, Ill.: J. F. Page, 1919.

Puffer, J. A. *The boy and his gang.* Boston: Houghton Mifflin, 1912.

Rudolph, F. *The American college and university.* New York: Knopf, 1962.

Russell, T. H. (Ed.). *Stories of boy life.* No location; Fireside Edition, 1914,

Seton, E. T. *Boy Scouts of America: A handbook of woodcraft, scouting and life craft.* New York: Doubleday, Page, 1910.

Shaw, A. *The outlook for the average man.* New York: Macmillan, 1907.

Small, A. The bonds of nationality. *American Journal of Sociology,* 1915, *10,* 629–83.

Smuts, R. W. *Women and work in America.* New York: Columbia University Press, 1959.

U.S. Department of Commerce. *Ninth census of the United States, 1870: Population and social statistics* (Vol. 1). Washington, D.C.: U.S. Government Printing Office, 1870.

West, J. E. The real boy scout. *Leslie's Weekly,* 1912, 448.

chapter 11

Progressivism and the Masculinity Crisis

by Joe L. Dubbert

The Progressive period of American reform brought to the surface submerged tensions about the proper roles for women and men. There was no more dynamic symbol of masculinity than the Rough Rider himself, an American president who had earlier been a boxer, rancher, big game hunter, and war hero. Progressive reformers generally supported the women's suffrage campaign as one of the democratic reforms they were espousing, but they often worried that the "New Woman" had gone too far. Some of them like the journalist William Allen White, voiced concerns about emasculation which were little more than shrill cries of misogyny. It is interesting to note that these fears preceded by more than a decade the introduction of Freudian theory into America. A fear of feminization seemed to originate in a national psychic crisis of the 1890s, doubly provoked by the announcement of the closing of the frontier and the strident militarism so characteristic of the age. But if the origins of these fears can be dated as early as the 1890s, the intensity in them was probably greatest in the new century. No more useful case study of this kind of male threat could be offered than an analysis of the writings of Progressive reformers, such as Willian Allen White, which Joe L. Dubbert offers here.

Fourteen years ago William Langer stated that the next assignment for professional historians ought to be to deepen the comprehension of the past "through the exploration of the concepts and findings of modern psychology."[9] The historical literature since Professor Langer's address to the American Historical Association in 1957, however, makes it apparent that historians have generally continued to be inattentive to the possibility of making important discoveries through the use of psychology. This is most unfortunate, because it has prevented historians from knowing more about important factors pertinent to understanding not only individuals but sociohistorical movements and climates of opinion as well. Moreover, to neglect personal feelings is unwarranted, since a variety of autobiographical materials exists on many individuals, material containing many insights, hunches, self-doubts, anxieties, exaggerated concerns, and fears. Too often historians have dismissed these data as unimportant reflections on the game of life, in favor of the more typical career information.

Historians of progressivism in particular have been notably preoccupied with social, economic, and geographic factors, social status anxieties, religious affiliations, ideological interpretations of history, and the organizational techniques employed by progressive reformers. Still lacking is an adequate awareness of personality, that is, of the *totality* of a man's or a woman's emotional and social characteristics and identity. If the past decade has been instructive at all, it should have taught us that people, men and women of all ages, colors, and creeds, do not necessarily respond to issues

"Progressivism and the Masculinity Crisis" by Joe L. Dubbert. Reprinted from *The Psychoanalytic Review*, Vol. 61, No. 3, Fall 1974, through the courtesy of the Editors and the Publisher, National Psychological Association for Psychoanalysis, New York, N.Y.

Superscript numbers in this chapter correspond with numbered references at the end of the chapter.

and national political figures according to articulated political philosophies on the issues but rather out of personal feeling for the national figures involved. John F. Kennedy, Martin Luther King, and Theodore Roosevelt touched sensitivities within individuals. At a time when "image projection" and "personal charisma" have been found to be so important, it is ironic that the past is not being more carefully studied for what these traits may suggest about the national temper and imagination. Certainly caution must not be thrown to the wind and all history rewritten from a psychoanalytical viewpoint, but the evidence is sufficient for us to believe that more should be known about personality types and the impact of psychological factors within political and social movements.

James R. McGovern is one historian who has recognized this neglect and has called attention to it in a commendable study of the muckraker David Graham Phillips.[10] According to McGovern, Phillips was personally obsessed by an overwhelming impulse to be a mature and complete male. He lived a passive life, largely dependent on strong-willed, domineering women who drove him into flights from reality, during which he tried to compensate for his "lack of maleness" by turning out an extraordinary amount of work. Reform politics interested him because he hoped it would eradicate those signs of effeminacy which deeply disturbed him. That such signs existed at the turn of the century cannot be doubted given the concern shown by many men at the quickening tempo of the women's rights movement, the debate about educated women, and the growing number of "home in peril" articles.

McGovern's thesis that this nagging virility impulse that plagued Phillips helps explain his personal political and social views now needs to be set in a broader framework from which amplification and further case studies can proceed. One of the by-products of the present "discovery" (actually it is a rediscovery) of the "woman problem" is the simultaneous discovery of a crucial identity crisis for the American male during the period 1880–1920. "In point of fact," Myron Brenton noted in *The American Male* (1966), "the contemporary American male who looks back to his nation's history for confirmation of what the American male once supposedly was may be in for a shock."[3] Although a patriarchal social structure developed in the nation's formative years, the walls of the male establishment began to crack by the mid-nineteenth century. Whereas originally Puritanism emphasized faith *and* works, by the late nineteenth century works alone had become the predominant goal of American males. According to the capitalistic ethos, men were expected to promote industry and commerce, which they did in abundance, often spending long hours at the office, at the plant, or in the fields and forests. With their energies spent, they came home too weary and worn to devote much time and interest to family or friends. The tasks of rearing the children therefore fell to females, who guaranteed the continuity of American moral standards as well as the patronizing of certain social and cultural events and activities, especially among the urban middle class. According to an article in *Christian Family Magazine,* "The solicitous mother, like the skillful culturist who anxiously watches the first mellowing rays of Spring . . . eagerly seizes the first tender years of childhood, and improves them as the golden seedtime of life," fixing in them the tone of the "moral culture."[19] In this role American women succeeded all too well to suit many American men, who by the late ninteenth century were becoming increasingly fearful of female moral, social, and cultural pre-eminence, to say nothing of growing female interest in politics.[12,4,20,17]

In the February 1869 issue of *Putnam's Monthly* the editor registered a stern early warning about this new woman who was interesting herself in culture, including German philosophy, poetry, and even Bismarck's foreign policy.[11] The new woman was making excessive demands on her husband, expecting responses and interests which were simply impossible and even out of his natural character, given his mission as a free and natural producer at the marketplace. In time this situation was bound to have serious consequences, according to Cyrus Edson in the *North American Review*.[7] Marriages would fail, insanity would increase, and violence would become commonplace unless prissy American females backed off a bit. A shrill editorial appearing in the *Living Age* in 1902 hysterically predicted the Europeanization of America if women continued their present interest in culture.[1] Threatened was the simple, natural growth of a nation whose very nationalism was based on the fact that it had escaped European civilization. "Men and women who breathe habitually an atmosphere of social form and convention gradually lose all spontaneity."

Culture, then, had become a distinctively female preoccupation for American middle-class women, and many men felt threatened by it. Some men became defensive about certain male domains, lest they succumb to women reformers. "The popularity of athletic sports at the present time will prove most useful to us as a race" wrote one commentator who explicitly feared an effeminization of youth if the efforts exerted by some women to abolish such sports as boxing succeeded. The football field is the "only place where masculine supremacy is incontestable," noted the *Independent* in 1909. And for young men about to enter courtship it was argued that brute strength was still the most admired trait in American men, the thing most likely to impress young ladies seeking a husband. Theordore Roosevelt believed that athletics was one of the best things to happen in a boy's life, for it developed the kind of rugged individualism that fostered a strong national character. Roosevelt took a personal interest in encouraging rule revisions in football to make the sport more palatable to anguished humanitarians who thought it barbaric. Viewed in this light, athletics has been much more than just a pastime. It has important connotations that should not be missed by those seeking to understand the national temper and imagination. During the progressive era it was an important line of defense against effeminization for American men whose destiny it was to propagate a superior race.[6,18]

Theodore Roosevelt preferred to see the relationship of the sexes in America restored to its pre-Civil War status; "The woman must be the housewife, the helpmeet of the homemaker, the wise and fearless mother of many healthy children." The relationship of men and women was fundamental to the rugged Rough Rider, who saw in the hands of women "the destiny of the generations to come after us." Grover Cleveland agreed completely with Roosevelt and feared that "liberated women" threatened the preordained progress of the race—"the sacred mission of womanhood." The good wife was defined as one who loved her husband and her country but had no desire to run either. This did not mean that Cleveland or Roosevelt objected to female suffrage as long as it did not have a "dangerous undermining effect on the characters of the wives and mothers of our land." Women must not eschew their obligation to protect the morals and manners of the civilization lest it lose its "favored nation" claim in heaven.[5,11,15,16]

True to his word, Grover Cleveland conspicuously remained a man's man in his personal life, according to Allan Nevins. He shunned polite society, dined out infrequently, always preferring instead card games, smoke-filled rooms, and hunting.[13]

By 1900, then, a severe sociosexual wrench was evident which had profound effects upon the personal attitudes of many men in their twenties and thirties, men who were seeking to identify not only as successes in business but as successful husbands and fathers and above all as successful *men*. These men, raised by strong-willed Victorian women, who had disciplined their sons in the ways of righteous living, were now themselves married to Victorian offspring.

But many men began to feel that too many women were taking too seriously their duties as mothers in pledging to protect America's moral integrity when they criticized sports, agitated for prohibition, became socially and culturally sophisticated, and even became politically informed. These mothers and wives were vital to the preservation of the race, men would admit, but their role was beginning to transcend its accustomed domain and threaten not just the masculine establishment but the whole of masculine identity.

The evidence clearly suggests that around 1900 tensions between American men and women were building considerably, judging by the frequent discussions of marital tensions so well outlined by William O'Neill's *Divorce in the Progressive Era.* One of the best examples of these conflicting crosscurrents is a book by Albert Beveridge written in 1906 entitled *The Young Man and the World.* "Be a man" is the main point Beveridge has to make. Be persistent but above all be yourself, advised the Indiana Senator. Avoid books, in fact avoid all artificial learning, for the forefathers put America on the right path by learning from completely natural experience. It was important to know your father, according to Beveridge, because he was a creature of experience—the school of hard knocks was his classroom, where he learned how to win and be a success. Other men should be consulted too in the clubs and pubs where they talked about things, not accomplishments. But a glaring ambiguity existed in Beveridge's mind, because in the very same volume he advised obedience to a mother's moral direction.[2a] Nothing in the home could match the radiance and love of a mother,[2b] for there was something transcendent about her. To her all should be confessed, for she alone served as the guide for righteous living. How can one be expected to effectively balance the honorable American drive toward success "according to your natural abilities" and the stern moralism of the cultured mother confesser? No easy task is this, and Beveridge himself finally admitted that it is best to "get out of the exclusive atmosphere of your perfumed surroundings; join the hardest working political club of your party in your city; report to the local leader for active work; mingle with those who toil and sweat."[2c] Put another way, one writer exclaimed, "For if a man, at certain periods and in certain moods, strongly desires to meet the standards set for him by women, he also desires, almost all the time, and in almost every mood, to meet the standards set for him by men."[27]

Embodied in Beveridge's dilemma is a basic personality trait of the American progressive. Recognizing the claims of moral strength and cultural sophistication of the American female, males yearned for natural masculine fulfillment, which they could never be certain of achieving given the accelerating tempo of change around 1900. But how, one must ask, did the quest for masculine fulfillment manifest itself? Did it have any direct or even indirect bearing on the political attitudes and social behavior of the progressives? It would be helpful to know more about family histories here, the manner in which children were raised, and the frequent marital and sex-identity tensions that exhibited more than just familiar differences of opinion. Unquestionably detailed answers to this kind of inquiry would vary among individuals, but judging from available biographical data and the personal reflections of some of the figures who matured in the last third of the nineteenth century, an exaggerated concern about masculinity is quite apparent. McGovern has supplied an excellent study of David Graham Phillips along these lines. A study of the Kansas editor William Allen White provides another fascinating example. Even before his father's death when White was fourteen, White's mother's influence over him was clearly established. A strong-willed, cultured wonan, she had a keen sense of puritan righteousness, a point of view which had been strengthened in her at Knox College, where she had been a student in the 1850's. On the Kansas plains, although bored, according to her son, she discharged her obligations as a good mother by raising her son according to the dominant moral precepts of the day. Young Willie went to three different Sunday Schools each week, performed his lessons faithfully under his mother's direction, diligently practiced the piano, and, like most rural children, dutifully executed several assigned chores around the farm and home. In his autobiography White recalled romping in the woods and retreating to his favorite hideaway, the barn, where he acted out his childhood fantasies. These experiences provided the material for *The Court of Boyville* (1898), a collection of short stories of boys. In these stories, however, a latent tension exists (similar to that in Beveridge's book) between the naturally free, primitive insincts of boyhood and the moral governance of stern parents, especially mothers, who failed to understand the importance of allowing adolescent males to follow their natural instincts. Mealy Jones' mother, for example, had been "a perfect little lady in her girlhood and . . . [now] was molding her son in forms that [had] fashioned her."[22b] The premise of these stories is that boys needed the freedom to run wild across the landscape to develop individual ruggedness, characteristic of strong-willed men. "There is a tincture of iron that seeps into a boy's blood with the ozone of the earth, that can come no other way," White wrote.[22a] Natural instinctiveness, not the artificial governance from a cultured feminine viewpoint, was the key to the triumph of a new race of men. Absent from the lives of too many boys was an awareness of fatherhood, a masculine viewpoint gained from the examples and experiences of a successful father. In White's case it had been his mother's Republicanism, her yen for music, her theology, and her choice books that had surrounded him. When he went to the University of Kansas, she left her El Dorado home and accompanied him. After he married, she lived with her son and daughter-in-law, and when the *Gazette* became successful, White purchased the house next door for his mother and visited her every day he was in town until she died at ninety-four.[21b,8a]

In June 1897 White found a new father. While in Washington, D.C., he was introduced to Theodore Roosevelt. The way White tells it, few first impressions could ever rival the dramatic chemistry of this meeting. "He sounded in my heart the first trumpet call of the new time that was to be." "Such visions, such ideals, such hopes, such a new attitude toward life and patriotism and the meaning of things" made White ecstatic "with the splendor of [Roosevelt's] personality." White praised Roosevelt's masculinity, his hard muscled frame, his crackling voice, "the undefinable equation of his identity." "It was something besides his social status . . . quite apart from reason" which won White to Roosevelt.[21c]

Roosevelt became a national hero to millions who saw in him a savior delivering a once free and natural state from the ravages of an artificial economic and social hierarchy which resembled European society in its structure and technique. What needs to be emphasized is that to men like White, Roosevelt also symbolized a restoration of masculine identity at a time in national life when it appeared to be jeopardized. Thus for White, Roosevelt was a success not so much because he was able to cut the Gordian Knot of reform, but because he could do it by resorting to manly, commonsense realism typical of the "Western spirit," as opposed to the emotional fear and trumpeting of crusading nineteenth-century reformers. Theodore Roosevelt was above both: above the sentimental proclamations of aggrieved women and above boastful exploitative paternalism. Roosevelt was simply too rugged, too courageous, too manly to be so negatively affected. In *The Old Order Changeth*, a collection of White's political essays, he theorized that in so far as progressivism was instinctive and emotional it was feminine, but to the extent it had power and dominance it was masculine.

Theodore Roosevelt brought the two together, supplying the power, dominance, and masculinity to make reform appealing to a generation of men disturbed about the national trends toward plutocracy and an effeminate society and culture.[24a,25]

White demonstrated his concern for the development of proper masculine traits by an urgent plea for more male teachers in public schools. Like many progressives, White emphasized the value of education to "direct the conscience of the people toward wisdom" and "turn their hearts to that common sense . . . conduct known as righteousness." But women, according to White, because of their peculiar circumstances, tended to be too abstract, too theoretical, too artificial in the classroom—void of a man's commonsense realism. White contended that the desire for male companionship was so strong among teen-age boys that many left female-dominated schools to seek companionship in such typical male haunts as the local pool hall. Although White was a thorough champion of male juvenile freedom, he could not countenance a pool-hall atmosphere for fear of immoral contamination and the danger of inseminating untrustworthy social and political judgments. The necessity of a proper education from male instructors was all the more acute considering the number of immigrants, mostly male, that had come to America since 1880. America had been made strong through natural competition among its producers, but could one be sure that this noble, virile, Aryan tradition would be sustained if corrupt aliens were not at once properly trained by precept and example? White firmly believed that to live in a man's world and have firsthand experience with a man's roughness was essential if a boy was to lead a productive life. For this very important reason male teachers were essential if the national prophecy was to be fulfilled.[24b]

White's concern that there be a realization of masculine identity and a restoration of a natural culture did not mean that he was unappreciative of American mothers or female schoolteachers. In the past America's mothers had served the nation well by presiding over a democratically run home; White described this as the true spirit of self-sacrifice. His own mother was an excellent example of a woman who devoted her life to her home and son although she was bored with the bleak existence on the bucolic Kansas plain. In other countries, where women were "half-castes," the artificiality of state and church prevented an appreciation of what America's puritan mothers were about to envision: Moral progress depended on a free and natural home life. America's mothers had done a magnificent job of rearing the nation's children, but there is a strong indication that William Allen White and other men reaching early middle age after 1900 could not help but feel that American women had been too successful in shielding their sons from reality by inculcating artificial views about polite society and encouraging cultural creativity. White, who fainted at the sight of blood, was never athletically inclined, refrained from visits to smoke-filled rooms, and, although he took his annual vacations in Estes Park, Colorado, a veritable hunter's paradise, neither hunted nor fished there—hardly the typical, rugged, manly type he admired.[8b] What White and his contemporaries seemed to long for was a new sense of brotherhood and a realization of truly masculine identity. Even the modern conceptualization of Christ had been corrupted to the point of viewing the Nazarene as "pale, feminine, wishy-washy, an otherworldly Christ that has grown out of the monkish idea of religion."[26a] White pleaded to these women who had grown restless and bored with home responsibilities and had escaped to return to the home where they obviously belonged. He had nothing but praise for Kathleen Norris's *Mother*, published in 1911. Little Margaret, the heroine, who lived with her family in a small New York town, grew bored and restless at the dull and routine pace of life. ("Nothing ever happens to us.") Her longed-for escape was realized when a prominent "society woman" employed Margaret as her secretary. But it finally dawned on Margaret (and this pleased White immensely) that her mother's life of devotion to her family and the performance of her routine home duties was the most meaningful for a woman. The commonplace life was, after all, the *Natural* life, truly richer than the artificial existence of women who sought status, culture, and mobility. In a letter to Theodore Roosevelt, White strongly recommended he read the novel and was pleased to learn that the former President had already read it and was equally impressed with it.[26a]

That White should mention such a novel to Theodore Roosevelt is not surprising because as good friends they exchanged many ideas and Roosevelt, more than any other public figure of his time, helped make possible the renewed quest for masculine fulfillment. White saw Roosevelt's importance as beyond that of being a successful, honest statesman whose efforts were bringing more equity to American life. He was successfully rescuing the American male from a threat of too much femininity. American men were now capable of sustaining a masculine identity; adolescence was over—the youth had been made strong thanks to Roosevelt's splendid example of male vigor and assertiveness. In 1912 William Allen White did not at first encourage the presidential aspirations of the man from Oyster Bay. Better it would be for the entire nation in the long run if the new, mature generation of men fought whatever devils were sent to it rather than follow Roosevelt for another four years. "We need a brother and not a master nor a servant," said White. Roosevelt had been a good father but now the sons, experienced and adept, were primed for their own manly heroics. Nevertheless, Roosevelt ran in 1912 and, of course, White supported him, as did some four million other Americans, a million of which, according to White, were "Teddy votes—votes of men who had confidence in you personally without having any particular intelligent reason to give why;

except that you were a masculine sort of a person with extremely masculine virtues and probably masculine faults."[26b]

White's last major contribution to the literature of the progressive era was a novel, *In the Heart of a Fool*, published in 1919, long enough after the progressive tide had receded so that it received negligible attention. Grant Adams, the hero, was White's ideal prototype. Rugged, handsome, intelligent, he became a powerful, dominant community leader and heroically sacrificed his life in the struggle against materialism. He fathered a son, Kenyon, who was born out of wedlock to a materialistic, compulsive, dominating German servant girl, Margaret Muller. She rejected her son, however, preferring instead to seek "better things," leaving him finally to be raised by Laura Nesbit, who was a perfect self-sacrificing, devoted, honest, and naturally cultured woman who knew her place in the scheme of life. But White prevents Laura Nesbit from controlling Kenyon's life by portraying a certain "magical quality" deep within his soul that insulated him from her total domination.[23]

It is not the intent here to propose a new interpretation of progressivism based on an analysis of one man during the tumultuous years betwen McKinley and Harding. However, it should be apparent that the record of these years is still far from complete, considering the valuable potential contribution of social psychology and the wider appreciation of the dynamics of personality composition. Historians would do well to examine more carefully the personal biographical information and anecdotes for leads that will reveal more about their subjects as individual human beings instead of beginning with a set of standards to measure their presumed liberalism, radicalism, or conservatism. What explains the extraordinary attraction to Theodore Roosevelt by American men like William Allen White, who in social and geographical background and personal temperament were quite different from the Rough Rider? Why were physical prowess and exaggerated concerns for masculinity such a frequent item of discussion? In what ways were young men of the period affected by the apparent rise of the new woman? In other words, the progressive era must be seen as more than a political reform movement. It would seem particularly appropriate that closer attention be paid to these factors for the light it may shed on many other issues confronting social historians, since it was, after all, during these years that men and women experienced a profound readjustment which had profound side effects not only on progressivism but on some of the long-range problems which remain unsettling in American life. Perhaps a writer for the *New Republic* summed it up best by noting that the male sex had been historically endowed with inferiority complexes but that these were being successfully turned into a defense mechanism against the assumed-to-be-superior female. William Allen White's answer was for woman to return to their historic place in the home, but with a new appreciation of the nature of a boy's and a man's world, by allowing them freedom of interaction so as to build the strong national character championed by Theodore Roosevelt. White was to be disappointed in the decade that followed, for as an anonymous contributor to *Harper's* pointed out in 1921 those men who longed for such normalcy, where women were dependent on men, were a bore. How stifling and oppressive!

REFERENCES

1. The Anglo-Saxon Society Woman. *The Living Age*, Vol. 232, 1902, pp. 513–522.

2. Beveridge, A. J. *The Young Man and the World*. New York: Appleton and Co., 1906, pp. (a) 61; (b) 78; (c) 353–354.

3. Brenton, M. *The American Male*. New York: Coward McCann, 1966, p. 123.

4. Calhoun, A. W. *Social History of the American Family*. New York: Noble, 1917.

5. Cleveland, S. G. *Women's Mission and Women's Clubs. Ladies' Home Journal*, Vol. 22, 1905, pp. 3–4.

6. Cope, E. D. The Effeminization of Man. *Open Court*, Vol. 7, 1893, p. 33–47.

7. Edson, C. Concerning Nagging Women. *North American Review*, Vol. 160, 1895, pp. 29–37.

8. Hinshaw, D. A. *A Man from Kansas*. New York: G. P. Putnam's Sons, 1945, pp. (a) 31–43; (b) 34–35; (c) 109–119.

9. Langer, W. L. The Next Assignment. *The American Historical Review*, Vol. 63, 1958, pp. 283–304.

10. McGovern, J. R. David Graham Phillips and the Virility Impulse of Progressives. *New England Quarterly*, Vol. 39, 1966, pp. 334–355.

11. Men's Rights. *Putnam's Monthly*, Vol. 8, 1869, pp. 212–224.

12. *Mrs Whittelsey's Magazine for Mothers*. New York: Henry Whittelsey, 1850–51.

13. Nevins, A. *Grover Cleveland*. New York: Dodd, Mead, 1934, pp. (a) 5–6 (b) 13; (c) 23; (d) 57; (e) 71.

14. Roosevelt, N. *Theodore Roosevelt: The Man As I Knew Him*. New York: Dodd, Mead, 1967, p. 27.

15. Roosevelt, T. The American Woman: A Mother. *Ladies' Home Journal*, Vol. 22, July 1905, pp. 3–4.

16. ———. The Strenuous Life (1900). *Memorial Edition*, New York: Charles Scribner's Sons, 1926, p. 5.

17. Sunley, R. Early Nineteenth Century American Literature on Child Rearing. In M. Mead and M. Wolfenstein (Eds.), *Childhood in Contemporary Cultures*. Chicago: University of Chicago Press, 1955, pp. 150–167.

18. The Uncultured Sex. *Independent*, Vol. 67, 1909, pp. 1099–1100.

19. The Weight of Female Influence. *Christian Family Magazine*, 1842, pp. 107–108.

20. Welter, B. The Cult of True Womanhood. *American Quarterly*, Vol. 18, 1966, pp. 151–174.

21. White, W. A. *Autobiography*. New York: Macmillan Company, 1946, pp. (a) 4; (b) 5–6; (c) 298; (d) 345 ff.; (e) 423; (f) 427–430; (g) 472–474.

22. ———. *Court of Boyville*. New York: Doubleday and McClure, 1899, (a) Preface; (b) p. 4.

23. ———. *In the Heart of a Fool*. New York: Macmillan Company, 1919.

24. ———. *The Old Order Changeth*. New York: Macmillan Company, 1910, pp. (a) 165–168; (b) 177–189.

25. ———. Roosevelt: A Force for Righteousness. *McClure's Magazine*, Vol. 28, 1907, pp. 386–394.

26. ———. *Selected Letters of William Allen White*. Ed. W. Johnson. New York: Holt, 1947, pp. (a) 130–131; (b) 144–145.

27. Woodbridge, E. The Unknown Quantity in the Woman Problem. *Atlantic Monthly*, Vol. 113, 1914, p. 514.

chapter 12

In Time of War

by Peter Gabriel Filene

In this excerpt from his larger study, Him/Her/Self: Sex Roles in Modern America, *Peter Gabriel Filene continues the theme developed by Jeffrey Hantover's study of the Boy Scouts. As a result of the perception that work (and the entire culture) were becoming feminized, American men sought other means of validating their masculinity. World War I gave it to them; it was, in Filene's words, "the ultimate test of manliness." At the same time, the ideology of male sexual purity continued to ask men to control their sexual passions. Victorian moral reformers also found in World War I an opportunity to extend their viewpoint. Thus, dominant Victorian social ideals of manhood, far from being altered by the war, were given even more concrete expression.*

"You are going into a big thing: a big war: a big army: stand-ing for a big idea," wrote "Dad" to "Tom" in a letter pub-lished as an editorial by the *Ladies' Home Journal.* "But don't forget that the biggest thing about a principle or a battle or an army is a man! And the biggest thing that a war can do is to bring out that man. That's really what you and the other chaps have gone over for: to demonstrate the right kind of manhood, for it is that which weighs in a fight and wins it."[1]

When Congress declared war on Germany in April 1917, the American public responded with almost ferocious zeal. The nation launched a campaign to destroy those Huns who had mutilated Belgian women and children and who sought to crush freedom under their iron heels. It was a venture in which, as President Wilson had so nobly declared and a mil-lion publicists repeated, the United States wanted nothing for itself except the rights and happiness of people around the world—a peace without victory. It was a crusade.

This disinterested idealism was sincere. But middle-class American men also wanted some satisfactions for themselves from the war. Basically they envisioned the battlefield as a proving ground where they could enact and repossess the manliness that modern American society had baffled. Beneath the tidal wave of war propaganda issued by the government's Committee on Public Information and its imitators, the theme of manliness protruded again and again during 1917–1918. Nowhere more graphically than in the hundreds of enlistment posters, such as the one depicting a gleeful sailor riding a torpedo into the ocean like a cowboy.

Americans entered the Great War to achieve not simply political principles, but psychological reassurance as well. And not simply for the doughboys in actual battle, but also for the citizens on the home front. Indeed, the incessant propaganda that filled newspapers, magazines, auditoriums, and street corners focused primarily on those who were not in uniform. The trenches represented only one part of the war's meaning; the rest of it took place among civilians. As Americans translated the ideals of progressivism to the international sphere, they hoped thereby to restore within the United States their Victorian values of pure, strenuous manhood. That had been William James's objective as he offered his essay "The Moral Equivalent of War." But, instead, there were rampant materialism, licentious sexuality, and stifled individual opportunity. Now men turned to real war for the virtues that they had failed to find in symbolic substitutes.

The most immediate and tangible consequence of belligerence was rationing. Led by Herbert Hoover's Food Administration, civic leaders and publicists from New York to Keokuk to Seattle implored families to eat meatless meals, to walk instead of driving automobiles, and to patch their pants instead of buying new ones. "Four-minute men" exhorted theater audiences and sidewalk crowds to serve the national cause by buying Liberty Bonds. The rich were urged to volunteer their energy in government jobs and Red Cross work, while giving up servants and limousines. Many people welcomed self-denial. Thrift would be "a fine experience for us," they announced. It would save the American soul from "the leprosy of materialism," end the mad "extravagance and luxury" that had contaminated civilization.[2] In short, according to these writers, the economic sacrifices would produce contrition and purification after an era of materialism.

The war was more than an economic emergency; for males over the age of seventeen, it became a matter of sacrificing job or education, an arm, a leg, perhaps life itself. But that was, for many commentators, precisely its value. Through the crucible of combat a boy would emerge a man. Even as improbable a boy as Neil Leighton, the hero of a

Saturday Evening Post story entitled "The Feminine Touch." He was the son of an actor, who had died soon after Leighton's birth, and a Fifth Avenue milliner. As a teenager, he worked in his mother's establishment, developed a taste for opera and ballet, and was teased by girls for being a sissy. Finally, he enlisted to fight in France, in order to "show them the sort of man I am!" Ironically, however, he found himself stationed not as a doughdoy in the trenches, but as an assistant in a French doctor's office. In fact, he agreed to take a woman's role in a play being produced by the soldiers. So far so bad for Leighton. But suddenly the Germans invaded during a rehearsal. Disguised in his female costume, Leighton managed to shoot three enemy soldiers with a pistol concealed in a muff. He then proceeded to save the town by discovering the German's code for retreat (church bells to be rung three times). By the end of the story, he had won several medals and the love of a French girl, while enduring an arm wound with manly stoicism.[3]

Almost all young boys suffered the anxiety of being considered sissies, and reluctantly or not, they fought fist fights to prove their masculinity.[4] The world war provided a larger arena for the same proof. At least, this is how civilian observers liked to interpret it. To risk one's life for America signified more than patriotic idealism; it defined manly character. When the poet Joyce Kilmer died as he was reconnoitering on a battlefield, a mass-circulation magazine offered this eulogy: "Kilmer was young, only thirty-two, and the scholarly type of man. One did not think of him as a warrior. And yet from the time we entered the war he could think of but one thing—that he must, with his own hands, strike a blow at the Hun. He was a man."[5]

But manliness included more than physical courage. It included those moral qualities that Victorians had in mind when they spoke of "character." Whoever would save his soul must be willing to lose his life. The Great War became a "crusade" because Americans proclaimed enormous moral consequences for those who went off to fight. Consider Kelsey, the protagonist of a *Saturday Evening Post* story published in 1917. Throughout his life this ship's fireman had wanted only to drink, fight, and earn as much money as he could. If anyone talked about defending freedom and democracy against Germany, he sneered at such sentimentality. "Mr. Nietzsche would have approved of Kelsey," the author remarks. "To look out for number one was his gospel." When a German submarine torpedoed his ship during an Atlantic crossing, however, Kelsey went out of his way to save a woman and child whom he had met previously. On the lifeboat during the icy night he gave them his warm fur coat. Eventually they reached England, whereupon he donated to the Red Cross a gold-filled purse that he had stolen from a dead passenger. In the end, Kelsey gruffly signed up to fight against the Huns who were killing women, children, and freedom.[6]

He had proved himself "a true man," the Victorians would have said, demonstrating not only strength, but honor as well. Like the heroes of countless wartime stories and essays and sermons, he had vindicated the ideal of manliness that the Beveridges, Roosevelts, Stimsons, and other patriarchs so earnestly espoused. For them the war represented a crusade—more precisely, a chivalric crusade, and adult version of what the Boy Scouts embodied in more artificial terms. And as more and more Americans went into uniform and into battle, as the casualties increased, these civilian commentators were convinced that their hopes were coming true. "The slouching, dissipated, impudent lout who seemed to typify young America has disappeared," a *Washington Post* editorialist announced in 1918. Service to the nation, he said, had molded a youth who was serious, active, courageous, "with the ideals of his country stamped upon his heart."[7] When such men returned home they would not be content with desk jobs or more education, those unmanly options that prewar America had offered.

No, said the narrator in one novel of 1918, "there will be a new movement toward the ever-vanishing frontier, a setting westward in the search for wider ranges, for life in the open air."[8]

Such was the meaning of the Great War as defined by observers at home, interpreting to the American public the bloody events across the ocean. But how did the soldiers themselves understand their experience? Did they see themselves as chivalric knights riding tanks or planes in the name of democracy and manhood? As one might expect, no single generalization holds true for more than 2 million men of diverse backgrounds and temperaments. For some, war was simply another job, one that they took with the same dispassionate attitudes that they had applied to their civilian jobs. Russell G. Pruden, for example, never once, throughout his wartime letters and diaries, betrayed any ideological interpretation or personal feeling beyond compassion and humor. Similarly, several doughboys recounted the ferocious battles of the Argonne without a trace of emotional flourish, working stoically to win or at least survive. For others, however, the experience of Woodrow Wilson's war aroused very vivid feelings. "Darling dear this is the most tiresome trip that I have even taken or ever expect to take again," one soldier wrote en route to France. "Sophia if I could only get back to you and have some of your mothers [sic] regular meals you cannot realize how I would eat." But beyond disgust at sugarless porridge and tainted fish was the pain in his heart. "It seems as fate has dealt us an awful blow, and some times dear, the old tears are bound to come to my eyes, and if I wasn't a man I certainly would cry. If I look at your picture once darling, I look at it thousands of times."[9]

Many never surmounted this sense of personal deprivation. Others certainly did. "War is not a pink tea." Arthur Guy Empey conceded in this best seller, *"Over the Top,"* "but in a worthwhile cause like ours, mud, rats, cooties, shells, wounds, or death itself are far outweighed by the deep sense of satisfaction felt by the man who does his bit." It may have been cliché, but it was a sincere cliché. Some performed their "bit" modestly. "Mother you asked if I dreaded my trip across," Sergeant Thomas Cole wrote home while with the AEF, "and in ans. I shall say I did not. I feel about this thing as every other true American feels and that is; It is an honour to be here and to fight for such a country as we have." Some tended toward self-grandeur. A young army lieutenant declared in one letter: "You know, I think soldiering makes real men." Alan Seeger, the ill-fated poet, echoed this sentiment with his characteristically romantic flair. "Be sure that I shall play the part well," he wrote to his mother from France, "for I was never in better health nor felt my manhood more keenly."[10]

However breezy or brassy the rhetoric, it expressed genuine emotions. After all, more than 25,000 American men—Empey and Seeger among them—enlisted in the Canadian, British, and French forces before 1917.[11] Their zeal was authentic. Yet it alone does not explain the propelling motives. Which needs in them were seeking the "deep sense of satisfaction" that Empey mentioned? Again, any generalization is presumptuous. But perhaps the example of John Dos Passos is suggestive, in exaggerated form, of what prompted other young combatants.

In August of 1916, months before the United States entered the war, the twenty-year-old Dos Passos wrote to his friend Arthur McComb: "I am dying [!] to get to Belgium & exhaust surplus energy." Almost a year later, still not having reached his destination, Dos Passos expressed the same frustrations, but now specifying their source.

> *I think we are all of us a pretty milky lot,—don't you?—with our tea-table convictions and our radicalism that keeps so consistently within the bounds of decorum—Damn it, why couldn't one of us have refused to register [with the draft*

board] and gone to jail and made a general ass of himself? I should have had more hope for Harvard. . . .

And what are we fit for when they turn us out of Harvard? We're too intelligent to be successful businessmen and we haven't the sand or the energy to be anything else.

Until Widener is blown up and A. Lawrence Lowell assassinated and the Business School destroyed and its site sowed into salt—no good will come out of Cambridge.

It's fortunate I'm going to France as I'll be able to work off my incendiary ideas.

By enlisting in the ambulance corps, Dos Passos finally found release for the "incendiary" feelings that burned so impatiently within him. Writing from a small village in Champagne after experiencing his first attack, he announced to McComb: "I've not been so happy for months." But from what precisely did this happiness derive? From the violence surrounding him. The war's havoc fed the fire of his aesthetic romanticism. An entry in his notebook, dated August 1917, almost vibrates with passionate delight in the violence.

. . . But gosh I want to be able to express, later, all of this, all the tragedy and hideous excitement of it. I've seen so very little. I must experience more of it and more—the grey crooked fingers of the dead, the dark look of dirty mangled bodies, their groans and joltings in the ambulances, the vast tomtom of the guns, the ripping tear shells make when they explode, the song of shells outgoing like vast woodcocks—their contented whirr as they near their mark—the twang of fragments like a harp broken in the air and the rattle of stones and mud on your helmet. . . .

In myself I find the nervous reaction to be a curious hankering after danger that takes hold of me. When one shell comes I want another, nearer, nearer, I constantly feel the need of the

*drunken excitement of a good bombardment—I want to throw
the dice at every turn with the old roisterer Death . . . and
through it all I feel more alive than ever before—I have never
lived yet.*[12]

Dos Passos had come closer than ever before to fulfilling
his thwarted energies—and did so in literary rendition of
suffering. Between the real violence and his imagery, he
found resolution of those "incendiary ideas" that had driven
him to France.

"I know these men will return finer, cleaner, straighter
men," a Harvard alumnus wrote from a French battlefront.[13]
In the light of Dos Passos's attitudes, however, one wonders. Finer and cleaner? Perhaps only because purged of the
furious energy that so many adolescents turned against the
enemy and, in suicidal heroism, against themselves. For
many, especially the fervent romantics like Dos Passos and
Seeger, war meant the ultimate test of manliness—at the
edge of death. Nothing short of that could satisfy them. "A
night attack is a wonderful thing to see . . .," wrote Charles
Nordhoff. "Into the maelstrom of sprouting flames, hissing
steel, shattering explosions, insignificant little creatures like
you and me will presently run—offering, with sublime courage, their tender bodies to be burned and mangled."

For others, less compelled by the need for total self-
definition, war meant physical action and adventure
sanctioned in the name of patriotism. And, for some, it gave
the opportunity to enact a more bluntly physical violence
than the aesthetic college men could admit. "I do not mind
saying," wrote the author of *Gunner Depew*, "that I was glad
whenever I slipped my bayonet into a Turk, and more glad
when I saw another one coming." And an infantryman wrote
home about killing three Germans: "Why I just couldn't kill
them dead enough it seemed like. Believe me it was some
fun as well exciting." Finally, there were those whose feelings were much more prosaic. A private, afer being

wounded at the Argonne and therefore withdrawn from action, remarked: "I was happy to be hit again, because life in
the trenches, plugging through the mud and water up to the
waist, sleeping in wet, damp dugouts is unspeakable." This
same private would receive the croix de guerre for earlier
bravery in an Argonne raiding party that had captured
forty-one German machine guns and fifty-seven prisoners.[14]

Whether any of these experiences produced "finer" and
"cleaner" men is dubious. Yet Americans insisted vehe-
mently that the war purified the young men who took part.
War produced not simply stronger, more courageous, more
honorable men, but purer men. Indeed, many Americans
made it an extension of the purity crusade that Victorian
reformers had been directing for half a century against vice.
This was the last dimension of manliness, which Americans
hoped to vindicate by means of the war.

And they thought that they had. According to one reporter in 1918, "Our fighting force to-day is not only the
cleanest body of fighting men the world has ever seen, but
the cleanest group of young men ever brought together outside a monastery." Others, particularly those working in the
social-hygiene movement, made the same boast. Venereal
disease among the armed forces, they claimed, had been
virtually eradicated.[15] They credited two factors for this
achievement. First of all, the American Social Hygiene Association had persuaded the secretary of war to create a
Commission on Training Camp Activities that would suppress vice in military camp areas. With the co-operation of
other government agencies as well as groups like the Young
Men's Christian Association, the War Department under-
took a $4 million campaign to keep prostitutes (and alcohol)
away from the recruits, to abolish red-light districts near the
camps, to require soldiers to obtain medical examinations if
they had sexual relations, and to disseminate information on
venereal disease. "How much sweeter and cleaner would

our home lives be," remarked one lieutenant, "if we were to live like these [army] boys do."[16]

But prohibition was not the whole reason for this uniformed purity. No, the soldiers themselves rejected sexual temptation; they were clean not only in body, but also in mind. Or so the American public was told. Even when they came into contact with the proverbially promiscuous French women, these American men remained true to their principles and to their sweethearts back home, doing no more than to stroll with the *mademoiselles*. And again the civilian writers argued that the war itself sublimated the male passions. The hero of Willa Cather's novel *One of Ours*, for example, enlisted after suffering the humiliation of marriage to a women of stronger will than his own. Thereafter he never again turned to women for erotic satisfaction. Instead, he reasserted his masculinity by embracing battle and making love to war.[17]

That civilians, especially the social hygienists, proclaimed the purity of the chivalric doughboys is not surprising. After decades of service in moral-reform movements, they wanted and needed to believe that Wilson's war was, in all its dimensions, a crusade—a culmination to their tireless efforts and energies. More surprising is the fact that so many soldiers also insisted on this theme. A group of engineers and medical students at the University of Minnesota, for example, drafted a resolution as they enlisted in April 1917: "Aware of the temptations incident to camp life and the moral and social wreckage involved, we covenant together, as college men, to live the clean life and to seek to establish the American uniform as a symbol and guarantee of real manhood." During the next eighteen months, soldiers at the front wrote home with assurances that they had not succumbed to sexual temptation.[18]

What had happened to the notion and practice of "sowing wild oats"— Had the Great War abruptly destroyed an attitude that decades of earnest Victorian moralizing and purity movements had failed to destroy? Hardly. Whatever people believed or professed to believe, the American men who fought during the First World War were not essentially different from those in other wars. According to the reminiscences of a madam operating a New Orleans whorehouse, the war had not at all inspired men to find "true manhood," courageous and celibate. "Every man and boy wanted to have one last fling of screwing," she declared, "before the real war got him. Every farm boy wanted to have one big fuck in a real house before he went off and maybe was killed. . . . The idea of war and dying makes a man raunchy. . . . I dreamed one night the whole city was sinking into a lake of sperm." From a training camp in Plattsburgh, New York, meanwhile, one soldier estimated that most of his comrades were "unchaste" and that one-half had contracted venereal disease. More precisely, the Surgeon General of the Army reported a venereal disease rate of 114 per thousand enlisted men in 1917, rising a year later to 150 (as compared to 81 per thousand in 1898).[19]

The vast majority of these patients had contracted the disease in civilian life, before they enlisted. Conditions were better after the men came under army supervision. Not much better, though, and certainly far from the life of a monastery. Strenuous efforts by military officials in France—including prohibitive regulations, propaganda, and medical treatment—kept the loss of manpower among the American Expeditionary Force to a lower rate than in any previous war. Of approximately 2 million fighting men, an average of 18,000 were out of action each day because of venereal disease (as compared to an average of 606 men incapacitated during the Second World War). Nevertheless, 18,000 daily cases constituted a medical problem serious enough that, in mid-1918, the army created a venereal-disease detention camp in France. The men of the AEF may indeed have been "cleaner" than previous armies, but they were not monks, either in body, or, more important, in mind. "Wandering through dark streets," one lieutenant wrote in his diary. "Ever-present women. So mysterious and seductive in darkness. . . . A fellow's got to hang on to himself here. Not many do." According to one officer's study, 71 per cent of the Americans stationed in France engaged in sexual relations.[20]

Obviously the spokesmen of purity were deceived by their own hopes or propaganda. The Victorian crusade for chastity had not abruptly achieved victory in the war to end wars. Soldiers' bodies may have been less contaminated, but not their minds. Nor had the Victorian male dilemma of ambivalance regarding continence and wild oats been resolved; if anything, it had intensified as the gap between public allegations and actual behavior widened still further. The prewar dilemma of manliness persisted—but not entirely. Some of its features had changed because of the war. For one thing, men had at last found, it seemed, an opportunity for the strenuous life that the corporate economy and vanishing frontier had been steadily stifling. To this extent they could win manliness, even if some of them in the process failed to transcend brutality and sexual vice. Second, the prevailing myth portrayed the warriors as chivalric knights (while the public at home forsook materialism in a patriotic campaign of thrift). Whatever the facts of how the soldiers were behaving, people did not know those facts or refused to believe them. Until the Armistice and even beyond, the American public believed that the crusade for world-wide democracy was also purifying their soldiers and themselves. And many of the doughboys, too, insisted romantically on this interpretation. In war Americans found, for the time being, peace of mind about their national morality—in large part because men were manly again. . . .

NOTES

[1]"Tom," *LHJ*, XXXIV (October 1917), 7.

[2]Quotations from Charles V. Genthe, *American War Narratives, 1917–1918: A Study and Bibliography* (New York, 1969), p. 29; Arthur C. Train, *The Earthquake* (New York, 1918), p. 279.

[3]George Weston, "The Feminine Touch," *Saturday Evening Post* (1918), reprinted in *War Stories*, ed. by Roy J. Holmes and A. Starbuck (New York, 1919), 299–321.

[4]E.g., *The Autobiography of William Allen White* (New York, 1946), pp. 49–50; William G. McAdoo, *Crowded Years: The Reminiscences of William G. McAdoo* (Boston, 1931), p. 25.

[5](Editorial) "To Joyce Kilmer," *Delineator*, XCIV (January 1919), 3.

[6]Norman Springer, "A Recruit," *Saturday Evening Post*, CXC (November 10, 1917), 15–18, 98–105.

[7]Ira E. Bennett, *Editorials from the Washington Post, 1917–1920* (Washington D.C., 1921), p. 197. See also Genthe, *American War Narratives*, pp. 29, 68–69.

[8]Train, *Earthquake*, p. 201.

[9]Russell G. Pruden Papers, Sterling Library, Yale University; James M. Merrill, ed., *Uncommon Valor: The Exciting Story of the Army* (New York, 1964), pp. 312, 327–342.

[10]Arthur Guy Empey, *"Over the Top"* (New York, 1917), pp. 279–280; Sgt. Thomas R. Cole to Mrs. J. W. Elliott, with the AEF in France, July 24, 1918, in Cole Papers, SHC; letter from Albert Angier, June 5, 1918, in *On the Field of Honor: A Collection of War Letters of Three Harvard Undergraduates Who Gave Their Lives in the Great Cause*, ed. Paul B. Elliott (Boston, 1920), p. 22; Alan Seeger to his mother, October 17, 1914, in *Letters and Diary of Alan Seeger* (New York, 1917), p. 8; Genthe, *American War Narratives*, pp. 40–45, 87.

[11]Genthe, pp. 25–26.

[12]Dos Passos to Arthur K. McComb, August 26, 1916, and July 31, 1917, both quoted in Melvin Landsberg, *Dos Passos' Path to U.S.A.: A Political Biography, 1912–1936* (Boulder, Colo., 1972), pp. 48, 56; Dos Passos to McComb, spring 1917, quoted in Landsberg, p. 52, and in Daniel Aaron, *Writers on the Left: Episodes in American Literary Communism* (New York,

Avon ed., 1965), pp. 358–359; Dos Passos Notebook, August 26, [1917], reprinted in introduction to Dos Passos, *One Man's Initiation: 1917* (Ithaca, N.Y., 1969), p. 22.

[13]Letter from Francis Reed Austin, August 16, 1918, in *On the Field of Honor*, ed. Elliott, p. 62.

[14]Charles Bernard Nordhoff, "More Letters from France," *Atlantic Monthly*, CXXI (January 1918), 123; Albert N. Depew, *Gunner Depew* (New York, 1918), p. 159, quoted in Genthe, *American War Narratives*, p. 80; Frank Freidel, *Over There: The Story of America's First Great Overseas Crusade* (Boston, 1964), pp. 197, 290.

[15]Frank Parker Stockbridge, "The Cleanest Army in the World," *Delineator*, XCIII (December 1918), 8; Kate Waller Barrett, head of the Florence Crittenton movement for unwed mothers, quoted in Paul S. Boyer, *Purity in Print: The Vice-Society Movement and Book Censorship in America* (New York, 1968), pp. 63–64; M.J. Exner, introduction to *Sex and Life: A Message to Undergraduate Men*, by Thomas Walton Galloway (New York, 1919), p. x; B. S. Steadwell, "Modern Campaign Against Venereal Disease," *Light* (January–February 1920), in Ethel Sturges Dummer Papers, SL, folder 403.

[16]William F. Snow, "Social Hygiene and the War," *Journal of Social Hygiene*, III (July 1917), 420–422; Rachelle S. Yarros, "'Shall We Finish the Fight?,'" *Life and Labor*, IX (January 1919), 19–20; Harold Hersey, quoted in Boyer, *Purity in Print*, pp. 55–57.

[17]Stanley Cooperman, *World War I and the American Novel* (Baltimore, 1967), pp. 227, 132–134; Genthe, *American War Narratives*, pp. 44–45; Floyd Gibbons, *"And They Thought We Wouldn't Fight"* (New York, 1918), pp. 93, 272; Luther H. Gulick, *Morals and Morale* (New York, 1919), p. 43.

[18]Quoted in Snow, "Social Hygiene and the War," 499; letter from Albert Edgar Angier, June 5, 1918, in *On the Field of Honor*, ed. Elliott, pp. 22–23.

[19]Stephen Longstreet, ed., *Nell Kimball: Her Life as an American Madam: By Herself* (New York, 1970), p. 279; Eugene A. Hicken to Grace A. Johnson, September 22, 1917, in Johnson Papers, SL, folder 119; *Report of the Surgeon General, U.S. Army, to the Secretary of War* (Washington, D.C., 1920), fig. 44, p. 181, and (1918), pp. 196–197, 200–201.

[20]*Report of the Surgeon General* (1919), pp. 1312, 1634; P.M. Ashburn, *A History of the Medical Department of the United States Army* (Boston, 1929), pp. 336–337; Freidel, *Over There*, pp. 80–81; Victor Hicken, *The American Fighting Man* (New York, 1969), p. 302.

period

IV

(1920-1965)

Companionate

Providing

chapter 13

The Breakdown of the Husband's Status

by Mirra Komarovsky

The Great Depression, the worst economic catastrophe in the twentieth century, was a major social catastrophe as well, because it deprived many men of their roles as family breadwinners. In the 1930s, Mirra Komarovsky interviewed 59 couples on relief, where the husband had become unemployed. Her study provides the fullest documentation of the effect of male unemployment on marriage in the 1930s. In the following selection, she presents complete case studies of the Patterson, Adams, and Holman families, as well as gives brief examples from her interviews with several other families. She finds that as the husband lost status, his wife lost more than she gained. Because both husband and wife believed the male should have been the provider, neither was satisfied when they were forced to accept nontraditional arrangements. Still, in the three types of families she identifies, she finds that some husbands coped with unemployment better than others, especially the husbands with male friends and emotionally supportive wives.

THE FREQUENCY OF BREAKDOWN

Unemployment does tend to lower the status of the husband. It has had this effect in 13 out of 58 families included in the study. . . .

In some families the hitherto concealed contempt for the husband came into the open; in others unemployment has reversed the husband–wife relation—dominance of the husband having been changed to his complete subordination; in still others the husband suffered a loss of respect, a change which is best described in the words of the wife: "I still love him, but he doesn't seem as 'big' a man."

That only 13 families were thus affected may appear to indicate that being the provider plays some, but after all only a small, part in determining the prestige and powers of a husband. It might be pointed out, however, that relief does not completely free the wife of economic dependence upon the husband. The relief allowance is so meager that the husband continues to be at least a potential provider. By taking families on relief we have excluded those now supported by a wage-earning wife. The importance of the economic factor for the husband's status would probably be fully revealed only by such a complete reversal of economic roles. Families in which the deterioration of the husband's status has led to the separation of the couple were also excluded from our study, since we have taken only complete families.

It must be remembered, furthermore, that most of our couples are middle-aged people married for 15 to 20 years. Attitudes become crystallized in marriages of such duration. Even had the prestige of the husband derived in part from his function as a provider, sheer force of habit may protect it for some time against the impact of unemployment. . . .

Excerpted from *The Unemployed Man and His Family* by Mirra Komarovsky, New York: Dryden Press, 1940, 23–47. © 1940 by the Dryden Press.

THREE PATTERNS OF BREAKDOWN

To give a general picture of the changes wrought by unemployment in husband-wife relations, we shall present three cases, each illustrating a particular pattern of change. In the first pattern, that of *crystallization of an inferior status*, unemployment has merely made more explicit a previously existing inferior status of a despised husband. Another pattern may be best described as the *breakdown of a more or less coercive control*. In this pattern unemployment has undermined the authority of a more or less dominant husband over a subordinate and resentful wife. Finally, in other cases unemployment has *weakened the authority of a husband over a loving wife*.

Unemployment crystallized the inferior status of the husband. In families illustrating this pattern the woman dominated the family prior to the depression. Furthermore, she neither loved nor respected her husband.

The depth of her contempt or antagonism for her husband differed from case to case. Thus, Mr. Dorrance was thoroughly despised by his wife for being a shiftless drunkard. Bitter fights characterized most of their married life. Mrs. Baldwin, on the other hand, concealed her contempt for her husband and preserved some decorum in daily relations with him.

The families within this group also varied in the degree of dominance of the wife. In one family the husband was completely beaten. He seldom tried to assert his power. The wife had won all their battles. Her only concession was to keep him in the house. Another wife was frustrated in her attempt to improve her husband's attitude toward the children and to correct some of his other faults. Nevertheless, she had her way in most of the spheres of family life.

Unemployment, in so far as it affected such families, has caused the concealed lack of respect for the husband to come into the open or, if the antagonistic sentiments were openly expressed prior to the depression, to increase the aggression toward the husband. The manifestations of the above changes were in increased conflicts, blaming the husband for unemployment, constant nagging, withdrawal of customary services, sharp criticism in front of the children, irritability at hitherto tolerated behavior, indifference to his wishes, and so on. The story of the Patterson family will illustrate the decline in the husband's status in families in which his position was low even prior to unemployment.

The Patterson Family

	Age
Mr. Patterson	47
Mrs. Patterson	43
Girl	18

Family on relief for a year and one half. . . .

Reaction to Unemployment and Relief. Prior to the depression Mr. Patterson was an inventory clerk earning from $35 to $40 a week. He lost his job in 1931. At the present time he does not earn anything, while his 18-year-old girl gets $12.50 a week working in Woolworth's, and his wife has part-time work cleaning a doctor's office. Unemployment and depression have hit Mr. Patterson much more than the rest of the family.

The hardest thing about unemployment, Mr. Patterson says, is the humiliation within the family. It makes him feel very useless to have his wife and daughter bring in money to the family while he does not contribute a nickel. It is awful to him, because now "the tables are turned," that is, he has to ask his daughter for a little money for tobacco, etc. He would rather walk miles than ask for carfare money. His daughter would want him to have it, but he cannot bring himself to ask for it. He had often thought that it would make it easier if he could have 25 cents a week that he could depend upon. He feels more irritable and morose than he ever did in his life. He doesn't enjoy eating. He hasn't slept well in months.

He lies awake and tosses and tosses, wondering what he will do and what will happen to them if he doesn't ever get work any more. He feels that there is nothing to wake up for in the morning and nothing to live for. He often wonders what would happen if he put himself out of the picture, or just got out of the way of his wife. Perhaps she and the girl would get along better without him. He blames himself for being unemployed. While he tries all day long to find work and would take anything, he feels that he would be successful if he had taken advantage of his opportunities in youth and had secured an education.

Mr. Patterson believes that his wife and daughter have adjusted themselves to the depression better than he has. In fact, sometimes they seem so cheerful in the evening that he cannot stand it any more. He grabs his hat and says he is going out for a while, and walks hard for an hour before he comes home again. That is one thing he never did before unemployment, but he is so nervous and jumpy now he has to do something like that to prevent himself from exploding.

Mrs. Patterson says that they have not felt the depression so terribly themselves, or changed their way of living so very much.

Changes in Husband–Wife Relations Since Loss of Employment. The wife thinks it is her husband's fault that he is unemployed. Not that he doesn't run around and try his very best to get a job, but he neglected his opportunities when he was young. If he had had a proper education and had a better personality, he would not be in his present state. Besides, he has changed for the worse. He has become irritable and very hard to get along with. He talks of nothing else, and isn't interested in anything else but his troubles. She and her daughter try to forget troubles and have a good time once in a while, but he just sits and broods. Of course that makes her impatient with him. She cannot sit at home and keep him company, so that during the past couple of years she and her daughter just go out together without him. It isn't that they leave him out—he just isn't interested and stays at home.

Mr. Patterson insists that his child is as sweet as ever and always tries to cheer him up, but the tenor of his conversation about his wife is different. She does go out more with the daughter, leaving him alone. He cannot stand it, worrying so and having them so lighthearted. "When you are not bringing in any money, you don't get as much attention. She doesn't nag all the time, the way some women do," but he knows she blames him for being unemployed. He intimates that they have fewer sex relations—"It's nothing that I do or don't do—no change in me—but when I tell her that I want more love, she just gets mad." It came about gradually, he said. He cannot point definitely to any time when he noticed the difference in her. But he knows that his advances are rebuffed now when they would not have been before the hard times.

The wife gives the impression that there might have been some decrease in sex relations, but declines to discuss them. She tells the following episode:

The day before the interview she was kissing and hugging the daughter. "I like to keep the girl sweet and young, and in the habit of kissing her mother good-night." The father walked in and said, "Don't you get enough of that?" Mrs. Patterson went on at great length as to how terribly that statement hurt her.

The interviewer also witnessed another episode. Towards the end of the interview with the wife, the husband walked into the living room and asked his wife if she thought the interviewer would be interested in talking to their neighbors. The woman said, "Don't bother us, we are talking about something else just now." He got up quietly and went into the kitchen. In a moment she called after him, "Oh, you can sit in here if you *want* to." Nevertheless, he stayed in the kitchen. . . .

Unemployment undermined a more or less coercive control

exercised by the husband over the wife. This group of wives was also characterized by absence of love or respect for the husband. But these husbands were stronger than their wives. His dominance was accepted with resentment varying from deep hatred to milder antagonism. A few cases were included in which there was continuous conflict between husband and wife with no clear-cut dominance of either. These conflicts meant that the wife could not get a permanent and secure victory and, therefore, resented her husband for frustrations in the regions of conflicting interests.

In so far as unemployment affected these families, it resulted in partial or complete emancipation of the wife from the husband's coercive authority. In some cases the relations were completely reversed; the dominance of the husband was changed to his complete subordination. In other cases the husband suffered defeat in particular spheres. Thus a Protestant man married to a Catholic refused, in spite of his wife's persistent efforts, to send the children to a Catholic school. After two years of unemployment the children were transferred to a parochial school. "After two years of unemployment I just could not fight her any longer," said the husband.

The pattern of breakdown of coercive control will be illustrated by the Adams family.

The Adams Family

Mr. Adams	60	Girl	19
Mrs. Adams	49	Boy	17

Family on relief for two years. . . .

Reaction to Unemployment and Relief. The family suffered many ups and downs in its economic life, even before the final unemployment. In 1926, Mr. Adams lost his job because of drink. Since then he has gone into several more or less unsuccessful ventures. From 1930 on Mrs. Adams contributed to the family income as a superintendent in an apartment house, taking in boarders, selling doughnuts and vegetables. Since 1933 the family has been on relief. The family's income is at present secured partly from boarders, partly from the small earnings of the two children. (It is doubtful that the family is entitled to relief.)

Mrs. Adams doesn't know what to say about the effect of the depression because in the last five years she has been more secure than in any other period of her life. When the family applied for relief she insisted on getting the relief check herself. She also controlled the money that was coming in from the boarders and from the children. Thus, for the first time in her life she knew exactly how much she had instead of just getting what was left after Mr. Adams' saloon bill was paid. She doesn't feel the humiliation of being on relief and is quite well satisfied with the present status.

Mr. Adams confirms Mrs. Adams' story of his work history. He feels that he could certainly get a job if he were not so old and sick. He attributes his broken health to heavy drinking. About relief and unemployment he says this: "I want you to put it down in black and white the depression in my case is due to drink."

Changes in Husband–Wife Relations. Mr. Adams said, "There certainly was a change in our family, and I can define it in just one word—I relinquished power in the family. I think the man should be boss in the family. I have old-fashioned ideas on the subject. I tried to be boss in the beginning, but you can't be boss with an English wife. But now I don't even try to be boss. She controls all the money, and I never have a penny in my pocket but that I have to ask her for it. The boarders pay her, the children turn in their money to her, and the relief check is cashed by her or by the boy. I turned down a good deal as a result of it. How did it all come about? Very simple. I stopped earning money, and most of the money that was coming in was coming in through her. Well, I'll be frank with you. Maybe if I had listened to her a long time ago we would have been better off now. But it certainly is hard—the hardest thing in the world is never to have an extra cent."

According to Mrs. Adams, the most important change in the family since unemployment is that she controls the money, and that Mr. Adams doesn't have any to get drunk on. The interviewer witnessed the following episode:

At the conclusion of the interview with Mr. Adams the interviewer put his dollar on the table in the presence of Mrs. Adams. She picked it up and said, "This dollar is mine, just as I told you." Mr. Adams did not argue about it, but as he was on the point of leaving he said to Mrs. Adams, "I have to make a telephone call to So-and-so." She gave him a nickel. "I need some cigarettes." She gave him fourteen cents. "Well, tomorrow I have got to get up early and finish re-painting the kitchen." Mrs. Adams said, "No you won't; there are other things to do."

Control over money is not the only change in the family. The sweetest victory for Mrs. Adams is her revenge over her mother-in-law. Her mother-in-law has no home now, and lives first with one and then another of her children. When her turn came, Mrs. Adams refused to take the mother-in-law in.

The interviewer heard the following exchange of words between the two:

Mrs. Adams said to Mr. Adams: "You always go to your mother in preference to me."

He answered, "Do I now take mother's advice in preference to yours?"

"Well," she said, "not now, but you used to, and you would have been better off if you had stopped long ago."

There are other ways in which Mrs. Adams has the better of her husband. They have some differences of opinion about the son's working, but the boy does what Mrs. Adams wants him to do. If she wants to buy some furniture, she just goes ahead and buys it. If he says anything, she tells him it is her money, not his.

Mrs. Adams is sorry she got wise so late in her life. "If I had only not been so soft in the beginning. If I had only set my will against his. But there was no use in trying before." If she had insisted on taking his wages away from him when he was earning, she is sure he would just have deserted the family and she would have been left with the two children.

"How does Mr. Adams take all this?" asked the interviewer. Mrs. Adams answered, "He still wants to be boss. That is his nature, even though he knows it wouldn't be for the best. He says he is treated like a dog in the house, but that's not true. He is good for a time, but once in a while the old trouble returns. Last week he came home drunk. She didn't know where he got the money. He didn't have much. He can't stand much now—it makes him sick. She thinks he got drunk last Saturday as revenge, because she said she wouldn't have his mother in the house. He is a very revengeful man. He came in and she didn't talk to him. That doesn't work with Mr. Adams. He goes right out of the house and gets drunk. So he started out of the house and she met him at the saloon door. She got hold of him and started talking to him, and just took him away by the hand. He cursed and pleaded but she brought him home just the same. It was the first time she got him out of the saloon. Why hadn't she done this before? He would not have stood for it before; he just wouldn't have paid any attention to her. . . ."

Unemployment lowered the status of a loved and respected husband. The first two cases described the effect of unemployment upon what might be generally described as unsatifactory marriages. The third pattern refers to marriages which were characterized by some love and admiration for the husband or, at the very least, by the absence of any very serious dissatisfaction on the part of the wife. A few marriages in this group were indeed far from harmonious. Thus, for example, one husband was irresponsible, unfaithful to his wife, and an indifferent father. The couple quarreled frequently, the wife complaining of his negligence and cruelty to her. But she continued to be deeply in love with him and was ready to forgive him at the slightest sign of improvement.

As to the relative status of the husband, this group of families consisted of all kinds; in some the husband was the true head of the family, others were dominated by the wife. But, while the woman was the matriarch, the husband accepted her leadership without apparent humiliation or hostility. He was a satisfied husband and thought his wife had good sense and was a good wife.

The decline in the husband's status took the form of the husband's defeat in certain spheres of the marriage relation. In another family subtle changes in the attitudes of the wife resulted in more equalitarian relations in a family hitherto led by the husband. The story of the Holman family will illustrate this pattern.

The Holman Family

Mr. Holman	37	Girl	18	Boy	10
Mrs. Holman	40	Girl	14	Boy	2

Family on relief for two years.

Husband–Wife Relations Prior to Unemployment. Mr. Holman is a young-looking and active man. He is not very intelligent, but he is good-natured and sociable, the kind who must have been the life of the party in "the good old days." He is, on the whole, a good family man. He must have been well adjusted to his job as traveling salesman of hardware articles. This job, while not putting too much demand upon his intellect, provided an outlet for his social interests. Mrs. Holman looks older than her husband. She is a thin and a fretful little woman, but a tireless housekeeper and a devoted mother. She is somewhat more "genteel" than her husband. Mr. Holman tells the following story of their courtship, which, in a way, gives a clue to their predepression relations:

"I was the one for having a little fun. Even when I courted her she would always want to stay at home or go to some quiet, dark spot where there wouldn't be any people. I think she was self-conscious as to how thin she was. Once I went out with another girl—a pretty one—and she asked me, referring to Mrs. Holman, where did I get such a skeleton. That was the end of that girl, because I really loved Mrs. Holman. She was good to me—really like a mother. And she still is."

Their married life was very satisfactory prior to unemployment. It is true that Mrs. Holman was more economical and less sociable. They did not have conflicts over it, because Mr. Holman earned good money, and besides, his work took him away from home for several days of the week.

Mrs. Holman was deeply in love with her husband. She apparently admired him, too. "He is certainly quick with his head. He knows the hardware business. Sometimes I would take the hardware manual and just call out any page and he would tell me exactly what was on that page."

No conflicts existed in this family. Mrs. Holman's attitude was maternal, while her husband's sentiments were those of gratefulness for her devotion. Both were devoted to each other and to the children. She admired him enough to consult with him about various decisions. With regard to money, or children, or church going, there seens to have been a good deal of consultation and joint decisions.

Reaction to Unemployment and Relief. Both Mr. and Mrs. Holman are mystified about the unemployment situation. Their economic philosophy does not offer them an adequate explanation in terms of external factors. Neither do they blame Mr. Holman. At first, Mr. Holman thought of it just as a stretch of bad luck that might turn any day. It was a reassurance to know that this bad luck was of a general character. Mr. Holman said to Mrs. Holman now and then, "I found out today that the So-and-sos are on relief. Well, I guess we're not the only ones. If such people as they are on relief, perhaps we shouldn't talk."

Mr. Holman reacted to unemployment with tireless search for work. He was active all day looking for odd jobs, washing windows for neighbors, and what not, or helping Mrs. Holman when he had nothing else to do. He is a man who likes to brag a bit and does not admit defeat so easily. But with continued unemployment he had periods of discouragement. "He doesn't say anything," says his wife, "but I know he gets so discouraged at times he begins to worry whether he will ever get a job again, we have been on relief so long."

Mrs. Holman does not blame her husband in the slightest for his unemploynent. She does not understand why such an energetic and bright man cannot find a job. Depression has been hard on the family because they have been forced to move into a two-room, backyard apartment and deny their children many necessities. Especially is it hard for their eldest daughter, an undernourished, nervous, genteel little girl, who is a senior in high school and deeply humiliated by the plight of the family.

Changes in Husband–Wife Relations. The major conflict since unemployment is over social life and is described by Mr. Holman as follows: Mrs. Holman is of a much quieter disposition and does not like amusements at all. When she spends 15 cents on a movie, she is so worried that she does not get any fun out of the movie. They decided to celebrate New Year's Eve. They got some one to stay with the children and went to a movie and had coffee and sugar buns afterwards. When they got back she said, "Now that it's done, I wonder if we wouldn't have been better off to have used the money for some of the things we need." But he is different. He likes good times. But they have conflict even when the amusement does not cost any money, because Mrs. Holman is jealous. For example, they broke up with their best friends because she was jealous of the woman for no good reason at all. The Holmans used to meet with the other couple, and the woman would just "kid" and dance and make merry, and Mrs. Holman would sit and sulk in a corner. Sometime ago, Mr. Holman joined a WPA club. He thought he could get a job through them. Well, they drank a bit. Once he came home late and she was furious. Mrs. Holman confirms this story. She says that they are of different temperaments. She likes to stay at home and he likes a good time. She confirmed her irritation with regard to the club. "It isn't right for a married man to stay out so late, is it? Besides why should he have a good time and spend money when I am going crazy trying to make ends meet on a relief allowance?"

All of these conflicts were resolved in Mrs. Holman's favor; Mr. Holman no longer attends the club and they stopped seeing their friends. The conflicts have arisen as the result of unemployment because, as Mr. Holman explains it, in the past he had had his share of good times on the road away from the family. Furthermore, Mrs. Holman could not use their poverty as an excuse to restrain his social life. At the present time, whenever he suggests some recreation that might cost a few pennies, she invariably reminds him of the manifold needs of the family, and this is the only time she speaks of his unemployment with a hint of reproach. . . .

This general description of the breakdown of the husband's status will be followed now by the discussion of the process of change as it bears upon two questions: which aspects of unemployment proved decisive in the deterioration of the husband's status, and what was his own reaction to the change.

THE VARIOUS WAYS IN WHICH UNEMPLOYMENT LED TO THE LOSS OF THE HUSBAND'S STATUS

Unemployment is a complex of conditions, and it affected the status of the husband in a variety of ways. This was clearly revealed in the attempt to discern the relation between unemployment and the changes in the attitudes of the wife. Not all aspects of unemployment were equally disruptive of the husband's status.

In some cases unemployment affected the husband's status because of the loss of earning power. The husband could no longer control the wife as heretofore by granting or withholding economic benefits.

The *weakening of economic coercion* occurred in cases in which the wife did not love her husband and tolerated him as a price for advantages of marriage. We do not assume, of course, that every time the wife deferred to her husband's wishes she was consciously aware of the possibility of his withdrawing support. It is only with the children that it is as simple as that. The father says, "I'll give you a nickel if you will go to the store for me," or, "If you don't behave, you will not go to the movie." With the wife, economic coercion exists as a general background of adjustment in marriage.

Loss of earnings and failure to provide for the family affected marital relations in still another way: they *lowered the prestige of the man* and lessened the respect that the wife had for him.

Possession of money carried with it power and prestige, but it apparently played still a third role in marriage. For some husbands *money has provided a margin of tolerance*, an area within which his authority was not put to severe tests because conflicting interests could be satisfied. Loss of money has narrowed this area, and for the first time necessitated choices and hence created new tests of the husband's authority.

It is not always possible to decide which of these three economic aspects of unemployment was the decisive feature in a given case. It is particularly difficult to decide whether weakening of economic coercion or loss of respect as a result of economic failure of the man was the critical element in the case. Economic coercion takes subtle forms and is seldom admitted by the wife. If the husband loses his earning ability and with it his power, the wife is likely to rationalize the change in terms of the man's lack of responsibility for the family. Furthermore, change in the behavior of the wife as a result of both aspects of unemployment may take similar forms. Take for example the Baldwin and Patterson families. In both of these cases we find more open contempt for the husband, less consideration for his wishes, quarrels with him over unemployment. Mrs. Baldwin, prior to unemployment, controlled her irritation with her husband over his lack of interest in "education." After unemployment she did not hesitate to call her husband a "big lug," who, because he failed to make something of himself, was the cause of all their suffering. Mrs. Patterson had always been disappointed in her husband, but never treated him with as much contempt as since his loss of employment.

The change might be explained by various processes. Both Mrs. Baldwin and Mrs. Patterson may have, even in the past, felt as much resentment and contempt for their husbands as they do now, but restrained the expression of their sentiments because they owed their livelihoods to their husbands. Now they are free to talk. We might say that in such cases the change was due to the weakening of economic coercion. But another explanation is possible. A husband who was an insurance salesman with a small income may have been a big disappointment to Mrs. Baldwin, but an unemployed husband can command still less respect. In most cases, no doubt, both existed because one was likely to merge into the other. It is probably true that the very fact of economic power endowed the husband with some prestige. The wife may have thought, as did Mrs. Garland, that her husband had no personality, but after all she recognized the fact that the house, the car, her clothes, and the summer vacation were derived from him. This fact in itself must have endowed him with some prestige.

In still another situation, economic failure of the man has apparently provided the wife a convenient way of rationalizing her dissatisfactions hitherto concealed. It is less disturbing to Mrs. Baldwin's conscience to blame her husband for lack of education now that this lack can be held responsible for his failure as a provider. It is easier for the dissatisfied wife to rationalize all kinds of grievances in terms of unemployment. She seizes upon his unemployment as a socially accepted mode of voicing grievances which she had had to conceal prior to unemployment. It is merely that the wife finds in unemployment an acceptable pretext for voicing her dissatisfactions; she feels freer to voice them now that the man holds no economic whip over her.

Increased presence of the husband at home affected his authority in two ways. In some cases it led to disillusionment in the husband. Apparently, authority depends upon distance and absence in certain kinds of relations. Mr. Fucini says that "when a man is at home all day he cannot possibly command as much respect as when he returns to the family for a few hours of concentrated conversation." The husband feels that he is a "fallen idol" to his family, and attributes it largely to his presence at home. His wife has become more aware of his little weaknesses. As for the children, they used to meet him in the evening with a glad welcome, and now that he is at home all day they don't pay attention to him. Now when he comes in, they sometimes call out, "Hi, Dad," and again they may not even do that.

Increased presence at home meant also that potential differences and disagreements of husband and wife came into open conflict and, in some cases, resulted in the defeat of the husband.

Most wives testify to the increased irritability and conflicts due to the man's presence at home. These exist even in families which do not show any changes in authority relations. Conflicts that arise through daily contact are of all kinds. One husband does not approve of the wife's housekeeping. She likes to work and rest alternately, while he thinks that she should complete her duties before resting. Another frequent source of conflict is over the children. Now that the husband is at home all the differences in the attitudes of the couple come to the foreground. The disagreements might be over the eating habits of the children; whether or not the daughter should help with the housework; whether the baby should be taken out of the crib when she cries; whether the boy should be locked out of the house when he is naughty; how late the children should be allowed to play out of doors—and so on.

The husband's share of household duties is another source of irritation. Now that he is idle most of the time, how much should he be expected to help his wife? There may be conflicts over the hobbies of the husband, or the radio—the man likes speeches and his wife likes jazz. Another man gets so engrossed in a book that he doesn't pay attention to anybody for hours, which irritates his wife. In another case, the wife never wipes the dishes before putting them away, and that annoys her husband. Underlying it all is the deep anxiety of both husband and wife, which increases their nervousness and irritability.

While increased irritability is observed in most cases, in itself it does not imply a change in the husband's status unless the marriage was without conflict in the past, in which case the mere presence of conflict would testify to a kind of rebellion on the part of the wife. Ordinarily, however, increased conflict means that the man's authority is put to a severer test, and thus provides a fertile soil for disintegration of authority.

The fact that the unemployed man spends so much of the day with his family does not always undermine his authority, but it has other unfavorable effects. Again and again would the complaint be made by both husband and wife that his continuous presence at home puts a great strain upon their relations. Work relief is superior to money relief from this point of view as it is also in many other respects.

Changes in the man as the cause of his downfall were the most difficult feature to discern. The relation between changes in the man and changes in authority relations is a complex one. Changes in the man's personality may affect his relations with the family and changes in his relation with the family may affect his personality. One man may become panicky as a result of unemployment and lose his sense of security and dignity. This is likely to result in behavior which endangers his status. He may become apathetic or he may become overdominant and difficult to live with. Another man may keep his self-respect and equanimity, thus having a greater chance to preserve his authority. But while the man's behavior affects his family relations, the attitude of the family may in its turn affect his behavior. If a family, after four years of unemployment, would not sit down to the table without the man, no matter how late he might be, as is the case in one family, it goes a long way towards keeping up his morale.

The interviewer enters somewhere in the midst of this process and is confronted with the difficult problem of discovering the decisive feature in this circular causation. In assigning the initial cause to the changes in the man, the testimony of the whole case was taken into consideration. The analysis of the material reveals that in three cases the impetus to loss of authority apparently came from the man himself; that is, from changes in his personality.

One such case is presented by the Scott family. "Before the depression," said Mr. Scott, "I wore the pants in this family, and rightly so. During the depression I lost something. Maybe you call it self-respect, but in losing it I also lost the respect of my children, and I am afraid I am losing my wife." But there is other evidence than his own testimony that the decisive feature in deterioration of his status was his own reaction to unemployment, his broken morale and loss of self-respect. Mr. Scott is a man who feels that when he ceased providing for the family he lost all claims to their consideration. An individual who has this view would relinquish his authority as a result of unemployment before it was put to a test. He became discouraged and apathetic. After the first year of relief he withdrew from contact with the children and let his wife handle the financial and other affairs of the family. In the early days of unemployment the children kept asking him to play with them, but because of his constant refusal and irritability they gave it up. He spends most of the day in the corner candy store and has ceased to look actively for work. . . .

In summary, it must be stated that the downfall of the husband was due most frequently to the loss of his earning power. In three cases out of the thirteen, the change, it is true, came as a result of the deterioration in the husband's personality and his continuous presence at home. Had he been able to preserve his own morale, had he found some occupation that would keep him away from the family for part of the day, the attitude of his wife might not have changed. But in most of the cases the unemployed man was doomed by the very fact of unemployment. It was not his own reaction to his plight, neither his increased contact with the wife, but his failure as a provider and loss of money which undermined his status. Loss of earning ability has lowered the prestige of the man in the eyes of his wife. He could no longer hold the economic whip over her, and finally loss of money necessitated new choices and created new tests of the husband's authority.

As will be pointed out in the discussion of parental relations, the unemployed father has more control over the fate of his status than the unemployed husband. This is especially true with the younger children. A father who has kept his self-respect has a good chance of keeping the respect of his children in spite of his failure.

It is not to be supposed that the economic factor plays no role in cases in which the breakdown came as a result of changes in the husband's personality. If we were to investigate the manner in which these changes came about, we would certainly find that they were the result of the man's own reaction to his failure as a provider. Thus, whether directly or through giving rise to certain conditions, the economic factors played the major roles in every case of loss of status.

The unemployed husband who has suffered a loss of status with his wife is a tragic figure. Defeated in the outside world, he feels the ground slipping from under his feet within the home as well. What does he do, faced with a crumbling world? Does he struggle to maintain his authority, or does he relinquish all claims to it? With what means does he attempt to arrest the disaster? What escapes and compensations does he seek?

THE HUSBAND'S REACTION
TO HIS LOSS OF STATUS

The men did not relinquish easily their claims to authority. They fought bitterly to maintain them in the face of the growing contempt and rebellion of the family. Most men reacted to the loss of status in husband–wife relations as they did in the case of parental relations, by *demanding* that their wives continue to respect them. There was less physical violence and aggression towards the wife than towards the child, because physical force presupposes some power which the man is more likely to have over the child than over the wife. Such pressure as the husband exerted was psychological rather than physical.[1]

The struggle for status took various forms. It manifested itself in part in the increased "touchiness" and in overemphasis of his authority. The husband frequently becomes sensitive to the slightest threats to his status. Incidents which would have passed unnoticed now arouse his anger. Again and again the wife testifies that the husband became "bossy," that he "flies off the handle" at the slightest remark, however harmless. Apparently his sense of insecurity is so profound and ever-present that he views the most trivial incidents of daily life in relation to his status. The commonplace and familiar activities take the form of contests for status. The wife asks the husband to go and fetch the coal; she complains about the long waiting at the relief office; she tells of a relative who secured a good job; she asks her husband to call for the child at school; the dinner is not ready at the usual time; she is late from a visit with her relatives; she remarks about the torn curtains. His anxiety and insecurity make every incident a reminder of his defeat and a hidden threat and insult to which he reacts with irritation and bitterness. As one man put it, "My ears have become sharper. I hear too much. I take things to heart which before I wouldn't have even heard."

Increased stubbornness is another frequent kind of reaction. It seems as if the husband picks himself a few strongholds and does not yield power within them even though he may have been defeated in the fundamental areas of life. It appears as if a refusal to concede to the wife's wishes is a source of satisfaction to the man as a remnant of power over her. In part, it may be sheer spite, a way of avenging himself for the indignities showered upon him. Thus, Mr. Fucini admits the loss of his authority. His reaction to his wife's patronizing and domineering attitude is a withdrawal of customary services in the home. He refuses to help the wife with her heavy housework and in spite of his increased leisure is less helpful than he was prior to unemployment. Mrs. Roland once told her husband not to come home without any money. He says that he was lucky and earned some that day. Yet the wife is quite helpless against his stubbornness in one or two of their daily conflicts. He refuses to tend the fire, he refuses to do errands for her. She says that he won't be budged if he says "No."

It is perhaps not without significance that these strongholds frequently concern help with the housework. Housework is so closely identified with the woman's rather than the man's role in the family that performing it is a symbol of degradation.

Needless to say, such means of preserving authority as those described above do not achieve their end. Indeed, they get the couple into a vicious circle of quarrels and mutual irritation. Mrs. Fucini is disgusted with her husband's refusal to help with the housework while he is hanging around the house all day with nothing to do. In her exasperation she strikes at what she intuitively feels is his most vulnerable spot—she blames him for failure to provide for the family. This in turn deepens the bitterness and anxiety and makes him still more antagonistic to her demands. . . .

A very different reaction to loss of marital authority is one in which the husband attempts to placate his wife through increased helpfulness. Mr. Baldwin, while always helpful to his wife, is now completely at her service during the day. He hopes that his helpfulness will earn for him some gratitude from his wife. When his wife accuses him for his failure as a provider, he defends himself by reminding her of his complete devotion and helpfulness in the home. "There is nothing I wouldn't do for you, and you know it." . . .

The husbands described so far had one thing in common. Whether through aggression or increased services, they nevertheless strove to defend their hurt egos. Of 13 husbands, 5 have ceased to struggle. They may have occasional spurts of rebellion, but these spasmodic efforts do not change the general picture of relinquishment of auhority.

Mr. Adams says, "There certainly was a change in our family, and I can define it in just one word. I relinquished power in the family. Now I don't even try to be boss. She controls all the money, and I never have a penny in my pocket but that I have to ask her for it."

Undemanding as these men are as a general rule, they do occasionally attempt to assert their power. Thus, Mr.

Adams once in a while secures some money from somewhere and gets drunk in the old style. The wife says it happens after quarrels, and he does it as revenge. Now and then he tells her that he is treated worse than a dog in the family, but this does not happen often.

The humiliation within the home drives some men to seek compensation outside it. It might be remembered, incidentally, that sometimes the man finds compensations within the family. There are several cases of loss of authority over the children, but complete preservation of it in husband and wife relations. The reverse is very rare. There are only one or two cases in which the man has lost the respect of his wife while still maintaining authority over the children, though he may, of course, continue to receive sympathy from them. Where such situations exist the man finds solace in some members of the family from the antagonism of others.

In contrast to such compensation within the home, in the Dorrance family the man sought solace outside the home.

The marriage of the Dorrances was most unsatisfactory even prior to the husband's unemployment. The husband was apparently a shiftless and lazy man who had never been able to keep a job. The family accepted charity during the various periods of married life even prior to his final layoff. Bad as it was, there were indications that his unemployment made things still worse. Sex relations have been discontinued for the past three years. The husband said that the wife poisoned the children against him and criticized him in front of the children more violently than she ever did before. This was his reaction to it:

"Well, I'll tell you," he said to the interviewer, "after a while you get so you don't care a damn any more, and that's the way I feel. As far as I am concerned the kids can do what they please, and the wife, too, for that matter. It's just like I said, 'Love flies out the window when the money goes.'"

Mrs. Dorrance confirmed the picture of her husband's

indifference. Towards the children, however, he is cruel. He flies into a rage at the slightest provocation, beats the children, and throws things at them. One of the children may be talking, and the husband will tell him to shut up, for no reason at all. If the child happens to be in the middle of a sentence, he naturally finished it, but even this little delay causes her husband to go into a fit of rage, and he will throw something—a plate, for example—at the child. The children have learned to duck very quickly, and so he has never very seriously hurt any of them.

But while Mr. Dorrance is a "home devil," he is a "street angel." According to his wife, he can be very nice to other children. He always drank some, but during the last few years drinks more than ever before. The little money he has, he spends on being "a good fellow" in saloons. He spends more money in the saloons than she does on clothes for herself and the children. She suspects that he is unfaithful to her. . . .

The vicious circle of the conflict in which the couple find themselves is another striking feature of the process of loss. There are numerous illustrations of the circular and cumulative character of conflicts. Unemployment calls for some action or attitude on the part of the husband. The wife reacts to it in a manner which aggravates the original attitude of the husband. He hits back, and so the two are caught in a mounting wave of bitterness.

As will be pointed out, families in which no change in the marriage relation has taken place do not get involved in this cycle of conflict. There are conflicts, but one or the other of the spouses fails to take up the gauntlet. The reaction is such as not to call forth the hot retaliation of the other. The wife might complain of unemployment, but the husband, instead of avenging himself upon her for this reproach, tries to justify himself or console her for her hardships. The husband may be irritable and unfair to the wife, but she, instead of seizing unemployment as a weapon to hold over him, tries to alleviate his anxiety. Needless to say, such differences in the methods of conflict are in themselves results of personalities and preunemployment relations of the couple.

But the most striking fact, perhaps, concerning the reaction of the husband to loss of authority is that there are no cases in which the husband has completely accommodated himself to the new authoritarian relation. There is no case in which the husband and the wife had adjusted themselves completely to the realignment of power. The decline in the husband's status is satisfactory to none. . . .

NOTES

[1]It is not to be supposed, of course, that all of the behavior of the men is consciously designed to uphold authority. It was in part a spontaneous manifestation of humiliation and anxiety and only in part deliberately calculated to protect his status.

chapter 14

Men and Jobs

by Elliot Liebow

Anthropologist Elliot Liebow spent most of 1962 and 1963 interviewing a group of adult black men who came together regularly at a carry-out shop in a blighted section of Washington's inner city. Liebow's main informant was Tally, a 31-year-old ex-heavyweight fighter and veteran employed as a semi-skilled construction worker. Liebow's research challenged the common line of thinking that lower-class black men had their own subculture, with its own unique goals and values. He found that black streetcorner men wanted to be good providers, the way middle-class men were. They wanted to be good fathers and husbands, but their marriages often broke up, and their children saw them infrequently. To conceal their feelings of manly failure, these men designed a fictional presentation of themselves as hypermasculine super-men, a fiction which appeared to outsiders as a distinct lower-class subculture.

A pickup truck drives slowly down the street. The truck stops as it comes abreast of a man sitting on a cast-iron porch and the white driver calls out, asking if the man wants a day's work. The man shakes his head and the truck moves on up the block, stopping again whenever idling men come within calling distance of the driver. At the Carry-out corner, five men debate the question briefly and shake their heads no to the truck. The truck turns the corner and repeats the same performance up the next street. In the distance, one can see one man, then another, climb into the back of the truck and sit down. It starts and stops, the truck finally disappears.

What is it we have witnessed here? A labor scavenger rebuffed by his would-be prey? Lazy irresponsible men turning down an honest day's pay for an honest day's work? Or a more complex phenomenon marking the intersection of economic forces, social values and individual states of mind and body?

Let us look again at the driver of the truck. He has been able to recruit only two or three men from each twenty or fifty he contacts. To him, it is clear that the others simply do not choose to work. Singly or in groups, belly-empty or belly-full, sullen or gregarious, drunk or sober, they confirm what he has read, heard and knows from his own experience: these men wouldn't take a job if it were handed to them on a platter.[1]

Quite apart from the question of whether or not this is true of some of the men he sees on the street, it is clearly not true of all of them. If it were, he would not have come here in the first place; or having come, he would have left with an empty truck. It is not even true of most of them, for most of the men he sees on the street this weekday morning do, in fact, have jobs. But since, at the moment, they are neither working nor sleeping, and since they hate the depressing room or apartment they live in, or because there is nothing to do there,[2] or because they want to get away from their wives or anyone else living there, they are out on the street, indistinguishable from those who do not have jobs or do not want them. Some, like Boley, a member of a trash-collection crew in a suburban housing development, work Saturdays and are off on this weekday. Some, like Sweets, work nights cleaning up middle-class trash, dirt, dishes and garbage, and mopping the floors of the office buildings, hotels, restaurants, toilets and other public places dirtied during the day. Some men work for retail businesses such as liquor stores which do not begin the day until ten o'clock. Some laborers, like Tally, have already come back from the job because the ground was too wet for pick and shovel or because the weather was too cold for pouring concrete. Other employed men stayed off the job today for personal reasons: Clarence to go to a funeral at eleven this morning and Sea Cat to answer a subpoena as a witness in a criminal proceeding.

Also on the street, unwitting contributors to the impression taken away by the truck driver, are the halt and the lame. The man on the cast-iron steps strokes one gnarled arthritic hand with the other and says he doesn't know whether or not he'll live long enough to be eligible for Social Security. He pauses, then adds matter-of-factly, "Most times, I don't care whether I do or don't." Stoopy's left leg was polio-withered in childhood. Raymond, who looks as if he could tear out a fire hydrant, coughs up blood if he bends or moves suddenly. The quiet man who hangs out in front of the Saratoga apartments has a steel hook strapped onto his left elbow. And had the man in the truck been able to look into the wine-clouded eyes of the man in the green cap, he would have realized that the man did not even understand he was being offered a day's work.

Others, having had jobs and been laid off, are drawing unemployment compensation (up to $44 per week) and have nothing to gain by accepting work which pays little more than this and frequently less.

Still others, like Bumdoodle the numbers man, are working hard at illegal ways of making money, hustlers who are on the street to turn a dollar any way they can: buying and selling sex, liquor, narcotics, stolen goods, or anything else that turns up.

Only a handful remains unaccounted for. There is Tonk, who cannot bring himself to take a job away from the corner, because, according to the other men, he suspects his wife will be unfaithful if given the opportunity. There is Stanton, who has not reported to work for four days now, not since Bernice disappeared. He bought a brand new knife against her return. She had done this twice before, he said, but not for so long and not without warning, and he had forgiven her. But this time, "I ain't got it in me to forgive her again." His rage and shame are there for all to see as he paces the Carry-out and the corner, day and night, hoping to catch a glimpse of her.

And finally, there are those like Arthur, able-bodied men who have no visible means of support, legal or illegal, who neither have jobs nor want them. The truck driver, among others, believes the Arthurs to be representative of all the men he sees idling on the street during his own working hours. They are not, but they cannot be dismissed simply because they are a small minority. It is enough to explain them away as being lazy or irresponsible or both because an able-bodied man with responsibilities who refuses to work is, by the truck driver's definition, lazy and irresponsible. Such an answer begs the question. It is descriptive of the facts; it does not explain them.

Moreover, despite their small numbers, the don't-work-and-don't-want-to-work minority is especially significant because they represent the strongest and clearest expression of those values and attitudes associated with making a living which, to varying degrees, are found throughout the streetcorner world. These men differ from the others in degree rather than in kind, the principal difference being that they are carrying out the implications of their values and experiences to their logical, inevitable conclusions. In this sense, the others have yet to come to terms with themselves and the world they live in. . . .

When we look at what the men bring to the job rather than at what the job offers the men, it is essential to keep in mind that we are not looking at men who come to the job fresh, just out of school perhaps, and newly prepared to undertake the task of making a living, or from another job where they earned a living and are prepared to do the same on this job. Each man comes to the job with a long job history characterized by his not being able to support himself and his family. Each man carries this knowledge, born of his experience, with him. He comes to the job flat and stale, wearied by the sameness of it all, convinced of his own incompetence, terrified of responsibility—of being tested still again and found wanting. Possible exceptions are the younger men not yet, or just, married. They suspect all this but have yet to have it confirmed by repeated personal experience over time. But those who are or have been married know it well. It is the experience of the individual and the group; of their fathers and probably their sons. Convinced of their inadequacies, not only do they not seek out those few better-paying jobs which test their resources, but they actively avoid them, gravitating in a mass to the menial, routine jobs which offer no challenge—and therefore pose no threat—to the already diminished images they have of themselves.

Thus Richard does not follow through on the real estate agent's offer. He is afraid to do on his own—minor plastering, replacing broken windows, other minor repairs and painting—exactly what he had been doing for months on a piece-work basis under someone else (and which provided him with a solid base from which to derive a cost estimate).

Richard once offered an important clue to what may have gone on in his mind when the job offer was made. We were in the Carry-out, at a time when he was looking for work. He was talking about the kind of jobs available to him.

I graduated from high school [Baltimore] but I don't know anything. I'm dumb. Most of the time I don't even say I graduated, 'cause then somebody asks me a question and I can't answer it, and they think I was lying about graduating. . . . They graduated me but I didn't know anything. I had lousy grades but I guess they wanted to get rid of me.

I was at Margaret's house the other night and her little sister asked me to help her with her homework. She showed me some fractions and I knew right away I couldn't do them. I was ashamed so I told her I had to go to the bathroom.

And so it must have been, surely, with the real estate agent's offer. Convinced that "I'm dumb . . . I don't know anything," he "knew right away" he couldn't do it, despite the fact that he had been doing just this sort of work all along.

Thus, the man's low self-esteem generates a fear of being tested and prevents him from accepting a job with responsibilities or, once on a job, from staying with it if responsibilities are thrust on him, even if the wages are commensurately higher. Richard refuses such a job, Leroy leaves one, and another man, given more responsibility and more pay, knows he will fail and proceeds to do so, proving he was right about himself all along. The self-fulfilling prophecy is everywhere at work. In a hallway, Stanton, Tonk and Boley are passing a bottle around. Stanton recalls the time he was in the service. Everything was fine until he attained the rank of corporal. He worried about everything he did then. Was he doing the right thing? Was he doing it well? When would they discover their mistake and take his stripes (and extra pay) away? When he finally lost his stripes, everything was all right again.

Lethargy, disinterest and general apathy on the job, so often reported by employers, has its streetcorner counterpart. The men do not ordinarily talk about their jobs or ask one another about them.[3] Although most of the men know who is or is not working at any given time, they may or may not know what particular job an individual man has. There is no overt interest in job specifics as they relate to this or that person, in large part perhaps because the specifics are not especially relevant. To know that a man is working is to know approximately how much he makes and to know as much as one needs or wants to know about how he makes it. After all, how much difference does it make to know whether a man is pushing a mop and pulling trash in an apartment house, a restaurant, or an office building, or delivering groceries, drugs, or liquor, or, if he's a laborer, whether he's pushing a wheelbarrow, mixing mortar, or digging a hole. So much does one job look like every other that there is little to choose between them. In large part, the job market consists of a narrow range of nondescript chores calling for nondistinctive, undifferentiated, unskilled labor. "A job is a job."

A crucial factor in the streetcorner man's lack of job commitment is the overall value he places on the job. *For his part, the streetcorner man puts no lower value on the job than does the larger society around him.* He knows the social value of the job by the amount of money the employer is willing to pay him for doing it. In a real sense, every pay day, he counts in dollars and cents the value placed on the job by society at large. He is no more (and frequently less) ready to quit and look for another job than his employer is ready to fire him and look for another man. Neither the streetcorner man who performs these jobs nor the society which requires him to perform them assesses the job as one "worth doing and worth doing well." Both employee and employer are contemptuous of the job. The employee shows his contempt by his reluctance to accept it or keep it, the employer by paying

less than is required to support a family.[4] Nor does the
low-wage job offer prestige, respect, interesting work, opportunity for learning or advancement, or any other compensation. With few exceptions, jobs filled by the streetcorner men are at the bottom of the employment ladder in
every respect, from wage level to prestige. Typically, they
are hard, dirty, uninteresting and underpaid. The rest of
society (whatever its ideal values regarding the dignity of
labor) holds the job of the dishwasher or janitor or unskilled
laborer in low esteem if not outright contempt.[5] So does the
streetcorner man. He cannot do otherwise. He cannot draw
from a job those social values which other people do not put
into it.[6]

Only occasionally does spontaneous conversation touch
on these matters directly. Talk about jobs is usually limited to
isolated statements of intention, such as "I think I'll get me
another gig [job]," "I'm going to look for a construction job
when the weather breaks," or "I'm going to quit. I can't take
no more of his shit." Job assessments typically consist of
nothing more than a noncommittal shrug and "It's O.K." or
"It's a job."

One reason for the relative absence of talk about one's
job is, as suggested earlier, that the sameness of job experiences does not bear reiteration. Another and more important
reason is the emptiness of the job experience itself. The man
sees middle-class occupations as a primary source of prestige, pride and self-respect; his own job affords him none of
these. To think about his job is to see himself as others see
him, to remind him of just where he stands in this society.[7]
And because society's criteria for placement are generally the
same as his own, to talk about his job can trigger a flush of
shame and a deep, almost physical ache to change places
with someone, almost anyone, else.[8] The desire to be a person in his own right, to be noticed by the world he lives in, is
shared by each of the men on the streetcorner. Whether they
articulate this desire (as Tally does below) or not, one can see

them position themselves to catch the attention of their fellows in much the same way as plants bend or stretch to catch the sunlight.[9]

Tally and I were in the Carry-out. It was summer, Tally's peak earning season as a cement finisher, a semiskilled job a cut or so above that of the unskilled laborer. His take-home pay during these weeks was well over a hundred dollars—"a lot of bread." But for Tally, who no longer had a family to support, bread was not enough.

> *"You know that boy came in last night? That Black Moozlem? That's what I ought to be doing. I ought to be in his place."*

> *"What do you mean?"*

> *"Dressed nice, going to [night] school, got a good job."*

> *"He's no better off than you, Tally. You make more than he does."*

> *"It's not the money. [Pause] It's position, I guess. He's got position. When he finish school he gonna be a supervisor. People respect him. . . . Thinking about people with position and education gives me a feeling right here [pressing his fingers into the pit of his stomach]."*

> *"You're educated, too. You have skill, a trade. You're a cement finisher. You can make a building, pour a sidewalk."*

> *"That's different. Look, can anybody do what you're doing? Can anybody just come up and do your job? Well, in one week I can teach you cement finishing. You won't be as good as me 'cause you won't have the experience but you'll be a cement finisher. That's what I mean. Anybody can do what I'm doing and that's what gives me this feeling. [Long pause] Suppose I like this girl. I go over to her house and I meet her father. He starts talking about what he done today. He talks about operating on somebody and sewing them up and about surgery. I know he's a doctor 'cause of the way he talks. Then she starts*

talking about what she did. Maybe she's a boss or a supervisor. Maybe she's a lawyer and her father says to me, 'And what do you do, Mr. Jackson?' [Pause] You remember at the courthouse, Lonny's trial? You remember? I just stood there listening. I didn't say a word. You know why? 'Cause I didn't even know what you was talking about. That's happened to me a lot."

"Hell, you're nothing special. That happens to everybody. Nobody knows everything. One man is a doctor, so he talks about surgery. Another man is a teacher, so he talks about books. But doctors and teachers don't know anything about concrete. You're a cement finisher and that's your specialty."

"Maybe so, but when was the last time you saw anybody standing around talking about concrete?"

The streetcorner man wants to be a person in his own right, to be noticed, to be taken account of, but in this respect, as well as in meeting his money needs, his job fails him. The job and the man are even. The job fails the man and the man fails the job.

Furthermore, the man does not have any reasonable expectation that, however bad it is, his job will lead to better things. Menial jobs are not, by and large, the starting point of a track system which leads to even better jobs for those who are able and willing to do them. The busboy or dishwasher in a restaurant is not on a job track which, if negotiated skillfully, leads to chef or manager of the restaurant. The busboy or dishwasher who works hard becomes, simply a hard-working busboy or dishwasher. Neither hard work nor perseverance can conceivably carry the janitor to a sit-down job in the office building he cleans up. And it is the apprentice who becomes the journeyman electrician, plumber, steam fitter or bricklayer, not the common unskilled Negro laborer.

Thus, the job is not a stepping stone to something better. It is a dead end. It promises to deliver no more tomorrow, next month or next year than it does today. . . .

NOTES

[1]By different methods, perhaps, some social scientists have also located the problem in the men themselves, in their unwillingness or lack of desire to work: "To improve the underprivileged worker's performance, one must help him to learn to *want. . . higher social goals for himself and his children. . . .* The problem of changing the work habits and motivation of [lower class] people . . . is a problem of changing the goals, the ambitions, and the level of cultural and occupational aspiration of the underprivileged worker." (Emphasis in original.) Allison Davis, "The Motivation of the Underprivileged Worker," p. 90.

[2]The comparison of sitting at home alone with being in jail is commonplace.

[3]This stands in dramatic contrast to the leisure-time conversation of stable, working-class men. For the coal miners (of Ashton, England), for example, "the topic [of conversation] which surpasses all others in frequency is work—the difficulties which have been encountered in the day's shift, the way in which a particular task was accomplished, and so on." Josephine Klein, *Samples from English Cultures*, Vol. I, p. 88.

[4]It is important to remember that the employer is not entirely a free agent. Subject to the constraints of the larger society, he acts for the larger society as well as for himself. Child labor laws, safety and sanitation regulations, minimum wage scales in some employment areas, and other constraints, are already on the books; other control mechanisms, such as a guaranteed annual wage, are to be had for the voting.

[5]See, for example, the U.S. Bureau of the Census, *Methodology and Scores of the Socioeconomic Status.* The assignment of the lowest SES ratings to men who hold such jobs is not peculiar to our own society. A low SES rating for "the shoeshine boy or garbage man. . . . seems to be true for all [industrial] countries." Alex Inkeles, "Industrial Man," p. 8.

[6]That the streetcorner man downgrades manual labor should occasion no surprise. Merton points out that "the American stigmatization of manual labor . . . *has been found to hold rather uniformly in all social classes*"

(emphasis in original; *Social Theory and Social Structure*, p. 145). That he finds no satisfaction in such work should also occasion no surprise: "[There is] a clear positive correlation between the over-all status of occupations and the experience of satisfaction in them." Inkeles, "Industrial Man," p. 12.

[7]"[In our society] a man's work is one of the things by which he is judged, and certainly one of the more significant things by which he judges himself. . . . A man's work is one of the more important parts of his social identity, of his self; indeed, of his fate in the one life he has to live." Everett C. Hughes, *Men and Their Work*, pp. 42–43.

[8]Noting that lower-class persons "are constantly exposed to evidence of their own irrelevance," Lee Rainwater spells out still another way in which the poor are poor: "The identity problems of lower class persons make the soul-searching of middle class adolescents and adults seem rather like a kind of conspicuous consumption of psychic riches" (Work and Identity in the Lower Class," p. 3).

[9]Sea Cat cuts his pants legs off at the calf and puts a fringe on the raggedy edges. Tonk breaks his "shades" and continues to wear the horn-rimmed frames minus the lenses. Richard cultivates a distinctive manner of speech. Lonny gives himself a birthday party. And so on.

chapter 15

Vietnam and the Cult of Toughness in Foreign Policy

by Marc Fasteau

Ever since Theodore Roosevelt waved his "Big Stick," American presidents have defined and justified American military policy with verbal bravado and masculine imagery. For almost that long, upper-class Ivy League men have been defined by the rest of the country as effeminate, probably homosexual. Joseph McCarthy made use of this popular stereotype in red-baiting the State Department. Post-McCarthy American foreign policy has been enunciated in terms of weakness versus toughness, in what seems a code for concerns about effeminacy and/or homosexuality. Marc Fasteau ably establishes that the cult of toughness was a continuing image in Cold War foreign policy rhetoric. Given Fasteau's demonstration that the imagery of masculine toughness was used in explaining the reason for continued American involvement in the Vietnam war, how can we decide among the different ways of interpreting the coincidence? Does it mean, as Fasteau seems to imply, that the cult of toughness led to continued involvement? Or was continued military involvement made possible by the cult of toughness? Or, still another possibility, were both the result of other social changes common to the Cold War period?

The Vietnam war has been for me, as it has been for many other Americans, a central influence in the evolution of my political beliefs and personal values. One of my most sustained intellectual endeavors has been the effort in the early years to decide whether the war made sense and then the longer and more difficult attempt, once it became clear to me that it was a pointless and futile undertaking, to understand what it was that kept the United States in the war. The process began in 1963, when I graduated from college and went to work as a member of Senator Mike Mansfield's staff, where my responsibilities led me to try to articulate and examine the underlying premises and rationale of our involvement. They did not stand up under scrutiny: Vietnam was not another Munich and there was no empirical or solid theoretical support for the "domino theory." In fact, the explanations were so clearly weak, that I could never quite understand how so many obviously intelligent men could believe them. Six years later, when everyone in his or her right mind knew the war was a disaster and still we couldn't get out, this nagging question connected up with an embryonic awareness of the masculine stereotype.

The precipitating event for me in making the connection was the publication of the Pentagon Papers. Here, at last, was the inside story—a good chunk of it at least—a twenty-year long view of the policymaking process, free of political if not bureaucratic posturing. I scoured the Papers eagerly for the analysis and motivation behind our involvement. But the most striking revelation of the Papers was not what they did say but what they did not say. Even at the highest and most private levels of our government, the rationale and supporting analysis for the American objective of winning in Viet-

nam had been incredibly flimsy. Secretary of Defense Robert
S. McNamara wrote to President Johnson in March 1964:

> *Unless we can achieve [an independent non-Communist South
> Vietnam], almost all of Southeast Asia will probably fall under
> Communist domination (all of Vietnam, Laos and Cambodia),
> accommodate to Communism so as to remove effective U.S.
> and anti-Communist influence (Burma) or fall under the
> dominance of force not now explicitly Communist but likely to
> become so (Indonesia taking over Malaysia). Thailand might
> hold for a period with our help, but would be under grave
> pressure. Even the Phillippines would become shaky, and the
> threat to India to the west, Australia and New Zealand to the
> south and Taiwan, Korea and Japan to the north and east
> would be greatly increased.* [1]

This is the fullest supporting discussion of the "domino
theory" in the Papers. Even in memoranda discussing the
broad outlines of United States policy, only an introductory
paragraph (usually the shortest) is devoted to a discussion of
our national interest in Vietnam. The only lengthy and careful examinations of this question in the Papers were produced by Undersecretary of State of George Ball and by the
CIA in response to a question from President Johnson. The
CIA concluded that

> *with the possible exception of Cambodia it is likely that no
> nation in the area would succumb to Communism as a result of
> the fall of Laos and South Vietnam. Furthermore, a continua-
> tion of the spread of Communism in the area would not be
> inexorable, and any spread which did occur would take time—
> time in which the total situation might change in a number of
> ways unfavorable to the Communist cause.* [2]

Ball's memo examining the likely effect of U.S. withdrawal
from Vietnam on a country-by-country, area-by-area basis

concluded that only in Southeast Asia proper would there be an adverse effect and that this would be short-lived.[3] Both analyses were dismissed by the Adminstration without a response on their merits.

Why was there so little serious analysis or rethinking of United States objectives in South Vietnam by the men holding power? Not because their achievement was thought to be cheap. Fairly early in the Johnson Administration, the President and his advisers were far more pessimistic in private than in public about the actual results of past war efforts and the forecasts about the results of each new escalation. CIA analyses consistently predicted the failure of escalation in the air and on the ground. Each new escalation was undertaken because the Administration did not know what else to do— getting out was (except at one point for Robert Kennedy) unthinkable. A partial explanation for this attitude is that Presidents Kennedy and Johnson and their advisers misapplied the lessons of history.

In the spring of 1956 Johnson said privately to columnist James Wechsler, as he was to say to others: "I don't want to escalate this war, I want nothing more than to get our boys home. . . . But I can't run and pull a Chamberlain at Munich." This analogy was often drawn.[4] But it rested on a number of very doubtful assumptions: that Communist China created and controlled the Viet Cong in the South and could produce similar insurgencies elsewhere; or that North Vietnam itself had imperialist ambitions and the capacity to carry them out on a scale which would threaten the security interest of the United States; that a Communist regime would be worse for the people of South Vietnam than the government they had; that even if China did not create the insurgency in South Vietnam, the struggle there was still "a test case"—despite Vietnam's unique character as a divided country and a history which made the Communists the heirs of nationalist sentiment; that Indochina was strategically vital to U.S. security; that China would somehow be able to force national Communist regimes in Indochina into actions furthering Chinese ambitions but not their own; and, finally, that if the United States won in South Vietnam, Communist parties in other underdeveloped countries would roll over and die.

These propositions can be debated, although they do not stand up under careful review. The shocking fact, however, is that nowhere in the Papers do our policymakers even articulate any of these underlying propositions, much less examine them critically. The process by which United States defeat in South Vietnam would lead to catastrophe is described only in the conclusory terms of the McNamara memo quoted above.

I made this discovery in a more impressionistic way myself in 1965 by cornering William Bundy, then Assistant Secretary of State of East Asian and Pacific Affairs, at a cocktail party, and asking him to spell out how the loss of South Vietnam to the Communists would injure the security interests of the United States. He couldn't do it. Coldly calculating, realist to the core, rational examiner of all sides of every policy issue set before him, ostensibly a believer in the systems-analysis article of faith that if effect follows cause the steps in between can and should be articulated, he hadn't even thought about it, hadn't even stated for himself the assumptions underlying the conclusion. Among other things, that conversation ended for me the lingering faith that the insiders "knew" more than those of us outside the situation-room circuit.

This incredible lacuna suggests that the "domino theory" was primarily a rationale supporting a policy chosen for other, not fully conscious, motivations. Major decisions are not made on such a transparently thin basis unless another, unstated rationale and set of values are at work. No other reasons are spelled out in the Pentagon Papers, but the feeling that the United States must at all costs avoid "the humiliation of defeat" is the unarticulated major premise of nearly every document. For example, John McNaughton, Assistant Secretary of Defense, McNamara's right-hand man and head of International Security Affairs at the Pentagon, described United States aims in South Vietnam, March 1965, as

70%—to avoid a humiliating United States defeat (to our reputation as a guarantor). 20%—to keep South Vietnam (and the adjacent territory) from Chinese hands. 10%—to permit the people of South Vietnam to enjoy a better, freer way of life. [5]

The Task Force on Vietnam, created by President Kennedy the day after the collapse of the Bay of Pigs invasion of Cuba and headed by Roswell Gilpatric, Deputy Secretary of Defense, reported that allied efforts should impress friends and foes alike that "come what may, the U.S. intends to *win* this battle." [6] President Johnson said on many occasions that he would not be the first American President to lose a war. For Nixon, "peace with honor"—meaning "peace without losing"—was a goal worth any sacrifice which could be sold to the American public. And the repeated admonitions of Secretary of State Henry Kissinger that it mattered "how" the United States disengaged from Vietnam, as we shall see, amount in the end to the same thing.

Statements like those quoted, consistent discounting of reports that the adverse consequences of losing in Vietnam would not be substantial, and the absence throughout the twelve years of active United States involvement of any seriour analysis of the specific effects of defeat suggested that the Kennedy, Johnson, and Nixon Administrations have been emotionally committed to winning, or at least not losing, in Vietnam, regardless of actual consequences. It does matter sometimes whether a nation wins or loses, but whether it matters depends on the particular circumstances and on the specific consequences that flow from the defeat or victory. Avoiding the "humiliation of defeat," per se, is not automatically an important national objective. But for our Presidents and policymakers, being tough, or at least looking tough, has been a primary goal in and of itself.

The connection between the war and the cult of toughness has not been prominent in the flood of writings about Vietnam, but the evidence is there, subtler in the Kennedy Administration and more blatant under Johnson and Nixon.

There was the Kennedy emphasis on personal toughness. An excessive desire to prove this quality had taken early root in John Kennedy and showed itself first through wild recklessness in sports that led to frequent injuries.[7] This need was demonstrated again in the famous PT-boat incident during his Navy career. Kennedy's bravery in rescuing a shipmate after his boat was rammed and bringing the survivors to safety is well known. But during this rescue, some of his actions appear to reveal the same straining after heroics.

> *Trying to signal American PT boats which patrolled a nearby channel at night, Kennedy swam alone into the dangerous passage and was almost carried out to sea by the current. There was no need for such foolishness, which endangered not only Jack but the rescue of his crew. He had eight uninjured men with him, plus a plank, lifejackets, and the island growth from which to make some sort of float or raft (as recommended by Navy survival doctrine in the South Pacific at that time) on which Kennedy and another man could have put to sea.*[8]

Later, sharing his brother's values but being more outspoken, one of the first things Robert Kennedy would want to know about someone being considered as a Kennedy adviser or appointee was whether he was tough.[9] If he was—on to other questions; if not, he lost all credibility.

This attitude was reflected in the counterinsurgency fad that so captivated the Kennedy Administration. Americans, excellent specimens both physically and mentally, would be trained to be the Renaissance men of the twentieth century. They would be able to slit throats in Asian jungles, teach the natives in their own language how to use democracy and modern technology to improve their lives, and would quote Thucydides in their reports. President Kennedy once had the entire White House press corps flown to Fort Bragg, South Carolina, to watch an all-day demonstration of ambushes, counterambushes, and snake-meat eating.[10] The Special Forces epitomized, much more clearly than any civilian engaged in the messier business of politics, the ideals of the Kennedys. They were knowledgeable, they were progressive, up-to-date, they would do good, but above all they were tough, ready to use power and unaffected by sentiment.

Closely allied to the concern about toughness was the Kennedy drive to win at all costs. We have seen the efforts made by Joe, Sr. to drill this precept into the Kennedy sons. By all accounts he succeeded. Eunice Kennedy Shriver said of her brother:

> *Jack hates to lose. He learned how to play golf, and he hates to lose at that. He hates to lose at anything.* That's the only thing Jack really gets emotional about—*when he loses. Sometimes, he even gets cross.*[11]

Throughout his adult life, Kennedy's affable and deceptively casual manner concealed, as a friendly biographer commented, a "keyed-up, almost compulsive, competitiveness."[12]

Kennedy's actions in Vietnam can be understood only against the background of these values, which he brought with him into the Presidency and which strongly colored the interpretation he placed on certain events that occurred early in his Administration: the Bay of Pigs fiasco, his Vienna meeting with Khrushchev, and, closely tied to the summit meeting, the confrontation with the Soviet Union over Berlin.

He came into office looking for challenge in his chosen field of interest: foreign relations. In his inaugural address (which never once mentioned the domestic scene) he declared America ready to defend "freedom in its hour of maximum danger," willing to "pay any price, bear any burden, meet any hardship, support any friend, oppose any foe to assure the survival and success of liberty." David Halberstam has written,

> *Almost at the same moment that the Kennedy Administration was coming into office, Khrushchev had given a major speech giving legitimacy to wars of national liberation. The Kennedy Administration immediately interpreted this as a challenge (years later very high Soviet officials would tell their counterparts in the Kennedy Administration that it was all a mistake, the speech had been aimed not at the Americans, but at the Chinese), and suddenly the stopping of guerrilla war became a great fad.* [13]

Questions about the Soviet Union's or China's actual *capacity* to produce or control insurgencies around the globe, and about whether the success of a few nationally oriented Communist insurgencies would in fact affect the security of the United States were not asked. For Kennedy and his men, it was enough that they had been challenged. They believed that relaxation of tensions could come only after they had proved their toughness. [14]

The first Kennedy response—to a challenge his own Administration had created—was the Bay of Pigs invasion, an unqualified fiasco which added, as we saw in the Gilpatric Task Force Report, more fuel to the feeling that the United States had to win the next one, no matter what. [15]

The next challenge, as Kennedy saw it, was over Berlin. The division of Berlin was the remaining unresolved issue of

World War II, primarily because the Allies, pressured by West Germany, refused to give up occupation rights and sign a peace treaty recognizing East Germany. Until the U-2 affair ended plans for a summit meeting with Khrushchev, Eisenhower had been moving slowly toward negotiations on the subject. In 1961, the Soviet Union was under strong pressure to close off West Berlin as an escape route for East Germans and was pressing for negotiations on a treaty which would allow them to do this.

Kennedy's staff divided on the issue. Dean Acheson, the hard-liner appointed by Kennedy to study the problem, wanted to respond to any Russian demands with an immediate show of force. As Arthur Schlesinger observed, "For Acheson the test of will seemed almost an end in itself rather than a means to a political end."[16] Kennedy's experienced experts on Russia, including Ambassador Llewellyn Thompson and Averell Harriman, disagreed. They believed that Russian aims were defensive, an attempt to consolidate and prevent the erosion of their position in Europe rather than a preliminary to an aggressive takeover of Europe. Kennedy was much closer to Acheson's position than to that of his more realistic advisers. Nancy Gager Clinch, quoting Louise FitzSimons' careful, but critical study of Kennedy foreign policy, wrote:

President Kennedy had assumed in preparing for the summit that to fail to adhere firmly to the Western powers' occupation rights in Berlin would be to show weakness. Crisis planning in Washington was already under way and a sseries of military steps were under consideration to demonstrate the American will to risk war over Berlin. . . . Any Russian requests at this time seemed to be viewed as encroachment [on the Free World] by Kennedy and his most influential advisers.[17]

Harriman, the American with the longest experience and demonstrably the best judgment in dealing with the Russians, an early dove on Vietnam, and a man long past concern with proving his own toughness, advised Kennedy not to view the meetings with Khrushchev as a personal confrontation. He told him,

> *Don't be too serious, have some fun, get to know him a little, don't let him rattle you, he'll try to rattle you and frighten you, but don't pay any attention to that. Turn him aside, gently. And don't try for too much. Remember that he's just as scared as you are. . . . Laugh about it, don't get into a fight. Rise above it. Have some fun.*[18]

When Khrushchev, true to form, blustered and threatened in pursuit of his objectives, Kennedy disregarded Harriman's advice and retaliated in kind. After their last meeting, Kennedy met privately with James Reston of *The New York Times*. As reported by Halberstam, he told Reston of Khrushchev's attacks:

> *"I think he did it because of the Bay of Pigs, I think he thought that anyone who was so young and inexperienced as to get into that mess could be taken, and anyone who got into it, and didn't see it through, had no guts. . . . So I've got a terrible problem. If he thinks I'm inexperienced and have no guts, until we remove those ideas we won't get anywhere with him. So we have to act."* Then he told Reston that he would increase the *miliary budget and send another division to Germany. He turned to Reston and said that the only place in the world where there was a real challenge was in Vietnam, and "now we have a problem in trying to make our power credible and Vietnam looks like the place."*[19]

Shortly after his return to the United States, he requested 3.25 billion dollars more in defense funds, large increases in the armed forces, a doubling then tripling of the draft, authority to call up 150,000 reservists, and a vastly enlarged bomb-shelter program. Certainly a large measure of this apocalyptic response was based on a personal reaction to an unpleasant confrontation.

Khrushchev was not so stupid as to risk all-out nuclear war over Berlin. He had threatened several times before to sign a separate peace treaty with East Germany, but had never done so.[20] If he did, it was uncertain whether the East Germans would have tried to cut the access routes to West Berlin. And if they took such actions, there were, as in 1947, many gradations of diplomatic and economic pressure that could be applied before an overt military response was threatened. Nevertheless, Kennedy leaped to describe the problem in cataclysmic terms. "West Berlin," he told the American public in July 1961, ". . . above all, has now become—as never before—the great testing place of Western courage and will, a focal point where our solemn commitments stretching back over the years to 1945 and Soviet ambitions now meet in basic confrontation. . . ."[21]

In October 1961, when it became clear that the Viet Cong were winning, Kennedy felt he had no choice. Vietnam was the place to prove his Administration's toughness. He sent two of his key advisers, Walt Rostow and General Maxwell Taylor, to Vietnam. Although the mission was said to be designed to give the President a first-hand, objective view of the facts, its composition reveals otherwise. Rostow and Taylor, as Kennedy well knew, were both hard-liners and leaders of the counterinsurgency movement. In particular, Rostow's eagerness to demonstrate the accuracy of his theories of guerrilla warfare was well known.[22] The mission included no one with countervailing views. The President had stacked the deck. No one would—and no one did, in the White House on their return—consider the option of doing nothing, or of removing the economic-aid mission then in place in South Vietnam. Although rejecting direct involvement of American troops (he had been burned once at the Bay of Pigs), Kennedy did accept the Rostow-Taylor recommendation to send combat support units, air-combat and helicopter teams, military advisers and instructors and Green Beret teams, an American involvement which had grown to more than 15,000 men by the end of 1963. The fact that a special national intelligence estimate prepared by U.S. agencies reported that "80–90 percent of the estimated 17,000 Viet Cong guerrillas had been locally recruited, and that there was little evidence that they relied on external supplies,"[23] thereby belying the "Communist monolith" theory of the war, was ignored by Kennedy (as Johnson would ignore, at great cost, other intelligence reports that pointed away from involvement). To "win the next one" Kennedy had taken the key step by committing American soldiers to the war, thereby giving the military a foot in the door and drawing press and national attention to the conflict and his Administration's commitment.

By the fall of 1963, when reports in the press that Viet Cong were doing very well against the South Vietnamese army and their American advisers could no longer be denied, Kennedy himself was unhappy with the commitment and—with Attorney General Robert Kennedy, his closest adviser—may have been looking for an opening to move away from it. By then the President was able to allow his natural skepticism somewhat freer rein. His handling of the Cuban missile crisis was considered at the time to be a great success* and he had gone a long way toward demonstrating not only to the public but to himself that he was tough and in command. It did for him—at the risk of Armageddon—what a career as a general in the army had done for Dwight Eisenhower: put his toughness and manhood beyond doubt.

There is also some indication that by 1963 Robert Kennedy too was changing. According to Halberstam, he began

---

*Recently, however, historians taking a second look have considered Kennedy's handling of the Cuban missile crisis to be a case of reckless, unnecessary heroics.[24]

to shed his simplistic, hard-line view of the world, and to develop "a capacity . . . to see world events not so much in terms of a great global chess game, but in human terms." He *felt* things, despite a conflicting attempt to maintain his cool. Virtually alone among the President's advisers, "his questions at meetings always centered around the people of Vietnam: What is all this doing to the people? Do you think those people really want us there? Maybe we're trying to do the wrong thing?"[25] And that fall, he was the first high official of the Administration to suggest that it was time to consider withdrawing from Vietnam.

Against these factors one must weigh President Kennedy's fear of domestic political reaction to a "pullout"—he foresaw a resurgence of the "soft on communism" charges hurled at the Democrats by Senator Joseph McCarthy during the fifties—and its effect on the impending Presidential election of 1964. Taken together with his personal emotional commitment to counterinsurgency and victory, and the growth of the American effort under his aegis up to November 1963, it seems unlikely that Kennedy would have quickly ended United States involvement.[26]

But if there was at least a chance that the Kennedys were growing away from the view that they had to win in Vietnam, President Johnson and the advisers he inherited from Kennedy were not. McGeorge Bundy and Walt Rostow, academicians who became, under Johnson, the key White House advisers on Vietnam, were believers in the ultrarealism school of government. "Its proponents believed that they were tough, that they knew what the world was really like, and that force must be accepted as a basic element of diplomacy. . . . Bundy would tell antiwar gadfly John Kenneth Galbraith with a certain element of disappointment, 'Ken, you always advise against the use of force—do you realize that?'"[27] Bundy also had an impulse toward action. Enormously confident, both in himself and in the power of the United States, he gloried in the challenge of taking a problem apart and mastering it. His instinct was always to try something. And, of course, power accrued to the "can-do" men, men whose mastery took the form of visible action, not those who expressed doubts and attacked the proposals of others. To answer, "Nothing," to the question, "What can be done about disagreeable development X?" was passive, the mark of a loser and a weakling.[28]

The tough, no-nonsense posture, common among professors of government and history in the late 1950s and 1960s, was also a kind of protection. University intellectuals have always been suspected in America of being a little soft; exclusive devotion to intellectual matters has been thought of as not quite manly. It's legitimate to attend the university to gather knowledge and technique and even to improve oneself, but after that the real man goes out into the harsh world of action and conflict and gets things done. A tough line in foreign affairs made one sound like a man of action—ven if the action was all on paper.

Johnson's single most influential adviser on Vietnam, Secretary of Defense Robert McNamara, had shown that he could get things done before he got to Washington by serving as president of the Ford Motor Company. But there was a split in his personality. His neighbors in Ann Arbor, where he had lived while at Ford, and his social friends in Washington knew him as a warm man of deep and humane feeling. But during the working day he was a different person, cold and machinelike, all emotion ruled out as antithetical to the task to be accomplished. His chief passion was rationality, a quintessentially masculine and, finally, narrow rationality based on the premise that anything worth knowing can and ought to be reduced to numbers and statistics.

One was always aware of his time; speak quickly and be gone, make your point, in and out, keep the schedule, lunch from 1:50 to, say, expansively 2 P.M., and above all, do not engage in any philosophical discussions, Well, Bob, my view *of* history is . . . *No one was going to abuse his time. Do not, he told his aides, let people brief me orally. If they are going to make a presentation, find out in advance and make them put it on paper.* "Why?" *an aide asked. A cold look.* "Because I can read faster than they can talk."[29]

This total distrust of feeling, of intuition, of nuance which can be conveyed only in personal contact was costly for McNamara. On his frequent early trips to South Vietnam, it led him to ignore the unquantifiable but real signs that the war was not going well, signs that, behind the body count and barrage of statistics about villages secured, the political structure of Vietnam was falling apart. It led him to disregard the repeated warnings from the CIA that things were not what the numbers made them seem, that the bombing would not, in the phrase of the day, "break Hanoi's will to resist."

Most important, McNamara kept his professional life separate from the "unmasculine" values and impulses that would have lead him to question the assumption that the United States had to win in Vietnam: compassion for our soldiers and the people of Vietnam; doubt about his mandate and ability to impose his view of the world on others; and the willingness to feel, through an act of empathy, what the other side is feeling and so understand that their "logic" might be different from his own. This schism made it impossible for him to challenge the objective of victory. Basic policy objectives, always grow out of underlying personal values. And values are closely linked to—in fact are the organized expression of—the emotions we consider legitimate and allow ourselves to express.

McNamara was not alone in his attempt to cut the "soft," "subjective" element out of his professional life. Secretary of State Dean Rusk cabled his ambassadors to stop using the word "feel" in their dispatches.[30] He and Rostow were not torn by the war. They were true believers. Rusk's career had been built on the cold-war dogmas of the late forties and fifties and he thought them eternal verities. They felt no conflict and, later, no remorse over the war.

McNamara's role, on the other hand, was tragic. He had great drive, an incredibly organized intelligence, and a strong commitment to public service. And he had deeply humane and liberal impulses—and what goes with them, a strongly held ethical framework. But this side of his personality was compartmentalized, walled off from his professional life. In this tension, he exemplified the *best* in American public men and, in the end, the war tore him apart. He could not bring the humane side of himself to bear in thinking about the war. Instead, the cult of toughness went unchallenged as the unarticulated major premise of all the systems analysis, war gaming, and policymaking. For all his other sensitivities, he was as much a victim of it as the others. His spontaneous response in a hostile confrontation with a group of students after a speech at Harvard in November 1966 was to shout at them that he was tougher than they were—although that had nothing to do with the issue in dispute.

In Lyndon Johnson there was no foil, no wellspring of opposing values and perspectives that would have allowed him to understand the limitations of these men. He was more openly insecure about his masculinity than John Kennedy and often made explicit the connection between these doubts and his decisions of state. No one has captured this better than Halberstam in his discussion of Johnson's decision to begin the bombing of North Vietnam:

> *He had always been haunted by the idea that he would be judged as being insufficiently manly for the job, that he would lack courage at a crucial moment. More than a little insecure himself, he wanted very much to be seen as a man; it was a conscious thing. . . . [H]e wanted the respect of men who were*

tough, real men, and these would turn out to be the hawks. He had unconsciously divided people around him between men and boys. Men were activists, doers, who conquered business empires, who acted instead of talked, who made it in the world of other men and had the respect of other men. Boys were the talkers and the writers and the intellectuals, who sat around thinking and criticizing and doubting instead of doing. . . .

As Johnson weighed the advice he was getting on Vietnam, it was the boys who were most skeptical, and the men who were most sure and confident and hawkish and who had Johnson's respect. Hearing that one member of his Administration was becoming a dove on Vietnam, Johnson said, "Hell, he has to squat to piss." The men had, after all, done things in their lifetimes, and they had the respect of other men. Doubt itself, he thought, was almost a feminine quality, doubts were for women; once, on another issue, when Lady Bird raised her doubts, Johnson had said of course she was doubtful, it was like a woman to be uncertain. [31]

Others played on Johnson's fear of not being manly enough. In late 1964 and 1965, Joseph Alsop, a prowar Washington columnist, wrote a series of columns which suggested that the President might be too weak to take the necessary steps, weaker than his predecessor was during the Cuban missile crisis. The columns hit Johnson's rawest nerve. He was very angry about them, but not unaffected. Bill Moyers, one of his closest aides, recalled that the President told him, after a National Security Council meeting, of his fear that, if he got out of Vietnam, McNamara and the other ex-Kennedy men would think him "less of a man" than Kennedy, would call up Alsop and tell him so, and that Alsop would write it up in his column. In dealing with a man with these anxieties, the military always had the advantage. "In decision making," Halberstam put it, "they proposed the manhood positions, their opponents the softer, or sissy, positions." [32]

Johnson was more open than the other men in his Administration about the connection between his views about the war and his preoccupation with aggressive masculinity and sexuality. The day after ordering the bombing of North Vietnam PT-boat bases and oil depots, the first act of war against North Vietnam, Johnson buoyantly told a reporter, "I didn't just screw Ho Chi Minh. I cut his pecker off."[33] Speaking of Johnson's psychological stake in the war, Moyers has said,

> It was as if there had been a transfer of personal interest and prestige to the war, and to our fortunes there. It was almost like a frontier test, as if he were saying, "By God, I'm not going to let those puny brown people push me around."

The tragedy of Vietnam for Lyndon Johnson was that he fought the war in part to protect the political capital he needed to push through his Great Society programs at home, and in the end it was the war that destroyed his credibility and brought the Great Society to a dead halt. Unlike John Kennedy and the men of the Eastern Establishment he brought into the government to run the country's foreign affairs, Johnson's real interest lay in the domestic sphere. He cared deeply about civil rights, education, and poverty; the place in history he wanted would come from progress on these fronts, not through the execution of grand designs in the international areas. But he thought he had to be tough in dealing with Vietnam or, even after his landslide victory in 1964, the Congress, sensing "weakness," would turn on him as he thought they had turned on Truman for "losing China."[34] But even his reading of domestic political history, like Kennedy's before him and Richard Nixon's later, was biased by his preoccupation with toughness.

Just as they did not examine carefully the question, "What exactly is the U.S. interest in Vietnam?", Kennedy and Johnson and their experts did not look to see if their fears about a reaction from the right were supported by the facts. If they had, the McCarthyite storm clouds would not have appeared so near and so dark. During the years that our Vietnam policy was shaped, 1954–1965, public awareness of and interest in Vietnam was low. Presidents Eisenhower, Kennedy, and, until 1965, Johnson, were not acting under pressure of aroused public opinion, even from the right.[35] Their Administrations *made* Vietnam into news, by treating events there as significant, by making predictions of victory which did not come true, and, ultimately, by sending in United States forces and their inevitable companions, the television and writing press.

Even after Vietnam was forced into the headlines, our Presidents have consistently dragged public opinion behind them. Support for United States policy has risen after dramatic military moves or initiatives which promised peace, and then trailed off as the war continued. In fact, a key concern which runs consistently through the Pentagon Papers is how to create and maintain public support for the war. Somehow it never struck Johnson, and later Nixon, as paradoxical that they should have to strain so hard to justify the war— preserving American honor; saving democracy in Southeast Asia; keeping our word; stopping the spread of communism—and at the same time fear a strong political reaction from the right if they withdrew.

In the 1940s and 1950s a powerful and vocal group of Americans naively believed that we had a special relationship with China which could be "lost." There were no comparable myths about South Vietnam. Joseph McCarthy's appeals took root during the Korean war and during a period of adjustment to the fact that victory in World War II was followed by the cold war instead of the tranquility we expected. The real lessons of the era—that Eisenhower was elected in large part to end the Korean war, and that the end of that war, even on the ambiguous terms of the armistice, decreased rather than increased McCarthy's influence—seem to have been ignored. Finally, political scientists examining the results of the 1952 elections have shown that, contrary to myth, McCarthy's charges of being "soft on communisn" did not translate into votes. Democrats whom McCarthy had attacked did no worse than the others. Senator William Benton of Connecticut, who was attacked by McCarthy and whose defeat was widely attributed to McCarthy's political clout, for example, lost no more support in the Eisenhower landslide than other Democratic candidates in Connecticut.

In short, Presidents Kennedy, Johnson, and Nixon and their advisers drew an analogy between the politics of the fifties and the politics of the sixties without examining the realities of either. This failure of analysis and the readiness to believe that the right, which might accuse them of being too soft and weak if they withdrew from Vietnam, had great political power, was in large part the result of their personal preoccupation with toughness and the projection of that preoccupation onto the voting public.

Another rebuttal to the suggestion that the cult of toughness directly influenced our policymakers is to suggest that individuals did not feel personally threatened by the idea of backing down in Vietnam but, rather, realistically recognized that advocating withdrawal would discredit them within the decision-making bureaucracy. As Richard Barnett has pointed out, one can be a "hawk," have one's advice rejected, and still maintain credibility in Washington, while unsuccessful advocacy of a "dovish" position is permanently discrediting. But this explanation only proves the point. What created the climate in which the "soft" position is riskier than the "hard" position? It grows out of the fear of the powerful individuals members of the bureaucracy that they themselves will appear soft.

The cult of toughness has also biased the Vietnam policies of President Nixon and Henry Kissinger, his chief foreign-policy adviser, but in a subtler and, in some ways, purer form than in previous administrations. Richard Nixon turned out not to be the rigidly doctrinaire anti-Communist we believed him to be. The *détente* with China and his willingness to deal with the Soviet Union on a broad range of issues from arms control to trade made that clear. There is no question that he is aware of the depth of the split beween the Soviet Union and China and that the Communist nations of the world do not now, if they ever did, constitute a monolith with a coordinated foreign policy aimed at subverting the non-Communist world. Henry Kissinger, his chief White House adviser and then Secretary of State, has an extraordinary sophisticated view of foreign affairs.

Kissinger became convinced in 1967–1968, as the result of his analysis of the political forces at work in Vietnam, that the United States could not win there in the sense of keeping a non-Communist government in power indefinitely.[36] And despite Nixon's public pronouncements, there is strong evidence that he shared this belief. Richard Whalen, a Nixon adviser and speechwriter during the 1968 campaign, quoted Nixon as saying in March of that year, "I've come to the conclusion that there's no way to win the war. But we can't say that, of course. In fact, we have to seem to say the opposite, just to keep some degree of bargaining leverage."[37] And, at least privately, Kissinger explained that a genuine victory was not a vital United States objective. What he and Nixon did believe was critical—critical enough to justify four more years of war, ten thousand American casualties, countless Vietnamese killed, maimed, and homeless, endangerment of the Arms Limitation Agreement with the Soviet Union, and social and political upheaval at home—was that the United States avoid the *appearance* of losing. It was vital, in Kissinger's off-the-record words, that there be a "decent interval" between United States withdrawal and the collapse of the Saigon government, a period of time which would allow the Communist takeover of the South to appear to be the result of political forces within the country rather than the failure of United States assistance.[38] Again the rationale was that this was necessary to prevent a right-wing McCarthyite backlash at home as well as to preserve American "credibility"—a favorite Kissinger term—abroad. Kissinger wrote, in January 1969, that

> *the commitment of five hundred Americans has settled the issue of the importance of Vietnam. For what is involved now is confidence in American promises. However fashionable it is to ridicule the terms "credibility" or "prestige," they are not empty phrases; other nations can gear their actions to ours only if they can count on our steadiness. . . . In many parts of the world—the Middle East, Europe, Latin America, even Japan—stability depends on confidence in American promises. Unilateral withdrawal or a settlement which, even unintentionally, amounts to it could therefore lead to the erosion of restraints and to an even more dangerous international situation.[39]*

The principal audience for the demonstration of credibility is the Soviet leadership and it is their restraint that is the focus of the Nixon–Kissinger foreign policy. So far so good; it is hard to argue with the premise that the United States has some responsibility for restraining the Soviet Union from efforts, however unlikely, to overrun Western Europe, from sending their own forces to fight in a "war of national liberation," or threatening Japan with nuclear weapons, or decisively shifting the military balance in the Middle East. Such actions are less likely if the Soviet Union, and this nation's friends, believe that the United States will respond, to the point of meeting force with force if necessary. But the other key premises of the Kissinger–Nixon foreign policy are more leaps of faith than applications of logic. "Credibility" is made into an absolute virtue, independent of the context in which it is demonstrated and the situations to which, like accumulated savings, it is later to be applied. Responding to a "challenge" where we have nothing at stake except credibility itself is considered just as important in maintaining this elusive virtue as responding firmly where national security is directly and immediately threatened; maybe, in the Nixon–Kissinger calculus it is even more important—if Americans are willing to fight over tiny, remote South Vietnam, maybe the other side will believe that we are ready to fight over anything. As Nixon wrote in *Six Crises,*

> *we should stand ready to call international Communism's bluff on any pot, large or small. If we let them know that we will defend freedom when the stakes are small, the Soviets are not encouraged to threaten freedom when the stakes are higher. That is why . . . all the . . . peripheral areas are so important in the poker game of world politics.* [40]

This is a very high-risk strategy, since it is based on the assumption that the Soviet Union will follow a "weaker" policy of *not* turning every confrontation with the United States into a test of its own credibility. In 1961, for example, Kissinger wanted our forces to invade East Berlin and tear down the Berlin Wall to maintain United States credibility, although he recognized the essentially nonaggressive motivation of the Soviet Union. [41] The second key premise of the Nixon foreign policy is "linkage," the idea that

> *all the world's trouble spots exist on a single continuum which connects the Soviet Union and the United States. In this context, the resolution of individual issues depends not so much on the merits of the specific issues as on the overall balance of power between the two sides. And the underlying assumption of linkage is that the settlement of a crisis in one area of the world can be predetermined by the strength and degree of resolution which one or both of the contending parties have shown in other areas.* [42]

As applied by Kissinger to Vietnam, this meant that if the United States appeared to fail there, the enemies of our allies elsewhere would feel less constrained in resorting to force; and even where our allies were not the object of armed attack, some might feel coerced into one or another form of voluntary submission.[43] It is indisputable that many international developments are in fact linked, or at least—in the phrase of James C. Thompson, Jr.—have "ripple" effects on each other depending on the geographical and conceptual distances between them.[44] But, as David Landau—writing in 1972, before our "peace with honor" exit from the Vietnam war and before the October war in the Middle East—prophetically suggested:

> *At a certain remove linkage becomes unjustified; it is silly to think that Soviet assistance to the Arab nations in the Mideast is in any way comparable to, or closer to a solution by virtue of, America's prosecution of a full-scale Indochina war. And it is even less reasonable to suppose that America's steadfastness in Southeast Asia measurably affects Washington's credibility in the European theatre, with the Soviet Union, or even with the West European Allies; from Europe's vantage point, the war is an exercise not in credibility, but in irrational and absurd theatricality.[45]*

> *Nixon and Kissinger cannot satisfactorily demonstrate to themselves or to anyone else that a high degree of "resolution" in one area will have the desired effect in other areas. From a detached outsider's view, it seems as plausible to say that this approach builds tension by encouraging Soviet toughness as to claim that it relaxes hostility by forcing Moscow to be more reasonable.[46]*

In short, the search for "peace with honor" in Vietnam, after Kissinger's sophisticated intellectual gloss and skilled diplomatic tactics are stripped away, was shaped and governed by the same tired, dangerous, arbitrary, and "masculine" first principles: one must never back away once a line is drawn in the dust; every battle must be won; and, if one fails to observe the first two injunctions and by some fluke the rest of the world doesn't care, the domestic right—the "real men"—will get you for being too soft.

Kissinger is too subtle and private a person for these underlying personal imperatives to be seen directly in what is known of his character and work. But the same is not true of Nixon.

Nixon's particular variant of the cult of toughness is, in Garry Wills' phrase, the "cult of crisis," the ultimate embodiment of the self-made man, he is always remaking and testing himself, watching from some disembodied vantage point to make sure his machinery is working. And the test that counts, the action that separates the men from the boys, that allows him to parade his efforts and virtue, and to experience his worth in the marketplace of competition most vividly, is the crisis. This can be seen in "his eagerness, always, to be 'in the arena,' his praise of others for being cool under pressure, for being 'tested in the fires.'"[47] The title and format of Nixon's book, *Six Crises*, also reflects this preoccupation. Each chapter describes a problem he faced, his efforts to deal with it, and the lessons he learned, mainly about his own reactions to pressure. Some of these lessons are quite revealing.

The most difficult part of any crisis, he wrote, "is the period of indecision—*whether to fight or run away.*"[48] But the choice, as he poses it, is not a real choice at all. What self-respecting man, let alone a President of the United States, can choose to "run away"? Even within the limited range of options he posits, he could have used other words—"walk away," "avoid the issue," for example—which encompass the possibility that retreat can be rational and dignified. "Run away" permits none of these overtones; it sounds just plain cowardly. More important, the *substance* of the issue, what is actually at stake (apart from honor and "credibility"), has dropped from sight. The emphasis is not on the problem at hand, not on trying to determine what objective is worth pursuing at what cost, but on *himself*—on his courage or lack thereof. In his October 26, 1973, press conference, for example, he said of himself in answer to a question about Watergate, "the tougher it gets the cooler I get"; he responded to another question about the Middle East conflict with "when I have to face an international crisis I have what it takes."[49]

During Nixon's 1958 tour through South America, he was told that violent anti-American demonstrations were likely at a planned visit to San Marcos University in Lima. There was real danger of physical injury. The decision: should he cancel the visit or go through with it? Here's how he saw it in *Six Crises:*

> *The purpose of my tour was to present a symbol of the United States as a free, democratic, and powerful friend of our South American neighbors. In this context, my decision became clear. If I chose not to go to San Marcos, I would have failed at least in Peru. But if I did go, I would have a chance to demonstrate that the United States does not shrink from its responsibilities or flee in the face of threats. . . .*

> *But the case for not going was also compelling. I would be risking injury, not only to myself but to others. If someone was hurt, I would be blamed. And if I took the easier and safer course of canceling the visit to San Marcos and going to Catholic University I might well be able to put the blame on both the Peruvian officials and the Communists.*

> *But my intuition, backed by considerable experience, was that I should go. . . . [If I did not go, it] would not be simply a case of Nixon being bluffed out by a group of students, but of the United States itself putting its tail between its legs and running away from a bunch of Communist thugs.*[50]

Two things stand out: first his view of the challenge to him—which was, after all, only a small, transitory, and propagandistic piece of the mosaic of relations with Latin America—as affecting the long-term realities of this country's fortunes; and, second, his tendency, like Kennedy and Johnson, to sweep away all complexities in a conflict and reduce the issue to the question of whether to stand up to the schoolyard bully. (In Caracas, another stop, Nixon's car was stoned by demonstrators and he was also physically threatened. Every year Nixon celebrates the anniversary of that brush with danger with a small party.)

In his meeting with Khrushchev while Vice-President, also described in *Six Crises*, he took the same approach, even in private sessions where propaganda was not involved. Khrushchev blustered away, boasting about the strength of the Soviet military. In that forum, Nixon said, "I could answer him and counterattack, point by point, and I proceeded to do so. It was cold steel between us all afternoon." His account of the meeting and his tactics read like a debating manual, Nixon describing how he countered this point with that, got the Premier off balance or was momentarily thrown off balance himself. Again, what is striking is the extent to which Nixon, like Kennedy in Vienna, identified the fate of the United States with his "showing" in the meeting and his ready assumption that the most important aspect in the meeting was to demonstrate, while not seeming belligerent, that he could not be pushed around.

Outstanding among Nixon's unacknowledged feelings, Bruce Mazlish pointed out in his psychohistorical study, *In Search of Nixon*, is his fear of passivity:

> *He is afraid of being acted upon, of being inactive, of being soft, of being thought impotent, and of being dependent on anyone else. . . . He is constantly talking about an enemy [the Soviet Union used to be he chief villain; these days it is "those who would use the smokescreen of Watergate . , ."] probing for soft*

spots in him (and thus America). To defend us or himself, Nixon must deny he is "soft" on communism, or Castro, or anything else.[51]

He compensates with an inordinate preoccupation with strength and fighting. The apparent ability to "hang tough" or "tough it out" appears to be the main conscious criterion on his choice of key advisers. A President needs, Mazlish recorded him as saying, "people who aren't panicking . . . somebody who brings serenity, calmness or strength into the room."[52]

In 1969, long after it became clear that "international communism" as a working entity did not exist and that the North Vietnamese could not create or control revolutionary movements in other countries, Nixon's rhetoric focused even more explicitly on credibility and face. Speaking to the nation after the invasion of Cambodia by American troops he declared, "It is not our power but our will and character that are being tested tonight." (Sounds like Kennedy's description of West Berlin as "the great testing place of Western courage and will.") And deeply moved by the vision of the United States acting like "a pitiful, helpless giant," he vowed that he would not see the country become a "second-rate power" and "accept the first defeat in its proud 190-year history." Mazlish noted,

> *In the first two short paragraphs of that speech, . . . the pronoun "I" is used six times. The speech as a whole is filled with "I have concluded," "I shall describe," "this is my decision," and other similar phrases. We also have "we will not be humilitated," "we will not be defeated," and the repetitive threat that if the enemy's attacks continue to "humiliate and defeat us," we shall react accordingly.*[53]

Vice-President Agnew, doing Nixon's gut work during the 1968–1972 Administration, compared then-Senator Charles

Goodell to Christine Jorgensen, a man surgically changed into a woman, literally an emasculated man, in describing Goodell's shift from hawk to dove.

Foreign affairs is an ideal area into which to project the need to be tough and aggressive. There are fewer constraints in that sphere than in domestic affairs. Domestic affairs are characterized by wide dissemination of information and fast political response which tends to check the transformation of psychological needs into policy. Basic objectives in foreign affairs are necessarily stated in highly abstract terms—"a world safe for diversity"—and are achievable, if at all, only in the long term, making strategy and programs difficult to evaluate. How, for example, could it be proven that progress toward the objective of an economically strong, politically liberal Latin America did or did not result from United States intervention in the Dominican Republic in 1965? In foreign affairs, one can more easily get away with labeling the other side in a confrontation as thoroughly evil, a description which justifies complete victory and makes a defeat less acceptable. There is less pressure to deal with the enemy up close, as human beings rather than abstractions. And only in foreign affairs can the President's advisers gather in the White House communications center at three in the morning to read freshly decoded cables describing battles in progress and use their analytical skills to map out "scenarios" involving aircraft carriers, generals and troops and real guns to "break the will of the enemy." For the foreign-policy intellectuals of the Kennedy and Johnson Administrations the Vietnam conflict was an opportunity to exercise overt, direct power usually denied to scholars and foundation executives. It was their chance to play in the big leagues.

The arms race is another area in which judgments have been distorted by male values. Two mistakes have characterized United States policy. First, our government has assumed that the Soviet Union would build as many and as advanced planes or missiles as was economically and technically possible—known among defense planners as "worst-case analysis." The illusory missile gap of 1959–1961 is an example. If American men are brought up to believe that they should be constantly aggressive and dominant, it is only natural that they assume their opponents will act the same way, regardless of the objective evidence. Second, despite strong indications that additional missiles are not necessary or particularly helpful as a deterrent, we have frequently made arms policy as though the key objective were to maintain a force larger in numbers or megatons of deliverable bombs than the Russians'. The United States rushed into equipping its missiles with multiple independently targeted warheads (MIRVs) while arms limitation talks were in progress. The rationale was that MIRVs were needed to establish a strong bargaining position. Since the United States was in fact in a position of strength before the MIRV program started, this suggests a commitment to competition for the sake of competition, the influence of the psychological need to feel bigger and more powerful than opponents regardless of actual national security needs. The result, predictably, was to make it inevitable that the Russians push ahead with their own MIRV program.

Not every male policymaker is driven by the masculine ideal, but most are significantly moved by it. Even among men who are subject to its pressures, however, decisions are the result of a complex set of influences, some of which, for particular individuals in particular areas, tip the balance away from the masculinist imperatives. Former Undersecretary of State George Ball, for example, who advised President Johnson against escalation, had a long history of diplomatic involvement with Europe and the idea of an American–European political and economic union. This helps explain why, of all President Johnson's senior advisers, he was most predisposed to play down the importance of conflict in Southeast Asia in favor of an emphasis on

Europe. I do not mean to denigrate in any way the value of Ball's courageous and clear-headed opposition to the Vietnam war, I am simply suggesting that a confrontation between the United States and the Soviet Union in Europe would have posed a greater test of objectivity for someone with his professional history.

It is fair to ask whether the need to dominate and win in every confrontation situation isn't likely to be characteristic of anyone, male or female, who climbs to the highest rank of government in our competitive society. The answer is a complicated no. Most women are not as personally threatened as most men by the suggestion that they are not tough enough. As Daniel Ellsberg pointed out, "In almost every case the wives of [the] major officials [directing the United States' participation of the Vietnam war] *did* manage to see both the impossibility of what their husbands were trying to achieve and the brutality of it and immorality of it."[54] The comprehensive Harris poll of American women's opinion conducted in 1970 supports Ellsberg's observation. Seven out of ten women and eight out of ten men are willing to go to war to defend the continental United States. But women are much less willing than men to go to war over actions that do not threaten the United States directly: invasion of Canada (78% of women willing compared to 84% of men willing); Communist invasion of Western Europe (42% to 60%); Russian takeover of West Berlin (37% to 50%); Communist invasion of Australia (37% to 54%); Communist takeover of South Vietnam (33% to 43%); takeover of South American country by Castro (31% to 43%); imminent Israeli loss in a war with the Arabs (17% to 28%). Significantly more women than men felt that the pace of Nixon's withdrawal of American forces from Vietnam was "too slow." Two out of three women but only 49% of men say they would become upset upon hearing "that a young draftee has been killed in Vietnam."[55]

Women have also been brought up to shy away from rigorous intellectual pursuits and vigorous initiative and leadership, so it *is* more difficult for a woman in this culture to maintain the self-confidence and drive needed to achieve a position of responsibility in government or elsewhere.

In the past women who did make it were able to do so only by adopting male values; it seems unlikely that these women would have done a better job on Vietnam, or the arms race. But, in the last five years under the influence of feminism, substantial numbers of women have broken away from the traditional female self-images and roles without adopting the compulsive toughness of the male stereotype. These women, and the smaller number of men who have begun to question the validity of the traditional male sex-stereotype, have the self-confidence to achieve positions of responsibility and power without feeling a personal need to respond to every challenge. Female or male, this kind of human being might well have kept us out of Vietnam.

The reasoning of this chapter will sound strange and illegitimate to many readers. American foreign policy is almost never analyzed in terms of the psychology of its makers. By unwritten consensus, this influence on public policy has been regarded as too personal and too subjective to be reliable. In fact, the taboo exists because the men who make the policy and analyze it are often uncomfortable with and ill-equipped to understand the role that their personal feelings and values play in decisions of state. As a result, men tend to be not only unwilling to focus on the role that their own psychology plays in their decisions but also only dimly aware that they have distinct psychological biases. Feeling that way about themselves, government officials and their male critics are more comfortable dealing exclusively with the "objective" elements of public policy, despite a growing awareness that analyses of military strength, political support, and cost-benefit ratios often involve leaps of subjective intuition.

Armchair psychoanalysis of public figures is unreliable.

Conclusions are usually drawn about personality characteristics and problems unique to the individual on the basis of inadequate evidence and, for that reason, are useful neither to the individual involved nor to society at large. But analyses of the influence of widely shared psychological biases which are created by common conditioning steers clear of these pitfalls. As psychohistorian Mazlish wrote,

> [The] "style" of politics may be vastly different among political leaders—for example, John F. Kennedy and Richard Nixon—while the substance of personality may be greatly alike. From different backgrounds and different life experiences, political figures may arrive at the same character traits of competitiveness, fear of softness, and so forth. The reasons must be sought in the fact that they all emerge from the same mold of American values; in short, from the constant corresponding processes and the basic "character" of the American people as it has been up to now. [56]

Analyses of this kind will not alone fully explain complex governmental decisionmaking. Along with the failures of judgment examined here, our nation's long involvement in Vietnam was grounded on our World War II role as defender of the Free World; our attempt in the early fifties to barter aid to the French in Indochina for France's membership in a projected European Defense Community; Cardinal Spellman's lobbying, during the Eisenhower Administration, for United States support of Diem, a devout Catholic; and the bureaucratic inertia created once officials staked their careers on recommendations that we intervene. But these other causes, like the "objective" arguments for and against United States involvement, have been exhaustively and repeatedly analyzed over the last decade. And all those articles, war games, area studies, and systems analyses—the accepted tools for exploring public issues—have not dented the basic attitudes of men like Richard Nixon who, as late as 1968, could describe the Vietnam war as "one of America's finest hours." Nixon got our troops out of Vietnam, but only because their withdrawal was required for his political survival and because he was able to avoid, at least in his eyes, the appearance of losing.

We may even avoid exact, carbon-copy Vietnams of the future. But the lesson of enduring value—the lesson that our policy is in danger of being pushed in stupid, costly, and dangerous directions by the cult of toughness—has not and will not be learned from public debate which does not focus critically on the existence and influence of the biases created by the masculine ideal. A decade of traditional dialogue and interpretation of the Vietnam experience did not stop Nixon from continuing to support the prosecution of war—at a cost of two billion dollars a year and a million new refugees; it didn't stop him from bombing Cambodia; it didn't stop him from believing that our prestige required an SST which was a disaster from every other point of view;* and it didn't stop him from adding MIRVs to the nation's existing nuclear overkill capacity.

To learn the real lessons of Vietnam for our foreign policy, we need desperately to broaden the scope of public debate. Let us make mistakes at the outset if we must, but let us begin to talk about what is really going on in the minds of the men who spend our blood and our treasure to save their sacred honor.

---

*Vice-President Ford, Nixon's choice, said, arguing in Congress for the SST, that the vote would determine whether each Congressman was "a man or a mouse."[57]

Excerpts within chapter: from *Kissinger: The Uses of Power* by David Landau are reprinted by permission of Houghton Mifflin Company and Anthony Sheil Associates Ltd. Copyright © 1972 by David Landau.

From *Six Crises* by Richard M. Nixon, by permission of Doubleday & Company, Inc. Copyright © 1962 by Richard M. Nixon.

From *The Best and the Brightest* by David Halberstam by permission of Random House Inc. and Elaine Greene Ltd. (published in British Com-

NOTES

[1]The New York Times (ed.), *The Pentagon Papers* ([Quandrangle: 1971] Bantam ed.: 1971), p. 278.

[2]CIA Memorandum, June 9, 1967, reprinted in *The Pentagon Papers. op. cit.*, p. 254.

[3]*The Pentagon Papers, op. cit.*, pp. 449–54.

[4]See the author's article, "Munich and Vietnam: A Valid Analogy?" *Bulletin of the Atomic Scientists* (September 1966), p. 22. for a full statement and critical discussion of this analogy.

[5]*The Pentagon Papers, op. cit.*, p. 432.

[6]*Ibid.*, p. 89.

[7]Nancy Gager Clinch, *The Kennedy Neurosis* (Grosset & Dunlap: 1973), p. 100.

[8]Ibid., p. 114.

[9]David Halberstam, *The Best and the Brightest* (Random House: 1972), p. 273.

[10]*Ibid.*, p. 124.

[11]Clinch, *op. cit.*, p. 98 (emphasis added).

[12]Joe McCarthy, *The Remarkable Kennedys* (Dial: 1960), p. 30, quoted in Clinch, *op. cit.*, p. 131.

[13]Halberstam, *op. cit.*, p. 122.

[13]*Ibid.*, p. 151.

[15]See also Halberstam, *op. cit.*, p. 72.

[16]Arthur M. Schlesinger, Jr., *A Thousand Days* (Houghton Mifflin: 1965), pp. 380–81.

---

[17]Louise FitzSimons, *The Kennedy Doctrine* (Random House: 1972), pp. 97–98, quoted in Clinch, *op. cit.*, p. 192.

[18]Halberstam, *op. cit.*, p. 75.

[19]*Ibid.*, p. 76.

[20]Clinch, *op. cit.*, p. 194.

[21]*Ibid.*, p. 195.

[22]Halberstam, *op. cit.*, pp. 156–62.

[23]*The Pentagon Press, op. cit.*, p. 98.

[24]Richard J. Walton, *Cold War and Counterrevolution* (Viking: 1972); Louis Heren, *No Hail, No Farewell* (Harper & Row; 1970); FitzSimons, *op. cit.*; Sidney Lens, *The Military Industrial Complex* (Pilgrim Press: 1970).

[25]Halberstam, *op. cit.*, p. 274.

[26]Clinch, *op. cit.*, pp. 219–21.

[27]Halberstam, *op. cit.*, p. 56.

[28]*Ibid*, p. 63.

[29]*Ibid.*, p. 215.

[30]*Ibid.*, p. 312.

[31]*Ibid.*, pp. 531–32.

[32]*Ibid.*, p. 178.

[33]*Ibid.*, p. 414.

[34]*Ibid.*, p. 425.

[35]Charles Yost, *The Conduct and Misconduct of Foreign Affairs* (Random House: 1972), pp. 39–40.

[36]David Landau, *Kissinger: The Uses of Power* (Houghton Mifflin: 1972), pp. 155–58.

[37]Richard Whalen, *Catch the Falling Flag: A Republican's Challenge to His Party* (Houghton Mifflin: 1972), p. 137.

[38]Landau, *op. cit.*, pp. 158, 180–82.

[39]Kissinger, *American Foreign Policy* (W.W. Norton: 1969), p. 112, quoted in Landau, *op. cit., pp. 186–87.*

[40]Richard M. Nixon, *Six Crises,* (Doubleday: 1962), p. 273.

[41]Landau, *op. cit.,* p. 71.

[42]*Ibid.,* pp. 118–19.

[43]*Ibid.,* p. 158.

[44]*Ibid.,* p. 120.

[45]*Ibid.,* pp. 119–20.

[46]*Ibid.,* p. 125.

[47]Garry Wills, *Nixon Agonistes* (Houghton Mifflin: 1970), p. 166.

[48]Nixon, *op. cit.,* p. xv (emphasis added).

[49]*The New York Times,* October 27, 1973, p. 14.

[50]Nixon, *op. cit.,* p. 199.

[51]Bruce Mazlish, *In Search of Nixon* (Basic Books: 1972), p. 116.

[52]*Ibid.*

[53]*Ibid.,* p. 117.

[54]*New York Post,* June 22, 1971, p. 67.

[55]Virginia Slims American Women's Opinion Poll, Louis Harris and Associates (1970), pp. 74–77.

[56]Mazlish, *op. cit.,* p. 170.

[57]*Boston Globe,* March 19, 1972, p. 2.

chapter 16

Men's Power with Women, Other Men, and Society:

A Men's Movement Analysis

by Joseph H. Pleck

In this short essay, written by an active participant in the men's movement, Joseph Pleck offers a contemporary analysis of male power relationships. He attempts to join current feminist thinking and men's liberation analysis by arguing that "patriarchy is a dual system, a system in which men oppress women, and in which men oppress themselves and each other." Pleck is especially interested in the psychological reasons why contemporary American males seek power over women. He also distinguishes between the power dynamics in male–female and male–male relationships and analyzes several ways in which these dynamics interact. Finally, he considers the world of men's work, where most American men, far from being power wielders, find themselves relatively powerless.

My aim in this paper is to analyze men's power from the perspective afforded by the emerging anti-sexist men's movement. In the last several years, an anti-sexist men's movement has appeared in North America and in the Western European countries. While it is not so widely known as the women's movement, the men's movement has generated a variety of books, publications, and organizations,[1] and is now an established presence on the sex role scene. The present and future political relationship between the women's movement and the men's movement raises complex questions which I do not deal with here, though they are clearly important ones. Instead, here I present my own view of the contribution which the men's movement and the men's analysis make to a feminist understanding of men and power, and of power relations between the sexes. First, I will analyze men's power over women, particularly in relation to the power that men often perceive women have over them. Then I will analyze two other relationships men are implicated in—men's power with other men, and men's power in society more generally—and suggest how these two other power relationships interact with men's power over women.

MEN'S POWER OVER WOMEN, AND WOMEN'S POWER OVER MEN

It is becoming increasingly recognized that one of the most fundamental questions raised by the women's movement is not a question about women at all, but rather a question about men: why do men oppress women? There are two

"Men's Power with Women, Other Men, and Society: A Men's Movement Analysis" by Joseph H. Pleck, in Dana V. Hiller and Robin Sheets (eds.), *Women and Men: The Consequences of Power*, Cincinnati: Office of Women's Studies, University of Cincinnati, 1977. Copyright © 1976 by Joseph H. Pleck.

general kinds of answers to this question. The first is that men want power over women because it is in their rational self-interest to do so, to have the concrete benefits and privileges that power over women provides them. Having power, it is rational to want to keep it. The second kind of answer is that men want to have power over women because of deep-lying psychological needs in male personality. These two views are not mutually exclusive, and there is certainly ample evidence for both. The final analysis of men's oppression of women will have to give attention equally to its rational and irrational sources.

I will concentrate my attention here on the psychological sources of men's needs for power over women. Let us consider first the most common and common-sense psychological analysis of men's need to dominate women, which takes as its starting point the male child's early experience with women. The male child, the argument goes, perceives his mother and his predominantly female elementary school teachers as dominating and controlling. These relationships *do* in reality contain elements of domination and control, probably exacerbated by the restriction of women's opportunities to exercise power in most other areas. As a result, men feel a lifelong psychological need to free themselves from or prevent their domination by women. The argument is, in effect, that men oppress women as adults because they experienced women as oppressing them as children.

According to this analysis, the process operates in a vicious circle. In each generation, adult men restrict women from having power in almost all domains of social life except child-rearing. As a result, male children feel powerless and dominated, grow up needing to restrict women's power, and thus the cycle repeats itself. It follows from this analysis that the way to break the vicious circle is to make it possible for women to exercise power outside of parenting and parent-like roles and to get men to do their half share of parenting.

There may be a kernel of truth in this "mother domination" theory of sexism for some men, and the social changes in the organization of child care that this theory suggests are certainly desirable. As a general explanation of men's needs to dominate women, however, this theory has been quite overworked. This theory holds women themselves, rather than men, ultimately responsible for the oppression of women—in William Ryan's phrase, "blaming the victim" of oppression for her own oppression.[2] The recent film *One Flew Over the Cuckoo's Nest* presents an extreme example of how women's supposed domination of men is used to justify sexism. This film portrays the archetypal struggle between a female figure depicted as domineering and castrating, and a rebellious male hero (played by Jack Nicholson) who refuses to be emasculated by her. This struggle escalates to a climactic scene in which Nicholson throws her on the floor and nearly strangles her to death—a scene that was accompanied by wild cheering from the audience when I saw the film. For this performance, Jack Nicholson won the Academy Award as the best actor of the year, an indication of how successful the film is in seducing its audience to accept this act of sexual violence as legitimate and even heroic. The hidden moral message of the film is that because women dominate men, the most extreme forms of sexual violence are not only permissible for men, but indeed are morally obligatory.

To account for men's needs for power over women, it is ultimately more useful to examine some other ways that men feel women have power over them than fear of maternal domination.[3] There are two forms of power that men perceive women as holding over them which derive more directly from traditional definitions of adult male and female roles, and have implications which are far more compatible with a feminist perspective.

The first power that men perceive women having over them is *expressive power*, the power to express emotions. It is well known that in traditional male–female relationships, women are supposed to express their needs for achievement only vicariously through the achievements of men. It is not so widely recognized, however, that this dependency of women on men's achievement has a converse. In traditional male–female relationships, men experience their emotions vicariously through women. Many men have learned to depend on women to help them express their emotions, indeed, to express their emotions for them. At an ultimate level, many men are unable to feel emotionally alive except through relationships with women. A particularly dramatic example occurs in an earlier Jack Nicholson film *Carnal Knowledge*. Art Garfunkel, at one point early in his romance with Candy Bergen, tells Nicholson that she makes him aware of thoughts he "never even knew he had." Although Nicholson is sleeping with Bergen and Garfunkel is not, Nicholson feels tremendously deprived in comparison when he hears this. In a dramatic scene, Nicholson then goes to her and demands: "you tell him his thoughts, now you tell me *my* thoughts!" When women withhold and refuse to exercise this expressive power for men's benefit, many men, like Nicholson, feel abject and try all the harder to get women to play their traditional expressive role.

A second form of power that men attribute to women is *masculinity-validating* power. In traditional masculinity, to experience oneself as masculine requires that women play their prescribed role of doing the things that make men feel masculine. Another scene from *Carnal Knowledge* provides a pointed illustration. In the closing scene of the movie, Nicholson has hired a call girl whom he has rehearsed and coached in a script telling him how strong and manly he is, in order to get him sexually aroused. Nicholson seems to be in control, but when she makes a mistake in her role, his desperate reprimands show just how dependent he is on her playing out the masculinity-validating script he has created. It is clear that what he is looking for in this encounter is not so much sexual gratification as it is validation of himself as a man—which only women can give him. As with women's expressive power, when women refuse to exercise their masculinity-validating power for men, many men feel lost and bereft and frantically attempt to force women back into their accustomed role.

As I suggested before, men's need for power over women derives both from men's pragmatic self-interest and from men's psychological needs. It would be a mistake to overemphasize men's psychological needs as the sources of their needs to control women, in comparison with simple rational self-interest. But if we are looking for the psychological sources of men's needs for power over women, their perception that women have expressive power and masculinity-validating power over them are critical to analyze. These are the two powers men perceive women as having, which they fear women will no longer exercise in their favor. These are the two resources women possess which men fear women will withhold, and whose threatened or actual loss leads men to such frantic attempts to reassert power over women.

Men's dependence on women's power to express men's emotions and to validate men's masculinity have placed heavy burdens on women. By and large, these are not powers over men that women have wanted to hold. These are powers that men have themselves handed over to women, by defining the male role as being emotionally cool and inexpressive, and as being ultimately validated by heterosexual success.

There is reason to think that over the course of recent history—as male–male friendship has declined, and as dating and marriage have occurred more universally and at younger ages—the demands on men to be emotionally inexpressive and to prove masculinity through relating to women have become stronger. As a result, men have given women increasingly more expressive power and more masculinity-validating power over them, and have become increasingly dependent on women for emotional and sex role validation. In the context of this increased dependency on women's power, the emergence of the women's movement now, with women asserting their right not to play these roles for men, has hit men with special force.

It is in this context that the men's movement and men's groups place so much emphasis on men learning to express and experience their emotions with each other, and learning how to validate themselves and each other as persons, instead of needing women to validate them emotionally and as men. When men realize that they can develop themselves the power to experience themselves emotionally and to validate themselves as persons, they will not feel the dependency on women for these essential needs which has led in the past to so much male fear, resentment, and need to control women. Then men will be emotionally more free to negotiate the pragmatic realignment of power between the sexes that is underway in our society.

MEN'S POWER WITH OTHER MEN

After considering men's power over women in relation to the power men perceive women having over them, let us consider men's power over women in a second context: the context of men's power relationships with other men. In recent years, we have come to understand that relations between men and women are governed by a sexual politics that exists outside individual men's and women's needs and choices. It has taken us much longer to recognize that there is a systematic sexual politics of male–male relationships as well. Under patriarchy, men's relationships with other men cannot help but be shaped and patterned by patriarchal norms, though they are less obvious than the norms governing male–female relationships. A society could not have the kinds of power dynamics that exist between women and men in our society without certain kinds of systematic power dynamics operating among men as well.

One dramatic example illustrating this connection occurs in Marge Piercy's recent novel *Small Changes*. In a flashback scene, a male character goes along with several friends to gang-rape a woman. When his turn comes, he is impotent; whereupon the other men grab him, pulling his pants down to rape *him*. This scene powerfully conveys one form of the relationship between male–female and male–male sexual politics. The point is that men do not just happily bond together to oppress women. In addition to hierarchy over women, men create hierarchies and rankings among themselves according to criteria of "masculinity." Men at each rank of masculinity compete with each other, with whatever resources they have, for the differential payoffs that patriarchy allows men.

Men in different societies choose different grounds on which to rank each other. Many societies use the simple facts of age and physical strength to stratify men. The most bizarre and extreme form of patriarchal stratification occurs in those societies which have literally created a class of eunuchs. Our society, reflecting its own particular preoccupations, stratifies men according to physical strength and athletic ability in the early years, but later in life focuses on success with women and ability to make money.

In our society, one of the most critical rankings among men deriving from patriarchal sexual politics is the division between gay and straight men. This division has powerful negative consequences for gay men and gives straight men privilege. But in addition, this division has a larger symbolic meaning. Our society uses the male heterosexual–homosexual dichotomy as a central symbol for *all* the rankings of masculinity, for the division on *any* grounds between males who are "real men" and have power and males who are not. Any kind of powerlessness or refusal to compete becomes imbued with the imagery of homosexuality. In the men's movement documentary film *Men's Lives*,[4] a high school male who studies modern dance says that others often think he is gay because he is a dancer. When asked why, he gives three reasons: because dancers are "free and loose," because they are "not big like football players," and because "you're not trying to kill anybody." The patriarchal connection: if you are not trying to kill other men, you must be gay.

Another dramatic example of men's use of homosexual derogations as weapons in their power struggle with each other comes from a document which provides one of the richest case studies of the politics of male–male relationships to yet appear: Woodward and Bernstein's *The Final Days.* Ehrlichman jokes that Kissinger is queer, Kissinger calls an unnamed colleague a psychopathic homosexual, and Haig jokes that Nixon and Rebozo are having a homosexual relationship. From the highest ranks of male power to the lowest, the gay–straight division is a central symbol of all the forms of ranking and power relationships which men put on each other.

The relationships between the patriarchal stratification and competition which men experience with each other and men's patriarchal domination of women are complex. Let us briefly consider several points of interconnection between them. First, women are used as *symbols of success* in men's competition with each other. It is sometimes thought that competition for women is the ultimate source of men's competition with each other. For example, in *Totem and Taboo* Freud presented a mythical reconstruction of the origin of society based on sons' sexual competition with the father, leading to their murdering the father. In this view, if women did not exist, men would not have anything to compete for with each other. There is considerable reason, however, to see women not as the ultimate source of male–male competition, but rather as only symbols in a male contest where real roots lie much deeper.

The recent film *Paper Chase* provides an interesting example. This film combines the story of a small group of male law students in their first year of law school with a heterosexual love story between one of the students (played by Timothy Bottoms) and the professor's daughter. As the film develops, it becomes clear that the real business is the struggle within the group of male law students for survival, success, and the professor's blessing—patriarchal struggle in which several of the less successful are driven out of school and one even attempts suicide. When Timothy Bottoms gets the professor's daughter at the end, she is simply another one of the rewards he has won by doing better than the other males in her father's class. Indeed, she appears to be a direct part of the patriarchal blessing her father has bestowed on Bottoms.

Second, women often play a *mediating* role in the patriarchal struggle among men. Women get together with each other, and provide the social lubrication necessary to smooth over men's inability to relate to each other non-competitively. This function has been expressed in many myths, for example, the folk tales included in the Grimms' collection about groups of brothers whose younger sister reunites and reconciles them with their king-father, who had previously banished and tried to kill them. A more modern myth, James Dickey's *Deliverance*, portrays what happens when men's relationships with each other are not mediated by women. According to Carolyn Heilbrun,[5] the central message of *Deliverance* is that when men get beyond the bounds of civilization, which really means beyond the bounds of the civilizing effects of women, men rape and murder each other.

A third function women play in male–male sexual politics is that relationships with women provide men a *refuge* from the dangers and stresses of relating to other males. Traditional relationships with women have provided men a safe place in which they can recuperate from the stresses they have absorbed in their daily struggle with other men, and in which they can express their needs without fearing that these needs will be used against them. If women begin to compete with men and have power in their own right, men are threatened by the loss of this refuge.

Finally, a fourth function of women in males' patriarchal competition with each other is to reduce the stress of competition by serving as an *underclass*. As Elizabeth Janeway has written in *Between Myth and Morning*,[6] under patriarchy women represent the lowest status, a status to which men can fall only under the most exceptional circumstances, if at all. Competition among men is serious, but its intensity is mitigated by the fact that there is a lowest possible level to which men cannot fall. One reason men fear women's liberation, writes Janeway, is that the liberation of women will take away this unique underclass status of women. Men will not risk falling lower than ever before, into a new underclass composed of the weak of both sexes. Thus, women's liberation means that the stakes of patriarchal failure for men are higher than they have been before, and that it is even more important for men not to lose.

Thus, men's patriarchal competition with each other makes use of women as symbols of success, as mediators, as refuges, and as an underclass. In each of these roles, women are dominated by men in ways that derive directly from men's struggle with each other. Men need to deal with the sexual politics of their relationships with each other if they are to deal fully with the sexual politics of their relationships with women.

Ultimately, we have to understand that patriarchy has two halves which are intimately related to each other. Patriarchy is a *dual* system, a system in which men oppress women, and in which men oppress themselves and each other. At one level, challenging one part of patriarchy inherently leads to challenging the other. This is one way to interpret why the idea of women's liberation so soon led to the idea of men's liberation, which in my view ultimately means freeing men from the patriarchal sexual dynamics they now experience with each other. But because the patriarchal sexual dynamics of male–male relationships are less obvious than those of male–female relationships, men face a real danger: while the patriarchal oppression of women may be lessened as a result of the women's movement, the patriarchal oppression of men may be untouched. The real danger for men posed by the attack that the women's movement is making on patriarchy is not that this attack will go too far, but that it will not go far enough. Ultimately, men cannot go any further in relating to women as equals than they have been able to go in relating to other men as equals—an equality which has been so deeply disturbing, which has generated so many psychological as well as literal casualties, and which has left so many unresolved issues of competition and frustrated love.

MEN'S POWER IN SOCIETY

Let us now consider men's power over women in a third and final context, the context of men's power in the larger society. At one level, men's social identity is defined by the power they have over women and the power they can compete for against other men. But at another level, most men have very little over their own lives. How can we understand this paradox?

The major demand to which men must accede in contemporary society is that they play their required role in the economy. But this role is not intrinsically satisfying. The social researcher Daniel Yankelovich[7] has suggested that about 80% of U.S. male workers experience their jobs as intrinsically meaningless and onerous. They experience their jobs and themselves as worthwhile only through priding themselves on the hard work and personal sacrifice they are making to be breadwinners for their families. Accepting these hardships reaffirms their role as family providers and therefore as true men.

Linking the breadwinner role to masculinity in this way has several consequences for men. Men can get psychological payoffs from their jobs which these jobs never provide in themselves. By training men to accept payment for their work in feelings of masculinity rather than in feelings of satisfaction, men will not demand that their jobs be made more meaningful, and as a result jobs can be designed for the more important goal of generating profits. Further, the connection between work and masculinity makes men accept unemployment as their personal failing as males, rather than analyze and change the profit-based economy whose inevitable dislocations make them unemployed or unemployable.

Most critical for our analysis here, men's role in the economy and the ways men are motivated to play it have at least two negative effects on women. First, the husband's job makes many direct and indirect demands on wives. In fact, it is often hard to distinguish whether the wife is dominated more by the husband or by the husband's job. Sociologist Ralph Turner writes: "Because the husband must adjust to the demands of his occupation and the family in turn must accommodate to his demands on behalf of his occupational obligations, the husband appears to dominate his wife and children. But as an agent of economic institutions, he perceives himself as controlled rather than as controlling."[8]

Second, linking the breadwinner role to masculinity in order to motivate men to work means that women must not be allowed to hold paid work. For the large majority of men who accept dehumanizing jobs only because having a job validates their role as family breadwinner, their wives' taking paid work takes away from them the major and often only way they have of experiencing themselves as having worth. Yankelovich suggests that the frustration and discontent of this group of men, whose wives are increasingly joining the paid labor force, is emerging as a major social problem. What these men do to sabotage women's paid work is deplorable, but I believe that it is quite within the bounds of a feminist analysis of contemporary society to see these men as victims as well as victimizers.

One long range perspective on the historical evolution of the family is that from an earlier stage in which both wife and husband were directly economically productive in the household economic unit, the husband's economic role has evolved so that now it is under the control of forces entirely outside the family. In order to increase productivity, the goal in the design of this new male work role is to increase men's commitment and loyalty to work and to reduce those ties to the family that might compete with it. Men's jobs are increasingly structured as if men had no direct roles or responsibilities in the family—indeed, as if they did not have families at all. But paradoxically, at the same time that men's responsibilities in the family are reduced to facilitate more efficient performance of their work role, the increasing dehumanization of work means that the satisfaction which jobs give men is, to an increasing degree, *only* the satisfaction of fulfilling the family breadwinner role. That is, on the one hand, men's ties to the family have to be broken down to facilitate industrial work discipline; but on the other hand, men's sense of responsibility to the family has to be increased, but shaped into a purely economic form, to provide the motivation for men to work at all. Essential to this process is the transformation of the wife's economic role to providing supportive services, both physical and psychological, to keep him on the job, and to take over the family responsibilities which his expanded work role will no longer allow him to fulfill himself. The wife is then bound to her husband by her economic dependency on him, and the husband in turn is bound to his job by his family's economic dependence on him.

A final example from the film *Men's Lives* illustrates some of these points. In one of the most powerful scenes in the film, a worker in a rubber plant resignedly describes how his bosses are concerned, in his words, with "pacifying" him to get the maximum output from him, not with satisfying his needs. He then takes back this analysis, saying that he is only a worker and therefore cannot really understand what is happening to him. Next, he is asked whether he wants his wife to take a paid job to reduce the pressure he feels in trying to support his family. In marked contrast to his earlier passive resignation, he proudly asserts that he will never allow her to work, and that in particular he will never scrub the floors after he comes home from his own job. (He correctly perceives that if his wife did take a paid job, he would be under pressure to do some housework.) In this scene, the man expresses and then denies an awareness of his exploitation as a worker. Central to his coping with and repressing his incipient awareness of his exploitation is his false consciousness of his superiority and privilege over women. Not scrubbing floors is a real privilege, and deciding whether or not his wife will have paid work is a real power, but the consciousness of power over his own life that such privilege and power give this man is false. The relative privilege that men get from sexism, and more importantly the false consciousness of privilege men get from sexism, play a critical role in reconciling men to their subordination in the larger political economy. This analysis does not imply that men's sexism will go away if they gain control over their own lives, or that men do not have to deal with their sexism until they gain this control. I disagree with both. Rather, my point is that we cannot fully understand men's sexism or men's subordination in the larger society unless we understand how deeply they are related.

To summarize, a feminist understanding of men's power over women, when men have needed it, and what is involved in changing it, is enriched by examining men's power in a broader context. To understand men's power over women, we have to understand the ways in which men feel women have power over them, men's power relationships with other men, and the powerlessness of most men in the larger society. Rectifying men's power relationship with women will inevitably both stimulate and benefit from the rectification of these other power relationships.

NOTES

[1] See, for example, Deborah David and Robert Brannon, eds., *The Forty-Nine Percent Majority: Readings on the Male Role* (Reading, Mass.: Addison-Wesley, 1975); Warren Farrell, *The Liberated Man* (New York: Bantam Books, 1975); Marc Feigen Fasteau, *The Male Machine* (New York: McGraw-Hill, 1974); Jack Nichols, *Men's Liberation: A New Definition of Masculinity* (Baltimore: Penguin, 1975); John Petras, ed., *Sex: Male/Gender: Masculine* (Port Washington, N.J.: Alfred, 1975); Joseph H. Pleck and Jack Sawyer, eds., *Men and Masculinity* (Englewood Cliffs, N.J.: Prentice-Hall, 1974). See also the *Man's Awareness Network (M.A.N.) Newsletter*, a regularly updated directory of men's movement activities, organizations, and publications, prepared by a rotating group of men's centers (c/o Knoxville Men's Resource Center, P.O. Box 8060, U.T. Station, Knoxville, Tenn. 37916); the Men's Studies Collection, Charles Hayden Humanities Library, Massachusetts Institute of Technology, Cambridge, Mass. 02139.

[2] William Ryan, *Blaming the Victim* (New York: Pantheon, 1970).

[3] In addition to the mother domination theory, there are two other psychological theories relating aspects of the early mother–child relationship in men's sexism. The first can be called the "mother identification" theory, which holds that men develop a "feminine" psychological identification because of their early attachment to their mothers and that men fear this internal feminine part of themselves, seeking to control it by controlling those who actually are feminine, i.e., women. The second can be called the "mother socialization" theory, holding that since boys' fathers are relatively absent as sex role models, the major route by which boys learn masculinity is through their mothers' rewarding masculine behavior, and especially through their mothers' punishing feminine behavior. Thus, males associate women with punishment and pressure to be masculine. Interestingly, these two theories are in direct contradiction, since the former holds that men fear women because women make men feminine, and the latter holds that men fear women because women make men masculine. These theories are discussed at greater length in Joseph H. Pleck, "Men's Traditional Attitudes toward Women: Conceptual Issues in Research," in *The Psychology of Women: New Directions in Research*, ed. Julia

Sherman and Florence Denmark (New York: Psychological Dimensions, in press).

[4]Available from New Day Films, P.O. Box 315, Franklin Lakes, N.J. 07417.

[5]Carolyn G. Heilbrun, "The Masculine Wilderness of the American Novel," *Saturday Review* 41 (Jaunary 29, 1972), 41–44.

[6]Elizabeth Janeway, *Between Myth and Morning* (Boston: Little, Brown, 1975); see also Elizabeth Janeway, "The Weak are the Second Sex," *Atlantic Monthly* (December, 1973), 91–104.

[7]Daniel Yankelovich, "The Meaning of Work," in *The Worker and the Job*, ed. Jerome Rosow (Englewood Cliffs, N.J.: 1974).

[8]Ralph Turner, *Family Interaction* (New York: Wiley, 1968), p. 282.